REVISITING OUTCOMES ASSESSMENT IN HIGHER EDUCATION

Edited by
**Peter Hernon, Robert E. Dugan,
and Candy Schwartz**

LIBRARIES
UNLIMITED
A Member of the Greenwood Publishing Group

Westport, Connecticut • London

50.00

Library of Congress Cataloging-in-Publication Data

Revisiting outcomes assessment in higher education / edited by Peter Hernon,
   Robert E. Dugan and Candy Schwartz.
         p.   cm.
      Includes bibliographical references and index.
      ISBN 1–59158–276–8 (pbk. : alk. paper)
      1. Education, Higher—United States—Evaluation.   2. Educational tests and
measurements—United States.   I. Hernon, Peter.   II. Dugan, Robert E.,
1952–   III. Schwartz, Candy.   IV. Title.
      LB2331.63.R48   2006
      378.1'66—dc22   2005029422

British Library Cataloguing in Publication Data is available.

Library of Congress Catalog Card Number: 2005029422
ISBN: 1–59158–276–8

First published in 2006

Libraries Unlimited, 88 Post Road West, Westport, CT 06881
A Member of the Greenwood Publishing Group, Inc.
www.lu.com

Printed in the United States of America

The paper used in this book complies with the
Permanent Paper Standard issued by the National
Information Standards Organization (Z39.48–1984).

10 9 8 7 6 5 4 3 2 1

Copyright Acknowledgments

The editors and publisher gratefully acknowledge permission for use of the following material:

Excerpts reprinted from *Library and Information Science Research*, Vol. 26, Heidi Julien et. al, "Assessing Instructional Outcomes in Canadian Academic Libraries," pp. 121–139, Copyright © 2004, with permission from Elsevier.

Excerpts from Middle States Commission on Higher Education, *Student Learning Assessment: Options and Resources* (Philadelphia, PA: Middle States Commission on Higher Education, 2003) reprinted with permission.

Excerpts from Peer Review of Teaching Project, "The Peer Review Process: Inquiry Portfolio," (Lincoln: University of Nebraska) reprinted with permission.

Excerpts from Peter Newby, "Culture and Quality in Higher Education," *Higher Education Policy* 12 (1999): 264, reproduced with permission of Palgrave Macmillan.

Excerpts from Alverno College, "Institutional and Program Assessment" (Milwaukee, WI: Alverno College), 3, reprinted with permission.

Excerpts reprinted from *Advances in Librarianship*, Vol 25, Danuta Nitecki, "Quality Assessment Measures in Libraries," 133–162, Copyright © 2001, with permission of Elsevier.

Excerpts reprinted from *Journal of Academic Librarianship* 31, Thompson, Bruce, Colleen Cook, and Martha Kyrillidou. "Concurrent Validity of LibQUAL+™ Scores: What Do LibQUAL+™ Scores Measure?," forthcoming, copyright © 2005, with permission from Elsevier.

Excerpts from John P. Kotter, *Leading Change*. Boston: Harvard Business School Press, 1996, reprinted with permission.

Every reasonable effort has been made to trace the owners of copyright materials in this book, but in some instances this has proven impossible. The author and publisher will be glad to receive information leading to more complete acknowledgments in subsequent printings of the book and in the meantime extend their apologies for any omissions.

Contents

Illustrations   xiii

Preface   xv

**Chapter 1 Institutional Mission-centered Student
             Learning   1**
             Robert E. Dugan and Peter Hernon

Assessment for Educational Quality and
    Accountability in Higher Education   2
Planning Process   3
A Framework Model for Outcomes
    Processes   4
Student Learning   8
Cultural Transformation   9
Conclusion   10
Notes   11

Chapter 2 Accountability and Quality Improvement   13
             Linda Suskie

Understanding Accountability and Quality
    Improvement   13
Why the Focus on Accountability and
    Quality Improvement?   15
Demonstrating Accountability and Quality
    Improvement: It Begins with Goals   17
Evaluating How Well Goals Have Been Achieved   22
Promoting a Climate of Using Evaluation Results
    for Accountability and Quality Improvement   29
Conclusion   31
Notes   32

Chapter 3 Stakeholders of Higher Education Institutional Accountability 39
Robert E. Dugan

Overview 41
Conclusion 58
Notes 59

Chapter 4 The Assessment Matrix: Providing Evidence of a Sustainable Commitment to Student Learning 63
Cecilia L. López

Research Basis for the Assessment Matrix 67
Use of the Assessment Matrix 69
Practical Ways to Use the Assessment Matrix 70
Examples of Institutional Use of the
  Assessment Matrix 75
Conclusion 83
Notes 84
Appendix: Assessment of Student Academic
  Achievement: Assessment Culture Matrix 87

Chapter 5 Assessment Strategies for Institutional Accountability 97
Robert E. Dugan

"We Do It Because We Have To"—Imposed
  and Required Measures 98
"We Do It Because It Is a Tool in Helping
  to Improve" 103
Findings Concerning Accountability
  and Strategic Decisions 108
Conclusion 110
Notes 112

Chapter 6 Design and Methodological Considerations 117
Peter Hernon

Experimental Designs 117
Statistical Inference 118

Sampling   119
Quantitative or Qualitative Study   120
Descriptive Statistics   120
Normal Curve   123
Z-Scores   124
Inferential Statistics   124
Reliability and Validity   128
Example of Outcomes Assessment   129
Metrics   131
Conclusion   131
Notes   132

Chapter 7   Methods of Data Collection   135
           Peter Hernon

Framework   136
Different Methods   142
Conclusion   148
Notes   149

Chapter 8   Managing Electronic Portfolios   151
           Candy Schwartz

The Importance of Planning   152
E-portfolio Decisions   153
E-portfolio Benefits   158
Getting Underway   159
Conclusion   161
Notes   161

**Chapter 9   The Learning Organization: Assessment
              as an Agent of Change   165**
           Patricia M. Dwyer

Introduction to Shepherd University   165
Changing the Educational Focus   166
The Challenge to Create Change That Lasts   168
Making the Connections   168
Indicators of a Cultural Shift   175
Conclusion   179
Notes   180

**Chapter 10 Applying Student Learning Outcomes
to an Educational Program**   **181**
Peter Hernon and Candy Schwartz

The Setting   182
Leading Up to Outcomes   182
Stage One   183
Stage Two   189
Stage Three   190
Stage Four   195
Stage Five   195
Examples   196
Conclusion   197
Notes   197

**Chapter 11 An International Perspective on
Educational Excellence**   **199**
Peter Hernon

Quality Assurance and Outcomes Assessment:
   A Comparison   200
Examples   204
A Proposed Competitive Framework   214
Conclusion   215
Notes   217

**Chapter 12 Standardized Learning Outcomes:
Assessing and Recording Achievement
in Non-Accredited Adult
Education Courses**   **221**
Jutta Austin

A System of Standardized Learning
   Outcomes   223
Design Procedure   224
Assessment   236
Evaluation   237
Conclusion   238
Notes   239

Chapter 13 Outcomes Assessment in Canadian Higher Education   **241**
  Heidi Julien

General Calls for Quality Assessment   241
Assessment Efforts   244
Case Study of Outcomes Assessment in Canadian
   Academic Libraries   247
Conclusion   265
Acknowledgments   267
Notes   267

Chapter 14 Information Technology and Outcomes Assessment in Higher Education   **273**
  Renée N. Jefferson

Information Technology in Higher Education   274
Information Technology in Academic Libraries   275
Outcomes Assessment in Higher Education   277
Information Technology and Outcomes Assessment
   in Academic Libraries   280
Conclusion   282
Notes   282

Chapter 15 Some Techniques for Outcomes Assessment   **287**
  Gloriana St. Clair and Carole A. George

Planning and Goal-setting   288
Information Literacy   289
Information Behavior   290
Continual Review   292
Graduate Student Interviews   293
Think-aloud Protocols   298
Conclusion   301
Acknowledgment   301
Notes   301

Chapter 16 Collaborating on Information Literacy   **303**
  Elizabeth Carter and Renée N. Jefferson

The Citadel   304
Evolution of the Instrument   305

Procedures 308
Results 313
Relating the Findings to Student Learning Outcomes 323
Conclusion 324
Notes 324

**Chapter 17 Developing an Information Literacy
Assessment Instrument 327**
Terrence Mech

King's College 327
Library and Information Literacy 328
Evolution of the Instrument 331
Larger Context 341
Observations 346
Conclusion 347
Notes 347

**Chapter 18 Service Quality: A Perceived Outcome
for Libraries 351**
Martha Kyrillidou

Background 352
Service Quality as a Positive Organizational
Change Outcome 355
A View from the Trenches: Universal Library
Service Provision 363
Conclusion 364
Notes 365

**Chapter 19 Future Directions in Outcomes
Assessment 367**
Peter Hernon and Robert E. Dugan

Discipline-based Outcomes in a
Framework for Outcomes Processes 368
Research Agenda 373
Developing a Set of Comprehensive
Indicators 375
Perspectives on Future Directions 377
Conclusion 394
Notes 395

Appendix: Web Resources 397
  Candy Schwartz

Directories and Resource Collections 397
Organizations and Initiatives 398
U.S. Regional Accrediting Organizations 401

Bibliography 403

Articles 403
Books 410
Book Chapters 413
Guidelines, Standards, and Accreditation Documentation 417
Government Publications 418
Reports 418
Web Resources 419
Unpublished Works 430

Index 433

About the Editors and Contributors 447

Illustrations

FIGURES

1.1	Open-systems Model	4
1.2	Hierarchical Framework for Outcomes Processes	6
4.1	Assessment Matrix: Analysis Worksheet	65
7.1	Assessment of Teaching and Learning	136
7.2	Student Course Evaluation	139
7.3	Methods of Assessing Program Outcomes	143
7.4	Examples of Surveys and Tests	145
9.1	Eight-stage Process for Creating Major Change	169
10.1	Student Learning Outcomes	185
10.2	Formal Course Description Based on Template	186
10.3	Organization Cluster	187
10.4	Proposal for a New Course	188
10.5	Outcome Assessment Measures	191
10.6	Existing Assessment at GSLIS	193
12.1	Page from Outcome Book for Modern Languages	226
12.2	Page from Outcome Book for Modern Languages	227
12.3	Page from Outcome Book for Art and Design	229
12.4	Page from Outcome Book for Art and Design	230
12.5	Page from Outcome Book for Art and Design	231
12.6	Index of Outcome Book for Art and Design	233
12.7	Page from Outcome Book for Counseling	234
12.8	Index of Outcome Book for Counseling	235
13.1	Changes in Average Student Test Scores for Seven Participating Groups	254

16.1 Information Literacy Assessment, Free Response
Method 306

16.2 Information Literacy Assessment (Revised, 2004) 309

16.3 Previous Library or Media Center Use of
Freshman Cadets 314

16.4 Current Library or Media Center Use of
Freshman Cadets 315

16.5 Previous Library Use of Graduate Students 318

16.6 Current Library Use of Graduate Students 319

18.1 Exploring Appreciative Inquiry as a Framework
for Following Up on Your LibQUAL+™ Data 358

18.2 The Benefits of a Library Summit 360

TABLES

13.1 Statistically Significant Increases to Test Scores 255

13.2 Ways in Which Students Believed That Instruction
Influenced Their Educational Success 261

16.1 Freshman Cadet Feelings about Libraries and
Other Related Activities (by Pre-test and Post-test) 317

16.2 Graduate Students' Feelings about Libraries and
Other Related Activities (by Pre-test and Post-test) 321

17.1 Students' Self-Report of Information Skills 332

17.2 Instrument Evolution 334

17.3 Freshman Information Skills by Course (Fall 2002) 334

17.4 Freshman Information Skills by Standards (Fall 2002) 335

17.5 Seniors' Information Skills by Standard (Spring 2003) 336

17.6 Information Skill of Seniors and Graduate Students
from Three Northeast Pennsylvania Colleges by
Standard: Mean Scores/Percentage (Fall 2004) 337

17.7 Percentiles—Seniors (Fall 2004) 338

Preface

Within academe the concept of *excellence in teaching* now goes beyond merely the imparting of knowledge, where instructors do the imparting and students memorize, repeat, and understand that content. Excellence also encompasses learning and student transformation throughout programs of study. A central question of this view of excellence is "How do the various courses that students take fit together to develop the 'abilities, habits of mind, ways of knowing, attitudes, values, and other dispositions that an institution and its programs and services assert they develop,'[1] as are reflected in their mission statements?" Outcomes assessment, which Peggy L. Maki equates with assessment for learning, "is a systematic and systemic process of inquiry into what and how well students learn over the progression of their studies and is driven by intellectual curiosity about the efficacy of collective educational practices."[2] That inquiry process is linked to planning for continual improvements in learning, whether that learning relates to information literacy, critical thinking, problem solving, quantitative reasoning, becoming an effective and good global citizen, communication skills (oral, written, and presentation), or other worthy educational goals.

This book complements *Outcomes Assessment in Higher Education* (Libraries Unlimited, 2004). Both are edited works with contributors from various segments of higher education, including officers of institutional accreditation organizations, an academic vice president, academic deans, a higher education consultant, faculty members, and librarians. The purpose of these cross-disciplinary perspectives is to demonstrate that we can all learn from one another and can work together to create stimulating learning environments that produce profound changes in students. These books place what occurs within the United States into proper international perspective.

The nineteen chapters of *Revisiting Outcomes Assessment in Higher Education* provide examples of higher-order outcomes (application of conceptual knowledge and skills) and show how different units within academic institutions developed those outcomes and either assess or plan to assess their progress in achieving them. It is our belief that, together, these two books document what is known about outcomes assessment in the middle of the first decade of the new century, as institutions and their programs gather, analyze, and use data collected through a rigorous process, and not based on anecdotal evidence. Undoubtedly, others will (and should) build from the foundation that works such as these provide. At the same time, readers will appreciate the final chapter and the perspectives of seven leaders in outcomes assessment about the challenges that the near future presents. As well, they should find chapter one of interest for its portrayal of a complex model that envisions outcomes assessment in terms of both vertical and horizontal dimensions. Chapter nineteen also returns to that model and discusses it in terms of disciplinary frameworks—a direction that outcomes assessment is likely to take.

The audience for both books includes faculty, administrators, and librarians at all academic institutions; accreditation organizations and associations, including program accreditors; program officials in national associations; other stakeholders, including members of state and other governments wanting to see what academe is doing to link accountability with continuous quality improvement, especially improvement in the student learner; and educators and accreditors in the United States and other countries wanting to learn more about outcomes assessment.

In *Student Learning Assessment: Options and Resources*, the Middle States Commission on Higher Education emphasizes a point that is critical to this book and its companion volume: that "teaching lies primarily in the hands of faculty members, and good learning cannot happen without their commitment and dedication. *Assessment, first and foremost, is a tool for faculty members to use as they do their very best to teach their students well.*"[3]

Notes

1. Peggy L. Maki, *Assessing for Learning: Building a Sustainable Commitment across the Institution* (Sterling, VA: Stylus Publishing, 2004), 3.

2. Ibid., xvii.

3. Middle States Commission on Higher Education, *Student Learning Assessment: Options and Resources* (Philadelphia, PA: Middle States Commission on Higher Education, 2003), 81.

CHAPTER 1

Institutional Mission-centered Student Learning

Robert E. Dugan and Peter Hernon

Outcomes assessment, which is intended to foster a culture of student learning in higher education, involves an ongoing, collaborative effort between faculty members and others within the institution (e.g., librarians). With cross-disciplinary learning and scholarship on the rise, programs at both the undergraduate and graduate levels are likely to draw on faculty from different disciplines who convey complementary knowledge and who need to settle on a common set of learning outcomes. One area of institutional collaboration relates to information literacy. However, outcomes assessment also refers to a developmental process related to critical thinking, problem solving, communication skills, becoming a responsible global citizen, and so on.

As departmental, organizational, and institutional cultures undergo change, and as the focus of that change is less on teaching and more on learning, a commitment to sustainable outcomes assessment becomes essential. Accrediting organizations expect institutions of higher education to make a long-term commitment to improved student learning, and stakeholders, such as state governments, demand actual evidence (data-driven decision making), not anecdotes, to evaluate the extent to which institutions of higher education meet their missions. Outcomes assessment therefore focuses on student learning as expressed in the institution's mission and it asks academe to adopt accountability as "an institutional value."[1]

Outcomes assessment thus deals with both assessment and accountability. Assessment focuses on the process that an institution or program uses to gather evidence about the attainment of student learning outcomes as expressed at the program and institutional levels; the goal is to improve overall instruction, advance or deepen learning, and thereby meet the expectations of stakeholders and educate students. The challenge is to transform organizational and institutional cultures into learning cultures in which students absorb and apply subject content and achieve specific discipline and program learning outcomes. The learning culture recognizes that people learn differently and it helps all students (including those with disabilities as well as students who are less academically prepared to enter a college or university, and international students who lack the language and conceptual skills that others might have) to develop throughout a program of study. As a result, assessment—a collaborative responsibility—focuses on the extent to which students construct their own meaning from what their instructors present, that is, the extent to which they can apply, synthesize, demonstrate, and translate what they have learned.

ASSESSMENT FOR EDUCATIONAL QUALITY AND ACCOUNTABILITY IN HIGHER EDUCATION

As Richard Frye, a planning analyst for the Office of Institutional Assessment and Testing at Western Washington University, Bellingham, maintains, "Assessment derives its legitimacy from the quality of its measurements."[2] Institutions of higher education must link assessment to the planning process—through an assessment plan—and be concerned about the quality of the evidence gathered on an ongoing basis and how that evidence leads to educational improvement.

Frye also observes, "Accountability aims at improving fiscal efficiency, but is blind to issues of educational quality. Assessment aims at improving the quality of education, but is necessarily constrained by budgets."[3] Accountability, in fact, is a multi-dimensional concept, which, for instance, addresses the extent to which the priorities of different stakeholders are met.[4] U.S. Secretary of Education Margaret Spellings emphasized that colleges and universities should "want to be able to tell their story better" and that "they are served when they can do that with real data and no anecdotes."[5] Student learning outcomes, when connected to the institutional mission and educational goals, help to "tell that story," that is, if the indicators of institutional performance are reliable and valid. Student learning outcomes, when gathered longitudinally, reflect changes in overall institutional performance over time.

In a discussion of institutional and program assessment, Alverno College highlights both dimensions and the qualities of such assessment. For instance, assessment at both levels "is a means to achieve educational purposes, not an end in itself" and it "encourages coherence."[6] In conclusion,

> Institutional and program assessment is a process and system for assessing institutional or curriculum effectiveness through a study of individual and group patterns in student/alumna performance over time as a result of curriculum, and comparing these patterns to diverse criteria from various sources. This enables a community of judgment to look at student and alumna perspectives, to reflect on insights about how they learn and continue to develop, to learn how curriculum contributes to their learning, and to envision more effective curriculum and supports for learning, including the learning atmosphere of the college.[7]

PLANNING PROCESS

The sustainability of outcomes assessment depends on the extent to which:

- It is linked to planning processes; and
- The results are used to achieve stated outcomes, thereby improving the educational experience.

Simply stated, the planning process (related to the development and implementation of an assessment plan) adheres to a simple *open-system model* that starts with the identification of institutional or program outcomes and links them to inputs (those needed to carry out the agreed-upon plan). As Figure 1.1 illustrates, the stages of the model then progress from throughputs to outputs and the feedback stage loops back to a review of the program and inputs. Inputs relate to the resources committed (e.g., faculty, the technology available to accomplish specific outcomes, administrative support, and support staff), and throughputs might relate to the implementation of student learning outcomes. The feedback loop covers the assessment process (gathering information and using it to revisit the inputs and improve the extent to which outcomes have been accomplished) and the whole process provides insights into the development of students, for instance, as critical thinkers, effective

Figure 1.1
Open-systems Model

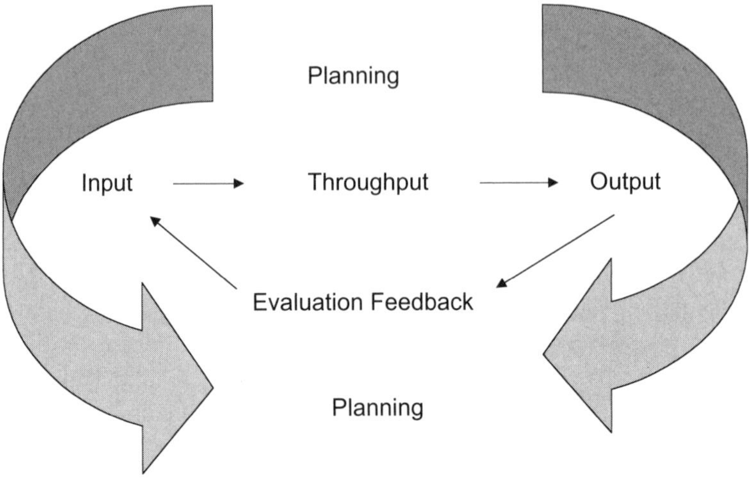

Input ⟶ Throughput ⟶ Output

Planning

Evaluation Feedback

Planning

communicators, and problem solvers. In effect, the assessment process could lead to change and new strategies for improving student learning.

Peggy L. Maki, a higher education consultant, views the planning process in terms of a collaborative *assessment cycle*,[8] and the planning process explains who will be assessed, how often, how the evidence will be gathered and interpreted (and by whom), and how the program or institution will follow up on implemented changes. The planning process should be transparent and address how academic programs and the institution foster a collaborative effort. That effort involves not only discussion and negotiation among all of the interested parties, but also investigation and reflection about what students learned and how to translate those results into action. The open-systems model, when applied to assessment, needs a written audit trail. In order to be sustainable and useful, the assessment process must occur at regular intervals and be continuous.

A FRAMEWORK MODEL FOR OUTCOMES PROCESSES

Institutions oftentimes deploy a systematic, hierarchical framework with horizontal and vertical levels to plan, gather, analyze, and report information, and to make changes to institutional and educational outcomes and objectives, as part of their effort to demonstrate accountability through assessment. This framework model demonstrates that the horizontal and vertical structures are integrated and dependent upon each other when the process involves the use of both. Institutional and organizational cultures play a role in both the horizontal and vertical processes. Additionally, the complexity of the framework helps to explain why institutions cannot respond to accountability demands as fast as stakeholders expect and want.

The characteristics of the framework model depicted in Figure 1.2 include:

- Hierarchy
  - It originates with the institution at the top and ends with individual courses taught by faculty at the bottom.
  - There is communication vertically between the horizontal levels and horizontally within the horizontal levels.
  - In almost every instance a resource (e.g., person, classroom, or service) simultaneously occupies both horizontal and vertical levels within this framework. For example, a faculty member belongs to a horizontal school (arts and sciences), a vertical discipline (sciences) and another horizontal level of science departments (e.g., physics, engineering, and chemistry). A science department then becomes a horizontal level for the numerous courses offered in this vertical structure.
  - It is systematic in that it involves inputs, processes, outputs, and evaluative feedback within horizontal levels, and between horizontal and vertical levels. It takes time to complete the largest systematic cycle from the beginning (institutional mission statement) to the end (consideration of, or changes to, the institutional mission statement).
- Planning
  - Planning, which often starts in the horizontal levels, is communicated down the hierarchy.
  - The horizontal levels plan, manage, identify, and refine expected educational outcomes and objectives.
- Educational outcomes and objectives
  - Goals and values originate from the institutional mission statement and shape the development of educational outcomes and objectives.

Figure 1.2
Hierarchical Framework for Outcomes Processes

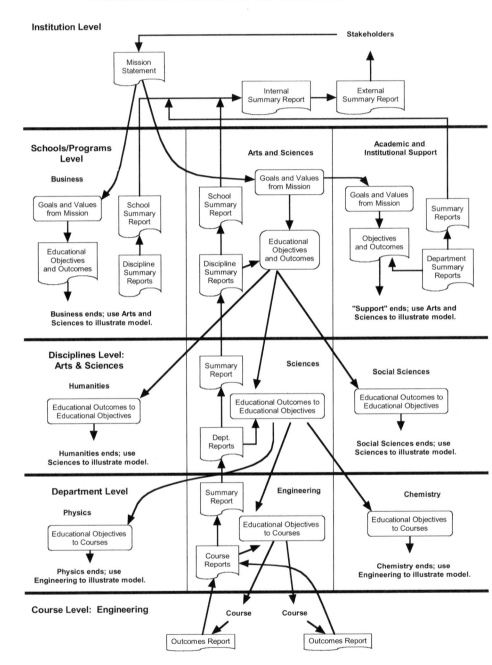

- The vertical levels receive the expected educational outcomes and objectives from the horizontal levels. These levels refine the expected educational outcomes and objectives for application to the next lower horizontal plane.
- The educational outcomes and objectives become course-embedded, measurable objectives (courses are vertical structures).
- Measurement and reporting
  - Measurements of the course-embedded objectives are often undertaken in the vertical structures, the results analyzed and then communicated via reports upwards to immediately higher horizontal levels.
  - The vertical and horizontal levels use the reports to measure progress towards meeting the identified educational outcomes and objectives.
  - Reports are summarized at the horizontal levels for communication upwards to the next horizontal level.
- Influences
  - In addition to documenting measured progress towards meeting expected educational outcomes and objectives, both horizontal and vertical structures can use the reports to recommend revisions and improvements of the expected outcomes and objectives, the curriculum of both general education and the disciplines, and educational content and delivery.
  - Summary reports inform internal and external stakeholders and eventually influence the institutional mission statement.

The culture of assessment, which is embedded in the horizontal and vertical levels of the framework, may include all perceptions and rationale from "we conduct assessment because stakeholders force accountability on us" to "we conduct assessment to improve institutional effectiveness and efficiency, especially concerning student learning outcomes." In this framework, the success of the assessment processes is dependent upon the cultural commitment to the assessment effort at each horizontal level and is communicated to the vertical levels, beginning with the senior institutional administration, including the president and the chief academic officer. Assessment can be delayed and even obstructed at any horizontal level.

Additionally, this framework is complicated; it involves several horizontal levels and hundreds if not thousands of faculty, academic and institutional support members, offices, and services. It takes considerable time to undertake one systematic loop from the identification of values and goals in the mission statement to the summary outcomes report(s) provided to the numerous and various stakeholders. However, stakeholders, especially those external to the institutional environment, demand and therefore expect a quicker turnaround for accountability than may be possible considering the complexity of this framework. It may be impossible to expect accountability from the institution as a whole. Accountability instead might be demonstrated from one or more specific vertical structures, especially by and within the disciplines.

STUDENT LEARNING

Historically, faculty members have relied on passive instructional methods (e.g., lecturing) instead of *"active learning* in which students solve problems, answer questions, formulate questions of their own, discuss, explain, debate, or brainstorm during class, and *cooperative learning* in which students work in teams on problems and projects under conditions that assume both positive interdependence and individual accountability."[9] Learning might also be characterized in such terms as deep and service learning. Deep learning relates knowledge gained from different classes, and it focuses on what is deemed significant within a program of study. Service learning, which is appropriate to many professional schools, involves experiential learning—developing critical thinking and problem solving skills.

Such types of learning should go beyond what occurs within a particular class and should focus on how student abilities progress throughout a program of study. For this reason, programs might establish rubrics, which "are explicit schemes for classifying products or behaviors into categories that vary along a continuum.... Rubrics can be used to provide formative feedback to students, to grade students, and/or assess programs."[10]

Student learning outcomes relate to the types of learning highlighted above and to the expectations conveyed from rubrics that characterize student learners at different phrases of their program completion. As *Knowing What Students Know*, a report published by the National Academies Press, notes, advances in understanding of how people learn reinforce the fact that assessment is evolving and new approaches to learning may emerge as rubrics address active, cooperative, deep, and service learning.[11] However, such learning necessitates a cultural transformation and alerting multiple educational constituencies to what academe is trying to accomplish. As the report explains,

> Assessments at the classroom and large-scale levels should grow out of a shared knowledge base about the nature of learning. Policy makers should support efforts to achieve such coherence. Policy makers should also promote the development of assessment systems that measure the growth or progress of students and the educational system over time and that support multilevel analyses of the influences responsible for such change.[12]

As Figure 1.2 indicates, support should also come from all levels of the institution.

CULTURAL TRANSFORMATION

Organizational and institutional culture is characterized by the values, norms, standards, beliefs, principles, philosophies, and ideologies that characterize an organization or institution, as well as the practices and behaviors that exemplify and reinforce those values, norms, and so forth. The culture encompasses the behavior and shared expectations that influence the way in which individuals, groups, and teams interact with each other and cooperate to achieve organizational or institutional goals. The culture of an organization may or may not be the same as the culture of an institution.

As librarians Amos Lakos and Shelly Phipps point out, "culture is the 'shared mental model' that the members of an organization hold and take for granted."[13] Organizational and institutional culture is often the cause of inflexibility. Members of the organization or institution might resist change that forces them to abandon established and approved ways of doing things; in effect, they are comfortable with the status quo. Lakos and Phipps note,

> For change to occur, the organization must recognize either a threat to its survival or a strong, positive external pressure that calls for adaptation and integration of new systems. Such systems provide the means to ensure continuation of the organization and the ability to achieve its

mission. Members must commit to strong organizational values for the organization to adequately change.[14]

It is important to gauge the extent to which the faculty's intellectual curiosity has shifted from teaching to learning by asking question such as

- How many academic units develop an assessment plan to improve learning?
- Who (and what) drives the assessment process?
- Is the process faculty-driven?

Perhaps the ultimate question is, "Would the process continue if certain administrators or faculty members retired or left the institution?" In other words, how sustainable is the assessment plan, and has the culture permanently transformed?

Evidence of cultural transformation appears in institutional cere-monies (e.g., rituals), practices, symbols (e.g., the arrangement of office space), slogans (e.g., phrases found in mission statements), group norms, and myths and stories (usually introduced to new staff to reinforce current or past values).[15] One indication of cultural transformation which is beginning to be common in higher education is an assessment day or week (e.g., a day or week each academic term or year), when students provide assessment information and faculty spend quality time focused on assessment issues, the assessment process, and the impli-cations of assessment data and information for improvement in peda-gogy, curriculum, student services, or instructional resources.

CONCLUSION

Assessment, which adheres to the open-systems model, is an on-going process that seeks to understand and improve student learning.

It involves making expectations explicit and public; setting appropriate criteria and high standards for learning quality; systematically gathering, analyzing, and interpreting evidence to determine how well performance matches those expectations and standards; and using the resulting in-formation to document, explain, and improve performance. When it is embedded effectively within larger institutional systems, assessment can help us focus our collective attention, examine our assumptions, and create a shared academic culture dedicated to assuring and improving the quality of higher education.[16]

Programs and institutions need to develop a strong and sustainable commitment to assessment as a process and as a means to improve leaning based on explicit student learning outcomes. External stakeholders might focus on retention and graduation rates as proxies for student learning, but internal constituents should not relegate student learning outcomes to a subordinate position. The commitment to student learning outcomes should be evident in how the institution goes about developing its set of intended student learning outcomes and implementing the planning process conforming to the open-systems model. The plan, which reflects the extent to which adherence to outcomes assessment leads to cultural transformation, might be created and implemented at different levels: institutional, school, program, discipline, departmental, or in academic support units (e.g., libraries).[17] Thus, assessment might involve team, simulation, and research projects, as well as case studies as students reflect on, as well as demonstrate, what they learned. The key to outcomes assessment is to move beyond reflection and self-perceptions to the demonstration phase.

Notes

1. Marilee J. Bresciani, "Undergraduate Assessment at North Carolina State University: A Collaborative Effort" (Raleigh: North Carolina State University, n.d.), 3. Available at http://www.ncsu.edu/provost/academic_programs/uapr/assess/sacs_report.html (accessed February 3, 2005).

2. Richard Frey, "Assessment, Accountability, and Student Learning Outcomes" (Bellingham, WA: Western Washington University, Office of Institutional Assessment and Testing, n.d.), 4. Available at http://www.ac.wwu.edu/~dialogue/issue2.html (accessed February 3, 2005).

3. Ibid., 5.

4. For an identification and discussion of the stakeholders, see Peggy L. Maki, *Assessing for Learning: Building a Sustainable Commitment across the Institution* (Sterling, VA: Stylus Publishing, 2004), 6–8.

5. Jeffrey Selingo, "President Plans No Price Controls or Strict Accountability Rules for Colleges, New Education Secretary Says in Interview," *The Chronicle of Higher Education: Today's News* (February 7, 2005). Available at http://chronicle.com/temp/email.php?id=ipm3fvtra5chlr4ewbs4fserlyxt2ali (accessed February 8, 2005).

6. Alverno College, "Institutional and Program Assessment" (Milwaukee, WI: Alverno College, n.d.), 3. Available at http://depts.alverno.edu/ere/ipa/ipa.html (accessed February 3, 2005).

7. Ibid.

8. Peggy L. Maki, "Developing an Assessment Plan to Learn about Student Learning," in *Outcomes Assessment in Higher Education: Views and Perspectives*, edited by Peter Hernon and Robert E. Dugan (Westport, CT: Libraries Unlimited, 2004), 89–101; Maki, *Assessing for Learning*, 3–6 (see also p. 179).

9. North Carolina State University, "Active and Cooperative Learning" (Raleigh: North Carolina State University, 2005). Available at http://www.ncsu.edu/felder-public/Cooperative_Learning, html (accessed May 7, 2005).

10. Mary Allen, "Student Learning Outcomes in the CSU: Using Scoring Rubrics" (Long Beach: The California State University). Available at http://www.calstate.edu/AcadAff/SLOA/links/using_rubrics.shtml (accessed May 7, 2005).

11. Committee on the Foundations of Assessment, *Knowing What Students Know: The Science and Design of Educational Assessment*, edited by James W. Pellegrino, Naomi Chudowsky, and Robert Glaser (Washington, D.C.: The National Academies Press, 2001).

12. National Academies Press, "Knowing What Students Know: The Science and Design of Educat..." (Washington, D.C.: The National Academies Press, 2001), 7 (of 7 pages). Available at http://www.nap.edu/books/0309072727/html/1.html (accessed May 17, 2005).

13. Amos Lakos and Shelly Phipps, "Creating a Culture of Assessment: A Catalyst for Organizational Change," *portal: Libraries and the Academy* 4 (2004), 349.

14. Ibid.

15. Bresciani, "Undergraduate Assessment at North Carolina State University: A Collaborative Effort," 9.

16. See University of Alaska, Fairbanks, Office of the Provost, "Student Learning Outcomes Assessment" (Fairbanks: University of Alaska, Fairbanks, n.d.). Available at http://www.uaf.edu/provost.outcomes/ (accessed February 3, 2005). The definition is taken from the American Association for Higher Education *Bulletin* 48, no. 2 (November 1995), 7–9. For a step-by-step guide to developing an assessment plan, see University of Alaska, Fairbanks, Office of the Provost, "Student Learning Outcomes Assessment: A Step by Step Guide to Preparing an Outcomes Assessment Plan" (Fairbanks: University of Alaska, Fairbanks, n.d.). Available at http://www.uaf.edu/provost/outcomes/StepByStep.html (accessed February 3, 2005).

17. See Robert E. Dugan, "A Local Institutional Assessment Plan," in *Outcomes Assessment in Higher Education: Views and Perspectives*, ed. Peter Hernon and Robert E. Dugan (Westport, CT: Libraries Unlimited, 2004), 103–134.

CHAPTER 2

Accountability and Quality Improvement

Linda Suskie

Institutions of higher education are increasingly called to demonstrate *accountability* and *quality improvement*. What do these terms mean? What forces are driving calls for accountability and quality improvement? How can institutions demonstrate accountability and quality improvement? This chapter provides an overview of these complex questions.

UNDERSTANDING ACCOUNTABILITY AND QUALITY IMPROVEMENT

The concepts of accountability and quality improvement are closely related. Dictionaries (e.g., *Webster's II New College Dictionary*)[1] define accountability as being responsible or answerable; within higher education, accountability has been defined as "the public presentation and communication of evidence about performance in relation to goals."[2] The concept of quality improvement, meanwhile, comes from the business world, where it was formalized many years ago by W. Edwards Deming, who studied systems used by the Japanese to improve continually their manufacturing processes.[3] He called this approach total quality management, a term that has largely been supplanted by the terms continuous quality improvement, continuous improvement, and quality improvement.

Accountability and quality improvement thus differ in that accountability refers to *demonstrating* quality, while quality improvement, of course, refers to *improving* quality. Here lies a conundrum. Imagine a supervisor asking employees both for documentation that they have been doing their jobs well and for information on steps they are taking to improve their performance. The two requests can easily be seen as contradictory. Employees would want to respond to the first request by documenting that they are doing a superlative job—after all, this way lies pay raises and opportunities for advancement. The second request, however, implicitly requires them to admit that they are *not* doing the best possible job. Employees might therefore be tempted to respond to the second request incompletely, by reporting only on minor areas for improvement—since acknowledging serious shortcomings might have serious consequences, perhaps including losing their job. Now imagine the supervisor requiring that all this documentation—both of the employees' current effectiveness and their efforts to improve their effectiveness—be made public, and the dilemma that the employees face only grows.

Institutions of higher education face exactly the same predicament, so it should be no surprise that Trudy W. Banta and Victor M. H. Borden have observed that "academics have not been able to identify indicators that would satisfy the twin purposes of accountability and improvement."[4] This seemingly unresolvable challenge has led Peter Ewell to suggest that quality improvement processes "should be removed, structurally and perceptually, from accountability."[5] Some accreditation associations are moving in this direction; the Commission on Colleges of the Southern Association of Colleges and Schools, for example, requires institutions to submit Quality Enhancement Plans that are separate from their documentation of compliance with accreditation requirements.[6]

Completely separating accountability and quality improvement efforts may be unnecessarily redundant and inefficient, however. Why conduct, for example, one assessment to demonstrate that students are writing adequately and a separate assessment to identify ways to improve their writing skills? Perhaps the answer is to *address* accountability and quality improvement efforts simultaneously but to *report* on those efforts in separate forums. Another key, as discussed later in this chapter, is to design incentives and rewards not only for good performance *results* but also for *efforts* to raise performance to new levels of excellence.

WHY THE FOCUS ON ACCOUNTABILITY AND QUALITY IMPROVEMENT?

Today a variety of stakeholders are calling for greater accountability and quality improvement. Legislators, government officials, accrediting agencies, board members, employers, and students and their families are increasingly asking for evidence that higher education institutions are providing programs and services of quality. Considering that American higher education has long been regarded by many as the best in the world—anyone who doubts this need only consider the thousands of international students who have sought an American education—why are these demands increasingly vocal?

The increased need for higher education has increased public attention to it. Higher education is no longer an optional indulgence but a necessity for economic well-being. Patrick M. Callan and Joni E. Finney have concluded that the American economy "will require college-level education throughout the workforce as a necessary condition of national prosperity,"[7] while the CHEA (Council for Higher Education Accreditation) Institute for Research and Study of Accreditation and Quality Assurance notes that "employers and elected officials have never been clearer in their demand that the graduates of U.S. colleges and universities should possess an increasingly specific set of higher-order literacies and communication skills."[8] Joseph C. Burke has concluded that this dramatic sea change "demands accountability."[9]

The success rates of low-income students and some students of color are especially worrisome.[10] As the Business-Higher Education Forum warned in 2004, "unless we do a better job of getting low-income students both *into* and *through* college, today's demographic trends could deepen social inequality and economic decline. Extending the diversity agenda from access to completion of a . . . degree is an economic imperative."[11]

The United States "no longer leads the world in the rate of college completion,"[12] especially in the education of scientists and engineers. According to the Organisation for Economic Co-operation and Development (OECD), the United States has been overtaken in the proportion of the population with a post-secondary education, as other countries increasingly recognize that post-secondary education is essential to sustained economic development.[13]

The costs of higher education—to students, their families, and taxpayers—is persistently growing faster than the general cost of living.[14] Like all consumers, students and their families want good value for their money and, as Susan Engelkemeyer notes, "a regular review of the return on an investment in education is not only reasonable but the least that students and their families can expect."[15] Taxpayers, meanwhile, want assurance that their tax dollars are spent on worthwhile needs. Banta and Borden note that there are "more questions about the relative contribution to society of higher education versus highways, prisons, and public schools."[16]

There are concerns about the quality of higher education's activities and products. As the National Commission on Accountability in Higher Education has noted, "employers report that too many graduates require additional training in the basic knowledge and skills required for sophisticated work."[17] According to Burke, critics have complained about "the quality and quantity of faculty teaching and student learning, the preoccupation with graduate studies and research, the neglect of undergraduate education . . . and the growth of 'mission creep' and 'program sprawl.'"[18]

The higher education community has been historically reticent about documenting and sharing what it does and what it accomplishes. Frank Newman has observed,

> The real reason we don't test is, we would rather not know. . . . We have a rhetoric about what we do . . . : when you come to our institution you get a great liberal education, you're going to learn to think, you're going to learn about the great traditions of Western thought. If we start measuring, we will start finding out that you didn't learn how to think, you didn't learn about the great traditions of Western thought. Then we have a nasty little problem on our hands.[19]

This reticence has led to what Ewell terms "'a crisis of confidence' in the eyes of external stakeholders; the point is not so much that outcomes are visibly deficient as the fact that no one seems to know *what* they are."[20]

The higher education community has also been habitually reluctant to acknowledge its shortcomings and improve what it does. Major foundations that have historically supported higher education now sense that higher education is slow to respond to change and that their gifts have consequently had little measurable impact. John Pulley has found that, as a result, foundations are redirecting their funds to projects in basic education and health where they can see more tangible results.[21]

DEMONSTRATING ACCOUNTABILITY AND QUALITY IMPROVEMENT: IT BEGINS WITH GOALS

Walter A. Shewhart developed a model that characterizes quality improvement as a continuous four-step cycle that Deming later popularized:

1. Establish clear, appropriate, and relevant goals and targets;
2. Design and implement programs, services, and other initiatives to achieve those goals;
3. Evaluate whether the goals have been achieved; and
4. Use evaluation results to improve the other three steps of the cycle: the goals, the programs and services, and/or the evaluation methods.[22]

This is a useful framework for engaging in accountability and quality improvement. The cycle begins with articulating goals, probably the most important step in the process. As Robert D. Behn observes, "You can't have accountability without expectations. If you want to hold people accountable, you have to be able to specify what you expect them to do and not do."[23]

Effective Goals Stem from Institutional Mission and Priorities

Accountability and quality improvement both aim to answer one fundamental question, "How well are we achieving what we aim to do?"[24] Accountability and quality improvement efforts and measures are thus valid only if they are based on meaningful, appropriate, and relevant goals.

What goals are most important to institutions of higher education? The higher education literature repeatedly mentions four types of goals:

- Educational quality and outcomes;[25]
- Responsiveness to "fundamental public priorities"[26] such as addressing regional economic, civic, and social needs;
- Responsible stewardship of resources and efficiency;[27] and
- Other aspects of institutional mission, especially scholarship and service.[28]

Of these four broad categories, the most important is "educational quality and outcomes," especially student learning outcomes, because goals should build on institutional missions, visions, and values,[29] and the fundamental mission of most colleges and universities is to foster student learning. As the Middle States Commission on Higher Education emphasizes, "because student learning is a fundamental element of the mission of most institutions of higher education, the assessment of student learning is an essential component of the assessment of institutional effectiveness."[30] The National Commission on Accountability in Higher Education concurs that, "to achieve excellent results, the focus of accountability . . . must be on learning [and] widespread student achievement,"[31] while the CHEA Institute for Research and Study of Accreditation and Quality Assurance notes that "evidence of student learning outcomes is becoming a principal gauge of higher education's effectiveness."[32]

While learning, scholarship, and service are at the heart of the missions of most institutions of higher education, this does not mean that institutions should have common goals. As the CHEA Institute for Research and Study of Accreditation and Quality Assurance notes, "institutions and programs will always differ appropriately with respect to mission and goals and diversity has been a historic strength of American higher education."[33] American higher education is not designed as "one size fits all." Indeed, one of its widely recognized strengths is the plethora of educational opportunities it offers to American students. Because it is a heterogeneous enterprise, there cannot be a common set of goals—or a common set of accountability measures—that apply with equal validity to all higher education institutions. The Business-Higher Education Forum concurs that "national capacity can be developed, and in fact is probably enriched, through multiple types of assessments."[34] Each institution has unique goals and must demonstrate accountability and quality improvement in unique ways.

Effective Goals Focus on the Ends, Not the Means

The National Commission on Accountability in Higher Education stresses that "better accountability for results at the institutional and state levels requires clearer goals (especially for student learning)."[35] Articulating clear goals is a bit like planning a road trip; travelers cannot plot their route until they know where they want to go and why they want to get there. If you want to visit Aunt Mary, for example, because she is very ill and may not linger long, you will want to take the fastest route to her town. If, on the other hand, Aunt Mary is hale and hearty and you want to see the beautiful region she lives in, you may choose a more meandering, scenic route.

Similarly, when establishing goals for a higher education institution, the institutional community should consider not only what it wants to accomplish but where this accomplishment will take the institution and *why* the community wants the institution to move in that direction. Root cause analysis[36]—repeatedly asking "Why?"—is a technique developed to solve process problems but is also useful for articulating goals. Consider three colleges, all of which have established apparently identical goals to renovate their student residence halls. When we ask each institution *why* it is renovating its residence halls, however, their true goals become quite different:

- The first college has experienced a rise in crime rates in and around its residence halls and wants to create a safer environment. This college's true goal is thus to reduce the crime rate in the vicinity of the residence halls.

- The second college is no longer filling its residence halls as students are increasingly drawn to off-campus apartments, so it wants to increase residence hall occupancy. In this instance, asking "Why?" a second time is useful: Why does the college want to increase residence hall occupancy? This elicits the college's true goal: to keep the residence hall operations financially self-sufficient.

- The third college wants to create more communal areas in its residence halls. Again, asking "Why?" a second time is useful; the college wants to use these communal areas for new programs and services on student civility. Here, asking "Why?" a third time is also useful: Why does the college want to create these new programs and services? This elicits the college's true goal: the college is concerned about the lack of tolerance and respect that its students demonstrate toward one another and wants to help them to develop greater sensitivity toward others.

Having goals that focus on the ends rather than the means helps identify appropriate measures to demonstrate accountability and quality improvement. These colleges might be tempted to "measure" their performance by simply documenting that the residence hall renovations have been completed, but that evaluates the activity, not the result.[37] In these examples, the first college might more appropriately evaluate the effectiveness of its residence hall renovation by tracking changes in the crime rate in the vicinity of the residence halls. Similarly, the second college might more appropriately monitor the financial self-sufficiency of residence hall operations, and the third might have students write about tolerance and respect for others.

Effective Goals Have Appropriate Targets

Many institutional goals are written in such vague terms that it can be difficult to tell whether they have been achieved. How can one tell, for example, whether an institution has achieved its goal to "improve the climate for diversity" or "give students a sense of civic responsibility"? An important part of the goal-setting process is therefore answering the question "How will we know when we get there?"[38] by setting targets that can be used to judge whether the goal has been achieved. These targets can take several forms:[39]

- A *standards-based* target simply sets a standard against which achievement is measured. An institution might aim, for example, to raise $8 million in private gifts, retain 85% of its students through the sophomore year, achieve a 95% pass rate on a licensure exam, or create a reserve fund for contingencies equal to 3% of its annual operating budget. The Association of American Colleges & Universities suggests setting three sets of standards, for basic, proficient, and advanced performance.[40]

- A *benchmark* target compares the institution against its peers. A community college might aim, for example, to have a sophomore retention rate above the average of community colleges in its state.

- A *best practice* target compares the institution with the very best of its peers. A liberal arts college might, for example, aim to have the best four-year graduation rate among peer institutions.

- A *value-added* target compares students' performance when they begin and complete their studies. A university might, for example, aim for its graduating seniors to demonstrate analytical skills that are significantly stronger than when they entered as first-year students.

- A *longitudinal* target compares the institution today against past performance. An institution might, for example, aim to raise 15% more in alumni gifts this year than last year.

All of these forms of targets have pros and cons. Standards-based targets, for example, may be difficult to establish rationally (although Samuel A. Livingston and Michael J. Zieky offer a number of methods).[41] Meanwhile, some institutions are so distinctive that it may be difficult or impossible to identify appropriate peers and set a meaningful benchmark target, while the value-added perspective may be difficult to implement at an institution that serves many transfer students. Often multiple perspectives give the most fair and complete picture of institutional performance.

Effective Goals Have Purposeful Plans and Initiatives Designed to Achieve Them

The second step of the Shewart/Deming cycle is planning and implementing programs, services, and other initiatives to achieve identified goals. This may seem self-evident, but goals are more likely to be achieved if the institution designs purposeful programs, services, and initiatives intended to help achieve them. Student retention rates, for example, will probably not increase without developing and implementing programs and services that have been carefully designed to promote student success.

Such initiatives will not happen without the committed involvement of faculty and staff, and that will not happen without the active support of institutional leaders. The National Commission on Accountability in Higher Education urges trustees and institutional leaders to "create the conditions, including necessary incentives and management oversight, for students and faculty to meet ambitious objectives in learning, research, and service."[42] Four conditions are especially important:

- Focus on only the most important institutional-level and program-level goals, because "if you try to be the best at everything, you'll be the best at nothing."[43] When accountability "focuses on a few priority goals . . . it acquires power to motivate and guide better performance," according to the National Commission on Accountability in Higher Education.[44]

- Provide adequate guidance and support for accountability and quality improvement efforts. Perhaps the three most important means of support are helping faculty and staff find the time to do these things (perhaps by suspending some other less important activities); providing technical support, coordination, and professional development opportunities; and giving faculty and staff direction and assistance. This takes time and effort; the Institute for Education Best Practices notes that "organizational cultures supportive of performance measures take time to develop, require considerable 'socialization' of the organization's members, and are enhanced by stable leadership."[45]

- Manage with a light touch. William F. Massy encourages institutional leaders to manage *for* quality—in a way that empowers faculty and staff—rather than *of* quality, which implies more direct and possibly micromanagement.[46] It is especially helpful to involve faculty and staff in identifying and developing tools and measures for accountability and quality improvement, as discussed earlier. As Banta and Borden note, "perhaps the surest way to ensure that [such measures] will be used is to involve the individuals who ought to use them in their initial selection and development" and have them specify "the kinds of data they will consider credible and helpful."[47]

- Use results appropriately, as discussed later in this chapter.

EVALUATING HOW WELL GOALS HAVE BEEN ACHIEVED

Effective tools and measures can help us answer not only the fundamental question, "How well are we achieving what we aim to do?" but also ancillary questions such as, "Are we focusing on the right things?," "Can we simplify what we are doing?," and "Can we do things better?" Linda Suskie describes several characteristics of effective tools for assessing student learning that also characterize effective tools and measures for accountability and quality improvement.[48]

Effective tools and measures provide useful information. Borden notes that the most useful measures are those that correspond to institutional mission and key institutional goals and values,[49] thereby demonstrating what psychometricians call content validity. Indeed, a study by the Institute for Education Best Practices confirmed that the best and, obviously, most useful "institutional performance measures communicate the institution's core values."[50]

Effective tools and measures are focused, simple and cost-effective, "yielding value that justifies the time and expense . . . put into them."[51] This means that accountability and quality improvement efforts should focus on only the most important institutional-level and program-level goals, as "more data is not more accountability," and when accountability "focuses on a few priority goals…it acquires power to motivate and guide better performance," as Susan W. Engelkemeyer suggests.[52] Accountability and quality improvement tools and measures are best kept simple and manageable; surveys should be very short, for example.

Effective tools and measures "give us reasonably accurate, truthful information"[53] of sufficient quality that it can be used with confidence to make decisions. While tools and measures should be designed using conceptually and methodologically sound procedures, Borden observes, "rare indeed is the single technique that is sufficiently reliable, valid, and comprehensive to provide all the information needed for making an important decision. Thus, several techniques should be used in a triangulation process to furnish a sound basis for judgment."[54]

Effective tools and measures are systematized, not once-and-done. A study by the Institute for Education Best Practices concluded that, to be effective, "performance measures must be…visible and consistent across the organization."[55] Nancy Kleiniewski stresses that faculty and staff are more likely to accept review processes and tools if they perceive them as "systematic, transparent, and consistent."[56]

Effective tools and measures are fair and ethical. They provide honest, balanced information on the institution's performance and, as discussed later in this chapter, they are used appropriately to inform decisions.

Effective tools and measures may be qualitative as well as quantitative, as some key institutional goals may be difficult to quantify.[57]

While a plethora of tools and measures is available to evaluate the achievement of institutional goals, none is the best choice for every situation. A tool that one institution finds very useful, for example, may be completely irrelevant at another, while a measure that one institution can implement easily may be too cumbersome or time-consuming at another. Possible tools and measures to examine and demonstrate accountability and quality improvement fall into several broad categories.

Accreditation Processes

According to the Middle States Commission on Higher Education, the accreditation process is "intended to strengthen and sustain the quality and integrity of higher education, making it worthy of public confidence and minimizing the scope of external control."[58] Accrediting associations may accredit an entire institution or an individual program.

While all accrediting associations establish and maintain standards for the institutions or programs that they accredit, they recognize that institutions of higher education are so diverse that their standards must be applied "within the context of [the institution's] own institutional mission and goals."[59] Accreditors therefore rely not on arbitrary standards or what Ralph Wolff calls "a single metric of effectiveness,"[60] but on the informed judgments that come from peer review.[61]

Accreditation processes generally include three elements: a self-study of the institution's strengths, weaknesses, and compliance with accreditation standards; a visit by a team of external reviewers; and recommendations or mandates for improvement based on the conclusions of the self-study and the review team. If serious concerns are identified, the accrediting association may require monitoring through follow-up reports or visits to ensure that identified concerns are addressed.

Assessments of Student Learning

Assessments of student learning, including tests, portfolios, projects, papers, and performances, provide information on how well the institution has achieved its goals for student learning, which are the key goals of most institutions of higher education. Because any one assessment strategy has inherent imperfections, the best evidence of student learning comes from multiple sources.[62] Published instruments, for example, show how students are performing compared to their peers across the country, but locally designed instruments are often a better match with institutional and program-level goals.

The CHEA Institute for Research and Study of Accreditation and Quality Assurance notes that "evidence of student learning can take many forms, but should involve direct examination of student performance— either for individual students or for representative samples of students."[63] The Middle States Commission on Higher Education explains:

> Suitable assessment measures . . . include **direct**—clear, visible, and convincing—evidence of student learning. Tangible examples of student learning, such as completed tests, assignments, projects, portfolios, licensure examinations, and field experience evaluations, are direct evidence of student learning. **Indirect** evidence, including retention, graduation, and placement rates and surveys of students and alumni, can be vital to understanding the teaching-learning process and student success (or lack thereof), but such information alone is insufficient

evidence of student learning *unless* accompanied by direct evidence. Grades alone are indirect evidence, as a skeptic might claim that high grades are solely the result of lax standards. But the assignments and evaluations that form the bases for grades can be direct evidence *if* they are accompanied by clear evaluation criteria that have a demonstrable relationship to key learning goals.[64]

Program Reviews

Program reviews are comprehensive reviews of an academic program or administrative operation. Like accreditation processes, they are designed both to demonstrate accountability and to foster quality improvement. They often include the same three elements as accreditation processes: a self-study conducted by the program's faculty and staff, a visit by one or more external reviewers, and recommendations for improvement based on the conclusions of the self-study and the reviewer.

Academic program reviews should aim to address three fundamental criteria:[65]

- *Quality*: What is the quality of the program, including its resources (e.g., faculty credentials, facilities, and library resources), its students (e.g., test scores and academic preparation), its activities (e.g., curriculum, faculty scholarship, and community service), and, most importantly, its outcomes (e.g., what its students have learned and how successful they are in their later pursuits). Lynn Arthur Steen offers provocative questions to consider, such as how well the curriculum meets the postgraduation needs of students, how the faculty's scholarship relates to the department's teaching mission, and how well the faculty is kept informed of research on how students learn.[66]
- *Need*: Is there sufficient demand for the program from students, employers, and others to keep it viable? Is demand anticipated to grow, diminish, or remain stable? How does this program compare with similar and competing programs? How central is the program to the institution's mission? Would the institution still be able to achieve its mission if the program did not exist? How might the institution be different if this happened?
- *Cost and cost-effectiveness*: How much does the program cost to operate, and how effectively and efficiently does the program use its

resources? The cost-effectiveness of academic programs can be evaluated in many ways, including student/faculty ratios, credit hours generated per full-time equivalent faculty member, cost per credit hour of instruction, space utilization, and so on.

These three criteria closely mirror the three major types of institutional goals discussed earlier in this chapter: educational quality and outcomes, responsiveness to fundamental public priorities, and responsible stewardship of resources and efficiency.

The Baldrige National Quality Program

The Baldrige National Quality Program, sponsored by the National Institute of Standards and Technology, might be considered a variation on the accreditation and program review themes. The Baldrige program was established by Congress in 1987 to "recognize U.S. organizations for their achievements in quality performance and to raise awareness of the importance of quality and performance excellence as a competitive edge."[67] To be considered for a Baldrige Award, an educational institution must provide thorough documentation of its efforts to improve and maintain the highest quality in seven areas: leadership; strategic planning; student and market focus; measurement, analysis, and knowledge management; faculty and staff focus; process management; and results. Examples of questions that applicants must answer include:

- How do senior leaders encourage frank, two-way communication throughout the organization?
- How do you keep your approaches to providing student, faculty, and staff access current with educational service needs and directions?
- How do you seek and use input from faculty and staff and their supervisors on education, training, and development needs?
- How is information on students used to engage all students in active learning?
- What are your results for key measures or indicators of ethical behavior in the senior leaders and governance of your organization?[68]

While the Baldrige National Quality Program is an intriguing concept, in practice it is difficult and time-consuming for higher education institutions to participate. Indeed, only two higher education institutions have received the award since the education category was introduced in 1999 through 2004: Kenneth W. Monfort College of Business and University of Wisconsin–Stout.[69]

Performance Indicators

Performance indicators, key performance indicators, performance measures, and performance metrics are all terms used to describe a set of quantitative measures of various aspects of institutional performance. Michael G. Dolence and Donald M. Norris define performance indicators as "measures that are monitored in order to determine the health, effectiveness, and efficiency of an organization" and that "tell stakeholders, managers, and other staff whether the college or university is accomplishing its goals using an acceptable level of resources."[70]

There are literally hundreds of potential performance indicators; Ewell has found that popular ones include:

- Student retention and graduation rates;
- Job placement rates;
- Racial/ethnic enrollment breakdowns;
- Dollar value of sponsored research grants;
- Licensure and certification examination pass rates; and
- Faculty workload (e.g., student/faculty ratios, average credit enrollments per full-time equivalent faculty).[71]

Many stakeholders, especially busy board members, legislators, and government officials, like performance indicators because they are numbers that are easy to understand and digest. James Honan observes, however, that performance indicators often do not reflect "what actually matters to the long-term well-being of the institution."[72] While Jean Avnet Morse emphasizes that "learning is the most important outcome" of most institutions of higher education,[73] performance indicators largely ignore much direct evidence of student learning and instead focus on financial measures,[74] other input measures such as student admissions standards and faculty credentials, or activity measures such as enrollments, time to degree, and graduation rates.[75] For example, of the ten viability indicators suggested by the American Academy for Liberal Education, six deal with finances and the remainder relate to enrollments.[76] Of the eight performance measures used by the Pennsylvania State System of Higher Education,[77] three deal with finances and productivity, three with student persistence, one with diversity, and one with faculty credentials.

Unfortunately, as the Business-Higher Education Forum notes, "it is possible to produce so-called improvements in these [kinds of] measures while actually hurting teaching and learning."[78] While some institutions have adopted a small set of performance indicators designed to provide more balanced information on key institutional goals—what Robert Kaplan and David Norton, David Oehler, and Brent Ruben call a balanced scorecard or dashboard indicators[79]—the Business-Higher Education Accountability Forum has concluded that measures of student learning are not yet common in higher education accountability systems.[80]

While performance indicators can be helpful in tracking some aspects of an institution's performance, they usually do not tell the full story of an institution's accomplishments. There is no simple, accurate performance indicator, for example, that indicates whether an institution is achieving its goals of improving the cultural climate of the region, linking budget decisions to institutional plans, giving students an appreciation of the arts, or graduating students with a sense of civic engagement. Even under the best of circumstances, when a performance indicator is clearly aligned with an important institutional goal, there is always a story behind the indicator and the indicator alone may be misinterpreted if the story is not shared.

Surveys

Surveys can be an important means of collecting information on the achievement of some goals, especially those concerned with meeting the needs of students or other groups. Surveys can help determine, for example, whether an institution has achieved goals to meet the needs of local employers, to provide a learning-centered environment for its students, or to offer user-friendly support for technologies. Both published and locally-designed surveys may provide useful information.

"Yes/No" Measures

Some goals can best be "measured" by simply noting that they have been accomplished: a new strategic plan has been adopted, a computer system has been upgraded. These types of yes/no measures should be used sparingly, as they often measure the tasks to be completed and not whether the underlying goal has been accomplished.[81]

Quality Improvement Tools

A variety of tools have been developed to study institutional processes and identify ways to improve them. A number of these tools, such as run charts, histograms, pareto analyses, and six sigma analyses, can be used both to study institutional processes and document improvements to them.

Online Institutional Portfolios

Online institutional portfolios are a relatively new way for institutions to demonstrate accountability and quality improvement. According to the Pew Forum, online institutional portfolios aim to enhance stakeholders' understanding of institutional mission, support institutional improvement, and communicate accountability within the context of the institution's mission[82] through a collection of Web sites with succinct information on the institution's goals and its success in achieving those goals. The Urban Universities Portfolio Project is perhaps the most significant effort to date in developing online institutional portfolios.[83]

PROMOTING A CLIMATE OF USING EVALUATION RESULTS FOR ACCOUNTABILITY AND QUALITY IMPROVEMENT

Accountability and quality improvement efforts are largely worthless unless the results are used to improve the institution and its programs and move them to new levels of excellence. Information from accountability and quality improvement efforts can be used to:

- Inform stakeholders of how well the institution is achieving its goals. The key here is what the Association of American Colleges and Universities calls transparency:[84] communicating results in terms that are relevant to and easily understood by each type of stakeholder and are devoid of higher education jargon.
- Revise institutional and program-level goals. Sometimes, for example, results show that current goals are too ambitious. A goal to raise $20 million in private gifts over the next three years may need to be rethought, for example, if this year brought in only $3 million and there are no major donor prospects in sight. Sometimes results

help show that the institution has too many goals, causing it to lose focus and diffuse its energies.[85]

- Plan modifications to current programs, services, and initiatives. Perhaps the curricula of some courses need to be rethought to help students better develop their critical thinking skills.

- Plan new programs, services, and initiatives. Disappointing student retention rates, for example, might indicate the need for a new first-year experience program or a new array of support services.

- Inform budget decisions. A new first-year experience program, for example, cannot succeed without a supporting budget. If students are graduating with inadequate computer skills, the institution may need to budget for upgraded computers and software to help them learn contemporary computer skills.

- Improve assessment and evaluation efforts. Sometimes assessment results are not what was expected because a survey question was not clear, students misunderstood a test question, or only a small, unrepresentative sample of students answered a survey. Revising assessment tools and strategies may lead to improved assessment results in the future.

Accountability and quality improvement efforts will obviously be more useful if faculty and staff see value in participating. Suskie describes several steps that administrators can take to promote a climate in which accountability and quality improvement efforts are seen as worthwhile activities, not pointless add-ons.[86] These steps include:

- *Use evidence as the basis for important decisions.* Obviously this implies adopting only those tools and measures whose results can contribute to significant decisions. "Good institutional performance measures ... point to action to be taken on results,"[87] while "indicators that are not used obviously have no meaning or value."[88] Before implementing any tool or measure, ask "What decisions will this tool help us make?" If the measure cannot be linked to any important decision, it is probably not worthwhile.

Another key to ensuring the use of accountability and quality improvement measures is to create an institutional "culture of evidence," in which decisions are based neither on whim nor anecdotes, but on systematic, compelling evidence. Sarah Carrigan, Jeremy Fisher, and

Philip Handwerk found that, if faculty and staff see that their assessment and evaluation efforts are not only valued but contribute to important decisions, they will be more likely to participate.[89] Lisa Petrides and Thad Nodine have confirmed this, finding that "the way data had historically been used had a significant effect on individuals' willingness to collect, share, and use data in decision-making."[90]

- *Use evidence ethically and responsibly.* This means recognizing that, because any one tool has inherent imperfections and, as the CHEA Institute notes, "judgments about quality are complex," the best approach is to use "multiple sources of information in a mutually reinforcing fashion."[91] As Suskie states bluntly, "Never base any important decision on only one assessment . . . Assessments shouldn't make decisions for us or dictate what we should teach; they should only advise us as we use our professional judgment to make suitable decisions."[92] Banta and Borden note that providing information from multiple sources has the added benefit of increasing the likelihood that it will be used by decision makers, because of its increased credibility.[93]

- *Do not use evidence punitively.* As Petrides and Nodine note, "How data are used in an environment of accountability—such as using data to explore program improvements as opposed to using data to justify cutbacks—can affect people's willingness to participate in data gathering and analysis."[94] As discussed above, major decisions should *never* be based on just one source of evidence, and decisions to terminate or cut back programs and services are certainly major for the people planning and implementing them.

- *Recognize and reward efforts to improve,* even if those efforts are not, at first, successful. Foster a climate that encourages appropriate levels of risk-taking and innovation and allows faculty and staff to stumble occasionally as they try their best to make improvements.

CONCLUSION

Will the forces calling for accountability and quality improvement ever go away? While it is entirely possible that some other issue may move to the forefront and consume everyone's attention, it seems doubtful that calls for accountability and quality improvement will soon disappear. As Robert Gabriner has noted, accountability is "a permanent part of our political and economic reality. The fiscal crises of the states, the growing demand for higher education, and the fierce competition for public funding are major factors driving the accountability movement."[95]

Higher education is simply too large an enterprise, with too many stakeholders keenly interested in it. While the way we define accountability and quality improvement and the ways we evaluate higher education's effectiveness may change, as long as higher education is viewed as a costly undertaking, there will be strong interest in ensuring that it offers effective programs and services and operates in an efficient manner. The National Commission on Accountability in Higher Education notes that the purpose of accountability is "to foster better-designed, better-implemented, adequately-supported, more successful educational programs."[96] The need for better higher education programs will not diminish, so neither will the need to give accountability and quality improvement efforts our continued full attention.

Notes

1. *Webster's II New College Dictionary* (Boston: Houghton Mifflin, 2001).

2. Business-Higher Education Forum, *Public Accountability for Student Learning in Higher Education: Issues and Options* (Washington, D.C.: American Council for Education, April 2004), 9.

3. W. Edwards Deming, *Out of the Crisis* (Cambridge, MA: Massachusetts Institute of Technology, 1987).

4. Trudy W. Banta and V.M.H. Borden, "Performance Indicators for Accountability and Improvement," in *Using Performance Indicators to Guide Strategic Decision Making*, ed. V.M.H. Borden and Trudy W. Banta (New Directions for Institutional Research, No. 82) (San Francisco: Jossey-Bass, 1994), 96–97.

5. Peter T. Ewell, "Developing Statewide Performance Indicators for Higher Education," in *Charting Higher Education Accountability: A Sourcebook on State-level Performance Indicators*, ed. S. S. Ruppert (Denver, CO: Education Commission of the States, 1994), 148.

6. Commission on Colleges of the Southern Association of Colleges and Schools, *Principles of Accreditation: Foundations for Quality Enhancement* (Atlanta, GA: Commission on Colleges of the Southern Association of Colleges and Schools, 2004).

7. Patrick M. Callan and Joni E. Finney, "State-by-state Report Cards: Public Purposes and Accountability for a New Century," in *Achieving Accountability in Higher Education: Balancing Public, Academic, and Market Demands*, ed. Joseph C. Burke (San Francisco: Jossey-Bass, 2005), 207.

8. CHEA Institute for Research and Study of Accreditation and Quality Assurance, *Statement of Mutual Responsibilities for Student Learning Outcomes: Accreditation, Institutions, and Programs* (Washington, D.C.: Council for Higher Education Accreditation, September 2003), 4.

9. Joseph C. Burke, "Preface," in *Achieving Accountability in Higher Education*, xi.

10. National Commission on Accountability in Higher Education, *Accountability for Better Results: A National Imperative for Higher Education* (Denver, CO: State Higher Education Executive Officers, 2005).

11. Business-Higher Education Forum, *Public Accountability for Student Learning in Higher Education*, 11.

12. National Commission on Accountability in Higher Education, *Accountability for Better Results*, 6.

13. Organisation for Economic Co-operation and Development, *Education at a Glance: OECD Indicators* (Paris: Organisation for Economic Co-operation and Development, 2003).

14. National Commission on Accountability in Higher Education, *Accountability for Better Results*.

15. Susan W. Engelkemeyer, "Institutional Performance Measures," *AAHE Bulletin* 51, no. 4 (December 1998), 5.

16. Banta and Borden, "Performance Indicators for Accountability and Improvement," 97.

17. National Commission on Accountability in Higher Education, *Accountability for Better Results*, 23.

18. Joseph C. Burke, "Reinventing Accountability: From Bureaucratic Rules to Performance Results," in *Achieving Accountability in Higher Education*, 217.

19. Kate Zernike, "Tests Are Not Just for Kids," *New York Times Education Life Supplement* (August 4, 2002), section 4A, 27.

20. Peter T. Ewell, "Can Assessment Serve Accountability? It Depends on the Question," in *Achieving Accountability in Higher Education*, 104–124.

21. John Pulley, "Crumbling Support for Colleges," *The Chronicle of Higher Education* 48, no. 29 (March 29, 2002), A28.

22. Walter A. Shewhart, *Statistical Method from the Viewpoint of Quality Control* (New York: Dover Publications, 1939, 1986). See also Deming, *Out of the Crisis*.

23. Robert D. Behn, *Rethinking Democratic Accountability* (Washington, D.C.: Brookings Institution Press, 2001), 7.

24. Middle States Commission on Higher Education, *Characteristics of*

Excellence in Higher Education: Eligibility Requirements and Standards for Accreditation, 12th ed. (Philadelphia, PA: Middle States Commission on Higher Education, in press).

25. Joseph C. Burke, "The Many Faces of Accountability," in *Achieving Accountability in Higher Education*; Brent D. Ruben, *Toward a Balanced Scorecard for Higher Education: Rethinking the College and University Excellence Indicators Framework* (New Brunswick, NJ: Rutgers University, Center for Organizational Development and Leadership, 1999); Richard Shavelson, "Assessing Student Learning: The Quest to Hold Higher Education Accountable." Seminar presented at the Center for Advanced Study in the Behavioral Sciences Seminar, Stanford University (2000). Available at http://www.stanford.edu/dept/SUSE/SEAL/Presentation/Presentation%20PDF/Assessing%20student%20CASBS%20Seminar%202000.pdf (accessed May 31, 2005).

26. National Commission on Accountability in Higher Education, *Accountability for Better Results*, 21.

27. Burke, "The Many Faces of Accountability"; Ewell, "Can Assessment Serve Accountability?"; Shavelson, "Assessing Student Learning."

28. National Commission on Accountability in Higher Education, *Accountability for Better Results*; Ruben, *Toward a Balanced Scorecard for Higher Education*.

29. Engelkemeyer, "Institutional Performance Measures"; National Commission on Accountability in Higher Education, *Accountability for Better Results*.

30. Middle States Commission on Higher Education, *Characteristics of Excellence in Higher Education*.

31. National Commission on Accountability in Higher Education, *Accountability for Better Results*, 12.

32. CHEA Institute for Research and Study of Accreditation and Quality Assurance, *Statement of Mutual Responsibilities for Student Learning Outcomes*, 4.

33. Ibid., 1.

34. Business-Higher Education Forum, *Public Accountability for Student Learning in Higher Education*, 9.

35. National Commission on Accountability in Higher Education, *Accountability for Better Results*, 15.

36. James J. Rooney and Lee N. Vanden Heuvel, "Root Cause Analysis for Beginners," *Quality Progress* 37, no. 7 (July 2004): 45–53.

37. Training Resources and Data Exchange Performance-Based Management Special Interest Group, *How to Measure Performance: A Handbook of Techniques and Tools* (Oak Ridge, TN: Oak Ridge Associated Universities, 2005). Available at http://www.orau.gov/pbm/handbook/ (accessed June 15, 2005).

38. Ibid.

39. Linda Suskie, *Assessing Student Learning: A Common Sense Guide* (Bolton, MA: Anker Publishing, 2004), 94–120.

40. Association of American Colleges & Universities, *Our Students' Best Work: A Framework for Accountability Worthy of Our Mission* (Washington, D.C.: Association of American Colleges & Universities, 2004).

41. Samuel A. Livingston and Michael J. Zieky, *Passing Scores: A Manual for Setting Standards on Performance on Educational and Occupational Tests* (Princeton, NJ: Educational Testing Service, 1982).

42. National Commission on Accountability in Higher Education, *Accountability for Better Results*, 21.

43. Training Resources and Data Exchange Performance-Based Management Special Interest Group, *How to Measure Performance*.

44. National Commission on Accountability in Higher Education, *Accountability for Better Results*, 13.

45. Institute for Education Best Practices, *Measuring Institutional Performance Outcomes: Consortium Benchmarking Study: Best-in-class Report* (Houston, TX: American Productivity & Quality Center, 1998), 61.

46. William F. Massy, "Academic Audit for Accountability and Improvement," in *Achieving Accountability in Higher Education*, 173–197.

47. Banta and Borden, "Performance Indicators for Accountability and Improvement," 103, 98.

48. Linda Suskie, "What Are Good Assessment Practices?," in *Assessing Student Learning*, 18–33.

49. V.M.H. Borden, "A Few Good Measures: The Impossible Dream?," in *Assessment to Promote Deep Learning: Insight from AAHE's 2000 and 1999 Assessment Conferences*, ed. Linda Suskie (Washington, D.C.: American Association for Higher Education, 2001), 31–40.

50. Institute for Education Best Practices, *Measuring Institutional Performance Outcomes*, 16.

51. Suskie, "What Are Good Assessment Practices?," 18.

52. National Commission on Accountability in Higher Education, *Accountability for Better Results*, 13.

53. Suskie, "What Are Good Assessment Practices?," 18.

54. Banta and Borden, "Performance Indicators for Accountability and Improvement," 101–102.

55. Institute for Education Best Practices, *Measuring Institutional Performance Outcomes*, 51.

56. Nancy Kleniewski, "Program Review as a Win-win Opportunity," AAHEBulletin.com (May 2003). Available at http://www.webs.uidaho.edu/ipb/pdf_files/Win-Win.pdf (accessed July 29, 2005).

57. Engelkemeyer, "Institutional Performance Measures."

58. Middle States Commission on Higher Education, *Characteristics of Excellence in Higher Education*.

59. Ibid., 2.

60. Ralph A. Wolff, "Accountability and Accreditation: Can Reforms Match Increasing Demands?," in *Achieving Accountability in Higher Education*, 88.

61. National Association of Independent Colleges and Universities, *Task Force Report on Appropriate Accountability: Regulations, the Responsibilities of Independence: Appropriate Accountability through Self-regulation* (Washington, D.C.: National Association of Independent Colleges and Universities, 1994).

62. Suskie, "What Are Good Assessment Practices?"

63. CHEA Institute for Research and Study of Accreditation and Quality Assurance, *Statement of Mutual Responsibilities for Student Learning Outcomes*, 5.

64. Middle States Commission on Higher Education, *Characteristics of Excellence in Higher Education*.

65. R. C. Shirley and J. F. Volkwein, "Establishing Academic Program Priorities," *Journal of Higher Education* 49 (1978): 472–488.

66. Lynn A. Steen, "20 Questions That Deans Should Ask Their Mathematics Departments (or, That a Sharp Department Will Ask Itself)," *AAHE Bulletin* 44, no. 9 (May 1992): 3–6.

67. National Institute of Standards and Technology, "Frequently Asked Questions about the Malcolm Baldrige National Quality Award," (Washington, D.C.: National Institute of Standards and Technology, 2004). Available at http://www.nist.gov/public_affairs/factsheet/baldfaqs.htm (accessed June 3, 2005).

68. Baldrige National Quality Program, *2005 Education Criteria for Performance Excellence*. (Washington, D.C.: Baldrige National Quality Program, 2005). Available at http://www.quality.nist.gov/PDF_files/2005_Education_Criteria.pdf (accessed July 1, 2005).

69. National Institute of Standards and Technology, "Frequently Asked Questions about the Malcolm Baldrige National Quality Award."

70. Michael G. Dolence and Donald M. Norris, "Using Key Performance Indicators to Drive Strategic Decision Making," in *Using Performance Indicators to Guide Strategic Decision Making*, 64.

71. Ewell, "Developing Statewide Performance Indicators for Higher Education."

72. James Honan, "Monitoring Institutional Performance," *AGB Priorities* 5 (Fall 1995).

73. Personal communication with Jean A. Morse (June 6, 2005).

74. Engelkemeyer, "Institutional Performance Measures"; National Commission on Accountability in Higher Education, *Accountability for Better Results*; Ruben, *Toward a Balanced Scorecard for Higher Education*.

75. Business-Higher Education Forum, *Public Accountability for Student Learning in Higher Education*, 13.

76. James C. Eck and John W. Harris, "AALE Viability Indicators: Warning Lights on the Institutional Dashboard," *Assessment Update* 12, no. 4 (July–August 2000), 1–2, 14–15.

77. Pennsylvania State System of Higher Education, *PASSHE Measures Performance and Rewards Success* (Harrisburg, PA: Pennsylvania State System of Higher Education, 2005). Available at http://www.passhe.edu/content/?/ performance (accessed June 10, 2005).

78. Business-Higher Education Forum, *Public Accountability for Student Learning in Higher Education*, 13.

79. Robert Kaplan and David Norton, "Using the Balanced Scorecard as a Strategic Management System," *Harvard Business Review* 74 (January/February 1996): 75–85; David C. Oehler, "Creating and Using a 'Dashboard' to Monitor Institutional Performance," unpublished paper presented at the American Association for Higher Education Assessment Conference, Denver, CO (2003); Ruben, *Toward a Balanced Scorecard for Higher Education*.

80. Business-Higher Education Forum, *Public Accountability for Student Learning in Higher Education*.

81. Training Resources and Data Exchange Performance-Based Management Special Interest Group, *How to Measure Performance*.

82. Pew Forum, *IUPUI, The Urban Universities Portfolio Project: Assuring Quality for Multiple Publics* (Washington, D.C.: Pew Forum, undated). Available at http://pewundergradforum.org/project11.htm (accessed July 1, 2005).

83. Barbara L. Cambridge, Susan Kahn, Daniel P. Tompkins, and Kathleen B. Yancey, *Electronic Portfolios: Emerging Practices in Student, Faculty and Institutional Learning* (Washington, D.C.: American Association for Higher Education, 2001).

84. Association of American Colleges & Universities, *Our Students' Best Work*.

85. Middle States Commission on Higher Education, *Characteristics of Excellence in Higher Education*.

86. Linda Suskie, "Promoting an Assessment Culture," in *Assessing Student Learning*, 34–48.

87. Institute for Education Best Practices, *Measuring Institutional Performance Outcomes: Consortium Benchmarking Study*, 26.

88. Banta and Borden, "Performance Indicators for Accountability and Improvement," 98.

89. Sarah Carrigan, Jeremy Fisher, and Philip Handwerk, "The Effectiveness of Institutional Effectiveness: Doing an Institutional Effectiveness Survey on the Web." Unpublished paper presented at the annual forum of the Association for Institutional Research, Cincinnati, OH (2000).

90. Lisa Petrides and Thad Nodine, "Accountability and Information Practices in the California Community Colleges: Toward Effective Use of Information in Decision Making," *iJournal: Insight into Student Services* (Issue No. 10) (Spring 2005). Available at http://www.ijournal.us/issue_10/print_version/ij_ issue10prt_07.htm (accessed July 1, 2005).

91. CHEA Institute for Research and Study of Accreditation and Quality Assurance, *Statement of Mutual Responsibilities for Student Learning Outcomes*, 4, 5.

92. Suskie, "What Are Good Assessment Practices?," 21.

93. Banta and Borden, "Performance Indicators for Accountability and Improvement."

94. Petrides and Nodine, "Accountability and Information Practices in the California Community Colleges."

95. Robert Gabriner, "The Significance of the New WASC Accreditation Standards for the California Community Colleges." Unpublished address to the State Academic Senate for California Community Colleges, San Francisco (April 15, 2004).

96. National Commission on Accountability in Higher Education, *Accountability for Better Results*, 23.

CHAPTER 3

Stakeholders of Higher Education Institutional Accountability

Robert E. Dugan

Higher education institutions do not operate in a political, economic, educational, or societal vacuum. Both internal and external constituents of higher education—the stakeholders—increasingly want institutions to be accountable by demonstrating and reporting on their efficiency and effectiveness. Stakeholders of higher education institutions include:

- Parents of prospective and enrolled students;
- Prospective and enrolled students;
- The internal community of the higher education institution at all governance levels;
- Regional, specialized/professional and national accrediting organizations;
- Federal and state governments;
- The business community;
- Education associations;
- The mass media (print, radio, video, and electronic media); and
- Taxpayers.

The stakeholders hold a multiplicity of perspectives concerning institutional effectiveness and accountability. When considering higher education accountability, stakeholders and others must acknowledge and understand these differing perspectives.

To complicate the discussion, more than one stakeholder perspective may influence an individual. For example, an employer in the business community is also a taxpayer, and could be a parent of a prospective or enrolled student, or even an enrolled student himself or herself. As a result, these differing, simultaneously held perspectives may actually conflict with one another.

What do the various stakeholders generally want? Despite their differing perspectives, stakeholders share common values when holding higher education institutions responsible for efficient and effective performance. Accountability focuses on results as institutions quantify and provide evidence that they are meeting their stated mission, goals, and objectives. Stakeholders want evidence that resources allocated from their taxes and personal income are used to produce individual benefits including learning, as well as benefits contributing to society in general and to the economy of the region, state, and nation. Specifically, stakeholders want to be assured that higher education institutions are accountable concerning accessibility, affordability, and quality.

Because of the value of higher education in terms of lifetime differentials (e.g., expected income), stakeholders want access to higher education institutions as an economically essential service.[1] Furthermore, stakeholders directly relate the value of accessibility to assurances of higher education as affordable. A shared value focuses on institutional accountability concerning the escalating cost for obtaining a higher education degree.[2] As such, stakeholders want to understand the financial management of higher education institutions when judging affordability: Are these institutions doing whatever possible to keep costs affordable, thereby increasing accessibility?

As important as accessibility and affordability is the matter of quality, especially concerning student learning. Stakeholders want assurances that student achievement, through learning, is occurring. They seek proof that students actually learn what they have been promised as graduates from these institutions:[3] those graduates should be able to communicate effectively, think critically, and solve problems, thereby raising the quality of the workforce to contribute to the economy and welfare of the locality and to compete regionally, nationally, and globally.

Stakeholders want higher education institutions to prepare educated citizens to participate in society. Graduates are expected to achieve broad public goals (e.g., educational attainment and economic well-being)[4] and assume leadership positions in the nation's democratic society.[5] Stakeholders also value information to demonstrate accountability. As higher education institutions are increasingly accountable for meeting their stated missions, goals, and objectives, they are expected to collect, analyze, and publicly report qualitative and quantitative measures and outcomes, and to rely less on self-reports and anecdotal evidence.[6]

Questions arise when stakeholders address common values. For example, which stakeholders are involved in determining and establishing the standards applied toward measuring institutional performance? Are the measures limited to traditional inputs and outputs—efficiency measures? Are outcomes measures including student learning outcomes included? How is the compiled and analyzed information reported, and to whom? How is the reported information used by stakeholders and others, and for what purposes?

Stakeholders feel powerless individually to confront higher education's existing practice to regulate itself through the accreditation process. Reports issued by accrediting bodies about the operations and general well-being of an institution, and the details therein, are not public; only the accreditation status of the institution is publicly available. An information gap exists between the information made available, and the information wanted by the stakeholders. As a result, the public has turned to the mass media for reports and packaged information about higher education and institutional performance measures.

What happens to those institutions if they do not meet the standards identified and thereby fail institutional accountability? Stakeholders want to reward those that meet identified and measured standards, and punish those that do not.[7] These punishments may take the form of reduced government funding allocations to individual higher education institutions. Additionally, prospective students and their parents may display their displeasure and concern by not applying for entrance, or vacating institutions in which there is a lack of assurances of shared stakeholder values.

OVERVIEW

Many stakeholders with differing roles and perspectives are interested in the accountability of higher education institutions. Because of the importance of higher education to society, culture, and the economy; because of the manner in which stakeholders may exert influence on other stakeholders; and because of the ubiquitous application of federal and state taxpayer funds to almost every higher education institution, who is not a stakeholder?

Mass Media

The mass media has undertaken at least two stakeholder roles in higher education:

1. Reporting information about higher education to the public; and
2. Compiling and packaging information about higher education institutions for interested consumers.

The mass media has discovered, reported, and analyzed performance information that higher education institutions collect and report, but these institutions may be unwilling to release information such as graduation or retention rates publicly. As a result, the media has come to play an important role in developing public support for higher education and institutional accountability and effectiveness issues, especially for the need for higher education institutions to identify, compile, and report performance measures.[8]

Additionally, the media has reported on information gathered, analyzed, and released by organizations and associations. An example is *Measuring Up: The National Report Card on Higher Education*, compiled and published by the National Center for Public Policy and Higher Education, an independent, nonprofit, nonpartisan organization with an identified public agenda. The biennially published information consists of a national report card for higher education and fifty state report cards. Its purpose is to provide the public and state policymakers with information to assess and improve postsecondary education in each state.[9] The mass media widely reported the availability of the national and state report cards, as well as online capability for site visitors to compare states in each performance category, and to view previous report cards from 2000 and 2002. In just two months after the organization's press release, *Measuring Up 2004* had been the subject of more than 125 articles as recorded by LexisNexis Academic![10]

In another role, media companies such as U.S. News & World Report have become attuned to the public desire for information concerning colleges and universities. Publications such as U.S. News & World Report's *America's Best Colleges* (http://www.usnews.com/usnews/rankguide/rghome.htm) and The Princeton Review's *The Best 357 Colleges* (http://www.princetonreview.com/) package information to meet consumers' desire and needs for performance measures, such as numerical ranks of institutions based on a number of traditional, quantitative measures.[11]

Higher Education Associations and Organizations

Dozens of profit and not-for-profit associations and organizations represent members who have varied interests and agendas concerning higher education. Most of these entities have a national presence, and several are supported regionally with affiliated chapters. Because of the entities' varied agendas, tensions exist among these stakeholders concerning higher education and accountability, particularly with regard to the application of performance measures.

The public availability of the content and quality of performance-based information, or the lack thereof, supporting accountability from higher education institutions creates tension. There is public demand, somewhat fueled by the media, for higher education to make institutional performance standards available. It has been stated that information is available but that its content, especially its economic basis, limits its public utility.[12] Other higher education officials argue that their institutions must develop a clearer means of communicating their value to lawmakers and the public in the effort to provide appropriate and adequate information supporting accountability.[13]

It is also argued that the public demand for the accountability of higher education institutions is a result of efforts aimed at elementary and secondary education reform, often involving education associations and organizations. Stakeholders, such as parents and federal and state governmental officials, expect higher education to measure student performance as is now expected from the K–12 levels.[14]

For many prospective students and parents, information to help choose a college can be found by visiting the campus and the institution's Web site, and from the media-produced guidebooks such as U.S. News & World Report's *America's Best Colleges*. However, some higher education associations want the federal government to require each higher education institution to compile and report performance-based information for public consumption.[15] For example, the membership of the Career College Association, representing for-profit colleges, wants Congress to require colleges to publish annual "institutional report cards" to help prospective parents and students make informed decisions about choosing a college, and to provide critical institutional information to education policymakers such as federal and state lawmakers. Published information would include retention, transfer, and graduation rates. The association also wants institutions to report aggregate outcome measures including job-placement rates, average starting salaries, graduate- and professional-school admissions data, passage rates of students on competency tests or certification examinations, student and alumni satisfaction surveys, and employer satisfaction surveys. Institutions would be required to compile and make this information available in order to participate in federal student-assistance programs.[16]

While some education associations seek federal intervention, others want to limit federal requirements for performance measures, arguing that such requirements should be left to the state level.[17] Yet others want to avoid governmental imposition of requirements altogether, and they argue that the educational associations should seek consensus concerning the identification and measurement of core accountability outcomes, and that institutions would then apply their own assessment and compliance systems to document and report achievements.[18]

Other educational associations are split over the content and availability of these report cards. The American Council on Education sees no real obstacles, and others note that higher education institutions already provide much of this information to federal and state governments, as well as to college guidebooks. However, other associations express concern because the missions of the institutions vary widely, and performance standards applicable to job training and career preparation would not be the same as those for liberal arts colleges. Additionally, community college officials contend that many students attend their programs to develop skills, not to graduate with a degree.[19]

Furthermore, Delmer D. Dunn notes that nationwide measures would result in standardizing institutional curriculums, thereby impeding an institution's flexibility to determine its own educational mission and learning objectives. Such standardization, he points out, would eventually jeopardize the academic freedom of the faculty member in the classroom, and the undertaking of research topics and scholarly writing.[20]

Education associations have compiled and released performance measures concerning accountability. One example is the independent, nonprofit, nonpartisan National Center for Public Policy and Higher Education, an organization founded in 1998 and responsible for compiling and publishing the biennial *Measuring Up: The National Report Card on Higher Education*, which includes information on both the national and states levels.[21] Another, the National Survey of Student Engagement (NSSE), is an accountability effort self-supported through higher education institutional participation fees and grants. It is designed to obtain information annually from hundreds of colleges and universities about undergraduate participation in learning programs and individual activities. The results provide an estimate of how students "spend their time and what they gain from attending college."[22] First compiled and reported in 1999, the results from the annual surveys are widely reported by the media. Higher education institution stakeholders, including prospective students and their parents, use the information to learn more about how students spend their time and what they gain from their experiences at participating institutions.

Consumers of Higher Education Institutions

Consumers are defined here as "the public in general" but are, for the most part, prospective and enrolled students and their parents. Other consumers of higher education, such as businesses and employers, are discussed later in the chapter.

The public wants higher education institutions to teach well and efficiently. As a result, consumers have increased their demand for higher education accountability concerning educational quality by wanting standard measures of performance, such as graduation rates, augmented and reinforced with evidence that students have learned what they were promised by the higher education institution. To be accountable, higher education institutions must identify learning objectives, apply methodologies to measure and analyze these objectives, and then share that information with the public by applying standard measures (e.g., graduation, transfer, and retention rates).[23]

Students and their parents use information when choosing a college that fits their perceived educational needs. Additionally, despite differing institutional missions, consumers use information to make comparisons among institutions. Information concerning the escalating costs of attending college is increasingly important; these increases are frequently reported in the media.

Cost information is important not only because of the aforementioned values concerning the accessibility and affordability of higher education, but also because prospective and enrolled students want assurances from the institution about a positive return on investment for their tuition dollars.[24] This need for a "return on investment" is an indicator that learners have assumed a consumer role, demanding more personal involvement in their higher education undertakings. In the past, higher education institutions controlled education, and processes (e.g., registration) have been practiced for the convenience of the institution.[25] Now, however, institutions seek to provide processes to meet the convenience of the consumer. As a result, consumers may view their relationship with the institution as lasting only as long as the transaction—the institution provides the product that the consumer requests to purchase.[26]

Businesses and Employers

It is widely recognized that economic development, especially in a global environment, requires educated and skilled individuals. Local, regional, and national business communities expect higher education institutions to meet the needs of the workplace and society in general. Essentially, the outputs of higher education—graduating students—are the inputs for businesses.[27]

Business leaders regard education as the key to competitiveness. Businesses want dependably trained, broadly knowledgeable graduates to become productive, contributing members to the economy. They expect the outcomes of higher education to focus on students' abilities to communicate effectively, think critically, and solve problems. These abilities are necessary to raise the quality of the workforce and to prepare educated citizens to participate in a democratic society.[28]

Higher education institutions of all classifications contribute to economic development.[29] Research universities help attract external research support, promote business start-ups, and make available academic experts for consultation in a multiplicity of disciplines. Comprehensive institutions respond to local and regional business needs by graduating students with skills in specific disciplines. Community colleges meet workforce needs through contract education with local businesses and certification in specific fields.[30] To facilitate this exchange of identifying needs and higher education institution response, members of the business community often have membership in higher education institution governing boards, or they participate in other fora. Additionally, colleges and universities are major vehicles for employment, upgrading job skills, and providing a means to attract employers who are interested in providing their workforce with opportunities for advancement and lifelong.

Higher Education Institutions

Higher education institutions are also stakeholders even though they are accountable to all of the stakeholders identified in this chapter. Most external stakeholders view all institutions, regardless of their status as private or public, as public property; they must demonstrate accountability.

Institutional stakeholder membership within higher education includes governing bodies (e.g., trustees), administrators, the faculty, and the academic and administrative support staffs. A primary concern is that of institutional autonomy—the ability and capability to provide curricula, programs and courses to students with few restrictions, limitations, and other obstructions imposed by federal and state governments, external review organizations both professional (e.g., accrediting organizations and education associations) and non-professional (citizen watch groups such as those focusing on budget and/or taxes), and laypeople in general.

Although accrediting organizations and other external stakeholders hold higher education accountable at the institutional level, it is the faculty who are responsible for delivering educational content in the classroom and for having an impact on students directly as consumers and indirectly through the workplace. Furthermore, the faculty are responsible for developing outcomes metrics and compiling those student learning outcomes promised in the institution's mission and value statements, and identified, designed, analyzed, and reported by the school/program/departmental level back to the institutional level as part of the accountability process.

Faculty are likely to characterize these accountability efforts as additional bureaucracy and as part of the current educational craze to appease vocal, external stakeholders. Faculty are opposed to government restrictions that, they claim, will decrease or relinquish entirely institutional autonomy, and they see the emergence of standardized testing, standardized curricula, and a loss of personal academic freedom concerning research and writing scholarship. Although faculty exert considerable influence in the classroom, they have, except in rare instances, little influence on educational policy at a governmental level. As a result, tensions exist as the higher education institution endeavors to address the accountability concerns of external stakeholders that are not shared by the faculty as a whole.

Many external stakeholders have concluded that the public interest is not served well if higher education institutions enjoy complete autonomy or exercise absolute internal accountability with no public oversight. Higher education institutions can sustain autonomy if they can meet public expectations for accountability by providing evidence to external constituents that learning outcomes are aligned with their stated educational missions, and by being more forthcoming publicly about their operations (e.g., budget and finances), practices (e.g., admissions) and internal governance (e.g., policies).[31]

Another accountability issue concerns setting institutional priorities, especially at state-funded institutions. When state funding for higher education institutions decreased in the first decade of the twenty-first century, internal institutional stakeholders had to consider setting higher priorities for some programs over others; an example would include re-allocating funding for graduate and professional education to undergraduate education.[32] Furthermore, such consideration would require an institution to align its allocations with its stated mission and education plan, and concurrently to meet external stakeholder expectations of learning objectives and outcomes (e.g., setting internal priorities to address regional economic development needs).[33]

Internal stakeholders are also increasing and expanding external stakeholder involvement in the institution. Because accountability issues are long term and will outlast individual stakeholders, institutions are establishing fora in which both external and internal stakeholders work together to implement responses to increasing accountability demands while meeting dynamic educational, societal, and economic needs.

Regional, Specialized/Professional, and National Accrediting Organizations

Society demands "product guarantees," and higher education accreditation processes in the United States provide a stamp of approval. Accreditors, indirectly monitored by the federal government, serve to identify potential problems within an institution or educational program and they provide a statement of quality to external stakeholders.

Higher education institutions have joined to form several organizations to coordinate regional and program accreditation through voluntary, self-regulatory processes. The regional accreditation process is intended to demonstrate the quality of the entire higher education institution to external stakeholders and particularly the federal government. When the federal Higher Education Act attached institutional eligibility for receipt of federal funding to regional accreditation, the voluntary nature of such accreditation became largely involuntary, although an institution may decide not to receive federal funds. Program accreditation is a means to verify the quality of academic programs, rather than the entire institution, to external stakeholders.

Through the mid-1980s, accrediting processes focused on the evaluation of input measures. The argument was that if the quality and quantity of an institution's inputs were assured, then the quality of its outputs was indirectly assured.[34] Stakeholders of higher education institutions hold higher education accountable for providing evidence that students receive the maximum yield possible from their personal, financial, and academic investment. As both consumers of higher education institutions and federal and state governments raised concerns over the accountability of how higher education institutions used resources, a shift began towards more student-centered and learning-oriented accreditation standards that linked, and later embedded, student learning outcomes assessment and accreditation. Higher education governing and monitoring bodies such as the Council for Higher Education Accreditation (CHEA), the federally approved umbrella organization that brings together the various forms of higher education accreditation (institutional, specialized/program, and national), and the accreditation organizations, recognized the obligation that institutions and each of the accrediting organizations had in responding to stakeholder pressure for evidence of student learning outcomes. These bodies called for increased awareness for measuring and reporting educational quality. Each institution was expected to prepare a plan to assess outcomes, to report its findings, and to incorporate the results of its evaluative processes into ongoing efforts to improve student learning.

The self-regulatory accrediting system has its critics. Assessment and accreditation are both premised on the importance of quality assurance. However, the accountability mechanisms used by higher education institutions are oftentimes created by the institution and/or the regional or program organization that accredits them. Furthermore, the information reported outside of the institution is little more than a statement of accreditation status. To the consumer, these self-referential measures (e.g., selectivity and retention rate) are difficult to understand, may not be applicable when comparing institutions, and provide little useful information.[35]

Government

Federal and state government may be the most visible stakeholders concerned with higher education institution accountability. The consumer is concerned about the availability and accessibility of higher education, especially with the escalating costs to attend and the perceived and realized benefits gained from that investment. Businesses and employers are concerned that college and university graduates have the abilities and skills to contribute positively to economic development. Both consumers and businesses want evidence that higher education is meeting the needs of society and the workplace.[36] Further, taxpayers with no specific or direct interest in higher education want government to use its financial and/or regulatory responsibilities to hold institutions and their administrators accountable for funding they received and educational programs offered.

The relationship between government and higher education institutions creates at least two tensions, the first of which concerns intergovernmental responsibilities. Historically, the provision, quality, and accountability at all levels of education have been viewed as a local concern,[37] and higher education has been situated at the state level. Additionally, much of the federal funding available for higher education is directed to the individual, not the institution. As a result, there is resistance to federal intervention from institutions primarily funded from the state level, and privately funded institutions.

A second tension exists between elected government officials and nonelected institutional administrators and faculty members. Elected officials are ultimately accountable to the voters, while higher education personnel are removed from direct public accountability. Furthermore, public higher education institutions depend on government funding. As a result, public colleges and universities are accountable to state legislators and policymakers who place increasing pressure on the institutions to demonstrate clear evidence of the value added as justification for the resources they consume.

To add to these tensions, elected representatives oftentimes do not have the necessary professional expertise or experience to lead or manage the highly specialized, nonelected education administrators. The conflicts between political and professional values create considerable tensions which, in turn, increase as elected officials require institutions of higher education to provide additional evidence of accountability that they can release to taxpayers through official and unofficial outlets (e.g., the media).

Federal Government

The federal government is an important stakeholder for accountability in higher education. It allocates taxpayer-provided funding to colleges and universities through grants such as those from the National Science Foundation and other federal departments and agencies, and to students through grants such as Pell Grants. As a result, the federal government, in its accountability role, has an interest in how this funding is spent.

Additionally, the federal government has concerns, raised by other stakeholders, about the accessibility and affordability of higher education. For instance, external stakeholders have asked Congress to discover why college costs rise faster than inflation, why it takes so long for a student to graduate, why graduation rates are lower than expected, and if graduates have the necessary skills and abilities to contribute to society and the economy.

Although not the primary funder of higher education, the federal government can influence colleges and universities. Congress, through the Higher Education Act, may impose federal requirements on institutions through legislation. For example, prior to 1972, federal aid allocated through the Higher Education Act was directly allocated to the institution in an effort to make college education more affordable by subsidizing an institution's educational costs. The 1972 amendments to the Higher Education Act authorized funding directly to students based on economic need and thereby enabled students to choose any accredited higher education institution.

Additionally, the 1972 amendments required institutions to track and report several identified efficiency and productivity measures to the federal government. In the late 1980s, the federal government requested that accrediting organizations incorporate student outcomes assessment as part of the accreditation process and criteria. CHEA has the responsibility to coordinate and monitor this accountability effort within the federally recognized accrediting system.

When drafting the reauthorization legislation of the Higher Education Act during the first term of President George W. Bush, the federal government recommended that the principles of accountability similar to those imposed on elementary and secondary education, such as "No Child Left Behind" also be applied to postsecondary education institutions. During reauthorization hearings, at least one education association had proposed that higher education institutions be required to file an accountability report card of more than a half dozen performance and outcomes measures with the federal government that, in turn, would be made available to external stakeholders including consumers and taxpayers. Such reporting would be a requirement for institutions to participate in federal student-assistance programs. Margaret Spellings, the Secretary of Education at the beginning of the second Bush administration, did not plan price controls on tuition or to extend K–12 federal testing standards to higher education. Her stated efforts concerning higher education were to focus on providing easily retrievable and better quality information from the federal government about colleges and financial aid options to parents and students, including graduation and retention rates, and costs.[38]

State Government

Stakeholders in state government include executives such as the governor and the governor's education aides; members of the state legislature, including the chairpersons of the education committees and budgeting/finance committees; and the members of the state's higher education board.[39] State executives and lawmakers are very interested because this governmental level subsidizes most of the costs of public higher education, facilitating its access and affordability, and, in turn, state government depends on higher education to contribute to the social and economic development and well being of the state.[40] Due to the allocation of state funding to public institutions, the taxpayer—oftentimes the source of most state funds—is an influential stakeholder in higher education.

Because of the state funding allocated to higher education, state governments have a vested interest in higher education accountability, and they assume an active role concerning institutional efficiency and educational effectiveness. State government does not focus solely on public institutions; some private institutions occasionally receive state funds, and the level and type of degrees awarded by state institutions, as well as most private higher education institutions, must often receive approval from a state governmental agency or board.

The current expectations that higher education be responsive to individual and personal, as well as general societal, needs have resulted in stakeholders such as students and parents demanding that state government hold institutions accountable for both what they teach and how much that experience costs.[41] As tuition and other related costs assessed annually by the institution exceed the increases in the cost of living, stakeholders and taxpayers have requested that these escalating costs be balanced with increased efficiency at the institutional level.

As a result, state governments demand more accountability; they place additional controls on institutional funding and spending to meet the publicly stated objective of improving quality and efficiency. Additionally, higher education institutions occupy a major role in regional and state economic and social development. As institutions request funding for programs or approval of degrees, states link the need for financial and operational controls to ascertaining that the institutions' outcomes positively affect the individual needs of the student as well as the state's economy, workforce, and social good.[42] Accountability is then, in part, accomplished by state government exercising a close, public monitoring of institutional practices and outcomes.

Governors and State Legislatures

State legislatures and governors play a critical role in higher education policy, through the power of the budget and their influence on the agendas and membership of public governing boards. Governors often view higher education as a contributor to economic development, primarily by providing graduates with the appropriate knowledge, abilities, and skills to meet workplace needs. Directly answerable to the taxpayer, governors insist on institutional efficiency as well as quality. They hold institutions publicly accountable for eliminating waste and duplication in order to keep higher education accessible and costs affordable.

State legislatures as stakeholders oftentimes share the same statewide learning, social, and economic development objectives as the executive. Legislative accountability objectives for higher education are most often found in the appropriations levels and accompanying instructions to the institutions included in the state's budget.[43] State legislatures' policy role in public higher education may also be implemented through the appropriations process.

State Boards of Higher Education

Many state governments have created statewide boards to monitor systems of higher education, provide reports, and advise state policymakers. The structure and functions of these boards vary among the states. The most influential, usually referred to as regulatory coordinating boards, are authorized by their respective state governments to approve or eliminate academic programs at public institutions, and they can exert considerable influence on individual campus budgets. Other boards are advisory with authority to review and recommend, but with no statutory standing to force change. In most states, these coordinating boards also monitor and provide oversight over the academic program and degree offerings of independent and private colleges.

Membership on these public boards may include gubernatorial and legislative appointees, or may be elected by the state citizenry; consequently, membership provides indirect or direct academic accountability to the public's will. In most cases, appointed membership has been legislated to be nonpartisan, and members are likely to have an interest or experience with higher education. As a result, these state boards tend to be more supportive than critical of higher education. A citizen usually chairs the board. Boards are generally supported by an academically qualified and experienced professional staff who conducts the planning and analysis necessary for decision and policy making, and who provides operational continuity as membership and leadership of the board, and the state executive and legislature for that matter, periodically change. The board staff, directly accountable to the board but not to the taxpayer, does not supervise the institutions and cannot micromanage institutional efficiency and effectiveness efforts.

Performance Reporting and Budgeting

Performance reporting has become the preferred approach that state government applies to public colleges and universities for measuring and reporting accountability requirements. The governor and the legislature have imposed performance requirements in an effort to hold higher education institutions more accountable and to influence institutional behavior and priorities directly and indirectly, using these indicators to increase institutional efficiency, effectiveness, and institutional reporting to stakeholders. The state coordinating boards then work with the institutions to identify, compile, and report the measures. As accountability indicators that were generally voluntary in the past have increasingly become mandatory, higher education institutions claim a loss of institutional autonomy because of state government monitoring and oversight.

State government influence to hold higher education institutions accountable is based on funding, so accountability systems most often attempt to link state-based budget allocations to institutional performance. Performance-based budgeting is the allocation of resources to institutions based on the extent to which they achieve and report on state-established goals, objectives, and outcomes. Although differing from state to state, accountability systems are designed to capture measures of processes (inputs and outputs), resource efficiency and effectiveness (usage or key resources such as space), state need and return on investment (the alignment of academic programs to workforce needs), and customer need and return on investment (the alignment of academic programs to personal needs).[44] These performance measures may include enrollment figures; retention, persistence, and graduation rates; student-to-faculty ratios and faculty workloads; research budgets and administrative costs; and, scores on exit examinations.[45]

As mandated by the legislation creating the accountability performance reporting systems, governors and state legislatures are the recipients of the reports. Additionally, these quantitative and qualitative performance measures allow comparisons among institutions for public reporting to external institutional stakeholders, and are therefore quite different than the private reviews from regional and academic program accreditors that cannot be used for institutional comparisons.

Tensions

State government executives and legislatures, responding to higher education stakeholders (e.g., consumers and taxpayers), have proposed and implemented institutional accountability systems. As states increase their monitoring of institutions and apply performance reporting and budgeting measures, tensions between the institutions and state government have escalated. Internal stakeholders view and interpret the state's accountability efforts as a threat to their institutional autonomy and academic freedom.

Governors and institutional presidents usually differ on the rationale of the need for public accountability. For example, governors want the public institutions to prove how they contribute to the social and economic development of the states; conversely, campus presidents want to know what the state can do for their campuses. The differences may be rooted in the desire of higher education to exist outside of the politics of state government, whereas state government seeks a significant role in educational policy reforms, initiatives, and outcomes because of its responsibility for the approval of educational programs and degrees for both public and private secondary institutions, the level of funding allocated to public universities and colleges, and the reality of being directly and ultimately answerable to taxpayers.

The loss of institutional autonomy and academic freedom may be the most discussed issue concerning state accountability. Internal institutional stakeholders object to governmental requirements that they expect may result in a standardized curriculum, impede innovation and flexibility, and restrict their longstanding academic freedom concerning the content and teaching methods used in the classroom, and the nature of academic research and writing.[46] Conversely, many external stakeholders claim that the public interest is not served in an environment of complete institutional autonomy. However, it has also been argued that state-based accountability systems provide achievable and measurable goals and objectives for institutions to reach, while providing the institutions with the flexibility to achieve the performance results by whatever means work most effectively at the campus level. As a result, autonomy is somewhat preserved while state accountability is encouraged.[47]

State government intervention in the setting of priorities at higher education institutions is another source of tension. For example, state officials may want to determine that funds allocated for graduate programs be reallocated to undergraduate education. Institutions argue that this decision is better delegated to the institutional level. Additionally, state government enforces priority setting by requiring institutions to detail how their activities benefit the public by clearly explaining broadly labeled programs such as "instruction" or "research" in their budget requests.

State higher education boards may exert influence in reducing the interference and the tensions between the executive and legislative branches, and the institutions. Board staff can buffer the institutions from politically motivated monitoring while at the same time maintaining the state-mandated accountability systems and reporting.

Another tension is caused by the implementation of the state accountability system: Is the system intended to measure the performance (outcomes) at specific institutions or aggregated statewide outcomes? State executives and legislatures can use reports on institution-specific accountability performance measures for appropriations considerations to reward or punish colleges and universities. Aggregated statewide outcomes are suited for measuring and reporting performance on a broader basis, and are used to determine the status of meeting statewide policy goals that are important to its economy and citizen well being.[48]

Measuring Up: The National Report Card on Higher Education is an example of reporting aggregated statewide higher education outcomes.[49] When compiled in 2004, *Measuring Up* did not report on individual institutional performance. Instead, it covered five categories of performance for each state:

1. Preparation: How well are young people in high school being prepared to enroll and succeed in college-level work?

2. Participation: Do young people and working-age adults have access to education and training beyond high school?

3. Completion: Do students persist in and complete certificate and degree programs?

4. Affordability: How difficult is it to pay for college in each state when family income, the cost of attending college, and student financial assistance are taken into account?

5. Benefits: How do workforce-trained and college-educated residents contribute to the economic and civic well-being of each state?[50]

The stated purpose of the biennial report cards is to provide state government leaders, policymakers, researchers, and the public with information to assess and improve postsecondary education in each state, and for state-to-state comparisons.[51]

State government accountability for higher education involves many stakeholders, creating numerous tension and conflict points. Because of the importance of higher education to the economic and social well-being of states and their citizens, and the need to sustain accountability efforts as the elected terms of state executives and legislative members begin and end, government and higher education institutions should consider establishing working fora in which education leaders, state policymakers, and representatives from both the private and public sectors systematically identify, discuss, and coordinate a system of accountability of higher education to the public.

CONCLUSION

It is important to understand the shared and differing perspectives of the various stakeholders of higher education because, although not necessarily interacting directly, they intentionally or unintentionally influence each other in what might be called a systematic cycle. For instance, the mass media may relate a measure of higher education accountability (e.g., graduation rates) by reporting on an education association's findings— those of the National Center For Public Policy and Higher Education in its biennial *Measuring Up: The National Report Card on Higher Education* or those covered in publications (e.g., U.S. News & World Report's *America's Best Colleges*). Both sources are intended to be consumed by, and influence, existing or prospective stakeholders (e.g., parents and students).

Government may be the most visible stakeholder concerning accountability and may be the most reactionary in this systematic cycle of stakeholder influence. State and federal government officials (both legislative and executive), and other government policymakers, closely review consumer-targeted information, and they contemplate whether or not official governmental action should be considered because higher education institutions receive governmental funds. Actions may include scrutinizing higher education institutions' budgets requests, appropriations, and expenditures, as well as reviewing existing education policy.

State and federal legislation and education policy in the form of published regulations or even legislative intent initially influence the values and later the requirements of independent peer accreditors of higher education institutions. Regional and program accrediting organizations incorporate outcomes accountability measures into their criteria and requirements.

To comply with government-mandated accountability standards, to achieve or maintain accreditation that is critical to the higher education institution for receipt of governmental funding assistance, and to ensure consumer perception of quality, colleges and universities develop institutional practices to measure and report on these accountability standards. This accountability activity, in turn, directly influences internal institutional components, including academic schools and programs, departments and faculty, and academic support units that identify measures, conduct assessments, and report their findings to the institution.

These institutional assessments are then compiled and reported to the federal and state governments, and accreditors. In some instances, this institutional-based information is also provided to internal constituents and/or reported externally to satisfy stakeholder information needs (e.g., those of alumnae and prospective students).

The mass media, in turn, uses the institutional information reported to state or federal government agencies dealing with higher education, or the self-reporting activities of the institution, to compile and publish reports concerning accountability measures (e.g., graduation rates) for consumers seeking information concerning higher education. Then, the systematic cycle of stakeholders' influences renews.

Notes

1. Carol T. Christ, "How Can Colleges Prove They're Doing Their Jobs?," *The Chronicle of Higher Education* 51 (September 3, 2004): B9; William Zumeta, "Accountability: Challenges for Higher Education," *The NEA 2000 Almanac of Higher Education* (Washington, D.C.: NEA Communications Services, 2000), 58.

2. James C. Hearn and Janet M. Holdsworth, "Influences of State-Level Policies and Practices on College Students' Learning," *Peabody Journal of Education* 77, no. 3 (2002): 10.

3. Clara M. Lovett and Robert T. Mundhenk, "How Can Colleges Prove They're Doing Their Jobs?," *The Chronicle of Higher Education* 51 (September 3, 2004): B6.

4. Thomas D. Layzell, "How Can Colleges Prove They're Doing Their Jobs?," *The Chronicle of Higher Education* 51 (September 3, 2004): B8.

5. Edward S. Lubinescu, James L. Ratcliff, and Maureen A. Gaffney, "Two Continuums Collide: Accreditation and Assessment," *New Directions for Higher Education* 113 (Spring 2001): 18.

6. Lovett and Mundhenk, "How Can Colleges Prove They're Doing Their Jobs?," B6.

7. Michael Arnone, "New Commission Debates Accountability," *The Chronicle of Higher Education* 50 (May 21, 2004): A26.

8. Delmer D. Dunn, "Accountability, Democratic Theory, and Higher Education," *Educational Policy* 17 (January/March 2003): 67, 71.

9. The National Center for Public Policy and Higher Education, *Measuring Up 2004* (San Jose, CA: The National Center for Public Policy and Higher Education, n.d.). Available at http://measuringup.highereducation.org/default .cfm (accessed February 21, 2005).

10. Search conducted November 23, 2004 using the following search structure: "Measuring Up 2004 AND higher education."

11. Kathi A. Ketcheson, "Public Accountability and Reporting: What Should Be the Public Part of Accreditation?," *New Directions for Higher Education* 113 (Spring 2001): 88.

12. Marilyn Gittell and Neil Scott Kleiman, "The Political Context of Higher Education," *American Behavioral Scientist* 43 (April 2000): 1074.

13. Arnone, "New Commission Debates Accountability," A26.

14. Donald Stewart, "Considering the Public Interest," ed. Donald Stewart and Arthur W. Chickering, *Liberal Education* 81 (Spring 1995): 12 +, available from EBSCOhost Academic Search Premier (accessed November 14, 2004); Jane V. Wellman, "Assessing State Accountability Systems," *Change* 33 (March 2001): 49.

15. Stephen Burd, "Will Congress Require Colleges to Grade Themselves?," *The Chronicle of Higher Education* 49 (April 4, 2003): A27.

16. Ibid.

17. Dunn, "Accountability, Democratic Theory, and Higher Education," 71.

18. Lovett and Mundhenk, "How Can Colleges Prove They're Doing Their Jobs?," B6.

19. Burd, "Will Congress Require Colleges to Grade Themselves?," A27.

20. Dunn, "Accountability, Democratic Theory, and Higher Education," 71.

21. The National Center for Public Policy and Higher Education, *About Measuring Up: Questions and Answers about Measuring Up 2004* (San Jose, CA: The National Center for Public Policy and Higher Education, n.d.). Available at http://measuringup.highereducation.org/qa.cfm (accessed February 21, 2005).

22. National Survey of Student Engagement, "National Survey of Student Engagement: Quick Facts" (Bloomington, IN: National Survey of Student Engagement, The Indiana University Center for Postsecondary Research, January 20, 2005). Available at http://www.iub.edu/~nsse/html/quick_facts.htm (accessed February 21, 2005).

23. Charles B. Reed and Edward B. Rust Jr., "How Can Colleges Prove They're Doing Their Jobs?," *The Chronicle of Higher Education* 51 (September 3, 2004): B8.

24. Daniel T. Layzell, "Linking Performance to Funding Outcomes at the State Level for Public Institutions of Higher Education: Past, Present, and Future," *Research in Higher Education* 40 (April 1999): 235.

25. Michael L. Skolnik, "Higher Education in the 21st Century: Perspectives on an Emerging Body of Literature," *Futures* 30 (1998): 643.

26. Ibid.

27. American Accounting Association, Teaching and Curriculum Section, Outcomes Assessment Committee, "Summary of 'Outcomes Assessment,'" *Journal of Accounting Education* 12 (1994): 111.

28. Hearn and Holdsworth, "Influences of State-Level Policies and Practices on College Students' Learning," 7.

29. Gittell and Kleiman, "The Political Context of Higher Education," 1084; Layzell, "Linking Performance to Funding Outcomes at the State Level for Public Institutions of Higher Education," 235.

30. Nancy Shulock, "How Can Colleges Prove They're Doing Their Jobs?," *The Chronicle of Higher Education* 51 (September 3, 2004): B7.

31. Christ, "How Can Colleges Prove They're Doing Their Jobs?," B10

32. Kristin Conklin and Travis Reindl, "To Keep America Competitive, States and Colleges Must Work Together," *The Chronicle of Higher Education* 50 (February 13, 2004): B20.

33. Margaret M. Sullivan and Peggy C. Wilds, "Institutional Effectiveness: More Than Measuring Objectives, More Than Student Assessment," *Assessment Update* 13 (September–October 2001): 5.

34. American Accounting Association, Teaching and Curriculum Section, Outcomes Assessment Committee, "Summary of 'Outcomes Assessment,'" 108.

35. Reed and Rust Jr., "How Can Colleges Prove They're Doing Their Jobs?," B6.

36. Lubinescu, Ratcliff, and Gaffney, "Two Continuums Collide," 18.

37. Hearn and Holdsworth, "Influences of State-Level Policies and Practices on College Students' Learning," 7.

38. Jeffrey Selingo, "President Plans No Price Controls or Strict Accountability Rules for Colleges, New Education Secretary Says in Interview," *The Chronicle of Higher Education* (February 7, 2005). Available at http://chronicle .com/daily/2005/02/2005020701n.htm (accessed on February 12, 2005).

39. Joseph C. Burke, "Trends in Higher Education Performance," *Spectrum: Journal of State Government* 76 (Spring 2003): 23.

40. Wellman, "Assessing State Accountability Systems," 49.

41. Hearn and Holdsworth, "Influences of State-Level Policies and Practices on College Students' Learning," 10.

42. Ran Coble, "Trends in Higher Education: Changes in Governance," *Spectrum: The Journal of State Government* 74 (Spring 2001): 16; Dunn, "Accountability, Democratic Theory, and Higher Education," 70.

43. Gittell and Kleiman, "The Political Context of Higher Education," 1065.

44. Layzell, "Linking Performance to Funding Outcomes at the State Level for Public Institutions of Higher Education," 235.

45. Karen Adler, "Texas Universities to Be Tested: Accountability System for Higher Education Is Approved," *San Antonio Express News* (October 29, 2004): 7B. Available at LexisNexis Academic (accessed on November 2, 2004); Dunn, "Accountability, Democratic Theory, and Higher Education," 69–70.

46. Dunn, "Accountability, Democratic Theory, and Higher Education," 71.

47. Wellman, "Assessing State Accountability Systems," 49.

48. Shulock, "How Can Colleges Prove They're Doing Their Jobs?," B6.

49. The National Center for Public Policy and Higher Education, *About Measuring Up*.

50. James B. Hunt Jr. and Garrey Carruthers, "Foreword" (San Jose, CA: The National Center for Public Policy and Higher Education, n.d.). Available at http://measuringup.highereducation.org/foreward.cfm (accessed February 21, 2005).

51. The National Center for Public Policy and Higher Education, "Measuring Up 2004."

CHAPTER 4

The Assessment Matrix: Providing Evidence of a Sustainable Commitment to Student Learning

Cecilia L. López

The assessment matrix is a useful tool originally designed in 1997 to assist institutions accredited by the Higher Learning Commission of the North Central Association (HLC/NCA), to strengthen their assessment efforts and for HLC/NCA peer reviewers to use as they consider characteristics of institutional and departmental assessment programs that were sustainable.[1]

The assessment matrix was first described in a presentation by the author during the 103rd Annual Meeting of the HLC/NCA in March 1998 and later published in the March 2000 *Addendum to the Handbook of Accreditation, Second Edition,*[2] and the 2003 *Restructured Expectations: A Transitional Workbook.*[3] Originally called the "Levels of Implementation, Patterns of Characteristics," the title accurately reflected the three-by-four matrix that described three levels of incremental progress institutions demonstrated as they started to carry out their assessment plans that had been previously approved by the HLC between 1991 and 1995. The clusters of characteristics embedded in these patterns of characteristics were associated with each level and were intended to be descriptive and not definitive, dynamic and not static. The patterns of characteristics were divided into four clusters, each descriptive of institutional or academic unit assessment policies, procedures, practices, and activities that were being used to provide evidence of an assessment process and ultimately evidence of assessment outcomes, improvement in student learning and student achievement.

The assessment matrix is depicted in Figure 4.1 and the chapter appendix. The patterns within the assessment matrix are:

    I. Institutional Culture

        A. Collective/Shared Values

        B. Mission

    II. Shared Responsibility

        A. Faculty

        B. Administration and Board

        C. Students

    III. Institutional Support

        A. Resources

        B. Structures

        C. Students

    IV. Efficacy of Assessment

The characteristics within each pattern may be understood to be benchmark indicators of progress toward demonstrating evidence of a sustainable commitment to institutional improvement, student learning, and student achievement. The characteristics associated with level one, "beginning implementation of assessment programs," include a number of indicators consistent with assessment efforts that are in their infancy, that are progressing at a slower than desired pace, or that have stalled. Patterns of characteristics associated with level two, "making progress in implementing assessment programs," include descriptors consistent with the value that the institution (as represented by its academic departments and academic programs) places on measuring student learning, assessing outcomes against clearly specified goals and measurable objectives, and developing students' skills in the cognitive, behavioral, and affective domains. Patterns of characteristics associated with level three, "maturing stages of continuous improvement," include indicators that have been culled from those assessment programs that are structured, systematic, ongoing, and sustainable. In institutions that manifest characteristics consistent with level three in their assessment programs, assessment has become a way of life.

Figure 4.1
Assessment Matrix: Analysis Worksheet*

Where would you place your institution, division, department, or academic unit (circle focus of your evaluation) on the continuum of assessment program implementation? Using the Patterns of Characteristics as your reference, circle your response for each Pattern of Characteristics and give your reasons.

Patterns	Level One			Level Two			Level Three			Evidence / Rationale
I. Institutional Culture										
a. Collective / Shared Values	1	2	3	4	5	6	7	8	9	
b. Mission	1	2	3	4	5	6	7	8	9	
II. Shared Responsibility										
a. Faculty	1	2	3	4	5	6	7	8	9	
b. Administration and Board	1	2	3	4	5	6	7	8	9	
c. Students	1	2	3	4	5	6	7	8	9	
III. Institutional Support										
a. Resources	1	2	3	4	5	6	7	8	9	
b. Structures	1	2	3	4	5	6	7	8	9	
IV. Efficacy of Assessment	1	2	3	4	5	6	7	8	9	

Design concept by Richard K. Foral, Nicolet Area Technical College (WI) and Gloria M. Rogers, Rose-Hulman Institute of Technology (IN)

Adapted by Cecilia L. López, Associate Director, The Higher Learning Commission

Source: Levels of Implementation and the Patterns of Characteristics Analysis Worksheet (Chicago, IL: The Higher Learning Commission, March 2002). Available at http://www.ncahigherlearningcommission.org/resources/assessment/02-AnlysWksht.pdf (accessed February 19, 2005).

When assessment has become deeply embedded in the culture of an institution that demonstrates characteristics associated with level three, decision makers at all levels study the information they obtain from successive iterations of assessment. They monitor learning in areas in which students have previously demonstrated lower than expected mastery of knowledge, skills, and values to determine whether the changes that faculty have made in order to increase student achievement have had the desired effect. They probe into areas in which student attainment is persistently high in order to deepen their understanding of the circumstances that optimize student performance so that those particular areas can be replicated or further enhanced.

In maturing assessment programs, academic vice presidents, deans, and department heads identify, encourage, and reward faculty who apply the results of research on learning theories and constructing knowledge. They follow the results of ongoing assessment to observe the impact of their efforts on the learning of particular student populations. They use findings from direct and indirect assessment measures to recommend changes in teaching, curriculum course content, instructional resources, and in academic support services in an effort to make a positive, measurable difference on student learning and achievement. Once any proposed changes have been adopted, the academic leadership incorporates them into the regular departmental and institutional planning and budgeting processes, and ensures that they remain high on the list of priorities for funding and implementation. Furthermore, they incorporate assessment findings into reviews of all academic programs to document the growth in student knowledge over successive years. In short, the institution's academic decision makers demonstrate by word and action that they are leaders in an institutional culture of evidence where continual improvement of student learning is an institutional value, an institutional commitment, and an institutional priority.

Because the patterns of characteristics for each level are descriptive and not definitive, institutions should not regard them as simple checklists. It is important for those charged with responsibility for an institution's assessment program to understand that few assessment programs exhibit all of the characteristics associated with a particular level at any given time. They also need to remember that not all assessment programs progress sequentially through each level. The levels are both fluid and dynamic. They are fluid because within any one institution, different academic units and programs may exhibit characteristics associated with not one but two or all three levels. They are dynamic because a growing number of institutions and academic units within these institutions are displaying characteristics that go beyond those first associated with any one of the three levels, thereby demonstrating that over time, departments and academic units will have evolved patterns of characteristics unique to their own institutional cultures and assessment efforts. The evolving nature of the characteristics will also change as institutions become more fully engaged in achieving continuous improvement in the learning of their enrolled students. This in turn will create assessment programs and assessment activities that will grow increasingly more distinctive. Their assessment programs will be more expressive of each institution's unique mission, culture, and educational goals, and, accordingly, the characteristics that they describe will become more varied.

The patterns of positive characteristics for each of the three levels are assumed to be cumulative in nature. However, this may not be immediately apparent if someone attempts to follow any single characteristic from one level to the next. (It might be helpful to read the matrix in Figure 4.1 and the chapter appendix vertically rather than horizontally.) Because many characteristics associated with level one are not positive descriptors, they are no longer present in better developed or more fully implemented assessment programs. Hence, they do not appear in level two. Additionally, in order to have the space necessary to add the descriptors used only for assessment programs that are fairly advanced, not all of the characteristics associated with level two are restated in the column reserved for level three. This means that when members of an institution refer to the assessment matrix document *Assessment of Student Academic Achievement: Levels of Implementation,*[4] they need to assume that all the positive characteristics of an assessment program at level two are expected to continue to be either exhibited in that same program or enhanced as that program evolves and progresses by demonstrating characteristics associated with level three.

RESEARCH BASIS FOR THE ASSESSMENT MATRIX

The conceptual basis for the assessment matrix was derived from a study that the author conducted. She reviewed 432 team reports written from 1997 through fall 1999. That study demonstrated how far 432 of the 986 affiliated institutions (44%) had come in realizing the expectations of the Higher Learning Commission as they were first stated in its 1989

"Statement on Assessment of Student Academic Achievement." The "Statement" became an important description of the assessment process:

> The program to assess student learning should emerge from and be sustained by a faculty and administrative commitment to excellent teaching and effective learning; provide explicit and public statements regarding the institution's expectations for student learning; and use the information gained from the systematic collection and examination of assessment data both to document and improve student learning.[5]

As is the case in all six of the regional accrediting bodies, the Higher Learning Commission has been and remains committed first and foremost to the continuous improvement of student learning. From this commitment come all of its efforts to engage institutions in the assessment of student learning. It is also "committed to the tenet that assessment of student academic achievement is key to improving student learning... [and] is critical to... the educational accomplishment of students now and in the future." Affiliated institutions began to craft mission statements and "purposes that... speak clearly to the learning expected of students; support the commitment to educational breadth and depth typical of institutions of higher education; and commit the institution to the excellence in teaching expected of institutions of higher education."[6] They began to demonstrate a strong, readily identifiable relationship between overall institutional mission and purposes and the specific educational objectives of individual programs, departments, and units. They began to understand that the primary purpose of the assessment program is to ascertain whether students are learning what the institution and faculty intend.

Analysis of those 432 team reports and, subsequently, over 315 self-study reports written between 2000 and 2003 indicate that virtually all institutions accredited by the Higher Learning Commission have had their plans for assessing student learning approved and are now actively working to implement and improve their assessment programs. However, the research reveals that institutions have progressed at different rates and with varying degrees of success. Some institutions are still struggling to get their assessment programs started, whereas many others have elements of their assessment programs in place. These latter colleges and universities are continuing to educate and engage all levels of their leadership in the assessment of student learning and to involve each of their academic departments more fully, especially those that have lagged behind in implementing their portion of the institution's assessment program. Findings from the study of team reports and self-study reports suggest that the assessment programs of this sample of accredited institutions currently fall along a continuum. The progress that individual institutions have made toward fully realizing their assessment plans along that continuum is relative, being in all cases dependent upon their unique histories, cultures, missions, attitudes toward assessment, and the prevailing faculty perception of the feasibility of improving student learning across academic programs.

In preparing the study on which the patterns of characteristics for the three levels are based, the author studied the sections of the team reports where peer reviewers critiqued the assessment programs and those sections of the self-study reports that described both institutional and departmental assessment efforts and accomplishments. The author analyzed all of the comments and sections on assessment through the constant comparative method of qualitative research.[7] The results showed that the concentrations and distribution of assessment program characteristics across a broad continuum permitted any single program to be reasonably classified at one of three levels, each possessing distinguishable characteristics.

USE OF THE ASSESSMENT MATRIX

The assessment matrix is a tool for institutions to use to understand and strengthen their assessment programs. There are at least six ways that institutions may find the assessment matrix, with its levels of implementation and their patterns of characteristics, informative and of practical value. Institutions can use the assessment matrix to:

- Measure their progress toward their goals for a successful assessment program at the institutional level by comparing current characteristics at a particular level, to those recorded one year or several years earlier, or to those that emerged immediately after their assessment program was established, and then to the characteristics of the next higher level in the matrix;
- Identify the structural, procedural, and policy changes their institution needs in order for the institutional assessment program at the institutional, academic unit, and departmental levels to become fully realized, by comparing the present characteristics of the

program to those associated with the next higher level and deciding how best to close the gap;

- Carry out the agreed-upon changes that will serve to maintain existent positive attributes of the assessment program and to improve components that need to be strengthened, by creating and following an action plan, timetable, and budget;

- Determine how far they have come toward carrying on effective assessment programs at the academic program level by identifying the characteristics of the assessment programs that exist within each academic unit and comparing them with the clusters of descriptors associated with each level;

- Confirm or challenge the impression held by the institution's constituents about the quality of their assessment program at the programmatic level (general education, technical/vocational programs, the majors, and graduate and professional degree programs) by comparing the actual characteristics of each with the levels and the descriptors associated with them; and

- Include in their self-study reports a self-evaluation of both the assessment program for the institution as a whole and the assessment programs of the academic units, using as standards for all of them the patterns of characteristics described in the levels, and any additional patterns of characteristics they have identified as important to their own unique missions and purposes.

PRACTICAL WAYS TO USE THE ASSESSMENT MATRIX

There are a number of practical ways to use the assessment matrix. For example, the characteristics within each level might serve as the basis for a series of questions. Raising questions engendered by discussions of the characteristics within each level may stimulate the faculty and administration to decide on a plan of action that would raise the effectiveness of their present assessment activities enough for them to demonstrate the capacity to attain patterns of characteristics consistent with the next higher level. How might this work? For purposes of discussion, let us consider how an institution might use the assessment matrix to think about student understanding of the value the institution places on the assessment of their learning and about the value-added aspect when students participate in assessment activities. A number of questions might arise from a consideration of the patterns of characteristics in the assessment matrix that refer to students' roles in an effective assessment program, and that might lead to productive discussion. For example,

- Can a prospective parent or student find the words "student" and "learning" together in the same sentence anywhere in the viewbook, catalog, or other materials sent to potential students?

- Do undergraduate students receive printed materials that contain explicit statements of institutional goals for student learning, for expected outcomes for their complete undergraduate education, for the general education program, for the major or for each course in which they are registered? Furthermore, do post-baccalaureate students receive comparable materials appropriate to the graduate degree program in which they are enrolled?

- Do any of the documents provided to enrolled students describe the value the college places on student learning across the entirety of their undergraduate (or graduate) education and each academic program and major? Do any explain the ways in which assessment is an integral part of the teaching–learning process?

- What required course or experience gives first-year undergraduate students an understanding of the intended outcomes for their learning over the course of their entire undergraduate education, their learning in the core curriculum and their major, and an understanding of how learning obtained from the core curriculum is integrated with learning in the major?

- What is being done to ensure that transfer students are expected to meet the institution's stated goals for their learning (i.e., its anticipated learner outcomes), for students' undergraduate education as a whole, and for their learning in the core curriculum and in the major?

- In what ways are successive classes of students being educated about the need for them to be active partners with the faculty and academic administration in the assessment program at both the institutional and department/unit levels?

- By what means are students helped to reach an understanding of the importance of the institution's goals for their learning and the college's assessment program; of how the program is being carried out; of the role students play in its success; and of how useful certain assessment activities and outcomes are to them as individual learners and to future cohorts of students?

- Are students actively engaged in assessment programs at both the institutional and departmental levels? Do they participate in each phase of the assessment process (see Figure 4.1) and offer suggestions for changes in learning resources, support services, the curriculum, and the modes or styles of instruction that they think could help them learn more?

- Who is responsible for asking students directly what it would take for them to want to be involved in assessment efforts? Who is responsible for using their answers to create ways to interest and involve them in assessment activities?

- What is being done, and by whom, to arouse student excitement about the potential benefits of assessment to future cohorts of students and to get them to take their own participation in the assessment program seriously?

- What innovative ways are the assessment committee, academic officers, and department and program chairs using to involve students as well as faculty on teams to evaluate projects that can enhance student learning and to increase the participating students' first-hand knowledge and understanding of assessment efforts across campus?

- What provisions are being made in the assessment program, and by whom, for students to become familiar with the faculty's goals, objectives, and expected student learning outcomes for each academic program in which they are enrolled and for each course?

- What is being done, and by whom, to make the findings from assessment activities useful to students interested in improving their learning as individuals?

- What reporting mechanisms exist to provide students with timely feedback about the results of tests and surveys in which they have participated? Where are these published so that students and faculty are made aware of them?

- What requirements provide students the opportunity to reflect upon the work they have produced over the course of their academic program, to put their thoughts into writing, and to include judgments about how their work does or does not demonstrate attainment of the faculty's expected outcomes?

- What is being done and by whom to compare students' self-assessment of what they have learned with objective indicators of their performance and then to use the results of that comparison as the basis for introducing improvements?

These questions are suggestive of the value of using the assessment matrix to determine which patterns of characteristics already exist in the institution's assessment programs, which ones could exist if there were an adequate infrastructure, and which ones will need to be cultivated if the continual improvement of student learning becomes accepted as an institutional priority.

A second way to use the assessment matrix is to consider it as a template for constructing a matrix consisting of patterns of characteristics unique to the institution and its academic program. For example, the assessment committee could ask each department or academic unit to evaluate itself against one or more of the descriptors associated with each level, without regard to which level any given characteristic belongs. The assessment committee would ask the academic unit to:

- Come to an agreement on where the faculty as a group is in regard to this particular characteristic; and
- Brainstorm until they concur on where, if there were no barriers, they would like to be in regard to that particular characteristic.

The academic unit would then be asked to compare its present and desired characteristics with those in the assessment matrix and to decide on the level with which the assessment program currently corresponds most closely and the particular part of the organizational structure in which it would be if it were to attain its desired state.

The usefulness of this type of exercise is that a group of constituents achieve consensus on descriptors of its current assessment program, articulate what it would like to see in place, and then create the means to make its vision a reality. In this scenario, faculty use the assessment matrix to help academic departments speak candidly about the actual state of their assessment program and then stretch their imagination until they can envision what it would look like if they were to develop an assessment program to match their own concepts.

A third way to use the assessment matrix is to create a two-part survey of the institution's current assessment program, using each of the patterns of characteristics. The first part of the survey would ask faculty engaged in the institution-wide assessment program and those carrying on assessment at the academic program level to evaluate each of the characteristics of their particular assessment program by using the characteristics from level two and three as standards. For each characteristic, they would assign a rating on a scale of 1 to 5, with 1 indicating non-existence of the characteristic and 5 signifying that it is an institutional priority. The second part of the survey would ask each respondent to assign a 1 to 5 rating of the relative importance of each of the characteristics addressed in part one. Comparison of the results of these two survey questions will lead to lively and useful debate and might well be the catalyst the group needs to galvanize and function as a team capable of agreeing upon a viable action plan that could move the assessment effort forward at both the institutional and academic program levels.

A version of the survey suggested above was constructed by Moraine Park Technical College in Fond du Lac, Wisconsin. Using the characteristics within each of the four patterns, faculty members were queried on the extent to which they strongly agreed or strongly disagreed with each characteristic.[8] Information derived from the survey demonstrated that although the college's assessment plan was on target, some minor adjustments would strengthen it.

Central Michigan University (CMU) developed is own version of a suggested use of the assessment matrix. When the assessment committee constructed "a survey and conducted subsequent focus group discussions," the committee asked constituents "to identify those characteristics they felt were present at CMU, those they felt were not present, and those they felt were only inconsistently present."[9] The results of the survey and focus groups were then analyzed to determine how supportive the University's faculty perceived the culture to be of assessment as a process. At the 2004 Annual Meeting of the Higher Learning Commission, CMU reported that:

> This approach was an excellent way to share detailed information about the expectations surrounding assessment (what does it mean to say that the institutional culture values assessment?) in a way that did not promote as much defensiveness as it did analysis and problem solving. This is hard to achieve in assessment, which is one reason we highly recommend the tool to engage the community and communicate the values, responsibilities, and organizational support that would be characteristic of well-functioning (mature) assessment programs.[10]

EXAMPLES OF INSTITUTIONAL USE OF THE ASSESSMENT MATRIX

At the 2002 annual meeting of the Higher Learning Commission, the author presented her study of the self-study reports of ten randomly selected institutions that had recently undergone a visit by peer reviewers.[11] The author's purpose for selecting this relatively small sample was to determine if the assessment matrix's three levels still accurately reflected progress toward implementation of assessment programs and to determine what characteristics could be added to the assessment matrix based on their actual use by those involved in assessment activities. All institutions in the study had encountered challenges in implementing one or more components of their assessment program; all had employed patterns of characteristics associated with each of the assessment matrix's levels of implementation. Although the original sample consisted of ten institutions, for the purposes of this chapter, only eight of the ten are presented: Butler County Community (KS); St. Louis Community College (MO); Jamestown College (ND); Doane College (NE); Drury University (MO); Rose-Hulman Institute of Technology (IN); Southeast Missouri State University (MO); and Eastern Michigan University (MI).

Butler Community College (BCC) had abandoned its assessment plan as "unrealistic" two years before its accreditation review. "Buy-in" from faculty was described as virtually non-existent. Drawing upon pattern II, "shared responsibility," BCC's administration decided to encourage faculty ownership of the assessment program by involving faculty in every aspect of the assessment process. Faculty developed measurable learning outcomes, which were integrated throughout the curriculum. Faculty developed assessment instruments, including scoring rubrics, which were closely aligned with those learning outcomes, and they developed a process of overlapping, three semester cycles of rotated, targeted courses to assess general education skills. Faculty also learned to use the scoring rubrics effectively. They analyzed and discussed resulting assessment data and set about documenting subsequent modifications in teaching, the general education curriculum, and departmental planning and budgeting. The faculty, with financial support from the administration, participated in the Community College Survey of Student Engagement (CCSSE), first as a pilot and then as a field test. The BCC assessment committee found results of the CCSSE to be real "eye openers," providing the committee's members and other internal constituents with a basis for debate, workshops, and plans for that could make the environment more conducive to active student engagement in the life and curriculum of the college.

The BCC's assessment committee also began publication of a monthly assessment newsletter. The committee developed a faculty and student assessment handbook, hosted faculty in-service training, conducted regular faculty workshops to consider changes suggested by the assessment data, and formalized a structured feedback process of assessment results and activities to BCC students, faculty, and administrators. Additionally, the college instituted the practice of having a faculty member of the assessment committee formally represent the committee on the BCC's budgeting council; this was widely viewed as an important strategy for guaranteeing strong, ongoing financial support from the administration for assessment activities and outcomes.

In preparing for a focused visit on assessment, St. Louis Community College (SLCC) decided to try to strengthen its program by concentrating first on the assessment matrix's pattern I, "mission," and then on pattern III, "institutional support." Referring back to its mission statement, SLCC added as a goal to its strategic plan that it would seek to "continually assess the attainment of learning goals and make appropriate changes that lead to student success." SLCC's district administration then demonstrated its commitment to sustainable assessment by providing substantial financial support and human resources to the effort. The district appointed a full-time assessment coordinator reporting to the district's chief academic officer. The coordinator's primary job was to elicit faculty understanding of, enthusiasm for, and participation in assessment activities at the district, campus, and departmental levels. The SLCC district showed further support for the assessment coordinator by hiring an assessment associate for the Office of Institutional Research to assist in the analysis of assessment results. Each college within the district instructed department heads to name an assessment resource person (ARP). Nineteen ARPs, all faculty members, received release time to collect and monitor assessment results and serve as assessment consultants to their own department as well as serve as a resource for district-wide programs, such as nursing.

Understanding the importance of communication among and within each of the district's colleges, SLCC also focused on the infrastructure needed to support sustainable assessment activities. For example, SLCC's district developed a database reporting system; developed and maintained an intranet Web page dedicated to assessment; supported an assessment listserv and bulletin board; held district-wide assessment service days; required annual assessment reports from every college and every department; and issued a number of publications, including a monthly newsletter, *Assessment Notes*, and a monthly flyer, *Assessment Succeeds*.

Jamestown College (ND) offers liberal arts, teacher preparatory, and professional programs for a student population of about two thousand students. At the end of the 1996 focused visit on assessment, the peer review team had characterized implementation of the college's assessment plan as "leisurely." In preparing for its 2001 visit by the HLC/NCA, the college decided to use the assessment matrix as the basis for organizing its self-study report. Attentive to its own mission statement, the board of trustees approved a five-year strategic plan that emphasized the importance of outcomes assessment in achieving standards of quality and institutional effectiveness. The board also approved *quantitative* institutional goals for student learning and institutional benchmarks for student learning in general education and the major, and was the first independent institution accredited by HLC/NCA to take such an action. Finally, to ensure the board's mandate to establish and maintain a strong assessment program, the administration added a line item in its budget for funding assessment activities. Because the college had taken these steps to embed assessment efforts into its fabric, the 2001 comprehensive peer review team agreed with the college that outcomes assessment had indeed become the "centerpiece" of the college's strategic plan. The college had institutionalized assessment policies, practices, and activities to a level where its assessment program was guaranteed to continue and be effective.

At Jamestown College, the Dean of the Faculty, with input from departmental faculty, added an explicit statement about the value the college places on student learning and on assessment as a means to improve student academic achievement. The Dean also recognized those departments making significant progress in implementing their assessment programs in a newsletter, the *Dean's Weekly*. The faculty, in turn, found meaningful ways to involve their students in the college's assessment activities. For example, during the annual assessment day, departmental faculty and the juniors and seniors named college fellows now meet to evaluate changes implemented during the year and to review and update departmental assessment programs. Additionally, a member of the student senate is a formal member of the college's assessment committee and articles on assessment appear regularly in the student newspaper, the *Collegian*.

Jamestown College also created an assessment handbook, which is available to all students, faculty, and staff. Its preamble contains statements by the president, the chief academic office, and the director of assessment regarding the value that the college places on student learning and on assessment as a process and means to improve learning. The contents of the assessment handbook include: an affirmation of the college's commitment to student learning; an explanation of the logistics and rationale for assessment day, including students' responsibilities and benefits to be derived from their active participation; specific and measurable learning outcomes; the methods by which students will be assessed on each of those outcomes; an organizational chart of the assessment program; and an annual calendar for its implementation.

Doane College in Crete, Nebraska, a master's degree–granting institution with just over two thousand students, also used the assessment matrix to structure the section of its 2001 self-study report on assessment. The college worked hard to transition from an assessment program that in 1992 had been described as "fledgling" to one that the 2001 peer reviewers commended as having made substantive progress. Among the many accomplishments the college cited were: campus-wide support among the faculty through the appointment of a standing assessment committee; the funding of two part-time assessment positions; the creation of structured feedback loops; and the requirement of annual departmental reports describing assessment activities, their results, and the actions taken on the basis of those results.

Drury University (DU), an independent master's degree–granting institution with an enrollment of over 4,400 students in Springfield, Missouri, realized that faculty ownership of the assessment process was "uneven." To address this challenge, DU focused on pattern II: "shared responsibility," specifically the role of the faculty, and the need for strong support from the administration. The faculty recognized the formal establishment of the Assessment Review Council (ARC) to be an important shift from administrative to faculty oversight of the assessment program. The Council's formal charge was to support assessment activities in three ways: by facilitating ongoing assessment efforts, by acting as a catalyst for assessment discussions and experimentation, and by partnering with colleagues to improve assessment practices and utility. In order to achieve greater consistency in departmental and program reporting and feedback, ARC developed an assessment framework or procedure for providing consistent feedback to academic units and then conducted a faculty workshop to explain the framework and the rationale for its use.

ARC's assessment framework proved to be particularly useful to the university. It called for clearly and publicly stated learning outcomes, assessment strategies that were to be well matched to those learning outcomes, evidence that assessment data are being collected and that the information from those data is being shared with each department or academic unit, evidence that assessment information is being used to make curricular and/or pedagogical changes, and evidence that each department and academic unit is maintaining an annually updated assessment plan.

The Academic Administration and Assessment Committee at Rose-Hulman Institute of Technology in Terre Haute (RHIT), Indiana, felt that faculty commitment to the use of learning outcomes needed to be strengthened. To achieve this, the assessment committee, with student and faculty input, constructed an efficient and cost-effective Web-based survey to determine the degree of faculty use of core general education outcomes in their courses.[12] The online survey asked faculty respondents to indicate for each of the courses they teach which learning outcomes are explicitly taught, which do students have the opportunity to demonstrate, and what feedback is provided to students. The results obtained from analyzing the completed survey revealed that it was possible for students to graduate from several programs in which the Institute's agreed-upon learning outcomes had not been explicitly addressed. Global awareness and cultural sensitivity were among the learning outcomes that had been inadequately addressed. When publicized, the administration found that the results had a major impact on faculty. In response to the findings, the assessment committee developed a six-year plan to be used by each of the departments.

The plan focused on each of RHIT's learning outcomes and encouraged departments to use external program advisory committees to participate, online, in the review of RHIT's e-portfolio. The purpose of the e-portfolio is to document student attainment of each of the general education outcomes. The e-portfolio provided links from each learning objective to a list of courses faculty had identified as offering opportunities for achieving that specific competency. Finally, the assessment committee created an online tutorial for students on how to write reflective statements about which competencies they had gained that represented attainment of a specific learning outcome.

Southeast Missouri State University (SMSU) faced not one but two major challenges. First, "How do we assess the degree to which students were, in fact, meeting the faculty's agreed upon learning objectives, like critical thinking and writing?" Second, "How do we assess students' 'capacity to integrate the breadth and diversity of knowledge and experience' across the majors and the interdisciplinary general education program known as 'university studies'?"

To address these two challenges and guided by pattern II, "shared responsibility," the SMSU faculty developed their own assessment measures as a method of providing patterns of evidence in both areas. Faculty developed a performance-based, normed measure of critical thinking skills to be administered to students before the first-year seminar and after the composition course sequence (which functions as a composition capstone). They also developed a rubric they adapted from the work of Peter Facione and used trained interdisciplinary teams of faculty readers to score it. In addition, they developed a three-tiered scoring rubric for writing. First, the writing measure is administered as a placement requirement for all first-year students, as formative evaluation; second, after the completion of the capstone composition course; and third, as a summative graduation requirement after students have completed seventy-five credits. To assess student learning across the entire undergraduate curriculum, SMSU faculty collected and read over one thousand artifacts from the first-year seminar and the senior capstone seminars. Faculty developed a rubric to measure student achievement of four core objectives: information management and retrieval, critical thinking and reasoning, effective communication, and the integration of information. The artifacts are blind-scored by interdisciplinary teams of faculty readers representing all colleges within the university in order to assure that faculty fully participated in the judgments made and accepted the data gathered as credible.

The 2000 team report for SMSU found that students and faculty viewed the assessment process and its outcomes as firmly embedded in the university's culture. Peer reviewers found students and faculty to have a clear sense of ownership over the assessment process and a strong awareness that important decisions are tied to assessment results. They concluded that the distinguishing characteristics of SMSU's assessment program are: faculty and student involvement in the assessment process; a useful and functional feedback loop to students, faculty, and administration; and meaningful use of assessment results to inform pedagogy and decisions taken to improve the curriculum, and thereby, student learning and attainment. In short, SMSU provided ample evidence of an assessment process that is structured, systematic, ongoing, and sustainable.

Trying to develop and sustain shared responsibility (pattern II) among its faculty was a major challenge for Eastern Michigan University (EMU). A key milestone in changing faculty attitudes about the efficacy of assessment was the administration's appointment of a director of assessment and the creation of a formal standing Assessment Committee and the Assessment Task Force and Steering Committee. A highly respected senior faculty member was appointed director of assessment, and the Task Force and Steering Committee identified key assessment issues and proposed guiding principles of assessment for all departments offering undergraduate education.

When the director of assessment recognized that lack of communication about the assessment process and its usefulness for departmental faculty members were issues that needed to be addressed, the director met individually in one-on-one discussions with department heads. The discussions led to the director's writing and distributing a brochure entitled "Q&A about Assessment in the Academic Major at EMU" and "Assessment Information Papers" on key issues and topics identified by the Assessment Task Force and the department heads as needing to be addressed. The director also distributed over forty issues of a newsletter, *Assessment Matters*, held college-wide and university-wide roundtable discussions on assessment methods and measures, and instituted and conducted annual assessment expos to showcase departmental assessment efforts.

As peer reviewers stated, EMU's assessment program was on track and exhibited patterns of evidence consistent with an institution "making progress" toward a sustainable assessment program. In a recent presentation, EMU representatives described as "successful" the university's efforts to sustain a culture of useful assessment practice within each of its academic units. They attributed this success to the institution's commitment to five basic actions: stimulating assessment, documenting assessment, communicating assessment, validating assessment, and financing assessment.[13]

During the 108th Annual Meeting of the Higher Learning Commission, representatives from three universities, the University of Nebraska at Lincoln (UNL), Oklahoma State University (OSU), and Eastern Illinois University (EIU) described how each had applied the assessment matrix as part of their assessment efforts.[14]

After a peer review visit from the Commission on Assessment, University of Nebraska at Lincoln (UNL) decided to use the fourth pattern, "efficacy of assessment." Recognizing that most assessment efforts at UNL occurred at the level of the academic unit, UNL's assessment committee needed to find a way to describe and communicate the university's assessment activities as a whole while providing the additional level of detail needed to document accomplishments of the academic units. The committee applied the framework of the efficacy pattern by identifying seven indicators that not only paralleled the characteristics associated with Pattern IV but also represented what the university valued about outcomes assessment. The university found a reasonable way to analyze systematically the data and information provided in departmental annual reports, much of which were unique to the department or discipline submitting its report. The assessment committee asked the academic units to focus intentionally on two questions in their annual reports. They were:

- How has the outcomes assessment process and evidence informed decision making?
- How has the outcomes assessment process led (or will lead) to the improvement of your educational program?[15]

UNL also used pattern II, "shared responsibility," regarding faculty members' increased engagement in the assessment process to document the influence outcomes assessment activities have had on an academic unit's programs. To do this, the assessment committee analyzed the percentage of academic units that over time had demonstrated increases in the following assessment activities:

- Modifications of assessment plans;
- Discussion of programmatic issues highlighted by assessment activities;
- Consideration of actions to improve student learning; and
- Actions taken to improve student learning.[16]

UNL reported that the process substantiated "the contribution of outcomes assessment for those who question its value."[17]

When the faculty assessment council at Oklahoma State University (OSU) distributed the assessment matrix to each of its academic programs, assessment activities had stalled in many academic units and assessment information reported in the state-mandated annual program reports were inconsistent. Using the principles embedded in the assessment matrix, the OSU assessment council began a process of "peer review of outcomes assessment" and assisted academic programs to meet the expectations of the university regarding outcomes assessment. The assessment matrix also "provided a framework that the council used to develop its own scoring criteria appropriate for evaluating each academic unit's assessment documents." As a result of the constructive feedback that the council provided each department, 75% have improved their assessment plans and demonstrated a greater commitment to the usefulness of assessment as a process.[18]

Eastern Illinois University (EIU) found that the assessment matrix "aided in cutting across discipline-specific barriers in order to develop a reporting process and feedback loop suitable for all academic departments and comprehensible by all constituencies."[19] They also observed that assessment matrix encouraged "self-reflection, shared responsibility, and greater analysis at the department level about progress in assessing student learning outcomes."[20]

CONCLUSION

Can the assessment matrix point the user to evidence of a sustainable commitment to student learning? The answer is yes. Many institutions, such as Mesa Community College (MCC) in Arizona, have worked hard to develop a strong and sustainable commitment to assessment as a process and as a means to improve learning. In a 2003 presentation at the Annual Meeting of the Higher Learning Commission, MCC representatives stated that their assessment program was "credible and sustainable." The author agreed, based on her ten-year association with MCC's assessment efforts and her review of MCC's 2005 self-study report submitted to the Higher Learning Commission. MCC attributes its success, in part, to what the college learned over its decade-long assessment effort—namely, that the existence of certain organizational characteristics makes the difference in sustaining a credible and useful assessment program. The characteristics they name are also characteristics described by the assessment matrix. They are:

- Assessment is driven by college values;
- The college makes a long-term commitment to assessment;
- The administration understands assessment and believes in its value;

- Faculty lead the programs and own the results;
- Technical expertise and support are provided;
- Learning outcomes are defined programmatically;
- Measurement tools align with learning outcomes;
- A viable research design and sound research methodology are used;
- Results are used by faculty to improve learning; and
- Assessment is linked to college planning.[21]

Institutions have found that the assessment matrix, with its patterns of characteristics, can be used in multiple ways in helping them strengthen their assessment programs. They have discovered that the matrix's benchmark indicators are an effective and useful way to document progress over time. They have also learned that the assessment matrix is a valuable tool for documenting what students know and can do by measuring their achievement against explicit and publicly stated student learning outcomes. In addition, many institutions have found the assessment matrix to be a tool they can use to help them decide on the kinds of evidence that will document that their assessment processes lead to improvement in the educational programs the institution offers. Finally, used as a tool, the assessment matrix points the way to answering two basic questions: "Upon completion of this educational experience, what can our students know and do?," and "How do we know?" In sum, the assessment matrix is a guide that an institution can follow or adapt to document that it has developed a culture of evidence and that it is sustainable.

Notes

1. Cecilia L. López, "Assessing Student Learning: Using the Commission's *Levels of Implementation*," 105th Annual Meeting of the North Central Association of Colleges and Schools, Commission on Institutions of Higher Education (Chicago, IL, April 2000). Available at http://www.ncahigherlearning commission.org/resources/assessment/Lopez_Levels_2000.pdf (accessed February 19, 2005).

2. North Central Association of Colleges and Schools, "Assessment of Student Academic Achievement: Levels of Implementation." Addendum to the *Handbook of Accreditation*, 2nd ed. (Chicago, IL: Commission on Institutions of Higher Education, 2000), 6–13. Available at www.ncacihe.org/aice/assessment/index.html (accessed February 19, 2005).

3. "Assessment of Student Academic Achievement: Assessment Culture Matrix," in *Restructured Expectations: A Transitional Workbook* (Chicago, IL: Higher Learning Commission, 2003), 71–79. Available at http://www.ncahigher learningcommission.org/resources/assessment/AssessMatrix03.pdf (accessed February 22, 2005).

4. See North Central Association of Colleges and Schools, the Higher Learning Commission, *Handbook of Accreditation*, 2nd ed. (Chicago, IL: North Central Association of Colleges and Schools, 1997), 32–43. (The third edition of the handbook was published in 2003.)

5. Ibid., 32.

6. Ibid., 32–43.

7. See Barney G. Glaser and Anselm L. Strauss, *The Discovery of Grounded Theory: Strategies for Qualitative Research* (New York: Aldine de Gruyter, 1967); Anselm L. Strauss and Juliet Corbin, *Basics of Qualitative Research: Grounded Theory Procedures and Techniques* (Newbury Park, CA: Sage Publications, 1990).

8. Janice Collins and Josh Bullock, "Evaluating Assessment: Turbulent Flight in the Life of an Assessment Evaluation Pilot Process," in *A Collection of Papers on Self-Study and Institutional Improvement, 2003. Volume 3: Promoting Student Learning and Effective Teaching* (Chicago: The Higher Learning Commission, 2003), 61–63.

9. Catherine A. Riordan, Jennifer J. Fager, and Timothy S. Hartshorne, "Strategies for Building a Culture of Assessment in Decentralized Institutions," in *A Collection of Papers on Self-Study and Institutional Improvement, 2004. Volume 3: Assessment of Student Learning* (Chicago: The Higher Learning Commission, 2004), 35–40.

10. Ibid., 37.

11. Cecilia L. López, "What We Are Learning: Assessment Strategies from the Trenches." Unpublished PowerPoint presentation at the 107th Annual Meeting of the Higher Learning Commission (Chicago: The Higher Learning Commission, 2002).

12. Gloria M. Rogers, "Assessing Student Learning: Elegance in Simplicity," in *A Collection of Papers on Self-Study and Institutional Improvement, 2003. Volume 3*, 55–57.

13. Donald Bennion and Michael Harris, "Developing a Culture of Assessment at Eastern Michigan University," in *A Collection of Papers on Self-Study and Institutional Improvement, 2004. Volume 3*, 29–31.

14. Jessica Johnson, Julie Wallin, and Karla Sanders, "Assessing an Institution's Outcomes Assessment Efforts: The Application of the Higher Learning Commission Assessment Matrix by Three Institutions," in *A Collection of Papers on Self-Study and Institutional Improvement, 2004. Volume 3*, 51–57.

15. Ibid., 52.

16. Ibid.

17. Ibid., 53.

18. Ibid.

19. Ibid.

20. Ibid., 54.

21. Andrea Greene, Gail Mee, and Gayla Preisser, "Ensuring the Assessment Investment Pays Off: A Case Study," in *A Collection of Papers on Self-Study and Institutional Improvement, 2004. Volume* 3, 51–57.

Assessment of Student Academic Achievement: Assessment Culture Matrix

Introduction

The clusters of characteristics contained in the "Assessment Cuture Matrix" emerge from rigorously applied research analysis of content found in team reports, the source of Consultant-Evaluators' discussion of assessment at scores of institutions. The Matrix provides markers of the progress institutions have made in developing their assessment programs. As institutions and teams use the Matrix, it is unlikely they will find any assessment program exhibiting all of the characteristics associated with a particular pattern at any given time. Moreover, not every assessment program will progress through every characteristic before it becomes an effective, ongoing system of processes that results in the continuous improvement of student learning. The Commission's research continues, and as its learning grows, these characteristics will be modified and updated.

The complexity of the "Assessment Cuture Matrix" indicates fluid and dynamic patterns of characteristics, rather than a uniform structure. The patterns of characteristics are fluid because within any one institution, different individual units may exhibit characteristics that cut across two or even all three sections of the matrix. They are dynamic because the goal of assessment is continual improvement of student learning, not completion of items on a checklist. Clearly, though, there is a basic assumption that the characteristics are cumulative in nature. That is, while not all of the characteristics in one column are restated in the next, it is assumed that most of them continue.

March 2000
Revised: March 1, 2001
Revised: March 1, 2002
Revised: April 1, 2003

I. INSTITUTIONAL CULTURE: a. Collective/Shared Values

Beginning Implementation of Assessment Programs	Making Progress in Implementing Assessment Programs	Maturing Stages of Continuous Improvement
— Collective / Shared Values —	— Collective / Shared Values —	— Collective / Shared Values —
■ A shared understanding of the purposes, advantages, and limitations of assessment has not evolved or is just emerging.	• A shared understanding of the purposes, advantages, and limitations of assessment exists and is broadening to include areas beyond the instructional division.	♦ Assessment has become an institutional priority, a way of life.
■ There is not an institution-wide understanding of the strategies to be used in conducting an effective assessment program.	• Student learning and assessment of student academic achievement are valued across the institution, departments, and programs.	♦ Students, faculty, and staff view assessment activities as a part of the institution's culture and as a resource and tool to be used in improving student learning at all degree and program levels.
	• Some but not all academic programs have developed statements of purpose and educational goals that reflect the institutional mission and specifically mention the department's focus on improving student learning, and the importance they attribute to assessing student learning as a means to that end.	♦ Academic units and programs consider assessment of student learning to be integral to their educational operations.
	• The institution has yet to extend its assessment program to include all of its academic programs.	♦ Assessment of student learning is an integral component of each academic program offered by the institution, including distance learning, and non-traditional, off-campus, and adult degree programs.
	• Assessment of general education skills, competencies, and capacities is progressing but has not been fully implemented or was begun but has stalled.	♦ Academic units and programs regard assessment findings as a source of knowledge essential for continuous improvement in instruction and program offerings.
		♦ Institutional decisions are tied to assessment results.

88

I. INSTITUTIONAL CULTURE: b. Mission

Beginning Implementation of Assessment Programs	Making Progress in Implementing Assessment Programs	Maturing Stages of Continuous Improvement
— Mission —	— Mission —	— Mission —
■ Neither the institutional statements of Mission or Purposes nor statements of educational goals includes wording about student learning.	● The institutional statements of Mission or Purposes or statement of educational goals indicate the value the institution places upon student learning.	◆ The characteristics described in Level Two are continued, sustained, and where appropriate, enhanced.
■ The statement of departmental purposes and the statement of educational goals of some or all academic units do not show an easily identifiable relationship to the institutional mission and goals.	● Some but not all of the institution's assessment efforts are recognizably expressive of the sentiments about the importance of assessing and improving student learning found in the Mission and Purposes statements.	◆ Every academic program has a published statement of its purpose and educational goals, developed by the academic unit's faculty, which reflects the institution's Mission and Purposes statements, including those portions directly focused on assessing and improving student learning.
		◆ The assessment program materials developed at the institutional level reflect the emphasis of the Mission and Purposes statements on the importance of identifying learning expectations, on determining the outcomes of assessing student learning across academic programs, and on using assessment results to improve student learning.

II. SHARED RESPONSIBILITY: a. Faculty

Beginning Implementation of Assessment Programs	Making Progress in Implementing Assessment Programs	Maturing Stages of Continuous Improvement
— Faculty —	— Faculty —	— Faculty —
■ Only a few academic departments or programs have described measurable objectives for each of their educational goals.	● Faculty in many or most departments have developed measurable objectives for each of the program's educational goals.	◆ All of the characteristics described in Level Two are continued, sustained, and where appropriate, enhanced.
■ Most academic programs have not identified and used direct measures of student learning.	● Faculty members are taking responsibility for ensuring that direct and indirect measures of student learning are aligned with the program's educational goals and measurable objectives.	◆ Faculty members engage in effective assessment practices.
■ Programmatic or departmental faculty members depend exclusively on indirect measures of learning.		◆ Faculty members routinely collaborate to determine appropriate measures for publicly stated goals, objectives, and intended outcomes and to justify and recommend improvements based on corresponding results.
■ A few academic units have begun to expand assessment activities beyond teacher evaluation of student learning and grades awarded in courses.	● The Faculty Senate, Assessment Committee, Curriculum Committee, other faculty bodies, and individual faculty leaders accept responsibility for becoming knowledgeable and remaining current in the field of assessment.	◆ Faculty members speak both publicly and privately in support of assessment.
■ Faculty and staff are questioning the efficacy of the assessment program, and their buy-in to date is minimal.	● Faculty members are becoming knowledgeable about the assessment program, its structures, components, and timetable.	◆ Faculty members systematically educate persons unfamiliar with institutional and departmental assessment programs about their value.
■ Quantitative and qualitative measures are not aligned with academic program goals and objectives.	● Faculty members are learning the vocabulary and practices used in effective assessment activities and are increasingly contributing to assessment discussions and activities.	◆ Faculty members continually explore the uses of assessment in the context of research on learning theories, constructing vs. acquiring knowledge, and active learning strategies.
■ Assessment of student learning is limited to those programs whose professional agencies mandate it.	● After receiving assessment data, faculty members are working to "close the feedback loop" by reviewing assessment information and identifying areas of strength and areas for possible improvement of student learning.	◆ Faculty members routinely link their assessment findings to decision making and instructional and program improvement.
■ Many programmatic or departmental faculty are not engaged in assessment activities that get to the core of measuring student learning outcomes.		
■ A substantial number of faculty members across the institution do not differentiate between grading in individual courses and the broader measurement of student outcomes across an academic program.	● Groups of faculty identified by the institution receive assessment reports and provide suggestions and recommendations to appropriate constituencies.	

II. SHARED RESPONSIBILITY: b. Administration and Board

Beginning Implementation of Assessment Programs	Making Progress in Implementing Assessment Programs	Maturing Stages of Continuous Improvement
— Administration and Board —	— Administration and Board —	— Administration and Board —
■ Concerns about the assessment plan identified in the last Evaluation Team's Report and/or the APR review (assessment panel review) have not been addressed or not adequately addressed.	● The Board, the CEO, and the executive officers of the institution express their understanding of the meaning, goals, characteristics, and value of the assessment program, verbally and in written communication.	◆ All of the characteristics described in Level Two are continued, sustained, and where appropriate, enhanced.
	● The CAO has oversight responsibility for the ongoing operation of the assessment program and for promoting the use of assessment results to effect desired improvements in student learning, performance, development, and achievement.	◆ Board members routinely champion institutional and other improvement efforts that are based on assessment findings.
	● The CAO arranges for awards and public recognition to individuals, groups, and academic units making noteworthy progress in assessing and improving student learning.	◆ Board members advocate the continual improvement of student learning as an institutional priority.
	● Deans, directors, and other academic officers demonstrate their commitment to the assessment program by informing senior administrators about assessment results and needs to make improvements in instruction, staffing, curriculum, and student and academic services.	◆ Senior administrators annually provide resources for the assessment program and provide additional resources necessary to enhance assessment practices and improve faculty's understanding of assessment principles and use of assessment results.
	● Unit heads devise strategies to ensure that their academic departments/programs implement the assessment plans they developed or develop them more fully.	◆ Senior administrators routinely authorize various campus offices (e.g., institutional research) to provide the support services needed to carry out the assessment programs.
		◆ Senior administrators regularly provide resources for special projects to enhance the assessment program (e.g., pilot projects, summer stipends, departmental grants, and support for assessment symposia).

II. SHARED RESPONSIBILITY: c. Students

Beginning Implementation of Assessment Programs	Making Progress in Implementing Assessment Programs	Maturing Stages of Continuous Improvement
— Students —	— Students —	— Students —
■ Students know little or nothing about the assessment program. They do not understand how it will be carried out, their role in its success, or how it could be useful to them and future cohorts of students.	• Students are becoming knowledgeable about the institution's assessment program.	◆ Throughout their academic programs, students are provided formal occasions to reflect upon their academic work and express their thoughts, in verbal and written forms, about the levels of success they think they have experienced in achieving the learning outcomes identified and expected by faculty.
■ Prospective and incoming students are provided with few or no explicit public statements regarding the institution's expectations for student learning and the student's role and responsibility in that effort.	• There is student representation (undergraduate and graduate, as appropriate) on the assessment committees organized within the institution.	◆ Students are regularly required to present verbal and written explanations of how work products they have selected demonstrate attainment of publicly stated goals and objectives for their learning.
	• The institution effectively communicates with students about the purposes of assessment at the institution and their roles in the assessment program.	◆ Student leaders educate their peers about the assessment program through conversations, public presentations, and/or articles in the student newspaper.
		◆ Students routinely participate in discussions with the unit faculty about improvements that might be made in areas of learning where assessment results indicate a need for strengthening.

III. INSTITUTIONAL SUPPORT: a. Resources

Beginning Implementation of Assessment Programs	Making Progress in Implementing Assessment Programs	Maturing Stages of Continuous Improvement
— Resources —	— Resources —	— Resources —
■ The institution has not designated funds in its operating budget to support a comprehensive assessment program.	● The CEO and CAO annually negotiate a budget for the assessment program sufficient to provide the technological support, physical facilities, and space needed to sustain a viable assessment program and to make professional development opportunities available.	◆ All of the characteristics described in Level Two are continued, sustained, and where appropriate, enhanced.
■ The institution does not understand or clarify the difference between the evaluation of resources and processes and the assessment of student learning.	● In institutions without an Office of Institutional Research (OIR), knowledgeable staff and/or faculty members are given release time or additional compensation to provide these services.	◆ A budget line has been established and sufficient resources are allocated in the annual E&G operations budget to sustain a comprehensive assessment program.
■ Sufficient resources have yet to be allocated in the annual E&G operations budget to operate and sustain a comprehensive assessment program.	● Unit heads endorse the use of departmental funds for professional development in assessment, for faculty release time, and other expenses associated with the department's assessment activities and initiatives based on assessment findings intended to improve student learning.	◆ Funds are available and sufficient to support consultation, workshops, and professional development for faculty in the area of assessment of student learning.
■ The institution does not protect the assessment program from the funding vicissitudes of particular schools, colleges, and units.	● Resources are made available to support assessment committees seeking to develop skills in assessing student learning.	◆ The Assessment Committee solicits proposals and awards funding for programmatic and departmental assessment activities and initiatives.
	● Resources are made available to departments seeking to implement their assessment programs and to test changes intended to improve student learning.	◆ Individuals who have administrative assignments (including deans and department heads) are given the responsibility and authority to use budgeted resources to support academic changes based on assessment findings.
	● The institution provides resources to support an annual assessment reporting cycle and its feedback processes.	
	● Assessment information sources such as an assessment newsletter and/or an assessment resource manual are made available to faculty to provide them with key assessment principles, concepts, models, and procedures.	

III. INSTITUTIONAL SUPPORT: b. Structures

Beginning Implementation of Assessment Programs	Making Progress in Implementing Assessment Programs	Maturing Stages of Continuous Improvement
— Structures —	— Structures —	— Structures —
■ The structure of the assessment program is beginning to take shape.	• There is an organizational chart and an annual calendar of the implementation of the assessment program.	◆ All of the characteristics described in Level Two are continued, sustained, and where appropriate, enhanced.
■ There is little or no infrastructure to support the institution's assessment program.	• The assessment program is provided with a Coordinator/Director who reports directly to the CAO.	◆ Syllabi for courses being currently offered and all submitted courses and programs state measurable objectives for student learning and provide for the assessment of students' academic achievement.
	• The CEO or CAO has established a standing Assessment Committee, typically comprised of faculty, academic administrators, and representatives of the OIR and student government.	◆ The institution maintains a system of data collection that helps sustain an effective assessment program.
	• The administration has enlarged the responsibility of the OIR to include instruction and support to the Assessment Committee, academic unit heads, and academic departmental or program faculty.	◆ The comprehensive assessment program is evaluated regularly and is modified as necessary for optimal effectiveness.
	• The CAO delegates unit heads sufficient authority and resources to conduct an effective assessment program.	◆ Institutional and departmental assessment programs are annually reviewed and annually updated.
	• Unit leaders (department heads) have responsibility for maintaining successful assessment programs as a part of their formal position descriptions.	◆ The effectiveness of the changes in curriculum, academic resources, and support services made to improve student learning is evaluated and documented.
	• Some or many academic units and the Curriculum Committee are requiring that faculty members indicate on the syllabi of previously approved courses and in the proposal for new courses, and for new or revised programs, the measurable objectives for student learning and how student learning will be assessed.	◆ The institution, through its organizational structure, provides financial resources and other support for all aspects of the assessment program, including research and evaluation design, data collection and maintenance, decision making, and consultation services.
	• Members of the Assessment Committee serve as coaches and facilitators to individuals and departments working to develop or improve their assessment programs and activities.	◆ The institution, through its organizational structure, provides on-line access to assessment data for academic departments and programs.
		◆ The institution, through its organizational structure, continually fosters accountability by facilitating the integration of planning and budgeting processes with the results of assessment.

III. INSTITUTIONAL SUPPORT: b. Structures (continued)

Beginning Implementation of Assessment Programs	Making Progress in Implementing Assessment Programs	Maturing Stages of Continuous Improvement
	Structures — continued from previous page	*Structures — continued from previous page*
	• The Assessment Committee is working with unit heads and with faculty and student government leaders to develop effective feedback loops so that information (about assessment results and the changes tried where those results suggest improvement is needed) can be shared with all institutional constituencies and used to improve student learning.	◆ The institution, through its organizational structure, systematically and routinely links assessment outcomes to the allocation of resources for the improvement of student learning. ◆ Academic unit heads report annually to the chief academic officer on accomplishments and challenges relating to the unit's assessment program. ◆ Academic unit heads report annually to the chief academic officer on recommended and implemented changes in the previous year's assessment plan. ◆ Information about assessment activities and their results is communicated regularly to the campus community.

IV. EFFICACY OF ASSESSMENT

Beginning Implementation of Assessment Programs	Making Progress in Implementing Assessment Programs	Maturing Stages of Continuous Improvement
— Efficacy —	— Efficacy —	— Efficacy —
■ Implementation of the assessment program is in its infancy, is progressing at a slower than desired pace, or has stalled.	● Considerable program-level data about student and program performance are available, but individual units vary widely in the degree to which they are using this information to improve the quality of educational experiences.	◆ All of the characteristics described in Level Two are continued, sustained, and where appropriate, enhanced.
■ There is minimal evidence that the assessment program is stable and will be sustainable.	● Assessment data are inconsistently used as the basis for making changes across the institution.	◆ Student learning is central to the culture of the institution and finding ways to improve it is ongoing.
■ Confusion exists regarding the different purposes and relationships among: placement testing, faculty evaluation, program review, institutional effectiveness, and the assessment of student learning.	● The data the assessment program collects are not useful in guiding effective change.	◆ A "culture of evidence" has emerged, sustained by a faculty and administrative commitment to excellent teaching and effective learning.
■ Assessment of general education skills, competencies, and capacities has not been implemented or has stalled.	● Assessment data are being collected and reported but not being used to improve student learning.	◆ Explicit statements regarding the institution's expectations for student learning are widely publicized.
■ Reported learner outcomes do not correspond with publicly stated goals and objectives for student learning.	● Faculty members are increasingly engaged in interpreting assessment results, discussing their implications, and recommending changes in academic programs and other areas in order to improve student learning.	◆ Programmatic benchmarks are established against which students' learning outcomes are assessed.
■ Few academic programs and departments are collecting, interpreting, or using data about student learning beyond the level of the individual classroom.	● Many academic units or programs are collecting, interpreting, and using the results obtained from assessing student learning in general education, in undergraduate majors, and in graduate and professional programs.	◆ The institution publicly and regularly celebrates demonstrated student learning, performance, and achievement.
■ Few if any academic programs are using assessment results to improve student learning.	● Assessment findings about the state of student learning are beginning to be incorporated into reviews of the academic program and into the self-study of institutional effectiveness.	
■ The assessment program is not designed to provide useful data, which could impact change.	● The conclusions faculty reach after reviewing the assessment results and the recommendations that they make regarding proposed changes in teaching methods, curriculum, course content, instructional resources, and in academic support services are beginning to be incorporated into regular departmental and/or institutional planning and budgeting processes and included in the determination of the priorities for funding and implementation.	
■ The data are being collected but not disseminated to constituencies.		

CHAPTER 5

Assessment Strategies for Institutional Accountability

Robert E. Dugan

Higher education stakeholders want postsecondary institutions to demonstrate and report on accountability measures demonstrating institutional effectiveness and efficiency. These various stakeholders carry differing perceptions of why accountability is desired, and what measures should be compiled, analyzed, and reported (see chapter three). Higher education institutions have developed their own assessment programs inclusive of identified accountability measures. However, a gap exists between the results of institutional assessment efforts undertaken and the perceptions and expectations of performance held by the stakeholders.[1]

This gap may be partially explained by differing external and internal stakeholder perceptions as to the need for institutional accountability. The purpose for undertaking the assessment effort varies by stakeholder: Is institutional effectiveness assessed for evaluative purposes to satisfy an accountability requirement, or to identify institutional functions and services that need improving? Generally, institutional effectiveness is the measured extent to which an institution achieves its mission and goals. Assessment efforts for evaluation are analogous to reporting functions. The institution conducts the assessment processes required to comply with accountability mandates from stakeholders such as state government, or to file a report such as a self-study with an accrediting organization. Assessment efforts for improvement seek to discover the degree of success in advancing institutional effectiveness, to foster continuous improvement, and to align better the measured learning outcomes with the institution's stated educational mission and expected learning achievements to improve student learning.

A critical underlying perspective is the expected outcome of the assessment process: evaluation for accountability or for continuous improvement (increasing effectiveness to have a positive impact on student learning). What broad strategies are undertaken concerning institutional accountability efforts? The strategies undertaken to demonstrate accountability fall along a continuum of "we do it because we have to" to "we do it because it is a tool in helping the institution review, evaluate, and improve efficiency and effectiveness."

"WE DO IT BECAUSE WE HAVE TO"—IMPOSED AND REQUIRED MEASURES

A reactive strategy occurs when external stakeholders impose, or otherwise require, accountability measures on the higher education institution, and go so far as to identify the measures to compile and report. Elected and non-elected government officials often initiate accountability by the imposition of productivity and performance requirements.[2]

State governments have imposed statewide performance-based accountability by establishing goals and objectives for higher education institutions and periodically assessing progress toward meeting them.[3] The goals include motivating internal institutional improvement, encouraging institutions to address state goals, and strengthening the quality of consumer information about institutional performance.[4] The implementation of the accountability system involves four types of policy instruments: mandates, which are rules governing the actions of individuals and agencies, intended to produce compliance; inducements, the transfer of funds to individuals or agencies in return for certain agreed-upon actions; capacity-building, the transfer of funds for investment in material, intellectual, or human resources; and system-changing, the transfer of official authority among individuals and agencies to change the system through which goals and services are delivered.[5]

The imposed measures vary by state and include a wide variety of possibilities. For example, state government may establish goals and objectives for their state-funded higher education institutions, and may apply any or all of the following four approaches to measure progress:

1. Inputs, processes, and outcomes: a production process model aimed at measuring the value added to departing students perhaps through pre- and post-assessments. Examples of these measures include: average American College Testing Assessment (ACT) and Scholastic Aptitude Test (SAT) scores of entering freshmen; first-year retention rates; six-year graduation rates; time to degree; credits to degree; graduate records examination (GRE) scores; and pass rates on licensure exams.

2. Resource efficiency and effectiveness: an approach that is designed to measure the efficient usage of key resources (e.g., faculty, space, and equipment) using ratio analyses or similar techniques. Examples of these measures include: student–faculty ratios; average faculty contact hours; cost per credit hour by discipline and student level; and instructional space use by time of day (e.g., percent of classroom/lab space in use).

3. State need and return on investment: an approach that assumes that higher education is a strategic investment for states, measures the fit between higher education and state needs (e.g., workforce preparation). Relevant measures include: economic impact studies (e.g., the multiplier effect of state investment in higher education), degrees granted per 100,000 working age population by degree level, percent of state high school graduates enrolled in state institutions of higher education, and overall level of employer satisfaction with graduates.

4. "Customer" need and return on investment: an approach built on the notion of "consumerism" that is designed to measure the impact of higher education in meeting individual needs. Measures include: percent of graduates placed in a job related to their field or graduate/professional school one year after graduation; average starting salaries of graduates by field; overall level of student/alumni satisfaction with educational experience; and pass rate on licensure exams.[6]

On the other hand, state governments that impose institutional accountability measures may simply require four types of institutional measures: input, process, output, and outcome. Inputs include the number of enrolled students or the number of library volumes. Process measures indicate how an organization allocates resources, such as faculty teaching loads, class size, the proportion of full-time faculty teaching undergraduates, and the proportion of courses or faculty using new technologies. Outputs include the numbers of graduates, the amount of sponsored research funds secured, faculty publication counts, and student employment rates.[7] State-level performance indicators for student-learning outcomes usually identify retention, persistence, and graduation measures[8] which are actually outputs.

Some states may require institutions to meet certain targets and report data, and may even link the attainment of the targets to state funding appropriations. For example, accountability measures in Texas include enrollment figures, graduation rates, student-to-faculty ratios, research budgets, and administrative costs.[9]

State governments tend to favor process and output indicators that measure institutional efficiency, consumer satisfaction, job placement, and value for resources.[10] This focus on process and output measures reflects state government demands for financially measurable performance indicators, but also suggests that learning outcomes are difficult to measure.[11]

Compiling a multiplicity of required and reported measures from the states, the non-profit National Center for Public Policy and Higher Education issues a report card on the performance of higher education in the nation. *Measuring Up 2004* is the third biennial report in which each of the fifty states is graded and compared to other states along dimensions of college opportunity and effectiveness, from high school preparation through receipt of the bachelor's degree. *Measuring Up* does not assess the quality or prestige of particular colleges or universities, but gauges the educational health of the population of each state in terms of five categories of college opportunity and achievement:

1. Preparation: How well are young people in high school being prepared to enroll and succeed in college-level work?

2. Participation: Do young people and working-age adults have access to education and training beyond high school?

3. Completion: Do students persist in and complete certificate and degree programs?

4. Affordability: How difficult is it to pay for college in each state when family income, the cost of attending college, and student financial assistance are taken into account?

5. Benefits: How do workforce-trained and college-educated residents contribute to the economic and civic well-being of each state?[12]

State governments can use performance-based funding to link strategically identified performance indicators with accountability, institutional performance, and funding levels.[13] By targeting funds on desired learning indicators, state governments can strategically shape institutional performance behaviors by affecting the allocation and application of resources across and within institutions.[14]

There are some examples of state governments connecting institutional performance reporting to budgeting. Tennessee has connected its goal-oriented performance reporting with an incentive-funding process. The state's goals highlight enrollment and persistence, remediation, quality and performance, teacher education, research and service, and student assistance. The identified quality and performance measures are ACT test scores, pass rates on licensure examinations, accreditation recognition for accreditable programs, and library purchases.[15] About five percent of the budget for Ohio's higher education system is used to reward individual institutions for keeping tuition low, obtaining outside support for economically important research, and producing skilled graduates in a timely manner.[16] Colorado collects eight performance indicators statewide: baccalaureate graduation rates, faculty teaching workload, freshman retention, achievement tests on licensure, professional and graduate-school examinations, institutional support spending per student, availability of general education lower-division courses required of all freshmen, support for and success of minority students, and credits required for the degree. Additional optional measures are selected by each institution. Colorado establishes statewide targets based upon national data or measures from comparison groups. State-funded higher education institutions are expected to reach certain thresholds against these national benchmarks and are awarded points based on whether they meet their expected goals. Those institutions in which performance exceeds the benchmark receive bonus funding.[17]

Tensions and conflicts may arise among stakeholders as a result of the imposition of accountability requirements or measurements. For example, officers at higher education institutions oftentimes interpret the imposition of any requirement as a threat to institutional autonomy, while faculty may view accountability requirements as bureaucratic and ultimately a threat to their academic freedom.[18]

Tensions can also result from a lack of agreement or clarity concerning perceived economic or financial needs as institutions attempt to balance the numerous demands placed on them by their various constituencies. For example, as a response to employers pressing for appropriately trained and skilled graduates to fill labor needs, institutions initiate new programs. However, government officials may then complain that the new programs are wasteful examples of higher education institutions trying to be all things to all people.[19]

There is also doubt that imposed accountability outcome measures demonstrate effectiveness. Instead, these accountability efforts generate more information than government officials can absorb or appropriately use in setting education agendas, measuring progress, or making decisions concerning the allocation of resources.[20]

State government can impose various approaches and numerous measures related to higher education accountability. The process usually becomes a political negotiation requiring consensus about technical measures among stakeholders that may not agree with one another on the purpose or need of the measurements.[21]

Other sources of accountability requirements are the federally recognized regional and program accrediting organizations. Accreditors are interested in many facets of institutional accountability, including efficiencies and effectiveness, that are covered in their standards and criteria for accreditation. Although many state governments identify the measures which they wish higher education institutions to compile and report, accreditors recognize the diversity of missions of their members and, while requiring a stated mission statement, expect each institution to develop that statement based on its local purposes and resources. Accrediting organizations also have standards for evaluating an institution's administrative and educational support services.[22] As a result of the individuality of institutional missions, accreditors recognize that no single set of measures can be imposed onto all members.[23]

Accrediting organizations are interested in student learning outcomes as a longitudinal measure of accountability, and want their members to demonstrate and report the learning provided to, and achieved by, their students from the time they enter to the time they leave the institution. What has been the learning achievement produced by the educational institution's efforts? Has an educational program contributed to an improvement in students' abilities, knowledge, and skills?[24] To comply with these accountability requirements, accreditors expect institutions to evaluate student performance and to document improvements made in academic programs on the basis of results obtained through assessment.[25] At the same time, accreditors provide the flexibility to create measures that appropriately fit with an institution's mission.[26]

"WE DO IT BECAUSE IT IS A TOOL IN HELPING TO IMPROVE"

Recognizing that assessment must be conducted to meet requirements imposed by accreditors or government, and also may be frequently requested by other stakeholders, many higher education institutions have embraced the accountability process as a strategic opportunity to quantify and qualify institutional efficiency and effectiveness, and to analyze learning outcomes to improve educational quality through strategic change. Institutional effectiveness is defined as the extent to which an institution achieves its mission and goals. The institutional effectiveness process is an ongoing and inclusive process that articulates institutional purpose through its mission statement; empowers administrative and academic organizational sectors to create meaningful objectives to support the mission; assesses the success of the institutional community in meeting stated objectives through measurement and analysis; and expects that the academic and administrative units apply the information and experiences gained from the assessment process to make improvements that ultimately move the institution closer to realizing its mission.[27]

Assessment Planning and Its Implementation as Strategy

An assessment plan serves as the foundation for all assessment activity;[28] it identifies the assessment strategy.[29] Determination of effectiveness is based in the institution's statement of purpose—an institution demonstrates effectiveness through the accomplishment of goals and expected education and educational support results that are linked to the institution's stated purpose. There must therefore be a direct strategic alignment between the mission and goals of the academic departments and of each academic support service, and the goals of the institution.

As a result, outcomes assessment has placed shared responsibility on all institutional units and their members for providing evidence of their contributions to desired outcomes and for incorporating outcomes assessment into planning and improvement. A higher education institution consists of both horizontal and vertical organizations. The horizontal represents the provision of institution-wide services and functions such as student activities, library, and financial aid shared by two or more of the vertical structures, whereas the vertical structures include the faculty, staff, and students of the various schools, disciplines, and departments. Outcome assessment plans are usually created and implemented at three levels: the institution, academic departments, and academic support departments.

Outcomes assessment planning as a strategic and systematic process of planning, discovering, understanding, and improving the quality of student learning should answer the following questions:

- Who are we?
- What are we trying to accomplish?
- How well are we doing?
- How can we improve what we are doing?
- What evidence exists that we have improved?[30]

Planning begins with educational values. Goals for student learning are embedded within the context of the institutional strategic planning process and the development of its institutional mission. These goals broadly state what students are expected to learn, achieve, and master. The formal institutional mission statement publicly declares the institution's educational goals as well as its values and principles, and becomes a critical means of publicly communicating these goals as widely as possible to all external as well as internal stakeholders.

While the student learning goals may originate from the institutional level, educational quality and its assessment are primarily a program-based effort managed at the academic department level and implemented at the course level. Learning outcomes assessment plans most often originate from organizational discussion at the academic department level. That discussion identifies the educational goals found in the institutional mission statement and restates them as learning expectations. These expectations are then converted into measurable and meaningful educational objectives and standards for the core (general education) curriculum, and for the academic disciplines and their respective programs. Clear and understandable performance standards supporting the educational objectives are created and structured by faculty at the course level. Instruments or other methods for assessing achievement through direct and indirect measurement supporting the performance standards are identified. The expectations concerning learning outcomes, educational objectives, and performance standards are oftentimes made known to students by faculty via individual course syllabi. Progress toward meeting the educational objectives is measured and compiled at the course level, and results compare measured performance to the expected standards.

Faculty and other members of the organizational academic units review the information generated and use it to recommend strategic changes at the course, academic department, and academic program levels that will improve student learning by revising the stated standards, expectations, and objectives; and by revising course content, methodologies, and pedagogy. The findings are also reported by the academic departments and programs to the institutional level for summary compilation, analysis, and reporting to stakeholders to demonstrate a contribution to institutional effectiveness for accountability. Academic support units deploy a similar strategic assessment process.[31]

The demonstration of institutional effectiveness involves a comparison of actual results to the stated goals. The instruments, methodologies, and measures applied in the effectiveness assessment process are examples of institutional and organizational (e.g., departmental and programmatic) strategic decisions.

Differences exist among inputs, outputs, and outcomes in their definitions, data collection and compilation methods, and the use and analysis of the results. Efficiency measures generally employ inputs and outputs which quantify and relate the amount of work performed/service provided to the amount of resources consumed. Compilation methods most often employ counts of tangibles; for example, an input counts the available resources (e.g., number of instructors and classrooms) while an output counts the workloads (e.g., number of courses conducted). Effectiveness measures focus on the quality of results for both operational and educational services. For example, operational effectiveness includes indicators such as enrollment levels, financial and human resources, and facilities utilization to meet stated purposes, along with the effort to improve performance as results measured against expectations.[32]

Effectiveness measures from the learning outcomes assessment process can provide meaningful data to observe the degree to which student learning meets the educational goals stated in the institutional mission statement. Student learning outcomes provide evidence of what students can do or have learned as a result of having completed a course, program, or other experience. Measuring outcomes applies direct and indirect qualitative (subjective information) and quantitative (numeric data) methods. Direct methods and measures include capstone course evaluation, course-embedded assessment, tests and examinations (locally/faculty designed and commercially produced standardized tests), portfolio evaluation, pre-test/post-test evaluation, thesis evaluation, videotape and audiotape evaluation of performance, and licensure exams. Indirect methods include focus group interviews, external reviewers, student surveying and exit interviewing, self-assessment, alumni surveys, employer surveys, and curriculum and syllabus analysis.[33]

Analyses concerning inputs and outputs are used to make adjustments in allocated resource levels, such as revising the number of sections of a course to offer. Outcome analysis, on the other hand, identifies changes necessary to improve instructional content and methods and thereby enhance student learning results. While it is preferable to apply and analyze information from direct methods for outcomes assessments, indirect assessment information is also useful.

Prioritizing outcomes is a recomended implementation strategy for assessment planning. Rather than trying to assess every desired outcome, an institution should assess those that are most critical and would provide the most information[34] for analysis and reporting. Changes and improvements need not be exhaustive nor fully implemented simultaneously to be effective. Incremental changes can be applied and tested gradually to ensure that effectiveness is indeed improved rather than introducing a larger, untested, and unproven series of changes that may do more harm than good.[35]

Another strategy concerns the scope of participation in the assessment process. For example, involving external constituencies (including members of accrediting associations, legislative and executive public officials, and community and business leaders, among others) can help address the public's need for accountability information.[36] Another set of strategies is concerned with how the outcomes assessments can be conducted over time. For example, portfolios might capture student work over several semesters, and writing portfolios might document student growth as writers by demonstrating writing proficiencies over their academic careers.[37] Professional portfolios contain copies of a student's work that could be shown to a prospective employer during an interview. Academic portfolios, on the other hand, frequently contain other material, such as research reports, analyses, case studies, and other work completed at various stages of a student's academic program. By reviewing academic portfolios, internal or external evaluators can get a "before and after" look at where students began and how they progressed over time.[38] Electronic portfolios enable long-term and accessible storage of student work, while electronic institutional portfolios can facilitate access for accreditors and the public to information about an institution's achievement of student learning outcomes and quality improvement efforts.[39]

The means for student testing is another strategic decision. Faculty may propose that outcomes assessment employ off-the-shelf standardized tests administered at the institutional or school level rather than at the departmental or course level.[40] However, the application of standardized tests may not be as effective as locally developed instruments. Faculty-developed tests can focus on the identified educational objectives of the institution and may, in fact, yield better projections of student performance throughout the curriculum for general education and the specific discipline.[41] Some faculty members may believe that the assessment process does not meet its stated objective of demonstrating whether or not learning occurs.[42] When this perception prevails, it must be dealt with.

Although a national standardized test may not be as effective as a faculty-developed local test, it can serve several strategic purposes. As an example, consider the ETS ICT (Information and Communication Technology) Literacy Assessment from the Educational Testing Service (ETS). This simulation-based testing program measures a postsecondary student's ability to define an information need; access resources and information; manage, integrate, and evaluate information; create new information/knowledge; and communicate information to others in a technological environment.[43]

Score reports for the ICT Literacy Assessment provide institutions with aggregated data on the performance of the student population who complete the testing. This proficiency-level score measures the ICT literacy skills of specific groups, such as entry-level students, juniors, or graduating seniors. Score reports can also be produced for the purpose of subgroup comparisons, looking at major, race/ethnicity, or other characteristics as provided in sampling plans submitted by the institution. As aggregate outcomes, the test will help two- and four-year colleges and universities set institutional/department benchmarks, and then measure progress year-to-year across system campuses, across campus departments, and among student cohorts.[44] Furthermore, it will enable institutions to plan resource allocation better, identify group strengths and weaknesses, plan the curriculum to address measured ICT literacy gaps, focus on specific areas of student improvement, and provide evidence to accrediting agencies as increased value is placed in ICT proficiency.[45]

For an individual, scores from the ICT Literacy Assessment can be applied to satisfy a prerequisite to enroll in specific courses, to authorize entry in and graduation from an academic program, and to act as a certification on transcripts.[46] It will also make it possible to to demonstrate to an employer the measured extent to which students/graduates can apply higher-order thinking skills, ethical behaviors, and proficiencies in the use of digital technology, communication tools, and networks to solve information problems.[47]

Because many national standardized tests provide aggregated data, such tests can be used to determine institutional benchmarks (current grades of the students taking the test), to provide input data when creating departmental assessment plans inclusive of educational objectives designed to improve scores, and, subject to re-test, to determine the effectiveness of course content or instructional change. These tests can also be applied as competency tests for individual students, as motivators (a failed student may not be allowed to register for the next semester), and as a means to document the achievement of skills for post-graduate work, for admission into graduate school, or for employment.

FINDINGS CONCERNING ACCOUNTABILITY AND STRATEGIC DECISIONS

Findings in a U.S. Department of Education report based on case studies at eight higher education institutions illustrated strategic directions in assessment planning and analysis.[48] An important finding was that the primary goal of student outcomes assessment was to understand student competencies in order to facilitate improvements in curricula and teaching methods. Assessment was used most often by and within institutions for institutional improvement, by campus boards, and by accreditation agencies. Although state government mandated assessment for half of the institutions studied, legislative and executive branches and other bodies did not often use information derived from student outcomes assessment. Faculty members were involved in and supportive of the assessment process. This may be a result of campuses encouraging faculty development in the area of assessment through attendance at conferences and other activities. While there was general satisfaction with the assessment methods used, there were stated needs for additional methods, especially in general education, and for the design and application of computer-based assessment methods. Institutions also voiced a strong need to abandon a single assessment strategy (e.g., a single examination) by applying a hybrid of assessment approaches, and an interest was expressed in developing additional local assessment methods.[49]

Another study identified and reviewed specific assessment protocols. Grades were the most frequently used assessment technique, followed by a capstone experience and then a simulation or case study analysis. Other techniques included portfolio reviews, satisfaction surveys conducted with alumni, exit interviews with seniors, and job placement information. Least used were external reviews including professional board evaluation of program or of students, and post-graduation certification examination. The study's authors concluded that grades were blunt assessment instruments that fail to provide independent confirmation of any outcome being attained. They also noted that while the assessment protocols most used were conducted by faculty with limited practitioner input, the three most valued external input sources were from advisory boards and the accreditation and certification processes.[50]

The aforementioned Department of Education report identified expectations for strategic directions and higher education assessment. First, the increasing need to demonstrate public accountability will lead to the creation of more state mandates concerning institutional effectiveness, especially learning outcomes. States will use norm-referenced ranking measures for intrastate institutional comparisons, for performance budgeting, and for public reporting. Furthermore, while some states mandated assessment measures that could be interpreted as norm-referenced, these measures were later replaced by institutions seeking more up-to-date measures specific to their curricula. There was widespread use of, but still movement away from, the American College Test–College Outcomes Measures Project (ACT–COMP), College Level Academic Skills Test (CLAST), and New Jersey College Basic Skills Placement Test (NJCBSPT). In their place was more criteria-referenced interpretation in outcome measures that are useful to improving programs. For some institutions, this strategic direction will result in more locally developed measures. However, the report found that institutions may lack the internal expertise and resources to design such measures.[51]

Several of the institutions studied in the federal report had obtained state funds to improve instruction as a result of applying the assessment process to identify weaknesses and attempt to correct them. This strategy suggests that state governments view a proactive strategic assessment approach accompanied by factual reporting favorably during budget deliberations. Additionally, there was a measurable trend away from paper- and pencil-tests to computer-based tests. Computer-based tests can deliver multimedia-based questions or adaptive tests. Computer-adaptive tests tailor each test question to the student's ability as determined by performance on prior test questions. Those revising or creating national or locally developed tests would facilitate assessment testing by designing computer-based tests.[52]

Interestingly, these study respondents expect to see greater accountability demands in higher education in general, not just for individual institutions. While higher education administrators and faculty do not want a national or common set of accountability measures, the institutions concluded that a common set of mandated assessment methods was possible.[53]

CONCLUSION

From within the institution or from the outside, the strategic purpose and direction of either an imposed or proactive accountability system is to improve institutional performance. Institutions must be held accountable for performance. However, the intended and desired outcomes must be derived from overall state needs because each state's circumstances differ. State governments and public higher education institutions should strategically align education goals and objectives, along with their respective measures, with the public agenda.[54] For example, if data show shortages of graduates in technical fields that are important to a state's economy, money could be used to increase enrollment in those disciplines. Therefore, a system of accountability must be for state, not institutional, outcomes.[55] Additionally, private and independent colleges should be included in statewide accountability systems because those institutions play a central role in meeting state policy goals for higher education.[56] Furthermore, each post-secondary institution has individual and unique educational purposes stated in its mission statement. An imposed national accountability system of learning outcomes is therefore not an appropriate or practical strategic direction.[57]

Demand for accountability is driven, in part, by the needs of stakeholders to understand institutional performance concerning teaching and learning. However, without basic agreement on education goals and standards for student learning, and methods of measurement, accountability systems will not be effectively designed to measure performance or improve education.[58] All stakeholders need to work together to identify goals; to agree on standards, their measures, and their intended purpose; and to be clear as to how the measures will be applied and to whom they will be reported.

Charles B. Reed, chancellor of California State University, and Edward B. Rust Jr., chairman and chief executive officer of State Farm Insurance Companies, served as co-directors of a 2004 report issued by the Business-Higher Education Forum (http://www.bhef.com/), an independent non-profit membership organization of leaders from American businesses, colleges and universities, museums, and foundations. The report, *Public Accountability for Student Learning in Higher Education: Issues and Options*, proposes a framework for a systematic approach to accountability that defines specific roles for many of postsecondary education's stakeholders.[59]

Higher education institutions should define and clearly communicate their institutional goals for student learning and then provide evidence to public audiences as well as accreditors that they have met these goals. Regional accrediting agencies must continue to serve as bridges between individual institutional assessment and public accountability. Additionally, accreditors should continue their efforts at the national level with the Council for Higher Education Accreditation to develop better ways to measure student-learning outcomes and communicate their work to the public. State governments must delegate the responsibility for setting goals and documenting outcomes to the institutions, and must employ accountability systems that distinguish between institutional and aggregated statewide performance measures. Recognizing the economic opportunity provided by the availability of higher education, the federal government's role is to maintain its commitment to provide all students, regardless of their economic circumstances, access to college through federal need-based aid. The national research organizations should focus a component of their research efforts, including longitudinal studies, on student learning in higher education. The national data compiled and reported are input-, output-, and process-based, but they inadequately identify and reflect what students have learned.[60]

Several lessons can be learned from reviewing the design and implementation of accountability systems and performance measures. Oftentimes such a system is expected to accomplish multiple purposes, from informing consumers of the condition of higher education to fiscal/ financial/budget decision making. The purposes of the accountability system should be carefully articulated and followed. Furthermore, an accountability system with rigidly mandated measures may not be applicable to all types of higher education institutions in a state because of the differences in educational purposes.

The number of performance indicators should be kept to a minimum; it is not necessary to measure all learning activities to demonstrate institutional effectiveness. Additionally, it is inappropriate to characterize a learning activity that is neither measurable nor contributes to learning.[61] Performance measures should be developed with as much stakeholder involvement as practical. Involvement should include those who determine policy (e.g., lawmakers) and those who implement it (e.g., faculty). Stakeholders must acknowledge and accept differences in measures types. Policymakers tend to prefer quantitative over qualitative measurement, whereas accreditors expect qualitative measures from their institutional members. Finally, performance results must be communicated in a timely and understandable manner for policymakers and the consumer (the public) in order to satisfy accountability needs and requirements.

Notes

1. Charles B. Reed and Edward B. Rust Jr., "How Can Colleges Prove They're Doing Their Jobs?," *The Chronicle of Higher Education* 51 (September 3, 2004): B7.

2. James C. Hearn and Janet M. Holdsworth, "Influences of State-Level Policies and Practices on College Students' Learning," *Peabody Journal of Education* 77, no. 3 (2002): 29.

3. Daniel T. Layzell, "Linking Performance to Funding Outcomes at the State Level for Public Institutions of Higher Education: Past, Present, and Future," *Research in Higher Education* 40 (April 1999): 235.

4. Delmer D. Dunn, "Accountability, Democratic Theory, and Higher Education," *Educational Policy* 17 (January/March 2003): 69.

5. Hearn and Holdsworth, "Influences of State-Level Policies and Practices on College Students' Learning," 11.

6. Layzell, "Linking Performance to Funding Outcomes at the State Level for Public Institutions of Higher Education," 235–236.

7. William Zumeta, "Accountability: Challenges for Higher Education," *The NEA 2000 Almanac of Higher Education* (Washington, D.C.: NEA Communications Services, 2000), 63.

8. Jane V. Wellman, "Assessing State Accountability Systems," *Change* 33 (March 2001): 50.

9. Karen Adler, "Texas Universities to Be Tested: Accountability System for Higher Education Is Approved," *San Antonio Express News* (October 29, 2004): 7B. Available from LexisNexis Academic (accessed November 2, 2004).

10. Dunn, "Accountability, Democratic Theory, and Higher Education," 75.

11. Zumeta, "Accountability: Challenges for Higher Education," 63.

12. James B. Hunt Jr. and Garrey Carruthers, "Foreword" (San Jose, CA: The National Center for Public Policy and Higher Education, n.d.). Available at http://measuringup.highereducation.org/foreward.cfm (accessed February 21, 2005).

13. Layzell, "Linking Performance to Funding Outcomes at the State Level for Public Institutions of Higher Education," 240.

14. Hearn and Holdsworth, "Influences of State-Level Policies and Practices on College Students' Learning," 17.

15. Wellman, "Assessing State Accountability Systems," 50.

16. Ran Coble, "Trends in Higher Education: Changes in Governance," *Spectrum: The Journal of State Government* 74 (Spring 2001): 16.

17. Wellman, "Assessing State Accountability Systems," 51.

18. Dunn, "Accountability, Democratic Theory, and Higher Education," 71.

19. Joseph C. Burke, "How Can Colleges Prove They're Doing Their Jobs?," *The Chronicle of Higher Education* 51 (September 3, 2004): B9.

20. Nancy Shulock, "How Can Colleges Prove They're Doing Their Jobs?," *The Chronicle of Higher Education* 51 (September 3, 2004): B7; Wellman, "Assessing State Accountability Systems," 52.

21. Wellman, "Assessing State Accountability Systems," 52.

22. Margaret M. Sullivan and Peggy C. Wilds, "Institutional Effectiveness: More Than Measuring Objectives, More Than Student Assessment," *Assessment Update* 13 (September–October 2001): 5.

23. American Accounting Association, Teaching and Curriculum Section, Outcomes Assessment Committee, "Summary of 'Outcomes Assessment,'" *Journal of Accounting Education* 12 (1994): 109.

24. Ibid., 106, 109.

25. Sullivan and Wilds, "Institutional Effectiveness," 5.

26. Hearn and Holdsworth, "Influences of State-Level Policies and Practices on College Students' Learning," 29.

27. Cape Fear Community College, Institutional Effectiveness/Planning and Research Office, *All about Institutional Effectiveness* (Wilmington, NC: Cape Fear Community College, n.d.). Available at http://cfcc.edu/ie/allabout.htm (accessed March 4, 2005); Gregory L. Weiss, *Institutional Effectiveness and Assessment for Academic Majors and Programs at Roanoke College* (Salem, VA: Roanoke College, May 2002). Available at http://www2.roanoke.edu/inst-res/assessment/AcadMan.htm (accessed March 4, 2005); Sullivan and Wilds, "Institutional Effectiveness," 4.

28. Weiss, *Institutional Effectiveness and Assessment for Academic Majors and Programs at Roanoke College.*

29. Donald Rybacki and Dan Lattimore, "Assessment of Undergraduate and Graduate Programs," *Public Relations Review* 25 (Spring 1999): 69.

30. Cape Fear Community College, Institutional Effectiveness/Planning and Research Office, *All about Institutional Effectiveness.*

31. For examples of the process, see: Texas Women's University, Office of Institutional Research and Planning, "Institutional Effectiveness Management Plan for Academic Programs," *Institutional Effectiveness Handbook* (Denton, TX: Office of Institutional Research and Planning, June 2003): 3–4, 10–11. Available at http://www.twu.edu/iep/IEhandbook.pdf (accessed March 3, 2005); Cape Fear Community College, Institutional Effectiveness/Planning and Research Office, "All about Institutional Effectiveness."

32. Metropolitan Community College, *Effectiveness Reviews* (Omaha, NE: Metropolitan Community College, January 12, 2004). Available at http://metroweb.mccneb.edu/institutionaleffectiveness/reviews.htm (accessed March 4, 2005).

33. Texas Women's University, Office of Institutional Research and Planning, "Appropriate Outcome Measures of Student Learning," *Institutional Effectiveness Handbook* 9 (Denton, TX: Office of Institutional Research and Planning, June 2003). Available at http://www.twu.edu/iep/IEhandbook.pdf (accessed March 3, 2005).

34. Rybacki and Lattimore, "Assessment of Undergraduate and Graduate Programs," 75.

35. Henk Vos, "How to Assess for Improvement of Learning," *European Journal of Engineering Education* 25 (2000): 229.

36. Kathi A. Ketcheson, "Public Accountability and Reporting: What Should Be the Public Part of Accreditation?," *New Directions for Higher Education* 113 (Spring 2001): 88.

37. William Condon and Diane Kelly-Riley, "Assessing and Teaching What We Value: The Relationship between College-Level Writing and Critical Thinking Abilities," *Assessing Writing* 9 (2004): 58.

38. Rybacki and Lattimore, "Assessment of Undergraduate and Graduate Programs," 70.

39. Ketcheson, "Public Accountability and Reporting," 92.

40. Raymond Rodrigues, "Want Campus Buy-in for Your Assessment Efforts?" (Washington, D.C.: American Association for Higher Education, n.d.). Available at http://aahebulletin.com/member/articles/2002-10-feature02_pf.asp? (accessed March 7, 2005).

41. Cecilia L. López, "Assessment of Student Learning," *Liberal Education* 84 (Summer 1998): 36–44. Available from EBSCOhost (Academic Search Premier; accessed February 27, 2005).

42. Vos, "How to Assess for Improvement of Learning," 228.

43. Educational Testing Service, "ETS Launches ICT Literacy Assessment" (Princeton, NJ: Educational Testing Service, November 8, 2004). Available at http://www.ets.org/news/04110801.html (accessed March 5, 2005).

44. Educational Testing Service, "Using Scores" (Princeton, NJ: Educational Testing Service, February 21, 2005). Available at http://www.ets.org/ictliteracy/scores.html (accessed March 5, 2005).

45. Educational Testing Service, "ETS Launches ICT Literacy Assessment."

46. Educational Testing Service, "Using Scores."

47. Educational Testing Service, "Employees and Information Proficiency" (Princeton, NJ: Educational Testing Service, February 22, 2005). Available at http://www.ets.org/ictliteracy/employer.html (accessed March 5, 2005).

48. U.S. Department of Education, National Center for Education Statistics, *The NPEC Sourcebook on Assessment. Volume 2: Selected Institutions Utilizing Assessment Results*, NCES 2000-172 (Washington, D.C.: Government Printing Office, 2000), v. Available at http://www.nces.ed.gov/pubs2000/2000 196.pdf (accessed March 5, 2005).

49. Ibid., vi.

50. Rybacki and Lattimore, "Assessment of Undergraduate and Graduate Programs," 68–69.

51. U.S. Department of Education, National Center for Education Statistics, *The NPEC Sourcebook on Assessment. Volume 2*, vi.

52. Ibid., vii.

53. Ibid.

54. Thomas D. Layzell, "How Can Colleges Prove They're Doing Their Jobs?," *The Chronicle of Higher Education* 51 (September 3, 2004): B8.

55. Shulock, "How Can Colleges Prove They're Doing Their Jobs?," B7.

56. Wellman, "Assessing State Accountability Systems," 52.

57. Reed and Rust Jr., "How Can Colleges Prove They're Doing Their Jobs?," B7.

58. Wellman, "Assessing State Accountability Systems," 52.

59. Reed and Rust Jr., "How Can Colleges Prove They're Doing Their Jobs?," B7.

60. Ibid., B8.

61. Michael L. Skolnik, "Higher Education in the 21st Century: Perspectives on an Emerging Body of Literature," *Futures* 30 (1998): 640.

CHAPTER 6

Design and Methodological Considerations

Peter Hernon

Data analysis for either a quantitative or qualitative study involves more than merely number or data crunching. It requires an understanding of the types of issues that this chapter presents. An assessment plan addresses these issues and links the data gathered to a regular review of program outcomes and subsequent adjustments in the achievement of student learning outcomes. Research methods and statistics textbooks in numerous disciplines and fields of study amplify the issues highlighted in this chapter.

EXPERIMENTAL DESIGNS

Educators might engage in pre- and post-testing of students and that testing might involve the application of repeated measures to assess the impact of student learning outcomes at the program or institutional level. The purpose is to determine the extent to which students have mastered the program outcomes—learned what the program values. Impact evaluation should be systematic and rigorous if educators want to minimize the effects of both measurement errors and chance and maximize the estimate of effectiveness. Taking measurement error and chance into account necessitates an understanding of elementary statistics and the concepts presented in this chapter.

The choice of an appropriate design, in part, depends on constraints of time, finances, human and material resources, political concerns, and whether the faculty seek publishing opportunities. In selecting the proper design, the critical question is, "To what extent can learning (mastery of the student learning outcomes) be attributed to the collection of courses and learning opportunities within the institution, or might other variables account for the impact on learning?," or, as the Middle States Commission on Higher Education puts it, "Has meaningful learning occurred as a result of an educational experience?"[1]

Program impact might be depicted in terms of impact (the program as represented by its student learning outcomes) minus confounding factors (threats to reliability and validity) and plus or minus the effect of chance, random fluctuations, or measurement error. Peter Hernon and Robert E. Dugan identify research designs, especially experimental ones, applicable to outcomes assessment,[2] but data collection for outcomes assessment need not revolve around these designs. In *Student Learning Assessment*, the Middle States Commission on Higher Education supports the use of pre- and post-testing[3] and notes that educators might adopt "a longitudinal perspective," but cautions that such a perspective is not always warranted; it may "not be necessary and may not yield meaningful information."[4] Clearly, educators have choices about what they consider to be meaningful information and how they collect it. It is important to view the term "meaningful information" in the context of an assessment plan.

STATISTICAL INFERENCE

Statistical inference uses what is known about the sizes of sampling variations to infer the likelihood that a given observation is due to chance. A *sample* is a portion of a universe, and *sampling* refers to the methods for selecting that portion. If educators intend to generalize their findings from a sample to the population, they generally select samples representative of that population. They must define the population and ensure a reasonably complete and accurate representation of that universe. It is possible to determine the amount of error that arises because a sample does not correspond exactly to the universe. This is an important aspect of statistical sampling because it means that educators can be precise about the error introduced by the sampling process. They can then decide whether the amount of error is tolerable when weighed against trade-off factors, such as the cost (time or money) of obtaining a larger sample that introduces less error.

SAMPLING

Probability and nonprobability sampling are two basic types of sampling methods. As Ronald R. Powell and Lynn Silipigni Connaway note,

> the primary purpose of sampling is to select elements that accurately represent the total population from which the elements were drawn. Probability sampling enhances the likelihood of accomplishing this objective. . . . The crucial requirement of probability sampling is that every element [e.g., an individual member] in the population has a known probability of being included in the sample.[5]

Although nonprobability sampling is the least scientific and useful of the two, educators might rely on it to identify those students whom they will ask to provide evidence of their learning. With such sampling, it is not possible to state the probability of a specific element of the population being included in the sample. There is no assurance that the sample is representative of the population. Still, nonprobability sampling is often easier and cheaper to conduct, and, in some instances, might be the only feasible type of sample with which to work.

Powell and Connaway, as well as the authors of most other research methods textbooks, discuss both types of sampling.[6] One example of probability sampling is *simple random sampling*, the simplest and most common method of drawing a probability sample. Simple random sampling involves the selection of subjects so that each one has an equal and known chance of inclusion and the selection of one subject does not influence the selection of another.

Example

With course assessment, educators typically deal with the universe (e.g., everyone in a class). It is possible that they might select a portion of that class using either a probability or nonprobability sample. Turning to outcomes assessment at the program level, educators might want to review what students learned after their first term in the program. If they take *all* of the students and ask them to complete a survey or engage in some test of their performance, the educators are dealing with the universe, or the population. On the other hand, if they select a portion of that universe, then the question arises, "Do all of the students have an equal and known chance of inclusion (probability sample), or are the students selected due to their availability at a certain time (nonprobability sample)?" Additionally, if the program relies on portfolio assessment, do the educators draw a simple random sample of student work, or do they divide the population of work into categories (e.g., term papers, oral presentations that were videotaped, and PowerPoint slides that students created) and draw a sample from the different categories? Such a probability sample is known as *stratified random sampling*.

QUANTITATIVE OR QUALITATIVE STUDY

Because measurement, a specialized form of description, assigns numbers to specify differing characteristics of a variable, it provides a means for quantifying variables and making comparisons among them. Quantitative studies involve measurement, whereas qualitative studies do not. Perhaps a better way to distinguish between both types is to recognize that quantitative research involves "a problem-solving approach that is highly structured in nature and that relies on the quantification of concepts, where possible, for purposes of measurement and evaluation."[7] Qualitative research methods focus "on observing events from the perspective of those involved and attempt to understand why individuals behave as they do. They take a more natural approach to the resolution of research problems."[8]

Studies might even involve the mixing of quantitative and qualitative aspects. Some of the methods in the methodological tool chest for investigating outcomes assessment are quantitative and others are qualitative (see Figures 7.3 and 7.4). Each has its place; educators must decide which type of method is most appropriate for determining what they want to know.

DESCRIPTIVE STATISTICS

Descriptive statistics convert raw data into indices that summarize or characterize datasets; such statistics comprise a set of procedures for organizing, describing, and summarizing observations. In effect, they provide a means for making sense of numbers and for transforming large groups of numbers into a more manageable form. Descriptive statistics are the kind that often appear in annual and other reports of departments engaged in program assessment, and include frequency distributions and measures of central tendency (averages). The data might be presented as graphic representations that show data distribution patterns visually and highlight selected findings.

Frequency Distribution

Researchers might arrange data from the largest to the smallest (or vice versa) in relation to some quantifiable characteristic. They then produce a frequency distribution that displays the frequency of occurrence and highlights patterns in the distribution of scores. A frequency distribution groups data into predetermined categories and reports numbers or scores for individual categories. That reporting might include the frequency of occurrence for each category or component of the rubric, the criterion-based rating scale that educators use to evaluate student performance (e.g., levels of mastery ranging from unacceptable through exemplary).[9] For example, for a specified learning outcome students might develop a mission statement for a business, or education students might create educational goals and objectives. Reviewers might examine student work in terms of a rubric that has four choices:

1. Very clearly stated;
2. Stated with some clarity;
3. Stated, but generally lacking clarity; and
4. Not stated.

Then the number of students whose written work was "adequate" (largely a "2") or "exemplary" (largely a "1") could be calculated and presented in the form of percentages.

Measures of Central Tendency

Averages, or measures of central tendency, comprise a type of descriptive statistic, which indicates the most typical or representative score in the group. There are three types of averages: the mode, the median, or the mean. The mode, the point(s) at which the largest number of scores falls, indicates the most typical case. The mode, which is the least stable of the measures of central tendency, is the most frequently occurring score or the largest frequency in a distribution. When scores are tied or data are grouped into classes, more than one mode may emerge. Distributions with two, three, or more modes are known as bimodal, trimodal, or multimodal. The primary advantages of the mode are that it is easy to compute and offers a quick indicator of the central value in a distribution.

The median is the midpoint of a distribution or the point below which half of the scores fall. It is not influenced by how far extreme scores may range in a given direction. If there are a few extreme scores in one direction, the median provides the best representation of central tendency. The mean, which is typically the measure of central tendency that people associate with the "average" is a more precise measure than the other two measures of central tendency. It is the sum of all of the scores divided by the number of scores.

Measures of Variability

Measures of central tendency define a point around which other scores tend to cluster. Measures of variability indicate how widely the scores are dispersed around the central point or average. The range, for instance, is the difference between the highest and lowest values. It uses an ordinal measurement scale (see the section on "inferential statistics") and measures two values in a distribution; other measures of variability are more reliable.

The standard deviation (SD), which was the only measure of variability included in any of the institutional reports studied, measures the dispersion of scores around the mean. The greater the scatter of scores, the higher the standard deviation. If all the scores in a distribution were identical, the standard deviation would be zero. The standard deviation can range from zero to a small or large number. It takes into account the deviation of each score from the mean value of the dataset.

Graphic Depiction

People cannot always visualize patterns among data presented in a table. The table might contain too much data or be incorrectly set up. Readers might also experience problems in transferring numbers into proportional groupings that summarize the patterns. For such reasons, using spreadsheets or other software, data might be presented in graphic form such as in a histogram (bar graph or chart) or pie chart. The graphic presentation of data serves as a reminder that "a picture is worth a thousand words—and at least ten thousand numbers."[10] Everything on a graph should be explained. Different symbols should be easily distinguishable from each other, and both the lettering and shading should be distinctive and true to form.

Histograms are bars representing the frequency with which different values of a variable occur. Bar charts may take different forms. A clustered bar chart displays two or more variables, with the bars being either vertical or horizontal. A stacked bar chart includes two or more variables in one bar; each segment of the bar might represent different value labels for a particular variable. For example, one could show different levels of mastery of a program outcome for each undergraduate class rank.[11]

The frequency polygon is another type of graphing technique for frequency distributions. The coordinates of the variables under study are plotted and then connected with straight lines. The end points of a frequency polygon are placed on the horizontal axis. This type of graph reflects changes over time. Each line in a line graph, which is similar to the frequency polygon, represents a different variable. An area chart takes the line graph and shades each group in a different color.

The pie chart, another common form for graphing data, shows the proportion of each variable to the whole. That proportion is expressed in terms of percentages. A scattergram, or scatter chart, portrays the distribution of findings. And, finally, it is possible to mix types of graphs. For example, a line graph might be superimposed on a bar graph.

NORMAL CURVE

A normal distribution is a family of distributions that assumes the shape of a symmetrical, bell-shaped curve that extends infinitely in both directions on a continuum close to, but never touching, the horizontal axis or baseline. If a normal curve were folded along its central line, the two halves of the curve would coincide.

Normal curves can have different shapes; however, there is only one normal distribution per mean and standard deviation. In a normal curve, all three measures of central tendency are identical: half of the cases fall above the central point and half fall below it. If the measures of central tendency are not equal, the distribution is distorted. The tail (or end) of the curve might be either top or bottom heavy; the largest part of the tail goes to the right (top heavy) or the left (negatively skewed).[12]

Z-SCORES

The Z-score is a raw score converted to standard deviation units. Because standard deviations are measured from the mean, Z-scores begin at that point and proceed up and down the scale. The mean assumes a value of zero and deviations to the right of the mean are positive and those to the left are negative. For example, a score that is one standard deviation above the mean has a Z-score of $+1$, while a score one standard deviation below the mean has a Z-score of -1.

Because the Z-score is reported in standard deviation units, it is possible to locate points on the baseline of the normal curve. Thus, the portion of cases that fall above or below those points can be determined by calculating areas under the normal curve.

INFERENTIAL STATISTICS

Descriptive statistics provide a convenient and useful means for summarizing datasets. In contrast, inferential statistics comprise a set of procedures used in drawing inferences and generalizations based on a sample of cases from a population. These procedures are derived from the principles of probability theory. Many populations are too large to permit, for example, the examination of every student. Sampling distribution serves as a means for characterizing the population. There is little need for statistical inference if educators directly observe every student in the population.

The purpose of this section is not to identify and succinctly present numerous tests useful for drawing statistical inference. Rather, it focuses on the more prevalent ones discussed in the literature of outcomes assessment and the published program reports examined. Statistical tests aid in data interpretation. Educators and researchers use them to compare data and to determine the probability that differences between groups of data are based on chance.

To determine the appropriate statistical test, educators should consider various factors and make decisions prior to actual data collection. Examples of such considerations include:

- Deciding on whether to characterize students (provide descriptive statistics) and/or to draw inferences to the population (inferential statistics).

- Stating the level of significance (for hypothesis testing). The level, which is the probability of rejecting a true hypothesis, is often set at .05 or .01, "which means that the null hypothesis, or the prediction of no relationship, is to be rejected if the sample results are among the results that would have occurred no more than 5%, or 1%, of the time. Stated somewhat differently, a significance level of .05 means that there is a 5% probability that the researcher will reject a hypothesis that is actually true."[13]

- Determining the appropriate measurement scale(s) to use (nominal, ordinal, interval, or ratio):

  - Nominal scale, the simplest of the group, identifies or differentiates groups without placing them in numerical order. The categories are mutually exclusive—every member of the group can be placed in one and only one of the categories. Such measurement names, but does not order, groups. Gender of the students is an example of this scale.

  - Ordinal scale differentiates and ranks groups, from the lowest to the highest (or vice versa), according to some characteristic. These measures indicate whether a group falls into certain categories and the numerical order of the categories. Although the order of the category shows the relative position of something, that order does not indicate the amount of difference between the positions. The categories lie along a dimension and an observation placed in category one is greater than an observation placed in category two, an observation in category two exceeds one in category three, and so on.

  - Interval scale also differentiates and ranks groups. The categories fall in order along a dimension. The difference between ordinal and interval measurement scales is that interval scales also quantify the differences between categories. The categories have equal distance from each other. The range between the highest and lowest scores is divided into a number of equal units, like degrees on a thermometer. Interval scales, however, lack a true zero point.

  - Ratio scales are interval scales but they have an absolute zero point.

- Understanding whether the population is normal (adheres to a normal curve).

- Seeing whether the distribution has one tail or two tails. A tail appears at each end of a normal curve or where the curve approaches the baseline. In estimating the value of the population mean, educators might believe that the population mean is on one side of the sample mean. In such cases, they are dealing with only one tail of the sampling distribution. When the hypothesis does not predict the direction of the difference, educators only discover that the sample results differ from the null hypothesis.

- Deciding on the number of *independent* variables (the experimental or predictor variables that educators manipulate and that presumably produce change) and *dependent* variables (influenced by the independent variable).

- Seeing whether it is preferable to risk a Type I error (the possibility of rejecting a true null hypothesis) or Type II error (the possibility of accepting the null hypothesis when it is false).

- Knowing whether the statistical test is parametric or nonparametric. Parametric methods generally require interval- or ratio-level data and assume that the scores were drawn from a normally distributed population or that both sets of scores were drawn from populations with the same spread of scores. When scores are dichotomous or in the form of either categories or ranks, nonparametric statistics are more appropriate. Nonparametric statistical methods do not make assumptions about the shape of the population distribution.[14]

- Figuring out the number of groups to be analyzed.

Experienced researchers know which statistical tests to choose given the above-mentioned considerations. They are also familiar with experimental designs and the statistical tests appropriate to them.[15]

Analysis of Variance and T-test

Analysis of variance (ANOVA) uses variance, the spread of scores in a distribution, of group means as a measure of observed differences among groups. ANOVA is a family of inferential statistical procedures that test the hypothesis that the means of the groups sampled come from populations with equal means and that group means only differ because of sampling error. Both the t-test, a parametric test, and ANOVA compare mean scores. Analysis of variance protects against a possible Type I error, which can occur when using the t-test and the number of groups or categories increases. The t-test is limited primarily to instances in which researchers only compare two samples at a time. ANOVA is more versatile, because it can compare more groups.

ANOVA, a parametric procedure, is based on three primary assumptions. First, the samples are drawn at random. Second, the samples are derived from normally distributed populations. Third, both the variances and means of the sampled populations are equal or nearly so. ANOVA therefore may be inappropriate when the populations are skewed or the samples are not randomly drawn.

In ANOVA, the dependent variable is measured at the interval or ratio level. However, the independent variables, called factors, could be at the nominal level. One-way ANOVA is an investigation of the possible effects of a single factor. Studying the simultaneous effects of two or more factors involves two-way ANOVA or multivariate analysis.[16]

In computing the t-test, researchers calculate the mean for two groups, determine the difference between both means, compute the standard error, and divide the difference between the means by the standard error. In interpreting a hypothesis, researchers take into account whether they anticipate a distribution with one or two tails. One kind of parametric t-tests pertains to independent groups—those instances in which the samples are drawn independently from a population without any pairing or other relationship between the two groups.

Mann-Whitney U Test

The Mann-Whitney U test, which is the nonparametric counterpart to the t-test for independent groups, compares a random sample from two populations assumed to be identical to see whether the samples are indeed similar. In effect, the test examines the difference between the two population distributions.

Factor Analysis

Factor analysis explores the interrelationships and commonalities among a set of variables. More precisely, it explains how the variance common to interrelated measures can be counted by a smaller number of dimensions with which the variables are correlated. Factor analysis examines a correlation matrix, which is a visual display of the intercorrelations of a list of variables. The matrix presents all possible combinations of correlation for a set of variables and isolates the dimensions that disclose correlation patterns. Researchers use factor analysis to draw inferences about the construct presented by the dimension. Simply stated, factor analysis ascertains whether a small number of unobserved variables or factors explain the interrelationships among a set of observed variables.

RELIABILITY AND VALIDITY

Reliability and validity apply to both the research design and methodology. In quantitative research, reliability seeks to determine the degree to which the data are consistent; consistency is the extent to which different samples of the same population produce the same results. Alternatively, qualitative research might focus on issues of credibility, transferability, dependability, and conformability, as opposed to issues of generalization and replication.

Validity refers to the extent to which study findings are generalizable to a population (external validity) or to which the study accurately measures what it purports to measure (internal validity). Internal validity also asks whether the researcher makes a reasonable interpretation, and whether other factors, variables, or conditions have been considered or acknowledged. If the reliability and internal validity of the data are limited, so too is the degree to which the findings can be generalized, even within a particular setting.

In *Student Learning Assessment*, the Middle States Commission on Higher Education concludes that "three forms of validity are especially relevant to assessing student outcomes:"[17] content, criterion, and construct validity. Content validity is concerned with the representativeness of the measuring instrument in describing the content that it is intended to measure. The central question is, "How well does the content of the instrument represent the entire universe of content which might be measured?"[18] *Face validity*, which represents the researchers' appraisal that the content reflects what they are attempting to measure, comprises a type of content validity. Face validity is judgmental and subject to interpretation.

Criterion-related validity compares scores on the data collection instrument to certain criteria known or commonly believed to measure the attribute under study. The purpose is to determine the extent to which the instrument treats a criterion. Any criterion must display:

- Relevance;
- Reliability; and

- The "absence of bias" ("the scoring of a criterion measure should not be influenced by any factors other than actual performance on the criterion").[19]

There are two types of criterion-related validity: *predictive* and *diagnostic*. The purpose of the former is to estimate or predict a future result, whereas the latter type diagnoses the current situation. The central difference between the two relates to the time when the data depicting the criterion are collected. To qualify as predictive validity, the correlation between the test scores and the criterion must come at a later time. Diagnostic validity requires that the correlation not be delayed, but made at approximately the same time. For example, if educators administer a test about knowledge of information literacy to students who completed freshmen English, diagnostic validity is determined by a correlation of test scores with perhaps the grade that the students received on a term paper that required use of library collections. Predictive validity involves a correlation of their test scores with the grade from a term paper in a subsequent class. Longitudinal data gathered under a suitable research design definitely enables the determination of predictive validity.

Construct validity, which has the most generalized application of the three types of validity highlighted here, asks whether the theoretical construct or trait is actually measured. For example, does a study of creativity or cultural sensitivity actually measure the construct? One way to answer the question is to correlate items on locally produced tests to those on national, standardized tests. If the correlation is high, one assumes that the new instrument measures what is intended (the construct).[20]

The Middle States Commission on Higher Education concludes,

> The concepts of validity and reliability apply primarily to summative assessment, and not as directly to formative assessment, because instructor-created examinations and measures usually only exhibit "face validity," not the other forms of validity discussed here, and they are not usually subjected to rigorous pre-administration tests of reliability.[21]

EXAMPLE OF OUTCOMES ASSESSMENT

One program-wide student learning outcome for the Graduate School of Library and Information Science (GSLIS), Simmons College, is to "apply relevant research studies to tasks requiring problem solving and critical thinking." Once a random sample of course-prepared research proposals has been selected from student portfolios, a group of outside evaluators, using a data collection instrument that the faculty develop and that has been shown to be both reliable and valid, might evaluate those proposals to determine how well the students completed the task—grasped the outcome. Did the students identify key research studies, correctly synthesize them, and properly apply them to the procedures section in their proposals? The results might be reported with a frequency count and percentage (both the percentage for each item and the cumulative percentage); the cumulative percentage is determined by adding the percentage at a given frequency to the percentages below it. The results might also be presented in the form of a bar chart or line graph depicting the results from each data collection. For instance, how do the results studied from the sample of papers examined in spring 2004 compare to those examined in subsequent spring terms?

If a random sample of students completed a test, prepared a paper in a capstone course, or responded to a scenario developed to measure their ability to synthesize research and to apply the literature examined to problem solving, it might be possible to determine the measures of central tendency, standard deviation, and range. Depending on how the examination of student comprehension was planned (e.g., which students were included and how they were selected), inferential statistics might be applicable.

Turning to another GSLIS student learning outcome, "analyze, synthesize, and communicate information and knowledge in a variety of formats," there might be an annual or semi-annual assessment day in which all of the students enrolled in courses claiming to advance oral and written communication participate in a skills assessment. Perhaps upon entry into the program the students might write one-page papers that an outside jury could then review and score. During that assessment day, they might write another one-page paper and their written work could be compared to measure progress over time.

As an alternative, student performance—defined here as ability to communicate effectively in written form—on an examination might be correlated with scores on a test of writing skills given to "students at institutions with comparable populations. Scores higher than those of the benchmarked school would be convincing evidence that the . . . [focus on writing skills] of the target institution [or program] is successful."[22]

Of course, the assessment results must be integrated into departmental planning, which is intended to improve the curriculum and the instruction. In preparing that assessment report, it is important to identify the outcome(s) under review, the method of assessment (whether direct, indirect, or a combination of both), when the data will be collected, which students will be assessed, and who will conduct the review. Furthermore, relevant indicators of reliability and validity should be determined. Next, it is important to determine how the data will be linked to departmental planning.[23]

METRICS

Metrics refer to a relationship between two quantities that can adequately be represented as a ratio (with a numerator and denominator) and then converted to a percentage. Student outcomes (e.g., graduation and retention rates) are often presented as metrics. In *Student Learning Assessment*, the Middle States Commission on Higher Education identifies some indirect measures at the course level as metrics. These include:

- Percent of class time spent in active learning;
- Number of student hours spent on service learning;
- Number of student hours spent on homework; and
- Number of student hours spent at intellectual or cultural activities related to the course.[24]

For instance, let us assume that, for a given school term (fifteen weeks), students in a course spent 30 of the 180 minutes working in groups to complete activities that reinforce the content of that three-hour class period. Thus, one-sixth of each class involves active learning. This metric might also be calculated for the entire term.

CONCLUSION

What is the relevance of traditional grading in outcomes assessment? The Middle States Commission on Higher Education provides one answer:

> Grades have been, and will continue to be, an excellent indicator of student learning *if they are appropriately linked to learning goals*. . . .

> Grades are an effective measure of student achievement if there is a demonstrable relationship between the goals and objectives for student learning and the particular bases (such as assignments and examinations) upon which student achievement is evaluated.[25]

Furthermore,

> In and of themselves, however, grades are not direct evidence of student learning. That is, a numeric or a letter grade alone does not express the *content* of what students have learned; it reflects on the degree to which the student is perceived to have learned in a specific context.[26]

Grades do have value at the course level. However, a series of grades at the program or institutional level does not adequately capture the extent to which students achieved broader outcomes (e.g., those highlighted in the examples of outcomes assessment). The Middle States Commission on Higher Education maintains that, "in general, when large-scale assessments are being used, or when standardized tests are administered program-wide or institution-wide, statistical tests should be used to analyze the data."[27] To this position, one might add that the use of pre- and post-testing at the program level might also involve statistical testing.

As outcomes assessment becomes integral to institutional culture, more institutions will expect all academic programs to include assessment based on descriptive and inferential statistics as part of the feedback loop of the open-systems model (see Figure 1.1) and relate the evidence gathered to the planning process and improved student learning. Still, the value of evidence gathered through the use of qualitative research methods should not be minimized.

Notes

1. Middle States Commission on Higher Education, *Student Learning Assessment: Options and Resources* (Philadelphia, PA: Middle States Commission on Higher Education, 2003), 36.

2. Peter Hernon and Robert E. Dugan, *An Action Plan for Outcomes Assessment in Your Library* (Chicago: American Library Association, 2002), 87–92.

3. Middle States Commission on Higher Education, *Student Learning Assessment*, 36.

4. Ibid.

5. Ronald R. Powell and Lynn Silipigni Connaway, *Basic Research Methods for Librarians*, 4th ed. (Westport, CT: Libraries Unlimited, 2004), 96.

6. Ibid., 94–119.

7. Jack D. Glazier and Ronald R. Powell, *Qualitative Research in Information Management* (Englewood, CO: Libraries Unlimited, 1992), xi.

8. Powell and Connaway, *Basic Research Methods for Librarians*, 3.

9. Middle States Commission on Higher Education, *Student Learning Assessment*, 43.

10. Richard M. Jaeger, *Statistics: A Spectator Sport* (Beverly Hills, CA: Sage, 1983), 23.

11. See, for instance, William S. Cleveland, *The Elements of Graphing Data* (Monterey, CA: Wadsworth Advanced Books and Software, 1985); Jan V. White, *Using Charts and Graphs: 1000 Ideas for Visual Persuasion* (New York: Bowker, 1984); and Robert Spence, *Information Visualization* (Boston: Addison-Wesley, 2001).

12. Most statistics textbooks discuss the normal curve and provide illustrations of it. See, for instance, Powell and Connaway, *Basic Research Methods for Librarians*, 239.

13. Powell and Connaway, *Basic Research Methods for Librarians*, 242.

14. For a more detailed discussion, see Michael R. Harwell, "Choosing between Parametric and Nonparametric Tests," *Journal of Counseling and Development* 67 (September 1988): 35–38; Sidney Siegel and John Castellan Jr., *Nonparametric Statistics for the Behavioral Sciences* (New York: McGraw-Hill, 1988).

15. See, for instance, Powell and Connaway, *Basic Research Methods for Librarians*, 165–183.

16. The Kruskal-Wallis test is the nonparametric equivalent to ANOVA. The test ranks scores and determines if the sums of the ranks for each group are so disparate that they are not likely to be from samples drawn from the same population.

17. Middle States Commission on Higher Education, *Student Learning Assessment*, 35.

18. Donald L. Ary, C. Jacobs, and A. Razavich, *Introduction to Research in Education*, 3rd ed. (New York: Holt, Rinehart and Winston, 1985), 158.

19. Ibid., 216–217.

20. Correlation examines the extent of the relationship between two random variables within specified limits. These limits are stated as correlation coefficients. A correlation coefficient is a number that indicates the degree of relationship between two variables. It reflects the extent to which variations in one variable accompany variations in the other variable.

Correlation coefficients range from 0 to plus or minus 1. Plus 1 indicates that the relationship is a perfect positive 1 (as one variable changes, the other variable undergoes equivalent changes in the same positive direction). Minus 1 is a perfect negative correlation. The presence of a negative correlation does not signify the lack of relationship between the two variables. The positive and negative signs indicate the direction of the change expected to occur in one variable when the other variable changes. A negative (or minus) correlation indicates that changes in one variable are accompanied by equivalent changes in the other variable. However, the change is in the positive direction; as one variable diminishes, the other increases.

The closer the coefficient is to a perfect positive or perfect negative correlation, the stronger or higher is the correlation. There might be a correlation of 0. In this instance, changes in one variable have no relationship with changes in the other variable.

21. Middle States Commission on Higher Education, *Student Learning Assessment*, 35.

22. Ibid., 26.

23. For an example of the use of a number of the statistical tests covered in this chapter, see Appendix J, "Enhancing Skills through Technology," in *An Action Plan for Outcomes Assessment in Your Library*, edited by Hernon and Dugan, 170–182.

24. Middle States Commission on Higher Education, *Student Learning Assessment*, 29.

25. Ibid., 36–37.

26. Ibid., 37.

27. Ibid., 38.

CHAPTER 7

Methods of Data Collection

Peter Hernon

A s Peggy L. Maki observes, goals for student learning provide the basis for meaningful assessment.[1] That assessment involves the development of outcomes that focus on what the institution and its faculty expect students to learn at course and program levels. It is possible that some general outcomes extend from a program to a school (e.g., professional studies or arts and science) or even to an institutional level. At the program level, or beyond, when the faculty embrace outcomes assessment, they, in fact, shift their focus from one of thinking about teaching (or the imparting of knowledge and skills) to one of learning (encompassing, e.g., knowledge leading to understanding, abilities, habits of mind, ways of knowing, attitudes, and values).[2] The purpose of data collection is to provide the necessary evidence for the faculty to judge the *collective impact* on student learning at two levels:

1. Conceptual level (e.g., critical thinking, problem solving, being a good global citizen, and values); and
2. Skills (e.g., oral and written communication, foreign language communication, technological sophistication, qualitative reason ability, and leadership).

As with any formative evaluation, evidence should be linked to ongoing program review and to finding ways to ensure the realization of student learning outcomes. In this way, the evidence informs the planning process and enables programs and schools to demonstrate how they meet the institutional mission.

This chapter highlights different methods for gathering evidence related to determining the extent to which students acquire specified outcomes, which means that faculty relate the evidence to the planning process. Because the companion volume, *Outcomes Assessment in Higher Education*, provided extensive coverage of those methods, this chapter recasts them in terms of Figure 7.1, which demonstrates that, when judging teaching and learning, higher education might draw on either (or both) outcomes assessment and course-level assessment and evaluation.

FRAMEWORK

Figure 7.1 shows that outcomes assessment—be it perhaps for student learning outcomes or a subset known as research outcomes—applies at the program and course levels. The next section highlights different ways to gather evidence; evidence might be rigorously collected and strong inferences drawn from it, or faculty might collect evidence less rigorously and make weaker inferences. On the surface, the former type of evidence might seem preferable. However, it might be too time-consuming, expensive, and difficult to collect such evidence with minimal error (e.g.,

Figure 7.1
Assessment of Teaching and Learning

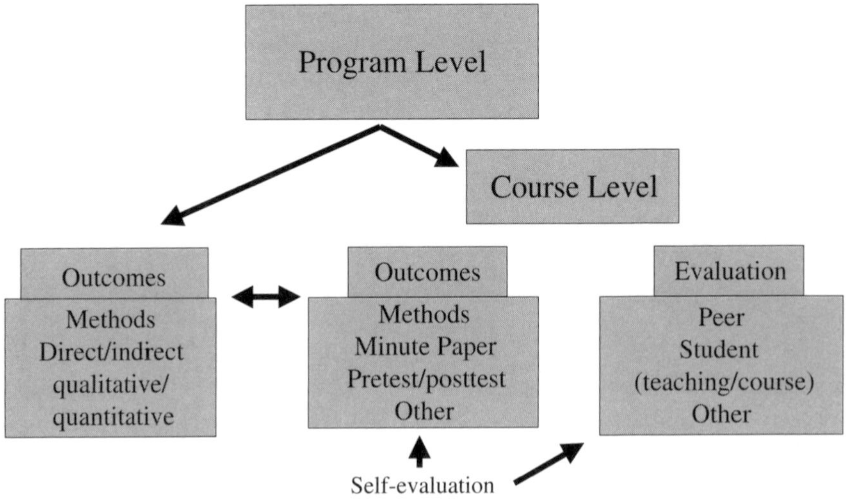

level of probability set at $p = .01$). Each type of evidence has its place, but institutions should not rely exclusively on either the latter type or what is known as student outcomes, which are aggregate statistics on groups of students (e.g., graduation, retention, and transfer rates). Student outcomes are institution-based and enable comparisons about internal institutional performance from year to year or about similarities and dissimilarities with peer institutions.

At the course level, faculty might set their own outcomes and measure the extent to which students achieve them. For instance, they might use a *minute paper* in which, in the few remaining moments of a class, they ask the students to answer a few questions (on paper):

- Do you find anything still confusing after today's class? Yes___ No___;
- If yes, what? (please explain).

Or,

- What was the most important thing you learned during class today?
- Does an important question remain unanswered for you? Yes___ No___;
- If yes, please explain.

Another method is to administer a pre-test and post-test. For instance, the first day of the course, before handing out and discussing the course syllabus, or before introducing the framework for understanding course content, they might ask the students to complete a signed pre-test (e.g., identifying five issues critical to comprehension of course content). The final day of the course, they might ask the students to complete the same form (post-test). Later, they can compare the pre-test and post-test for a measure of student comprehension or learning.

A third choice is to allow adequate time at the end of some (or perhaps all) classes for students to break into groups and address an issue central to the topic of the day. They might be asked to apply some aspect of a lecture or other method of delivering content. It is quite likely that faculty might select the minute paper or group work for a given class, and the pre-test and post-test for the school term.

The intent of outcomes at either the course or program level is to improve learning and not to evaluate teaching or the students' contribution to the course. Course evaluation, however, does involve these other aspects of the classroom experience. The goals of course evaluation might be to identify weaknesses for which corrective action might be taken or to demonstrate excellence in teaching for use in promotion and tenure decisions. Course evaluation might contain a component on student assessment of teaching and the teacher. It might also ask for students to assess their contribution to the success of the course (see Figure 7.2 for an example). Other methods of evaluation include peer review of teaching (e.g., from members of the rank and tenure committee), or review by outside evaluators, who are instructed to examine specific previously agreed-on points (e.g., the effective use of instructional media) or who visit classes as part of program or institutional accreditation. Those individuals conducting either peer review (for self-improvement or as part of promotion and tenure consideration) or accreditation review might examine course documentation (e.g., the syllabus and the explanation of assignments) and the grades for past years to detect grade inflation. This must be handled delicately so that (1) questions about the impingement on academic freedom are avoided, and, more important, (2) faculty do not withdraw or reduce their participation in outcomes assessment. The purpose of such assessment is not to judge individual faculty and their teaching styles; rather, it is to view the program holistically and identify areas needing improvement to meet program outcomes more effectively.

A better way to institute peer review of teaching is through the use of an *inquiry portfolio*, which might take more time to develop than most faculty members would be willing to devote. However, faculty might be prevailed upon to prepare abbreviated portfolios annually and more detailed ones perhaps every four or five years. The inquiry portfolio

focuses around a specific question or issue regarding teaching practices, course structures, and student learning over time.... [F]aculty initially write a benchmark portfolio which [provides a snapshot of students' learning within a particular course][3] to identify issues or questions within their teaching. They then develop an inquiry portfolio focusing specifically on that issue or question. An inquiry portfolio provides faculty with opportunities to document improvement in their teaching over time and to assess the long-term impact of teaching changes, the success of teaching approaches, and the accomplishment of student learning. The prompts that follow are designed to help faculty begin this scholarly investigation into their own teaching.[4]

Figure 7.2
Student Course Evaluation

School Term:	Fall [ ]	Spring [ ]	Summer [ ]

Course/Section No. _____	Instructor: _____

Number of students in the course: _____

This form, which is intended to collect your opinions about the course, only takes a few minutes to complete. Please place a check mark in the brackets that best matches your opinion. The scale includes values ranging from "strongly agree" to "strongly disagree"; NA refers to "not applicable."

	Strongly Agree	Agree	Neutral	Disagree	Strongly Disagree	NA
1. Program and any course outcomes were made clear (verbally) during the first week	[ ]	[ ]	[ ]	[ ]	[ ]	
2. The instructor:						
a. Communicated ideas and information clearly	[ ]	[ ]	[ ]	[ ]	[ ]	
b. Explained grading policy early in the course	[ ]	[ ]	[ ]	[ ]	[ ]	
c. Encouraged students to think for themselves	[ ]	[ ]	[ ]	[ ]	[ ]	
d. Encouraged the asking of questions and responded well to them, even when there was a disagreement of opinion	[ ]	[ ]	[ ]	[ ]	[ ]	
e. Presented course material in an organized manner	[ ]	[ ]	[ ]	[ ]	[ ]	
f. Treated students with respect	[ ]	[ ]	[ ]	[ ]	[ ]	
g. Was available during stated office hours	[ ]	[ ]	[ ]	[ ]	[ ]	[ ]
3. The assignments contributed to my understanding of course content	[ ]	[ ]	[ ]	[ ]	[ ]	
4. Criteria for evaluation of student performance (i.e., on graded assignments) were:						
a. Clear	[ ]	[ ]	[ ]	[ ]	[ ]	
b. Consistently applied	[ ]	[ ]	[ ]	[ ]	[ ]	
c. Written	[ ]	[ ]	[ ]	[ ]	[ ]	
5. I received *timely* feedback on graded:						
a. Oral presentation(s)	[ ]	[ ]	[ ]	[ ]	[ ]	[ ]
b. Written work	[ ]	[ ]	[ ]	[ ]	[ ]	

(*Continued*)

Figure 7.2
Student Course Evaluation (*Continued*)

	Strongly Agree	Agree	Neutral	Disagree	Strongly Disagree	N/
6. I learned from the feedback provided on graded assignments	[]	[]	[]	[]	[]	
7. I would encourage others to take this course from the instructor	[]	[]	[]	[]	[]	
8. I made a positive contribution to the class by:						
a. Asking questions	[]	[]	[]	[]	[]	
b. Doing the assigned readings	[]	[]	[]	[]	[]	
c. Participating in discussions	[]	[]	[]	[]	[]	
d. Other (please specify) _____	[]	[]	[]	[]	[]	

If you marked other than "strongly agree" any of the statements in question 8, why?

9. I have the following suggestions for:
   a. Activities and/or assignments that would strengthen the value of the course for future students

   b. Improving teaching/learning in the course

10. Other comments

11. I am a: Freshman []   Sophomore []   Junior []   Senior []   Undecided []

12. I took this course as a: Requirement []   Elective []

Peer review is a critical component if individual faculty members wish to continue to develop as good teachers. At the same time, "without the credibility of an independent evaluation comparable to the peer review of research, teaching will not be given equal importance"[5] or accorded higher status within universities. The peer review process might work in the following way:

> Once a faculty fellow completes his/her course portfolio, it is posted on an electronic workspace and a hyperlink to the material is made available to solicited external reviewers. External reviewers assess the portfolios based on criteria such as the intellectual content of the course, the appropriateness of teaching practices, levels of student understanding, and the portfolio author's effectiveness in documenting his/her teaching.[6]

Another effective way to improve teaching is to video- or audiotape a class in progress. Watching or listening to a tape can help faculty members identify teaching strengths and weaknesses. Many faculty members, however, find the assistance of a colleague or teaching improvement consultant more useful. A dean or departmental chair might want to invite a colleague or consultant for help in analyzing faculty performance, providing encouragement, and suggesting strategies for improving teaching. The goal is to improve teaching by identifying weaknesses and implementing strategies to offset them.

Self-evaluation, another method of course and teaching evaluation, can contextualize observations of students, peers, or external reviewers.[7] Faculty might also include in inquiry portfolios discussions of each course they teach, especially if they adopt different teaching styles in different courses. The honesty and insight of faculty members are critical components of the self-evaluation. If either component is compromised, greater weight might be attached to the inquiry portfolio or peer review.

Self-evaluation might ask faculty, for example, to:

- Discuss their teaching approach and philosophy (within and across courses);
- Explain their greatest strength and weakness in teaching;
- Identify the one thing they would most like to change about their teaching, if they made a change;
- Explain how they assess their teaching performance, in comparison to others in the department;
- Note changes that they have made since they last taught a specific course;

- Comment on how they think the course is going (do they see any problems in teaching that course and do they have any thoughts about how those problems might be resolved?);
- Identify any changes they anticipate making the next time they teach the course;
- Discuss whether or not technology is appropriate to a course and, if it is, what technology they use and for what purposes;
- Mention any recent teaching and learning innovations they have adopted or attempted; and
- Identify any aspects of their teaching they think needs improvement.

Self-evaluation might also include audio- and videotape analysis.

There are many kinds of teaching styles and methods, and even if the ideal system for improving teaching were in place, not all faculty would excel in all modes of teaching. Still, it is essential that faculty be held accountable for their teaching and be expected to meet program and perhaps course outcomes, thereby contributing more to learning.

DIFFERENT METHODS

Figures 7.3 and 10.5, which focus on the program-level outcomes highlighted in Figure 1.1, show that there are different options for collecting required evidence. Direct methods indicate whether a student "has command of a specific subject or content area, can perform a certain task, exhibits a particular skill, demonstrates a certain quality in his or her work (e.g., creatively . . .), or holds a particular value."[8] For example, a type of capstone experience might lead a student to integrate and synthesize knowledge about a field or discipline, and examine values and views of life. It might extend the student's knowledge and enable him or her to critique and apply relevant research and scholarly literature. Furthermore, that experience might address issues raised in an introductory course (or set of required courses), but at a higher level.[9]

Indirect methods, on the other hand, provide evidence that is "related to the act of learning, such as factors that predict or mediate learning or perceptions about learning but do not reflect learning itself."[10] Graduation rates, a student outcome, are an example of an indirect measure. However, Alexander W. Astin, professor emeritus of higher education

Figure 7.3
Methods of Assessing Program Outcomes*

Direct Measures	A culminating academic experience
	    Capstone experience (course, project, or get-together)
	    Thesis or dissertation
	Electronic portfolios
	Performance (task completion)
	    Internship
	    Licensure and qualifying examination for professional or
	        graduate school
	    Test
	Professional jurors or evaluators (outside examiners provide
	    feedback on students' written work or oral presentations)
	Theses/senior papers (reviewed by those jurors for content
	    analysis of writing and presentation)
	Videotapes and audiotapes of performances

Indirect Measures	Exit interviews Interviews (e.g., focus group interviews) Observation Surveys (e.g., of seniors or alumni) Tracking student data (student outcomes): graduation and retention rates, employment statistics, etc.

Producing Quantitative Evidence	A culminating academic experience
	    Capstone experience
	Performance (task completion)
	    Internship
	    Licensure and qualifying examination for professional or
	        graduate school
	    Test
	Professional jurors or evaluators (outside examiners provide
	    feedback on students' written work or oral presentations)
	Theses/senior papers
	Tracking student data

Producing Qualitative Evidence	Electronic portfolios Interviews (e.g., exit interviews and focus group interviews) Observation Surveys Videotaping of performance

*See Peggy L. Maki, *Assessing for Learning: Building a Sustainable Commitment across the Institution* (Sterling, VA: Stylus Publishing, 2004), 85–118.

and organizational change at the University of California at Los Angeles, cautions that, to reflect excellence, such rates need a context. He suggests that institutions need to develop a dataset on each student at the time of enrollment into a program and to update that dataset periodically throughout the program. "Such data would then provide a basis for learning how much any college actually contributes to, or detracts from, its students' chances of completing a degree, or of achieving many other types of outcomes." As a consequence, the data collected "would come much closer to assessing institutional quality and effectiveness than raw degree-completion rates would."[11] Austin also states that, "instead of simply comparing these rates, we should be asking ourselves: How can we help facilitate degree completion? What is it about certain institutions that enable them to retain their students at higher-than-expected levels? And what is it about certain other institutions that causes their students to drop out?"[12] However, any datasets so compiled should be governed by policies and practices which guarantee student privacy and ensure that the data are not subject to misuse.

For the types of direct and indirect assessment identified in Figures 7.3 and 7.4, the evaluation of student learning outcomes and research outcomes (see below) depends on either quantitative evidence (data that are represented numerically) or qualitative evidence (data that do not lend themselves to such clear expression; data expressed in narrative form or in prose). One type of evidence is not necessarily better than the other. The faculty will have to determine which type (or whether both types) provides the most relevant insights for gauging how well students learn.

Figure 7.4 provides examples of surveys and tests highlighted in the previous figure. Such surveys might be administered at the program, school, or institutional level. As discussed in *Student Learning Assessment*,

> If an institution finds that its students spend less time studying than the national average for study time, it might introduce curricular changes that link student evaluation (i.e., grades) more directly to the amount of time studied, perhaps by providing assignments that demand more out-of-class time and by using class examinations which test areas that are not learned simply by attending class.[13]

Commercially available instruments offer norm-referenced data (comparing a person's score against the scores of a group of people who have already taken the same examination, called the "norming group") for

Figure 7.4
Examples of Surveys and Tests*

Surveys	• College Student Experiences Questionnaire ("assesses the quality of effort students expend in using the resources and opportunities provided by the institution for their learning and development") • Community College Survey of Student Engagement (assesses the "quality in community college education") • The National Center for Higher Education Management Systems' Comprehensive Alumni Assessment Survey (helps "colleges and universities gain up-to-date information on a variety of issues. Your graduates can provide evidence of the effectiveness of your institution as well as a self-report of their own personal development and career preparation") • The National Center for Higher Education Management Systems' Student Outcomes Information Services (SOIS) ("is designed to help colleges and universities gain up-to-date information on student needs and reactions to their educational experiences") • National Survey of Student Engagement ("offers some insights into the relationships between effective educational practice and selected aspects of student success")
Tests	• Academic Profile ("a test of academic knowledge and skills. It is intended for use by colleges and universities in assessing the outcomes of their general education programs to improve the quality of instruction and learning") • CAAP (Collegiate Assessment of Academic Proficiency) Tests (cover reading, writing skills, writing essays, mathematics, science, and critical thinking) • College BASE Exam (might be required of all students obtaining their undergraduate degree—taken during the senior year) • Major field assessment tests (MFATs) (a "battery of undergraduate outcomes tests that is used by schools and departments at more than 600 colleges and universities globally to measure student academic achievement and growth") • Watson-Glaser Critical Thinking Appraisal (measures "an individual's critical thinking skills. The examinee is asked to evaluate reading passages that include problems, statements, arguments, and interpretations")

*See also North Carolina State University, University Planning & Analysis, "Internet Resources for Higher Education Outcomes Assessment" (Raleigh: North Carolina State University, n.d.). Available at http://www2.acs.ncsu.edu/UPA/assmt/resource.htm (accessed December 5, 2004); Peggy L. Maki, *Assessing for Learning: Building a Sustainable Commitment across the Institution* (Sterling, VA: Stylus Publishing, 2004), 114–118.

comparative or benchmarking purposes, and they offer some indication of reliability and validity. As an alternative to these instruments or to locally developed ones, institutions might collaborate to develop cooperative assessment instruments.

Research Outcomes

With undergraduate and graduate programs in the social and behavioral sciences trying to teach students an appreciation of research as an inquiry process, to critique published research, and to become researchers, these programs might adopt learning outcomes related to formal research. These outcomes might address the extent to which students have gained (and can apply) the knowledge necessary to engage in research as an inquiry process that centers on *problems* that have not been previously researched. The inquiry process consists of reflective inquiry (the problem statement, literature review, conceptual base of the study, objectives, and hypotheses and research questions), procedures (research design and methodology), quality indicators (e.g., reliability and validity), data collection and analysis, and effective report writing skills. For example, student learning outcomes related to research might deal with the difference between a problem and purpose statement, the extent to which the study indeed is original and adds substantially to the published literature, and the adequacy of the literature review. Direct measures of assessing student attainment of a research outcome might focus on the thesis or dissertation and its defense, and professional jurors might evaluate the final product. An alternative is to have students maintain a developmental portfolio that provides examples of their work so that professional jurors following some predetermined scoring rubric can determine if students progress throughout their program of study.

Lifelong learning is a complex issue. Novice researchers who have completed a thesis or dissertation will be likely to pursue opportunities that enable them to develop their knowledge of research and their skills with both qualitative and quantitative research. If outcomes focus on the adequacy of the initial experience (thesis or dissertation) to provide the necessary foundation, then qualitative evidence has a place.

Student Learning Outcomes

Such outcomes reflect both direct and indirect measures, and may involve the gathering of quantitative and qualitative evidence. In selecting an instrument to gather evidence either directly or indirectly, key questions to address include:

- Is the evidence provided by the instrument linked to important learning outcomes?
- Is a standardized instrument appropriate for the learning goals of the institution? Is the evaluation method appropriately comprehensive?
- Are important learning outcomes evaluated by multiple means?
- Do questions elicit information that will be useful for making improvements?
- Are questions clear and interpreted consistently? Does everyone interpret the responses the same way?
- Do the results make sense?
- Are the results corroborated by other evidence?
- Are efforts to use "perfect" research tools balanced with timeliness and practicality?
- Is evidence gathered over time and across situation? How much should be assessed?
- Are faculty and staff members who are knowledgeable about measurement serving as resources for developing assessment instruments?[14]

Studying lifelong learning and its impact of program graduates becomes a more difficult issue. How do faculty know that what they observe resulted from students' undergraduate or graduate education? How do individuals update their knowledge, and is there a learning continuum attributable to their formal program of study? Another approach is to include a module on lifelong learning that focuses on learning goals such as:

- Explain the importance of lifelong learning in your chosen career;
- Given a particular situation, identify what you need to learn; and
- Identify relevant resources, associations, and organizations that provide continuing education opportunities.

Given the learning objectives selected, what type of evidence—quantitative or qualitative—is more useful? Will that evidence be collected by a survey or other means specified in Figures 7.3 and 7.4?

Role of Libraries

Librarians might have a role in setting student learning outcomes and in gathering evidence for those outcomes. The Association of College and Research Libraries, a division of the American Library Association, has developed *Information Literacy Competence Standards for Higher Education* and *Objectives for Information Literacy Instruction: A Model Statement for Academic Librarians.*[15] One of the stated performance indicators, "The information literate student constructs and implements effectively-designed search strategies," has the following outcome, "Constructs a search strategy using appropriate commands for the information retrieval system selected (e.g., Boolean operators, truncation, and proximity for search engines; internal organizers such as indexes for books)." One of the measurable objectives for this outcome is "Demonstrates an understanding of the concept of Boolean logic and constructs a search statement using Boolean operators."

Evidence for this objective might be gathered through the use of course-level assessment. It is also possible that, when librarians know that students have already been exposed to the initial instruction, they might engage in pre-testing and post-testing, or might devise a test that requires a demonstration of that knowledge. In information literacy or fluency sessions, librarians might cover the Boolean operator "AND," gather database statistics for the "number of searches" and "the number of hits," and calculate the "number of hits per search." If the number drops over the school term, they might claim that their efforts in instructing students on this specific Boolean operation reduced the number of retrievals per search. Naturally, before advancing this assumption, they would have to develop a rationale for why the change is likely due to their instruction. This rationale would address the issue of validity—are we measuring what we think we are?[16] The validity of the claim might be strengthened if the library had gathered such statistics prior to the start of the term's instructional program (after the arrival of the new freshman class on campus) and the number of hits per search had not declined. The purpose is to see if the decrease only resulted once the librarians introduced Boolean searching in their instruction.

CONCLUSION

Both public and private academic institutions need to provide hard evidence that relates to accountability (quality and performance). That evidence should also be useful in improving programs and enhancing student learning. Individual institutions will assess student learning outcomes, including research outcomes, in different ways, but many of them share similar learning goals—helping students to develop into critical thinkers, problem solvers, and lifelong learners. Clearly, assessment calls for a shift from teaching (or the imparting of knowledge) to an emphasis on learning.

Regional accrediting organizations expect institutions to accept a shift to accountability and assessment and to improve the reliability and validity of the evidence collected to address the outcomes developed by institutions, programs, and courses. What type of evidence must be collected? Whose responsibility is it to collect that evidence? How much evidence must be collected? How will the evidence be used to improve student learning? Such questions become important as faculty and administrators select from the tool chest of methods to address the outcomes they select to characterize the program graduate.

Student learning outcomes, as well as research outcomes, generate self-referential data necessary to improve learning quality. However, these measures and the evidence gathered "are difficult both to translate to the public and to use in comparing institutions. Further, a connection between the quality of student learning and what federal and state governments spend on higher education is difficult to make."[17] Stakeholders still want institutions to collect and report student outcomes as ratios and percentages. As a result, student outcomes, student learning outcomes, and research outcomes—and evidence gathered quantitatively or qualitatively—have a place in improving the quality of learning and demonstrating accountability.

Notes

1. Peggy L. Maki, *Assessing for Learning: Building a Sustainable Commitment across the Institution* (Sterling, VA: Stylus Publishing, 2004).
2. Ibid.
3. Peer Review of Teaching Project, "The Peer Review Process: Benchmark Portfolio" (Lincoln: University of Nebraska, n.d.). Available at http://www.unl.edu/peerrev/process.html#benchmark (accessed December 3, 2004). One aspect of the benchmark portfolio involves having faculty members reflect on their course syllabus and answer questions such as "What is your course about?" and "What is the content area covered?"

4. Peer Review of Teaching Project, "The Peer Review Process: Inquiry Portfolio" (Lincoln: University of Nebraska, n.d.). Available at http://www.unl.edu/peerrev/process.html#inquiry (accessed December 3, 2004).

5. Ibid.

6. Ibid.

7. For an example of a self-evaluation form, see Karron G. Lewis, "Evaluation of Teaching: Self-evaluation Techniques" (Austin, TX: University of Texas at Austin, Center for Teaching Effectiveness, n.d.). Available at http://www.utexas.edu/academic/cte/sourcebook/evaluation2.pdf (accessed December 2, 2004).

8. Middle States Commission on Higher Education, *Student Learning Assessment: Options and Resources* (Philadelphia, PA: Middle States Commission on Higher Education, 2003), 30.

9. For an excellent discussion of the capstone course and experience, see T. C. Wagenaar, "The Capstone Course," *Teaching Sociology* 21 (July 1993): 209–214.

10. Middle States Commission on Higher Education, *Student Learning Assessment*, 32.

11. Alexander W. Austin, "Point of View: To Us Graduation Rates to Measure Excellence, You Have to Do Your Homework," *The Chronicle of Higher Education* 51 (October 23, 2004), B20.

12. Ibid.

13. Middle States Commission on Higher Education, *Student Learning Assessment*, 32–33.

14. Ibid., 39–42.

15. American Library Association, The Association of College and Research Libraries, *Information Literacy Competence Standards for Higher Education* (Chicago: Association of College and Research Libraries, 2000); American Library Association, The Association of College and Research Libraries, *Objectives for Information Literacy Instruction: A Model Statement for Academic Librarians* (Chicago: Association of College and Research Libraries, 2001).

16. Peter Hernon and Robert E. Dugan, "Institutional Example: Academic Librarians and Faculty: Information Literacy," in *Assessing for Learning: Building a Sustainable Commitment across the Institution*, ed. Peggy L. Maki, 108–110.

17. Charles B. Reed and Edward B. Rust Jr., "A More Systematic Approach," *The Chronicle of Higher Education* 51 (September 3, 2004), B7.

CHAPTER 8

Managing Electronic Portfolios

Candy Schwartz

The planning and implementation of an outcomes assessment program in an academic institution necessarily involves choosing among various methods for assessing the impact of the program on student learning. Figure 10.5, prepared for a graduate program seeking to undertake outcomes assessment, lists a wide range of both direct and indirect methods, including the portfolio. Chapter seven, which reviews methods of gathering data for assessment at many levels, discusses the inquiry portfolio as a way for teachers to engage in self-reflection and possibly external assessment. This chapter takes up the use of electronic portfolios (a family of products known variously known as e-portfolios, eportfolios, digital portfolios, and webfolios) for assessing student learning. The focus here is on e-portfolio management, and the issues which would need to be considered in preparing for an e-portfolio initiative.

"Paper" portfolios have been used in educational settings for many decades, but e-portfolios are relatively new, dating from the early 1990s.[1] As Trent Batson points out, the recent boom in e-portfolios is a matter of the timing being right: students (at least in the developed world) live, work, and learn in a digital world; the Internet is ubiquitous; and the Web is now commonly database driven and dynamic.[2] While this chapter considers their use in student learning assessment, e-portfolios are used in many other types of settings, especially those which involve credentialing or evidence of a body of work. The Web site of the recently established annual ePortfolio conference, sponsored by the European Institute for E-Learning (EIfEL), goes so far as to predict that "in 2010, every citizen will have an ePortfolio."[3]

THE IMPORTANCE OF PLANNING

An e-portfolio program is just one component of an overall assessment plan, but can be a very complex component, consuming time on a continuous rather than periodic basis. As with most undertakings involving the intersection of people and technology, the more forethought and planning the better. Careful consideration of purpose, process, and impact can go far in preventing costly investment in inappropriate software "solutions," or equally costly expenditure of time and goodwill among constituents. Initial groundwork should involve all stakeholders, including students, faculty, administrative staff, academic leaders, employers where appropriate, and representatives from partner services such the library, information technology, career center, and student support. Each of these groups has a role to play, and each will have differing insights and opinions as to what e-portfolios will mean for them, and what the impact will be on their community.[4]

If the preceding paragraph sounds somewhat cautionary, it is intentional. In these days when almost all student work is in machine-readable files or easily built Web pages, it is all too easy to decide to "put just a few resumes online," and perhaps to build a database or buy a software product to serve that specific purpose. It is then a small step to permit students to link from those resumes to course work they may have chosen to store on the public Web, or behind a password, or perhaps in their online journals or blogs (most of which are maintained not on institutional computers but on the servers of commercial Internet providers). This is not systematic, it is not controlled, and it does not serve the purpose of assessing student learning. Such activities may, in fact, detract from efforts to institute e-portfolios—"we've already done that," "we've already spent money on that," or "we don't want to ask the students to take the time to do differently what they are already doing anyway."

An e-portfolio is more than a resume and a few files. It is a complex tool, requiring thoughtful and informed policies for such aspects as content, access, confidentiality, and retention. The technological infrastructure may need to handle a wide variety of files, from simple Word documents and PDF files through interactive Web sites to image, sound, three-dimensional, and multimedia formats. Recordkeeping and tracking are necessary, as are the network checks and controls that characterize user authentication and authorization. A "learning portfolio," such as that envisioned by Gary Greenberg, incorporates communication services as well.[5] Furthermore, although e-portfolios may be viewed as "culminating experiences," and categorized with assessment tools such as capstone courses, in fact portfolios may begin even before the learner's progress through the program begins, growing and changing as the learner does, and perhaps continuing to serve lifelong learning after most ties with the institution have been severed.

E-PORTFOLIO DECISIONS

The following sections consider various decisions to be made in e-portfolio management, highlighting the issues and raising questions.

Goals and Uses

An e-portfolio program can serve many different goals, and decisions about other aspects of the program (i.e., content, use in assessment, retention, and technical management) will depend on the purposes and intended uses of e-portfolios. Some uses may have little to do with student learning assessment—for example, students might want to make selected portfolio content available to potential internship supervisors, employers, or graduate/professional schools (or, for that matter, family members and friends). E-portfolios intended primarily for this purpose can be called showcase, dossier, or training portfolios.[6,7] E-portfolios can also be used by advisors and students together in planning for careers or further education. Academic departments may use e-portfolios as an element in recruitment, and college-bound students (and their parents) might take e-portfolio programs into account during college selection. None of these functions is incompatible with the use of e-portfolios for assessing student learning, so long as assessment remains the primary purpose.

There are several kinds of assessment goals which might be served by e-portfolios:

- Assessment of the success of the program in bringing about desired learning (in this case the assessment might focus on aggregate data rather than individual: "How well are we doing in helping our students achieve the identified program learning outcomes?");
- Assessment of the success of a specific class and faculty member in achieving stated course learning outcomes (here again, the focus is

on an entire class rather than on the individual: "How well are the students learning in this class?");[8]

- Evaluation of an individual student; and
- Showcasing learning and achievement of outcomes to an external agency (e.g., an accrediting organization).

Content

The Middle States Commission on Higher Education suggests that planning for portfolios includes the following questions about content:

- How will students choose what to include in the portfolio?
- How and when will work be included in the portfolio?
- How will student and faculty reflection occur in the portfolio process?[9]

E-portfolios might include papers and project work from courses, independent studies, and extracurricular activities (especially community service). Students might be asked to include personal and professional goals, learning objectives, career plans, and self-reflective essays. The various items which normally document transition of students through an academic program (e.g., admissions essays, advising session records, recommendations, and resumes) might appear as well. Comments from faculty might be included, either in the context of a piece of work, or as separate reflections on a student's progress at one or many points in time. Where students engage in internships or practicum experiences, comments and evaluation by site supervisors could be added to the portfolio. Some program-wide documents (e.g., internship guidelines, and program and course descriptions) might be needed to provide the context for an individual student's achievement measured against policies in place at a specific point in time.

E-portfolio content is not only varied, it is also dynamic. Students should be able to annotate materials to highlight how the activities they represent contributed to learning. Some content might be the result of group work. Some might include both draft and final versions (e.g., versions of a major paper, demonstrating learning through various revisions). Other items might be transitory, to be replaced by final versions. An e-portfolio is not an electronic filing cabinet. Although some content may be required, students learn to be selective and to pick and choose appropriate materials.

Greenberg distinguishes between the showcase e-portfolio (where content creation is divorced from e-portfolio consideration, and structure is imposed post facto), the structured e-portfolio (presented as a template into which content is fit), and the learning e-portfolio (where structure develops along with content).[10] These can all include reflection, annotation, career aspirations, and course and extracurricular evidence of achieving identified or self-imposed learning outcomes, but learning e-portfolios, according to Greenberg, are the hardest to manage because they tend to incorporate a larger amount of discussion and feedback, and the organization of materials is principally left up to the author.[11] On the other hand, the comments, discussions, annotations, and self-reflection are generally held to be some of the most important aspects of an assessment portfolio.[12]

Retention

Institutions need to create policies regarding the length of time for which e-portfolio content will be available after graduation. As e-portfolios become more common across the entire educational spectrum, they may accompany individuals through every academic level and beyond (a scenario which would require considerable work in standards-making and interoperability). A related point has to do with ownership—does some or all of the content belong to the student, the institution, or the author (e.g., the internship supervisor)? Federal regulations govern the retention and accessibility of student records; presumably these laws might include some content in e-portfolios.

Other factors also influence retention. These days, evidence of learning might come in the form of text files (including Word, PDF, and other proprietary or open formats), digitized image or sound files, video formats of various kinds, Web pages, databases (e.g., a Microsoft Access file, or a small digital library using open source software), or program code representing anything from molecular models to computer games. In addition, e-portfolio content might hyperlink to external resources. Unfortunately, formats evolve and alter over time, as preservation experts and records managers well know, and externally referenced resources relocate and disappear. Although policies can recommend (or require) selected format standards for e-portfolio deposit, the problem of digital obsolescence has not yet been resolved. This raises interesting questions regarding the responsibility of an institution with respect to the continued accessibility of e-portfolio content.

Use in Assessment

E-portfolios are a tool for assessment of learning, and are also a subject of review themselves. As assessment tools, student e-portfolios can help to assess a program, a course, a faculty member, a student, or even a particular learning activity. It is critical that the intended use be made clear from the outset, and that assessment criteria be publicly distributed and well understood.

Formative assessment occurs during the process of a course or an activity, providing feedback and informing adjustment and progress. This is where the student engages in self-reflection, examines past work and related content, and discovers what he or she has learned. The role of the faculty member is to guide the student through the process, explain why it is important, and offer support and encouragement. Robert McCloud suggests activities and questions which can help the faculty member who has little experience in this activity.[13] Joan Vandervelde presents a rubric for evaluating an e-portfolio for its merits as a portfolio.[14] This would be a useful component in formative assessment, as students learn to manage content.

Summative assessment evaluates a body of work representing, for example, a student or group of students in a course or throughout a program. McCloud discusses the pros and cons of using rubrics in this stage of assessment.[15] Kathy Schrock's directory of resources on rubrics is a rich collection of links to guidelines, examples, and discussions.[16] This stage of assessment may call on external parties (e.g., alumni and potential employers). Brenda Johnston's overview of scholarly research into summative assessment using portfolios points out that there are many approaches, and that practice is "very complicated, messy, slippery, and ambiguous."[17] Helen C. Barrett and Judy Wilkerson also highlight the problems in using portfolios for summative assessment when it might be argued that content is too learner-centered and individualized to be used in this way.[18] They go on to recommend a model in which e-portfolios and assessment systems are separate but linked.

Software

Clearly, the technologies and processes which manage the dynamic and fluid content characterizing e-portfolios must be flexible and sophisticated. The software functions supporting an e-portfolio system could include:

- Authoring programs compliant with current standards for a variety of file formats;
- File import and export utilities;
- Database management;
- Metadata management for individual digital objects;
- Complex access control to objects and their associated commentaries;
- Flexible displays and reports, including representations which connect content to other content as well as to outcomes and standards;
- Version control;
- Group interaction and communication; and
- User-friendly interfaces for different types of users (students, faculty, and those who may contribute to or view the content).

Advanced functions might include dynamic resume creation, and measurement and assessment tools. Long-term commitment to maintaining e-portfolios also requires a large and continuously growing amount of dynamic storage on campus servers.

David Gibson and Helen Barrett's review of the advantages and disadvantages of using common office productivity tools or customized homegrown systems includes a detailed rubric which could be used to evaluate any system under consideration.[19] George Lorenzo and John Ittelson also evaluate these options as well as two others: open source and commercial systems.[20] Early-adopting institutions had to develop their own systems; their experiences have contributed to a growing collection of solutions, including standardization efforts and collaborations. The following are some examples:

- The IMS Global Learning Consortium maintains an XML-based open and interoperable ePortfolio specification.[21] It supports various portfolio types, including assessment, showcase, learning, and personal development, and can import, export, and manage many different kinds of content and processes.
- The Open Source Portfolio Initiative (OSPI) was established in 2003 and maintains an open source portfolio product (2.0 now in

release) which is now in use at several large institutions.[22] The project is derived from more than half a decade of development at the University of Minnesota.[23]

- ePortfolio.org, a service of the Connecticut Distance Learning Consortium (CTDLC), offers centralized hosting and management of student e-portfolios.[24] Eighteen institutions participate in this project, which was initiated under a grant from the Department of Education's Fund for the Improvement of Postsecondary Education (FIPSE). The latest version includes content import tools for students, dynamic resume creation, assessment and rubric-building tools for educators, and interactive functions for chat, advising, career counseling, and similar activities.

E-PORTFOLIO BENEFITS

Besides providing evidence of learning, e-portfolios serve students, faculty, and institutions in a number of other ways. Students are required to set goals and to think more actively about both formal and informal learning. They become more aware of the interrelationships between all of the elements that contribute to their growth, and they are directly exposed to the program and course learning outcomes that guide faculty and other participants in their education. E-portfolios reduce traditional dependence on one advisor and engage students with many faculty and other members of the extended academic community. From a very practical point of view, students can use portfolios to study for tests by reviewing work and reading comments.[25] Digital formats allow students to sort and aggregate content in different ways for different purposes,[26,27] and to work at their own pace and schedule, in a mode in which they are likely to be very comfortable. Remotely accessible portfolios are especially helpful for a commuting, part-time student body, or in a distance education setting.

Faculty, departments, and institutions gain a tool which can be used to assess students, courses, programs, and academic partners. It becomes easier to share course content and teaching philosophy with colleagues. Program review and self-study can shift from the narrow episodic lens of an individual course to the broader continuous consideration of the impact of an aggregated collection of curricular activities on student learning. E-portfolio systems can also be used to gather statistics, profile data, survey data, and other data useful for benchmarking and indirect assessment measures.

However . . .

Good intentions notwithstanding, an e-portfolio program is unlikely to be trouble-free in the initial stages. In surveying members of the New England electronic portfolio project (NEePP) one year after its founding, Trent Batson, Kim Chambers, and Eileen Palenchar found that the major pitfalls in developing an e-portfolio program were cited as problems in "faculty buy-in, policy development, selection of software, [and] integration and lack of staff resources."[28] Lessons extracted from the survey included the importance of developing and communicating a vision, running pilot programs, and developing and mandating data entry standards and policies. Siemens, on the other hand, suggests that over-regulation may inhibit adoption, and also argues that portfolio control should not reside in the institution, but should instead be managed by approved external portfolio providers.[29]

In addition to faculty concerns about increased workload and the difficulty of persuading students to focus on learning objectives rather than passing grades, Stephen Acker sees the problem of protecting intellectual property as a major obstacle to e-portfolio success.[30] He points to the inherent conflict between the objective of exposing content and the need to maintain ownership of that content, and recommends careful sharing of student work, even in the presence of typical policies regarding anonymous and aggregated use.

GETTING UNDERWAY

A one-day conference with outside speakers experienced in e-portfolio use can be a good way to jumpstart an initiative, especially if the entire academic community is invited to participate. This also presents an opportunity to recruit interested parties into local early-adopter efforts. Time will have to be spent reviewing technology options and developing policies, guidelines, tutorials, templates, and prototypes. Initial participation could be optional, or conducted by a volunteering department or unit. Content could be confined to text and images at first, with additional media accommodated once the program is running smoothly. Information technology and library services can be partners in addressing concerns about the information literacy of students and faculty, and in developing readiness training. Jafari is one of the few to suggest that attention also be paid to a robust sustainable business plan.[31]

More important than policies and technologies, faculty and students have to be willing to transform their ways of thinking and behaving. Faculty will have to rethink syllabi, assignments, and interaction with students in and outside of class. Students will need to become skilled at analyzing their learning in a conscious way. Every significant meeting between faculty and students, in person or virtual, may need to be documented for its contribution to that learning. It may take some time for e-portfolio activities to be integrated into the normal routines of student and faculty life, but the payoffs are worth the effort, as faculty and students and other constituents become partners in learning.

Douglas Love, Gerry McKean, and Paul Gathercoal present a useful taxonomy defining five levels of portfolio maturation, from the static scrapbook (level one) to "authentic evidence as authoritative evidence for assessment, evaluation, and reporting" (level five).[32] Similar to the assessment matrix presented in chapter four, portfolio project managers can use this taxonomy as a pathway to development of a program useful to students, teachers, administrators, employers, and other stakeholders. In earlier related work, Gathercoal, Love, Beverly Bryde, and Gerry McKean provide a stage-by-stage roadmap of activities and attitudes that can make for a successful transition into an e-portfolio culture.[33]

Respected e-portfolio programs are a good source for inspiration and encouragement. Alverno College was one of the first institutions to develop a Web-based portfolio system (http://ddp.alverno.edu/). The Diagnostic Digital Portfolio (DDP) is managed by a relational database and presents contents in a matrix which aligns a student's key performances (selected assessments and assignments) to the eight abilities which drive the Alverno learning experience. Content can also include ability definitions and levels, outcomes for all major and other areas, and digitized results from advising documents and learning style and interest inventories. Students can select works to showcase and can create electronic resumes. The Alverno site projects the feeling of a mature, well-established program.

LaGuardia Community College began its ePortfolio work in 2001, with funding from the Department of Education. The ePortfolio site (http://www.eportfolio.lagcc.cuny.edu/index.html) provides samples, templates, beginner and intermediate tutorials, an FAQ, an e-portfolio consultant, and an annotated bibliography of key readings. The process is described to the student as "collect" (your work), "select" (key materials to showcase), "reflect" (on learning), and "connect" (to your academic, community, and work experience). LaGuardia's e-portfolio site communicates excitement, enthusiasm, and collaboration.

CONCLUSION

Leaders in outcomes assessment emphasize that all members of the extended academic community should be involved in planning and implementation of assessment. However, much of what transpires in committees, task forces, and policymaking efforts may seem abstract and dry to students. In contrast, working with a personal e-portfolio puts students in direct and intimate contact with learning outcomes, and encourages them to be creative, to think beyond the box, and to become active learning partners rather than passive receptacles. Faculty can also be energized by new ways of thinking about teaching, and about their interactions with students. None of this is achieved without significant effort, but it is difficult to think of any other vehicle that can support the goals of learning outcomes assessment as well.

Notes

1. Australian Information and Communications Technology in Education Committee (AICTEC), *e-Portfolio* (Sydney, Australia: Australian Information and Communications Technology in Education Committee, 2005). Available at http://standards.edna.edu.au/standards/e-portfolio.html (accessed July 31, 2005).

2. Trent Batson, "The Electronic Portfolio Boom: What's It All About?," *Syllabus* (December 2002). Available at http://www.campus-technology.com/article.asp?id=6984 (accessed July 31, 2005).

3. European Institute for E-Learning, *ePortfolio 2005* (Champlost, France: European Institute for E-Learning, 2005). Available at http://www.eife-l.org/portfolio/ep2005/ (accessed July 31, 2005).

4. Ali Jafari offers insights into how each of these groups might view e-portfolios. Ali Jafari, "The 'Sticky' ePortfolio System: Tackling Challenges and Identifying Attributes," *EDUCAUSE Review* 39, no. 4 (July/August 2004): 40. Available at http://www.educause.edu/ir/library/pdf/erm0442.pdf (accessed July 31, 2005).

5. Gary Greenberg, "The Digital Convergence: Extending the Portfolio Model," *EDUCAUSE Review* 39, no. 4 (July/August 2004): 34. Available

at http://www.educause.edu/ir/library/pdf/ERM0441.pdf (accessed July 31, 2005).

6. Ibid., 31.

7. Kari Smith and Harm Tillema, "Clarifying Different Types of Portfolio Use," *Assessment & Evaluation in Higher Education* 28, no. 6 (December 2003): 625–648.

8. Faculty could also develop course portfolios or their own personal portfolios.

9. Middle States Commission on Higher Education, *Student Learning Assessment: Options & Resources* (Philadelphia, PA: Middle States Commission on Higher Education, 2003), 53.

10. Greenberg, "The Digital Convergence," 31.

11. Ibid., 34.

12. Ibid., 34.

13. Robert McCloud, *Using ePortfolios for Engaged Learning: A Handbook for www.ePortfolio.org* (Newington, CT: Connecticut Distance Learning Consortium, 2004). Available at http://www.eportfolio.org/EngagedLearning2.pdf (accessed July 31, 2005).

14. Joan Vandervelde, *Rubric for Electronic Portfolio (E-portfolio)* (Menomonie, WI: University of Wisconsin-Stout, 2005). Available at http://www.uwstout.edu/soe/profdev/eportfoliorubric.html (accessed July 31, 2005).

15. McCloud, *Using ePortfolios for Engaged Learning*, 15.

16. Kathy Schrock, "Assessment & Rubric Information," *Kathy Schrock's Guide for Educators*. Available at http://school.discovery.com/schrockguide/assess.html (accessed July 31, 2005).

17. Brenda Johnston, "Summative Assessment of Portfolios: An Examination of Different Approaches to Agreement over Outcomes," *Studies in Higher Education* 29, no. 3 (June 2004): 409.

18. Helen C. Barrett and Judy Wilkerson, *Conflicting Paradigms in Electronic Portfolio Approaches: Choosing an Electronic Portfolio Strategy That Matches Your Conceptual Framework*. Available at http://www.electronicportfolios.com/systems/paradigms.html (accessed July 31, 2005).

19. David Gibson and Helen Barrett, "Directions in Electronic Portfolio Development," *Contemporary Issues in Technology and Teacher Education* 2, no. 4 (2003): 559–576. Available at http://www.citejournal.org/vol2/iss4/general/article3.cfm (accessed July 31, 2005).

20. George Lorenzo and John Ittelson, *An Overview of E-portfolios* (Washington, D.C.: EDUCAUSE, 2005). Available at http://www.educause.edu/ir/library/pdf/ELI3001.pdf (accessed July 31, 2005).

21. IMS Global Learning Consortium, Inc., *IMS ePortfolio Specification* (Burlington, MA: IMS Global Learning Consortium, Inc., 2005). Available at http://www.imsglobal.org/ep/ (accessed July 31, 2005).

22. Open Source Portfolio Initiative, *About OSPI* (Minneapolis, MN: Open Source Portfolio Initiative, 2005). Available at http://www.theospi.org/modules/cjaycontent/index.php?id=3 (accessed July 31, 2005).

23. Paul Treuer and Jill D. Jenson, "Electronic Portfolios Need Standards to Thrive," *EDUCAUSE Quarterly* 26, no. 2 (2003): 34–42. Available at http://www.educause.edu/ir/library/pdf/EQM0324.pdf (accessed July 31, 2005).

24. ePortfolio.org, *About ePortfolio.org* (Newington, CT: Connecticut Distance Learning Consortium, 2005). Available at http://www.eportfolio.org/about.cfm (accessed July 31, 2005).

25. Batson, "The Electronic Portfolio Boom."

26. Greenberg, "The Digital Convergence," 30.

27. Helen Barrett, *Pedagogical Issues in Electronic Portfolio Development* (2002). Available at http://www.electronicportfolios.com/EPpedissues.pdf (accessed July 31, 2005).

28. Trent Batson, Kim Chambers, and Eileen Palenchar, *Who's Doing What? ePortfolio in New England*. Unpublished presentation at NERCOMP 2005, Worcester, MA. March 7, 2005.

29. George Siemens, *ePortfolios* (December 16, 2004). Available at http://www.elearnspace.org/Articles/eportfolios.htm (accessed July 31, 2005).

30. Stephen Acker, "Overcoming Obstacles to Authentic ePortfolio Assessment," *Campus Technology* (2005). Available at http://www.campus-technology.com/news_article.asp?id=10788 (accessed July 31, 2005).

31. Jafari, "The 'Sticky' ePortfolio System," 41.

32. Douglas Love, Gerry McKean, and Paul Gathercoal, "Portfolios to Webfolios and Beyond: Levels of Maturation," *EDUCAUSE Quarterly* 27, no. 2 (2004): 26. Available at http://www.educause.edu/ir/library/pdf/EQM0423.pdf (accessed July 31, 2005).

33. Paul Gathercoal, Douglas Love, Beverly Byrde, and Gerry McKean, "Web-based Electronic Portfolios," *EDUCAUSE Quarterly* 25, no. 2 (2002): 29–37.

CHAPTER 9

The Learning Organization: Assessment as an Agent of Change

Patricia M. Dwyer

H ow does change take hold on the university campus? Is change a top-down initiative, a grassroots movement, or some combination of the two? Successful assessment programs, and, more generally, many organizations that have experienced transformation, point to a model of change that taps the resources and talents of the group; the outcome is a common sense of purpose and responsibility—a vision that can be embraced by the entire community. This was the experience at Shepherd University as we formulated an assessment process that would engage the campus. The purpose of this chapter is to highlight our process and to introduce a model of change that may prove helpful in efforts to transform a campus culture.

INTRODUCTION TO SHEPHERD UNIVERSITY

Shepherd University is part of the public school system of West Virginia. Located in the historic Eastern Panhandle of the state and perched on the Potomac River, the university attracts students primarily from West Virginia, Virginia, Maryland, Washington, D.C., and Pennsylvania. Approximately 4,000 students are enrolled in 197 undergraduate majors, minors, and concentrations; the university has recently had selected graduate programs accredited.

165

In 1998, Shepherd University found itself in a predicament that many colleges and universities face: it was slated for an accreditation visit in 2002, but campus assessment efforts were stalled at every turn. As the new director of assessment, I was acutely aware of the resistance and, in some cases, outright hostility to assessment initiatives. Now, three years after our accreditation visit, that resistance and hostility are no longer prevalent. The university's assessment efforts have expanded into pedagogical reform, teaching and learning initiatives, and ultimately a thriving Center for Teaching and Learning that now houses the assessment process.

CHANGING THE EDUCATIONAL FOCUS

In *The Dance of Change*, Peter Senge and his colleagues define the kind of transformation that Shepherd University went through "as the capacity of the human community to shape its future, and specifically to sustain the significant processes of change required to do so."[1] The "human community" that they describe sustains a certain "creative tension," that is, "energy generated when people articulate the vision and tell the truth (to the best of their ability) about current reality."[2] Creative tension is central to the scenario that Georgine Loacker and Maria Mentkowski explore in their essay "Creating a Culture Where Assessment Improves Student Learning." They describe Alverno College president Sister Joel Read's call for the faculty to engage in a process of critical inquiry to inform curricular change. The key to success in moving through these turbulent waters, Alverno College discovered, was asking the critical question: "What kind of person are we as educators seeking to develop?" Both the faculty and administrators were involved in formulating an answer. Loacker and Mentkowski point to the sense of co-responsibility that contributed to the college's transformation.[3]

If fostering co-responsibility is essential to effecting change, then what role does leadership play in moving an organization forward? Senge and his colleagues describe the "subtle choice" that is necessary at the outset of any change effort when leadership determines whether the initiative will be authority driven, use the charismatic hero-leader model, or rely on a widespread commitment in which a variety of people share different aspirations and capabilities and join together to move the organization forward.[4] Whichever choice is made, the organization needs a leader "who appreciates the development of learning capabilities";[5] in other words, change should be driven by learning rather than by an authority figure.

There must be repeated opportunities for small actions that individuals design and implement themselves, first on a small scale and then with the involvement of increasingly larger numbers of people and activities. Participants learn from successes and failures and talk to each other candidly about the results. Participation builds commitment, and those with similar aspirations are naturally drawn into the collaborative process.[6]

Change driven by shared learning provides the essential infrastructure for implementing successful assessment processes in colleges and universities. While assessment has become firmly imbedded in the culture in elementary and secondary schools, higher education has been much more resistant to opening the doors to its classrooms, curricula, and successes or failures in meeting student learning goals. That resistance stems from faculty belief that assessment infringes on academic freedom, faculty complaints that "big brother" (i.e., government) is watching in menacing ways, a belief that accreditation organizations should not delve into matters such as learning (either in the classroom or program of study), the sense among many faculty members that assessment represents one more committee meeting or a time-consuming "extra," a tradition of having research and publication serve as the sole focus of accountability, and so on. Perhaps less articulated is a subtle but real sentiment among some faculty that assessment and practices that explore curriculum, pedagogy, and educational goals fall far beneath the lofty and esoteric aims of higher education. Often "covering" the content within a discipline becomes the focus, rather than exploring teaching methods or curriculum revisions that could enhance student learning, such as those that address different learning styles or encourage higher thinking skills (e.g., problem-solving and critical thinking).

Any successful assessment process must ensure that the organizational culture reflects dynamic learning, both for the students who gain when programs are continually assessed, and for staff and faculty who learn about new ways to assess programs or present course material that grow out of *educational* goals rather than discipline-specific content mastery. On our campus, departmental discussion about program learning goals was new territory for most. Envisioning programs as cohesive building blocks toward learning outcomes rather than merely a collection of courses prompted many of our faculty to restructure curriculum or rethink pedagogy. Thus, our assessment process, with components that included grassroots education and small group action that increasingly included more broad-based participation, mirrored the development of the "learning organization" that Senge and his colleagues describe and that assessment is meant to create.

THE CHALLENGE TO CREATE CHANGE THAT LASTS

Many of us have seen assessment programs created for an accreditation visit, only to have them quickly disintegrate as soon as the decision is rendered. The challenge every campus faces is incorporating an assessment program that will outlast the fear of losing accreditation, and indeed, become part of the campus culture. At the 2002 Professional Organizational Development conference in Atlanta, Ann F. Lucas, author of *Leading Academic Change*,[7] conducted a workshop on nurturing leadership skills in department chairs. She presented John Kotter's theoretical model for understanding ways that change takes hold and becomes effective in an organization. His model (see Figure 5.1), like the "learning organization" that Senge and his colleagues describe, effects change because a "guiding coalition" from within the organization leads and teaches in order to create the necessary buy-in for lasting change. Kotter, a professor at the Harvard Business School, describes this coalition as powerful enough to effect change and to work as a team to achieve a vision. On our campus, the small coalition's power was its understanding of assessment as a way to improve student learning. They were ambassadors, a support structure, and a resource. Thus, Kotter's model, with its elements of grassroots education, was very similar to the process that Shepherd University implemented for campus-wide assessment.

The eight-step process that Kotter outlines[8] (see Figure 9.1) also helps to explain why the assessment process at Shepherd University was sustained beyond the accreditation visit that created the initial call for action. The following section describes the connections between Kotter's steps and the successful process for implementing assessment at Shepherd University.

MAKING THE CONNECTIONS

Step 1: Establishing a Sense of Urgency

Facing an accreditation visit was all the urgency we needed. The "major opportunities" cited in this stage (see Figure 9.1) can provide a more positive spin to the "urgency" and get a campus to move forward with an assessment process. Some opportunities may include, for instance, a call for major curricular reform (as in the case of Alverno College), realignment

Figure 9.1
Eight-stage Process for Creating Major Change

Step 1: ESTABLISHING A SENSE OF URGENCY
- Examining the market and competitive realities
- Identifying and discussing crises, potential crises, or major opportunities

Step 2: CREATING A GUIDING COALITION
- Putting together a small group with enough power to lead the change
- Getting the group to work together like a team

Step 3: DEVELOP A VISION AND A STRATEGY
- Creating a vision to help direct the change effort
- Developing strategies for achieving that vision

Step 4: COMMUNICATING THE CHANGE VISION
- Using every vehicle possible to constantly communicate the change vision
- Having the guiding coalition role model the behavior expected of employees

Step 5: EMPOWERING BROAD-BASED ACTION
- Getting rid of obstacles
- Changing systems or structures that undermine the change vision
- Encouraging risk taking and non-traditional ideas, activities, and actions

Step 6: GENERATING SHORT-TERM WINS
- Planning for visible improvements in performance, or "wins"
- Creating those wins
- Visibly recognizing and rewarding those people who made the wins possible

Step 7: CONSOLIDATING GAINS AND PRODUCING MORE CHANGE
- Using increased credibility to change all systems, structures, and policies that do not fit together and do not fit vision
- Hiring, promoting, and developing people who can implement the change vision
- Reinvigorating the process with new projects, themes, and change agents

Step 8: ANCHORING NEW APPROACHES IN THE CULTURE
- Creating better performance through customer and productivity-oriented behavior
- Articulating the connections between new behaviors and organizational success
- Developing means to ensure leadership development and succession

Source: Reprinted by permission of *Harvard Business Review* from *Leading Change* by John P. Kotter. Copyright © 1996, p. 21, by the Harvard Business School Publishing Corporation, all rights reserved.

of schools or programs, and outside funding for a particular project that demands assessment. Urgency does not have to be equated with panic. The collection of data and reflection on the learning goals of a program are integral to a good assessment program. Often faculty and administrators need an impetus to make these activities a priority.

Step 2: Creating a Guiding Coalition

Shepherd University had formed a plethora of assessment committees but very little action had been taken. When putting together a guiding coalition, the director invited selected faculty and staff members who would work well together and would be good ambassadors for the assessment program. This small group represented the seeds of the "learning organization" that Senge and his colleagues describe. As this Assessment Task Force learned about assessment, they mentored others. These were the "small actions" designed and implemented with a few and then with increasingly larger numbers of people and activities. Participation builds commitment, and as more was learned about the benefits of assessment, more buy-in to the process was created.

In addition, the name change from "committee" to Assessment Task Force contributed to the different tone that the group hoped to communicate. Unlike other campus committees that tend to be top-heavy with administrators, the Task Force developed leaders at the faculty and staff level. One dean represented the other administrators on the Task Force, and thus staff, faculty, and, most important, students made up the core educators and support team for assessment initiatives. This was an important signal to the campus as to who "owned" the assessment process. The Task Force met once a month and planned assessment workshops, helped departments to construct assessment plans and reports, and generally offered assistance where needed. The role of the members as supporters rather than watchdogs was key to the success.

Step 3: Develop a Vision and a Strategy

This step was perhaps the most important in the assessment process at Shepherd University. Our vision took the form of connecting assessment to improving student learning. While this relationship might seem obvious to seasoned assessment practitioners, it was a "light bulb" moment for most on our campus. And, because the assessment director was also a faculty member at the time, the vision did not feel imposed as a top-down edict. It was more of a value that those "in the trenches" could embrace. Surely everyone cared about and was committed to student learning.

This connection of assessment to student learning became the mantra whenever the director was discussing assessment issues with chairs or faculty, staff, or students. The Assessment Office became the Office for Assessment of Student Learning—the administrative assistant answered the phone with that phrase, the office stationery communicated that message, and every newsletter and announcement always linked assessment and student learning. At this same time, the director proposed that a statement be included in the institutional mission that would highlight the importance of improving student learning. The following was added to the university mission statement in 2000: "Student learning is central to the culture of our institution, and finding ways to improve student learning is a continuous process."

While the newly revised mission statement communicated the vision, the Assessment Task Force recognized the need for a structure to help departments collect and review data immediately. With an accreditation visit in two years, we decided to create a yearly cycle for assessment plans and reports from each department and unit. While this cycle demanded a quick turnaround to complete the assessment loop, it also provided more immediate feedback (and deadlines) for departments that were starting assessment activities for the first time. We found that once faculty saw the value of the data to improving their programs, and that no top-down actions were taken to control or monitor the results, we gained more buy-in to the process.

In addition, we kept the assessment plans simple. Each plan needed to be linked to the institutional mission; departments identified no more than three learning goals to assess each year; two means of assessment were established for each learning goal; and departments determined a benchmark for success for each learning outcome.[9] This kept the process from seeming overwhelming, especially for beginners. With three learning goals and two means of assessing each, we had assessment plans that were manageable and yielded quick results.

Another strategy to achieve the vision was to create forums for departments or units to have more in-depth discussions in a pleasant and open atmosphere. The director invited departments and staff units to go off campus for an assessment retreat where they could enjoy a comfortable conference facility, share a good meal, and relax together away from the demands of office phones and e-mail. The Office for Assessment of Student Learning made the arrangements and paid for meals, and the director offered to facilitate a discussion with each department or unit about program learning goals.

Throughout the academic year, the director organized grassroots faculty development opportunities to continue educating the campus about assessment. Some departments were farther along in assessment than others, especially those with discipline-specific accreditation standards. Monthly lunches (free food is always a draw) provided the opportunity for individuals to share an assessment strategy that they were using, from student self-assessment to using primary trait analysis for course-embedded assessment goals.[10] Because the faculty and staff saw the presenters as "one of their own," they were much more open to the message—to transform the learning culture through assessment and dialogue.

Step 4: Communicating the Change Vision

To communicate the vision, the Office for Assessment of Student Learning created a newsletter, "Assessment of Student Learning at Shepherd," that showcased assessment's link to student learning; initiated a speaker series, "Focus on Student Learning," with faculty and staff as guest speakers presenting topics of interest; and organized a brown-bag lunch discussion group, "Food for Thought," on issues of teaching and learning. These forums were critical to the success of the process for several reasons. First, they brought faculty from a variety of disciplines together to discuss a topic in which everyone was interested—teaching. Before the focus on assessment, occasions were rare for interdepartmental discussions. Most faculty felt energized by this new forum for the exchange of ideas. Second, these monthly discussion groups also brought together academic affairs and student affairs personnel. Because the assessment process included every unit on campus, every one of them constructed learning goals, whether from the perspective of financial aid, admissions, or the registrar. Student affairs was vitally connected to assessment because of the wide variety of co-curricular activities it sponsored and assessed. Thus, the entire campus could see the ways each unit contributed to enhancing student learning.

The guiding coalition, the Assessment Task Force, served as support for the campus and, in communicating with departments or individuals, always linked assessment with student learning. The Task Force members reviewed yearly plans and gave feedback and advice about the format of the plans. Thus, they made sure that each plan was linked to the mission, had three learning outcomes to be assessed, had two means of assessing each outcome (both direct and indirect), and had a benchmark to determine success. Task Force members would not comment on the actual outcomes being assessed but only gave feedback on the components of a good plan.

Step 5: Empowering Broad-based Action

In his model, Kotter cites the need to remove obstacles. At Shepherd University, we were more likely to work around them. For example, the director called her team a task force rather than a committee. This kept the group from "stepping on the toes" of already established assessment committees that were not moving the process forward. In addition, the Task Force was housed under Strategic Planning rather than the Faculty Senate in order to streamline and facilitate the decision-making process.

Early on in the assessment process, the Task Force wanted to encourage departments to assess those outcomes that might be risky; in other words, departments should not assess only those outcomes that felt safe or ones that were guaranteed to produce good numbers. On April 24, 2000, the Task Force approved a campus *Philosophy of Assessment* in which it asserted that assessment results would not be used for punitive purposes. The following excerpt from the University Mission Statement provided the foundation of the *Philosophy of Assessment*:

> [T]he small residential setting of the college creates an environment in which students are able to work closely with faculty, staff, and administrators who encourage their intellectual growth, personal fulfillment, and academic and professional excellence. Student learning is central to the culture of our institution, and finding ways to improve student learning is a continuing process.

The *Philosophy of Assessment* statement noted that

- Promoting student learning is at the heart of every assessment initiative. Student learning is the common goal that drives every department and program.
- Assessment has the potential to promote an atmosphere of learning, cultural diversity, and curricular innovation.
- Assessment of student learning can build bridges between academic and student affairs, and between academic support programs and departments.

• Assessment results will be used to initiate or build service and academic programs and not for any punitive actions.

While the philosophy encouraged participation on a more abstract level, a more practical way to promote broad-based action is through funding. Initially, each department was automatically awarded $500 to defray the cost of assessment materials. At the end of the first year under the new director, very little of the money had been used; most departments did not have ideas, other than ordering tests, about how to use it. In the second year, the director shifted to mini-grant applications and encouraged departments to apply for projects. Applicants could be awarded grants up to $1,000 for an assessment-related project. These could include curricular revision based on assessment data, travel to an assessment-related conference, stipends for outside portfolio reviewers, or departmental retreats with outside consultants. After the initial year of awards, the Office for Teaching and Student Learning organized panel discussions of the grantees' assessment projects. This advertised and celebrated the accomplishments of those granted awards and also gave others ideas on ways to use assessment funds.

Step 6: Generating Short-term Wins

Our "wins" in the first year were simply getting assessment plans and reports completed for each department/program. While neither the plans nor reports were perfect, the completion of the assessment loop gave departments some data to work with. Furthermore, department members discovered that they could learn something about their programs that could be very valuable. Many departments received positive results from the use of standardized tests, and this encouraged further assessment. As assessment cycles afforded more information to the departments, the departments were encouraged by their deans and the Vice President of Academic Affairs to use results in seeking budget increases.

We visibly recognized these "wins" by showcasing departments' assessment efforts in the newsletter or through the speaker series. In addition, we started a Student Achievement Day; students submitted proposals to present projects or papers to the university community. These were often capstone projects, and entire departments would attend the session to recognize the students' achievement. In the last two years, as capstone presentations have grown and developed, we have moved to a more departmentally based recognition of student achievement.

Step 7: Consolidating Gains and Producing More Change

Increased credibility for the assessment process came with the "exemplary" rating we received on our assessment efforts from the North Central Higher Learning Commission accreditation team. By this time, all departments and units were using assessment to review learning goals and assess success in achieving them. In 2002, the university also restructured and created the position of Dean of Teaching and Learning to expand assessment activities and to develop a Center for Teaching and Learning.

Working with new faculty to communicate a campus culture whose focus is enhancing student learning has been a more recent initiative. Now, even before new faculty members begin their first semester, the Center for Teaching and Learning sends each of them a book about pedagogy and curriculum development, with teaching tips that will help them create a syllabus and prepare better for the upcoming semester. The letter of welcome that accompanies the book invites them to be part of a new faculty learning community. These monthly meetings, organized and facilitated by the Dean of Teaching and Learning, acquaint new faculty with the university policies and help them get acclimated. Of course, sessions that support teaching excellence are always a part of the program.

Step 8: Anchoring New Approaches in the Culture

A successful accreditation visit contributed to making assessment part of the culture of the institution. Our "better performance" included changes in the curriculum, prompted by assessment, to meet student needs. We have also completed several successful discipline-specific accreditations, established graduate programs, and continue to develop innovative teaching strategies and curriculum initiatives. New leadership has emerged through faculty learning communities, summer teaching institutes, and Task Force outreach.

INDICATORS OF A CULTURAL SHIFT

The eight-step process of change provides a dynamic framework for adopting new programs (e.g., the assessment process). Forming a "guiding coalition" and a vision provides the foundation and the inspiration for action; aligning resources to that vision and creating "wins" ensures that the change will last. Three years beyond the accreditation decision, several indicators point to the lasting change that took effect as a result of an assessment process that mirrored Kotter's model:

- Creation of a New Administrative Position: Dean of Teaching and Learning: Because our President and Vice President of Academic Affairs saw the value of what had been accomplished in preparation for the accreditation visit in the area of assessment, they decided to create a position to shepherd the projects that had been initiated and to develop those that would grow out of the assessment process. This move also signaled to the campus the importance of teaching and learning in the context of the university mission. The Dean of Teaching and Learning sits on the deans' council and brings to the table issues of curriculum change, pedagogy, technology and classroom development, and co-curricular activities that support teaching and learning.

- Assessment of Student Learning: Departments and academic support units continue to assess learning outcomes and explore ways to revise curriculum or change teaching strategies to improve student learning. After the accreditation visit in 2002, we moved to an eighteen-month cycle between assessment plans and reports. This revised schedule provides time for departments and units to collect more data and reflect on changes to be made in curriculum or programs.

- Development of an Intentional First-Year Program: Soon after the accreditation visit, we recognized that to improve student learning, especially in the first year, an infrastructure needed to be in place to support students in this important transition time. We started with the development of learning communities for first-year students. These are linked General Education courses where professors work together outside of class to encourage an interdisciplinary approach to the course work. Introductory writing courses were linked to music, political science, sociology and biology; the students responded enthusiastically to this more cohesive approach to learning. At the same time, a first-year task force was formed to explore components of an intentional first-year experience. In conjunction with the "Foundations of Excellence" discussion as outlined by John Gardner and the First-Year Policy Center, we continued to shape our options for first-year students. (See Fyfoundations.org

Web site for the Foundations of Excellence in the First College Year, a project sponsored by the Policy Center on the First Year of College and supported by the Lumina Foundation for Education.) Most recently, we have added interest groups, small groups of fifteen first-year students who are matched with a faculty or staff mentor. The students enroll in the course based on a topic that interests them and are acclimated to the university setting through large- and small-group learning experiences. The three large-group sessions focus on survival skills, wellness, and diversity; these sessions are planned and facilitated by upper-class leaders, and the format is interactive and engaging. Small group sessions enable students to explore the interest around which the group is focused as well as process some of the challenges they are meeting in the first semester. In 2003, we started with four learning communities, and in 2004, we initiated four interest groups; in Fall 2005, we offered five learning communities and twelve interest groups. Working closely with student affairs staff, we have made great strides, with very little budget, to create an intentional first-year experience. We are currently collecting data on retention, and already our efforts are proving to be successful, with the rate of attrition in the learning communities far less than our typical drop-rate among first-year students.

- Faculty Learning Communities: In an effort to draw new members into the learning organization, the Dean of Teaching and Learning initiated new faculty learning communities. Once a month the group meets to learn more about campus services, and topics like advisement, merit pay, promotion and tenure, and our student profile. These sessions help new faculty become more acclimated to the university, and they also get acquainted with colleagues from a variety of disciplines. When we have a number of new chairs assuming that leadership position for the first time, we arrange a learning community to address their unique concerns.

- Campus-wide Conversation about the General Education Curriculum: In 2002–2003, focus groups were organized to assess student awareness of the current general education learning goals. Assessment efforts had helped us identify educational outcomes, but we wondered how students experienced what was often seen as a "check-list" model of general education courses. An upper-division social work class facilitated the focus groups as part of the course curriculum. What we discovered was that students did not see coherence to the program, and wanted to have more diversity in the curriculum and more choice. At the beginning of 2004, the General Education Committee organized a campus-wide conversation on "liberal arts in the twenty-first century." Our kick-off event, which included a major speaker on general education reform, raised the important issues: first and foremost, who are our students and what do they need to be successful graduates? How can we better integrate general education with the major? Should general education be more skills-based or content-driven? Working groups met throughout the year, each focused on one of these questions. The next phase will be to examine the present curriculum based on the information gathered.

- Linking Curriculum to Student Development Theory: In 2004–2005, the Center for Teaching and Learning partnered with the staff of student affairs to present research on stages of student development. In monthly seminars, student affairs staff explored ways students develop over their university years and discussed characteristics unique to millennial students. Since then, both General Education Committee and department chairs have become more aware of shaping the major to suit students better at their varied levels of emotional and intellectual maturity.

- Teaching, Learning and Technology Roundtable: In 2004–2005, a broad-based coalition of faculty, administrators, staff, and students worked with outside consultants to develop a more cohesive vision for teaching, learning, and technology. This initiative started with a two-day retreat in which the group identified strengths and weaknesses of the present classroom infrastructure as well as obstacles in the area of faculty development. Working over the next few months in subgroups, the team put together a vision, mission, and values statement that would guide the group's decisions throughout the process. The Dean of Teaching and Learning acted as a co-leader with two faculty members and the director of information technology. In the next phase, the team will develop a strategic plan with a time-line for implementation of the objectives.

- Summer Faculty Teaching Institutes: In the summer of 2002, we started special summer institutes where faculty from a variety of disciplines could gather to review curriculum and discuss new teaching strategies. Initially faculty were paid to spend a week in July revising curriculum for one course based on Dee Fink's text on creating deep learning.[11] In the next year, we moved to a two-day institute during the week between the close of examinations and graduation. Many more faculty members were able to attend, and because they were on contract, no additional funds were needed for stipends. This time the institute focused on learning to use WebCT (our platform for computer integration), using group work to increase learning, and interactive lecturing.[12]

CONCLUSION

Because assessment is often associated with top-down scrutiny of programs or curriculum, it is all the more important to develop a process that incorporates grassroots education and broad-based participation to create a common understanding and purpose. The "learning organization" as described by Peter Senge and his colleagues articulates a model of leadership that was essential to our assessment program's success. We were all part of the learning—faculty, staff, administrators, and students, and as we developed incrementally a corpus of knowledge and understanding concerning assessment, the threat of program cuts or administrative interference in curriculum development diminished. Now our campus-wide conversations about assessment no longer focus on "Why?" Instead, they revolve around "How?"

While we were not aware of Kotter's model of change when we instituted the assessment process at Shepherd University, intuitively we knew that two key elements of Kotter's steps were critical to our success. First, we needed to communicate a common vision about assessment; for us, the vision was assessment as a way to improve student learning. Second, we knew that education at the grassroots level would gain buy-in, and that the more we actually collected and reviewed data, the more we would understand how assessment could help us achieve the vision. Thus, both academic departments and support units such as student affairs and the library saw themselves as contributing to the vision, assessing learning goals and not merely student satisfaction. Our assessment program helped us engage our entire campus in a common mission, breaking down barriers between departments, as well as between academic and student affairs. One could not hope for a better outcome.

Notes

1. Peter Senge, Art Kleiner, Charlotte Roberts, Richard Ross, George Roth, and Bryan Smith, *The Dance of Change: The Challenges of Sustaining Momentum in Learning Organizations* (New York: Currency/Doubleday, 1999), 6.

2. Ibid., 16.

3. Georgine Loacker and Maria Mentkowski, "Creating a Culture Where Assessment Improves Learning," in *Making a Difference*, edited by Trudy W. Banta (San Francisco: Jossey-Bass, 1993), 6–7.

4. Senge et al., *The Dance of Change*, 41.

5. Ibid.

6. Ibid.

7. Ann F. Lucas, *Leading Academic Change: Essential Roles for Department Chairs* (San Francisco: Jossey-Bass, 2000).

8. John P. Kotter, *Leading Change* (Boston: Harvard Business School Press, 1996).

9. James O. Nichols, founder of Institutional Effectiveness Associates, a private consulting firm, was the primary source for this template.

10. Primary trait analysis is a way to assess individual skills in class or departmental assignments. Instructors or departments identify the skills they want to assess, develop a rubric that would identify levels of competency, and assess individual skills in the project or paper. Rather than computing a grade that includes all the components of an assignment, instructors or departments assess "traits." Thus, they can assess how a class or randomly selected students in a department fare on a variety of skills. See Barbara E. Walvoord and Virginia Johnson Anderson, *Effective Grading: A Tool for Learning and Assessment* (San Francisco: Jossey-Bass, 1998) for a more detailed explanation.

11. L. Dee Fink, *Creating Significant Learning Experiences* (San Francisco: Jossey-Bass, 2003).

12. For more information about Shepherd University's Center for Teaching and Learning, see Shepherd University, Center for Teaching and Learning, home page (Shepherdstown, WV: Shepherd University). Available at http://www.shepherd.edu/ctl/ (accessed July 28, 2005).

CHAPTER 10

Applying Student Learning Outcomes to an Educational Program

Peter Hernon and Candy Schwartz

In chapter fourteen of the companion volume, Sandra Bloomberg and Melanie McDonald of the College of Professional Studies, New Jersey City University, describe the process that motivated the College faculty to understand, accept, and develop student learning outcomes. As they noted, "our progress at times has seemed glacial, our path circuitous, and our outcomes occasionally serendipitous—and that is simply how it is. We have planned, we have sought opportunities, and we have created and used synergy. This is our success."[1] The purpose of this present chapter is to continue the story about traveling through a long, dark tunnel and starting to emerge into daylight, but to use a different situation—the Graduate School of Library and Information Science (GSLIS), Simmons College, Boston—and to identify the outcomes that guide learning in the master's program.

Such outcomes should characterize program graduates and the basic knowledge (leading to understanding, "abilities, habits of mind, ways of knowing, attitudes, values"[2]) and skills they have gained through the program. In effect, the institution's and school's mission, as portrayed by these outcomes, "characterize a culture of inquiry that relies on evidence of student learning to inform institutional actions, decisions, and long- and short-term planning focused on improving student achievement."[3] Additionally, individual faculty might develop student learning outcomes at the course level, and other outcomes (students and research) will be created for the doctoral program. These outcomes round out the program's identity. Students become known for the educators that taught them and what they learned.

This chapter highlights the stages through which GSLIS has gone in developing its set of program outcomes, and it identifies the remaining stages through which the program might travel. Furthermore, the chapter presents paths that the program might visit as it implements the agreed-upon set of outcomes.

THE SETTING

Simmons College in Boston, Massachusetts, is a small, private liberal arts women's undergraduate college with four large graduate schools. GSLIS is one of those graduate schools, and is one of the country's longest-running academic programs in library and information science. GSLIS offers a master's degree (with an enrollment in the range of six hundred to seven hundred students) and a doctorate in library management (with about fifteen students). Master's students may take a general suite of courses or may choose one of three areas of specialization (including a state-accredited school library teacher program, and a concentration in archives management or preservation). The student body is largely composed of working adults (the median age is thirty-three) who take classes part-time and who may take from one to six years to complete the degree. Course schedules are developed with the working student in mind, and each student's sequence of progression through courses is dictated only by the presence of prerequisites (typically the core required courses).

LEADING UP TO OUTCOMES

Like all discipline-based academic units, and perhaps especially those in areas which are prone to rapid social and technological change, GSLIS constantly revisits the curriculum (the curriculum committee is made up of the faculty as a whole). The beginnings of a move to outcomes assessment can be seen in the period from 1996 through 1999, when the faculty began to meet frequently outside of faculty meetings to consider the core curriculum. During this period the faculty drew up a model that still serves as a framework for curriculum planning, evaluation, and revision. The next step took the form of a "Core Curriculum Planning Document" which drew on course syllabi and input from faculty to identify almost two hundred concepts (e.g., "ethical issues in research" and "client/server model") mapped to one or more of eight constructs: technology, users, research, ethics, information policy, management, reference, and organization. The faculty ranked the concepts to determine which ones should be addressed in the required core curriculum, and took the first steps toward revision of the core. Informed by these activities, in the following academic year the faculty thoroughly revisited and revised the GSLIS mission, vision, goals, and objectives, and reaffirmed the model. Students, alumni, and area employers were involved in this process, working with faculty on committees that used the curriculum model to guide discussion of the identified core areas of knowledge. While the work of these three years informed the next stage, the obvious missing element was any serious consideration of how to assess the success of curriculum revision from the student learning point of view.

STAGE ONE

In 2000, Simmons College prepared its self-study report for the New England Association of Schools and Colleges as part of the re-accreditation process, and that report introduced the institution to outcomes assessment. Soon thereafter, GSLIS started the preparation of its self-study report for master's program accreditation by the Committee on Accreditation of the American Library Association. Both accrediting bodies expected a greater emphasis on learning as demonstrated by the adoption of student learning outcomes and the linkage of any evidence gathered for continuous improvement in student learning. As Peggy L. Maki observes, "what an institution and its programs and services learn through students' work promotes programmatic and institutional dialogue and self-reflection about the processes of teaching and learning and their relationship to levels of student achievement." She then notes, "Dialogue and self-reflection, in turn, stimulate innovation, reform, modification, change, and revision or rethinking of educational practices and pedagogy to improve or strengthen student achievement."[4]

This was a period of great change in the department, with a surge in enrollment, a new dean and six additional faculty members, a move to a new building, and the accreditation activities. Nevertheless, curriculum review resumed after only a brief hiatus, and in fact offered a good opportunity to introduce the new community members to the program and to benefit from their fresh viewpoints. Although to long-standing members of the faculty the planning process did at times seem to be the glacial and circuitous path described by Bloomberg and McDonald, there were two significant differences this time. First, the process began with the development of a set of program outcomes, formally adopted in 2003 (see Figure 10.1), and second, the introduction of outcomes led necessarily to consideration of assessment. The program outcomes, as well as the model developed earlier, provided a framework for a systematic revision of curriculum, and led to a new set of required core courses, which were put into place with the 2005/2006 academic year. At faculty retreats, adjunct faculty members teaching either core or elective courses have been introduced to outcomes assessment, and the review extended to the elective courses and their relationship to the core.

The outcomes have been integrated into GSLIS curriculum materials and processes in a number of ways:

- Course template. As an aid during curriculum revision, the faculty developed and used a course description template (Figure 10.2) which included identification of the program outcomes addressed by the course. Collaborating in groups derived from the core course constructs, full-time and adjunct faculty created formal course descriptions for each core and required course, using this template. When more than one faculty member taught a course, the parties affected made a collective decision. The entire faculty reviewed each course for its continuation in the program. Course descriptions prepared by adjunct faculty revealed a tendency to lay claim to covering all or most of the outcomes, rather than a select few. This serves as a reminder that the list of outcomes met by each course must be reviewed to determine the accuracy of the claims. Once the course descriptions were complete, a matrix showing the ten outcomes and which courses met which outcomes was developed and reviewed. That information was then reviewed and the matrix was revised as necessary.
- Advising. These formal course descriptions will be made available to students for their assistance in course selection. During the process of preparing the descriptions, some of the groups also prepared graphic representations of possible course sequences in

Figure 10.1
Student Learning Outcomes

1. Demonstrate the ability to apply standards relevant to specific information service activities.
   - This includes standards which apply to the organization of information (Anglo-American Cataloguing Rules, Library of Congress Subject Headings, Library of Congress Classification, Dewey Decimal Classification, MARC formats, the Dublin Core, and the Encoded Archival Description) as well as to information delivery and presentation (including markup languages such as XML and XHTML).

2. Demonstrate knowledge of print and electronic information retrieval procedures.
   - This includes knowing how to find information in print reference resources, how to use online searching protocols for use in structured online databases, and how to exploit the tools offered by Web search engines, portals, and subject gateways.

3. Develop user-centered strategies for solving reference service problems, while demonstrating a command of current issues and trends.
   - This requires familiarity with a wide array of information resources and services, as well as the ability to analyze information needs of specific individuals and communities and to evaluate and select appropriate information resources for specific information needs.

4. Analyze, synthesize, and communicate information and knowledge in a variety of formats.
   - Formats include oral and written presentation and communication, and the ability to use presentation technologies (e.g., PowerPoint and the Web) effectively.

5. Recognize existing and potential problems in a workplace and devise strategies to resolve them.
   - This entails familiarity with management principles and best practices, and the ability to identify and resolve management problems.

6. Assess, create, and evaluate systems for managing content.
   - Content management systems include software and services for database management, Web content management, and online public access catalogues.

7. Apply relevant research studies to tasks requiring problem solving and critical thinking.

8. Demonstrate leadership abilities
   - Leadership abilities evidenced in learning contexts include team building and shared decision making, strategic planning, advocacy, and consensus building and collaboration.

9. Respond to diversity among individuals and communities through policies, collections, and services.

10. Analyze information problems and develop solutions, drawing from a wide range of information technology tools and practices.

Figure 10.2
Formal Course Description Based on Template

Course Number & Name: LIS 415, Information Organization

- **Description:** The phenomena, activities, and issues surrounding the organization of information in service of users and user communities. Topics include resource types and formats, information service institutions, markup, descriptive metadata, content standards, subject analysis and classification, and the information life cycle. Readings, discussions, examinations, and oral and written exercises. Required course.

- **Prerequisites:** None

- **Audience (level, environment/setting):** Beginning, all settings

- **Student Learning Outcomes** [by number]: 1, 4, 6 [see Figure 10.1]

- **Topics/List of Lectures:**
  - Introduction to information organization and the information life cycle
  - Resource types and formats
  - Information service institutions and retrieval systems
  - Information retrieval systems
    - history, current, database structures
  - Markup, descriptive metadata, and content standards
    - SGML/XML, MARC, MODS, et al.
    - Principles of entry convention and authority control
    - FRBR, AACR, EAD, TEI, Dublin Core
    - Interoperability (Z39.50, OAI, et al.)
  - Subject analysis (alphabetic, systematic, algorithmic)
  - The information life cycle revisited; preservation

- **Suggested Textbooks/Readings**
  - Caplan, Priscilla. (2003). *Metadata fundamentals for all librarians*. Chicago, IL: ALA.
  - Chu, Heting. (2003). *Information representation and retrieval in the digital age*. Medford, NJ: Information Today.
  - Hillman, Diane, & Westbrook, Elaine L. (Eds.). (2004). *Metadata in practice*. Chicago, IL: ALA.
  - Schwartz, Candy. (2001). *Sorting out the Web: Approaches to subject access*. Westport, CT: Ablex.
  - Taylor, Arlene G. (2004). *The organization of information*. 2d ed. Englewood, CO: Libraries Unlimited.
  - Taylor, Arlene G. (2004). *Wynar's Introduction to cataloging and classification*. 9th rev. ed. Englewood, CO: Libraries Unlimited.

each area (Figure 10.3). This work has been extended to all areas, and will prove useful to students in program planning. Additionally, clear and identifiable career tracks began to emerge from the core and elective portions of the program.

- Course syllabi. Beginning in the 2005/2006 academic year, course syllabi identify the program outcomes appropriate to the course, as well as any course-specific outcomes. If the relationship between the outcomes and the syllabus (and/or assignments) is unclear, individual faculty members have been asked for clarification.

Figure 10.3
Organization Cluster

Solid lines indicate that LIS 415 is a prerequisite
Dotted lines indicate that LIS 415 is recommended for this course or area of concentration

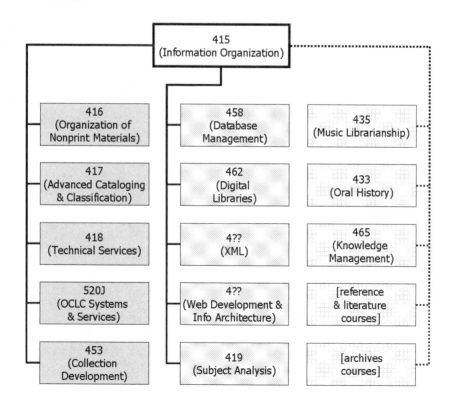

Figure 10.4
Proposal for a New Course

Please include the following items
1. Title
2. Description (as would appear on the Web in course listings)
3. Number of credits
4. Frequency with which course should be offered
5. Prerequisites
6. Audience (level, environment/setting)
7. Student learning outcomes (by number, see below)
8. Course outline (list of topics)
9. Suggested texts/Reading list
10. Discussion of relationship to existing courses and to program goals and objectives and learning outcomes.

Student Learning Outcomes

1. Demonstrate the ability to apply standards relevant to specific information service activities.
2. Demonstrate knowledge of print and electronic information retrieval procedures.
3. Develop user-centered strategies for solving reference service problems, while demonstrating a command of current issues and trends.
4. Analyze, synthesize, and communicate information and knowledge in a variety of formats.
5. Recognize existing and potential problems in a workplace and devise strategies to resolve them.
6. Assess, create, and evaluate systems for managing content.
7. Apply relevant research studies to tasks requiring problem solving and critical thinking.
8. Demonstrate leadership abilities. (Leadership abilities evidenced in learning contexts include team building and shared decision making, strategic planning, advocacy, and consensus building and collaboration.)
9. Respond to diversity among individuals and communities through policies, collections, and services.
10. Analyze information problems and develop solutions, drawing from a wide range of information technology tools and practices.

- Course proposal form. A faculty member proposing a new course for faculty vote must demonstrate its relationship to the outcomes (see Figure 10.4). The course proposal form facilitates creation of the formal course description and integration of the course into future planning and assessment.

STAGE TWO

GSLIS, which is currently in both stages one and two, is reviewing the new curriculum and deciding if there is need for either a capstone course or experience and what that course or experience will be. At present, both the school media center program and the archives concentration have internships that provide the necessary summative (final) assessment of the extent to which program outcomes have been met. However, even for that program and concentration, a clearly identified feedback loop of the evidence generated to the planning process has not yet resulted. How does the information generated through those internships relate back to the stated student learning outcomes? What changes within courses result? How do those changes advance learning?

Such questions are not transitory; rather, they guide self-reflection and future curriculum review. Undoubtedly, the challenges will increase as graduate education shifts from students comprising Generation X, who are born between 1965 and 1970, to students comprising the next generation, known as Generation Y, the Internet Generation, the Millennium Generation, or the Entitlement Generation. "[M]anaging an emerging workforce containing retiring Boomers, Generation Xers, and newly entering Nexters will be a challenge."[5] Paraphrasing Brian Smith, organization growth, during times of change management, requires a realization and acceptance about how both generations differ from previous generations and of how the entire workforce contributes to a productive, forward-thinking organization.[6] From an educational perspective, however, there are also learning differences and educational expectations between the different generations. The Millennium Generation, for instance, is self-directed but less interested in reading, especially long articles or books. Furthermore, they matured and learned in an environment that was dominated by passive education and entertainment, and they are comfortable with the digital environment. They may be at ease with presentation skills that focus on the application of technology, but less comfortable with outcomes centered on oral and written communication skills. Paradoxically, a number of them may require support for technology-based education.[7] As this example indicates, a faculty focused on learning needs to develop effective ways to educate different generations of students, often mingled together in the same class, and enhance the likelihood that learning (related to course content and the programmatic outcomes) indeed does occur.

This stage also involves another decision point—for each outcome should there be levels that students should reach as they progress through the program? For example, should students completing the core courses (or certain ones) have attained certain knowledge, attributes, and skills? How might a person who has completed a specific core course be characterized? How does that characterization change as the individual progresses through the program? In *Developing Research & Communication Skills*, the Middle States Commission identifies rubrics with four levels: "novice," "developing," "proficient," and "accomplished."[8] Bloomberg and McDonald suggest "novice," "proficient," and "accomplished."[9]

STAGE THREE

This stage, which actually overlaps the second one, involves a review of the methodological tool chest and a determination of which methods of formative (ongoing) assessment will become integral to the planning process. The purpose is to assess students periodically and to make adjustments in the presentation of the outcomes so that the students gain the most from the set of courses comprising their program of study. As well, that assessment and any adjustments in the delivery of course content will be applicable to the next cohort of students.

Shortly after the concept of outcomes assessment had been formally introduced into curriculum review, the faculty took up the issue of assessment measures. Figure 10.5 highlights the choices in the tool chest, and was distributed to GSLIS faculty along with Figure 10.6, which considered to what degree assessment activities were already present at GSLIS. From that list, GSLIS faculty are considering direct methods, especially the digital portfolio (see chapter eight) and the capstone course or experience. They are also considering the use of outside jurors or evaluators, and various indicators of performance (see chapter seven). For example, a capstone experience for those intending careers as academic reference librarians might involve giving a presentation related to an aspect of information literacy. Another choice might be to use random sampling to select some students to engage in simulated task performance whereby they demonstrate certain skills in critical thinking or problem solving. GSLIS faculty will face many choices and decisions as assessment plans move forward. If outside jurors or evaluators are

Figure 10.5
Outcome Assessment Measures

The Curriculum Working Group has compiled a list of possible measures for outcomes. This list attempts to include all possible measures, with the view that the faculty could discuss these and determine which ones might be appropriate in our setting. The list is compiled from the sources listed in the bibliography.

Direct Measures

- Course-based measures
  - Course-embedded projects, assignments, or exam questions that directly link to program-level expected learning outcomes and are scored using established criteria
  - Holistic written evaluations of student performances together with a set of rating scales
  - Observations of field work, internship experiences
  - Evaluations of student knowledge and skills from internship supervisors, faculty overseers, or students
  - Group problem-solving tasks
- Culminating experiences
  - Standardized testing (i.e., from external testing organizations)
  - Locally designed multi-dimensional or comprehensive standardized tests or exams
  - Portfolios (e.g., art, writing, and case studies), with scoring rubrics and external and internal assessment
  - Capstone experience (course, thesis, or field project) (should be linked with objectives and use internal and external evaluation teams; expectations must be made clear to students all the way along; might be done in association with baseline data gathered at program entry; might also require an oral defense or interview)
- Methods applicable within courses or in culminating experiences
  - Blind scored essays and texts
  - Oral proficiency examinations
  - Moral/ethical choice exercises
  - Concept Mapping—students construct their own maps, indicating concepts as labeled circles or boxes and showing the relationships among concepts
  - Gown's Vie—students are asked to construct a Vie diagram that displays the conceptual methodological elements involved in the knowledge acquired (frequently used in science laboratory instruction)
  - Simulated task performances—students must identify and solve typical problems within a case setting with responses directly observed by assessors, or by means of an essay or debriefing
  - Videotaped/audiotaped performances
  - Computer simulations
  - Think-aloud techniques
  - Rubrics or rating scales (e.g., simple checklists or holistic rating scales)

(Continued)

Figure 10.5
Outcome Assessment Measures (*Continued*)

- Self-reflection
- Qualitative internal and external juried reviews of projects/papers

Indirect Measures

- Surveys and interviews
  - Faculty surveys getting at perceptions of student knowledge and skills
  - Alumni surveys
  - Employer surveys
  - Current and former student surveys which ask students to self-report knowledge gains, changes in skill levels, and levels of involvement in the learning process
  - Open-ended interviews with individuals or groups
  - Structured interviews using a discipline-specific conceptual map to plan the interview
  - Exit interviews
  - Focus groups
  - Student logs (e.g., reflections on teamwork experience)
- Syllabus review
- Data gathering
  - Tracking student groups over time to determine term-to-term persistence, program completion, course passage rates, grade point performance
  - Job placement data
  - Retention/graduation rates

Note: The bibliography has not been included in the figure.

to be used, who serves as the panel and what documentation do they follow that is both reliable and valid? More important, how do those assessments lead to improved learning? From the outset, GSLIS faculty have expressed a desire for flexibility, wishing to avoid a "one size fits all" assessment method, and possibly undertaking many different methods.

In support of the assessment process, GSLIS has begun to work with outcomes expert Peggy L. Maki, who conducted one workshop for faculty and staff at the end of the spring 2004/2005 semester, and returned in the 2005/2006 academic year. Collaborating with someone external to the community, and especially someone who is knowledgeable about the process, makes it easier for the members of GSLIS to work together to

Figure 10.6
Existing Assessment at GSLIS

Direct Measures		Do We?	Notes
Course-based measures	Course-embedded projects, assignments, or exam questions that directly link to program-level expected learning outcomes and are scored using established criteria	All courses?	What about the "established criteria"?
	Observations of field work, internship experiences; evaluations of student knowledge and skills from internship supervisors, faculty overseers, students	Some courses	
	Group problem solving tasks	Some courses	
"Culminating" experiences	Portfolios (e.g., art, writing, or case studies), with scoring rubrics and external and internal assessment	Only in School Library Teacher Program	A trend in LIS and at Simmons
	Capstone experience (course, thesis, or field project) (should be linked with objectives and use internal and external evaluation teams; expectations must be made clear to students all the way along; might be done in association with baseline data gathered at program entry)	No	
Methods applicable in courses or culminating experiences	Self-reflection	No	
	Moral/ethical choice exercises	Some courses	
	Simulated task performances—students must identify and solve typical problems within a case setting with responses directly observed by assessors, or by means of an essay or debriefing	Some courses	
	Qualitative internal and external juried reviews of projects/papers	No	If we adopt portfolios?

(Continued)

Figure 10.6
Existing Assessment at GSLIS (*Continued*)

Indirect Measures		Do We?	Notes
Surveys and interviews	Employer surveys, alumni surveys	Yes	
	Current and former student surveys which ask students to self-report knowledge gains, changes in skill levels, and levels of involvement in the learning process	To some degree	
	Open-ended interviews with individuals or groups, focus groups	Yes	Occasional, not regular
	Student logs (e.g., reflections on teamwork experience)	Some courses	
Syllabus review	Implication is syllabus review by other than person responsible for course. We could do this for core courses and all technology courses.	Not systematically	
Data gathering	Tracking student groups over time to determine term-to-term persistence, program completion, course passage rates, grade point performance	Yes	
	Job placement data	Yes	
	Retention/graduation rates	Yes	

move through stage three, determining the best set of methods, into stage four.

STAGE FOUR

Upon the conclusion of the third stage, there is need to conduct a pilot study to see how the process works in practice. This stage might last for one school term and selectively focus on the accomplishment of student learning outcomes. What problems occurred? How are those problems resolved? How are those adjustments covered in the ongoing "cycle of inquiry": "identify outcomes," "gather evidence," "interpret evidence," "implement change"? That cycle occurs within the context of the institutional and school mission.[10]

STAGE FIVE

In this final stage, the process is regularized but remains flexible. The types of issues noted in stage two remain at the forefront. There is a realization that changes will continue to occur, and there might be other selections from the assessment tool chest.

Throughout all of the stages, there is a realization that the faculty decide what students should learn. Outcomes assessment at this stage focuses on four questions:

1. How well are students learning what the faculty impart (e.g., knowledge leading to understanding, ways of knowing, and formation of attitudes)?
2. What measures and procedures does the institution use to determine that the programs are effective?
3. Over time, is there a need to make adjustments in those measures and procedures?
4. What does the program do with the evidence gathered to improve its performance and student learning?

It is also important to ask (and answer), "To what extent does the school offer evidence that demonstrates its effectiveness to employers, the GSLIS profession and society, and those paying for the tuition?"

EXAMPLES

This section highlights two examples of student learning outcomes identified in Figure 10.1:

1. Analyze, synthesize, and communicate information and knowledge in a variety of formats; and

2. Apply relevant research studies to tasks requiring problem solving and critical thinking.

It is clear that these two outcomes are closely related. Both, for instance, include oral and written communication skills, as well as an ability to synthesize information; however, if students make oral presentations about research, the second outcome might include other presentation competencies (e.g., use of presentation technologies). As one example of an assessment method, a student might be asked to present key aspects of a problem statement for a research study orally in no more than four minutes (timed by stopwatch). A scoring rubric could focus on the clarity, originality, and importance of the problem identified (see Figure 8.1 of *Outcomes Assessment in Higher Education*). The first outcome could also be served by a timed oral presentation within which the student would have to explain a selected topic, its importance, and key aspects, accompanied perhaps by a one-page handout covering the scope, the importance, and a key reading. This could be required of a sample of students halfway through the program and another sample in their final term, using a paper the student had already prepared for a course. Assessment of the ability to synthesize information might focus on the literature review portion of a student research proposal and the works cited. How well do students synthesize the literature?

Some critical questions become:

• Who assesses the results?

• What scoring rubric is used?

• How are the results interpreted?

• In making those judgments, how is interscore reliability assumed?

• How are the results linked back to the planning process and improved learning for those students currently in the program as well as the next cohort of students?

Of course, faculty members teaching courses covering specific outcomes should not conduct the assessment. Other members of the faculty, or others, might conduct the assessment, but documentation covering "a criterion-based rating scale" should be developed to guide that assessment.[11] Most important, those individuals conducting assessment should not let their set of opinions guide their assessment.

Which methods will be selected from the methodological tool chest to collect the necessary evidence? Will the method be a direct or indirect one, or will a combination of methods be used? Digital portfolios providing a collection of student work and faculty commentary would address both outcomes. Timed presentations used within a course might be related to a course outcome. On the other hand, if a sample of students outside of specific courses is selected, then this speaks to program outcomes assessment. From the tool chest, it is important to select the most relevant method or methods; the goal is not to select and apply every conceivable method.

CONCLUSION

The regular assessment of faculty for promotion, tenure, and salary increases must remain separate from outcomes assessment. Faculty, deans, and committees on rank, tenure, and appointments must all be accountable for this separation. Linking outcomes assessment to faculty review diverts attention from learning and ensures that members of the faculty look after their own self-interests. Learning suffers and the institutional culture does not change. The goal of outcomes assessment should be viewed as positive (treating faculty as educators who collectively advance student learning), and negative (only reacting to pressure from regional accrediting organizations or program accrediting agencies).

Notes

1. Sandra Bloomberg and Melanie McDonald, "Assessment: A Case Study in Synergy," in *Outcomes Assessment in Higher Education*, ed. Peter Hernon and Robert E. Dugan (Westport, CT: Libraries Unlimited, 2004): 272.
2. Peggy L. Maki, *Assessing for Learning: Building a Sustainable Commitment across the Institution* (Sterling, VA: Stylus Publishing, 2004): 3.
3. Ibid.

4. Ibid.

5. Raul O. Rodriquez, Mark T. Green, and Malcolm James Ree, "Leading Generation X: Do the Old Rules Apply?," *Journal of Leadership & Organizational Studies* 9 (Spring 2003): 67–75.

6. Brian Smith, "Managing Generation X," *USA Today (Magazine)* 129 (November 2000). Available from Infotrac (accessed July 28, 2004).

7. Bizhan Nasseh, "Internet-Generation & Adult Learners Will Create Major Challenges for Higher Education Institutions in the 21st Century" (Muncie, IN: Ball State University, n.d.). Available at http://www.bsu.edu/classes/nasseh/study/learners.html (accessed January 4, 2005).

8. Middle States Commission on Higher Education, *Developing Research & Communication Skills: Guidelines for Information Literacy in the Curriculum* (Philadelphia, PA: Middle States Commission on Higher Education, 2003), 69–73.

9. Bloomberg and McDonald, "Assessment," 274–288.

10. Maki, *Assessing for Learning*, 5, 153.

11. Middle States Commission on Higher Education, *Student Learning Assessment: Options and Resources* (Philadelphia, PA: Middle States Commission on Higher Education, 2003), 43.

CHAPTER 11

An International Perspective on Educational Excellence

Peter Hernon

Outcomes assessment is primarily a term that applies to institutions of higher education in the United States. In part, such assessment places student learning in the context of what institutional mission statements espouse, and it seeks to enhance student learning and the quality of students' educational experience. Student learning assessment, which is a part of an ongoing process to document and improve student learning, might occur at the program level and describe field-specific skills, attitudes, knowledge, and abilities to be mastered by learners completing a program. In many other countries, quality assurance agencies exercise jurisdiction over institutional accreditation and work with professional associations in providing program accreditation. They focus on concepts related to outcomes assessment, namely quality assurance, quality enhancement, and the application of good (best) practices to higher education.

Both quality assurance and quality enhancement, which are part of the broader quality movement (often equated with total quality management and the establishment of the Malcolm Baldrige National Quality Award), link accountability to *fitness-for-purpose*—a clear statement of how the organization or institution meets its purpose (its mission) and is effective and efficient in meeting stated goals and objectives that reflect that mission. Although fitness-for-purpose focuses on "doing" enough to meet the goals, Peter Newby of the Centre for Higher Education Research, Middlesex University, London, argues that it should be reinterpreted as "doing better than before."[1] Perhaps a better characterization is that as institutional missions evolve and focus more on learning (and less on just the imparting of information and knowledge), fitness-for-purpose might also shift to outcomes assessment. Outcomes assessment, as practiced in the United States, seeks speedier transformation of organizational and institutional cultures.

The purpose of this chapter is to compare outcomes assessment and quality assurance and to provide a global perspective to any discussion of outcomes assessment. The examples relate to three countries, two of which were covered in the previous volume. The third country is South Africa; the author had an opportunity to deliver a keynote address there and to interact with different individuals, one of whom is a representative of the government's quality assurance agency. However, some examples from other countries are offered for the purpose of illustrating that the concepts of *outcomes* and *impacts* have different, but evolving, meanings. As a consequence, when educators in different countries use basic terminology such as *outcomes* they might not be referring to the same concept and its operationalization. Still, it seems that a number of other countries are moving in the direction of the Middle States Commission on Higher Education and other accrediting organizations and associations in the United States, and their emphasis on student learning outcomes and the involvement of the entire institution in making a commitment to achieving such outcomes.

QUALITY ASSURANCE AND OUTCOMES ASSESSMENT: A COMPARISON

Unlike outcomes assessment that focuses directly on student learning, quality assurance views learning from the perspective of teaching and the imparting of the message. As this chapter illustrates, there are differences between an approach centered on teaching and one focused on learning. The first approach does not challenge institutions to prize learning and to provide evidence that program graduates meet societal norms for a quality education or for an information literate individual who functions as an independent learner in an age of the global, interconnected village. The learning approach is broader in the type of evidence it requires; it examines teaching and teaching effectiveness; student satisfaction with courses, programs of study, and the institution itself; outputs related to class size, program retention rates, graduation rates, and so on; faculty productivity; financial commitments and priorities; administrator support for those priorities; the impressions of employers and others; the curriculum; technological support; and space considerations. Outcomes assessment may include some of the same metrics, but it also examines impacts—those on student learning (*student learning outcomes*) and the emerging capabilities of students as researchers who recognize research as an inquiry process and who are able to apply the specific steps and stages of that process (*student research outcomes*).

With the attention of accrediting organizations falling on processes more than structures, quality assurance and outcomes assessment view change as central to educational excellence and any characterization of quality. Quality is a relative concept in that different groups have different views on the quality of educational programs. For example, the teaching faculty might focus on the process of education,[2] whereas students might be more interested in their level of satisfaction with courses and the program, and whether they are able to gain employment upon graduation. Employers might be interested in the quality of the graduates, government bodies might focus on value for money, and accrediting organizations might concentrate on other matters that provide indicators of institutional accountability. In operational terms, quality involves defining goals (reflecting the mission), the process for achieving the goals, the results or the extent to which the goals are met, and the use of those results for improvement.

As Geoff Scott of the Office of Planning & Quality, University of Western Sydney, observes, fitness-for-purpose might more precisely be interpreted as "fitness for moral purpose. For example, a learning program or activity is of high quality if it is demonstrably relevant, desirable and feasible for those intended to benefit from it." He then defines quality assurance; it "aims to assure stakeholders that the appropriate policies, processes, structures and procedures are in place to guarantee that the design and delivery of core activities like learning programs or research projects are of consistently high standard."[3] Quality and quality assurance are terms broader in intent than outcomes assessment, which involves an assessment of the impact of the educational process on learning and the emergence of the educated (information literate and technology literate) graduate, who is able to engage in critical thinking and problem solving, and who demonstrates good communication skills. When quality assurance assumes the component of quality enhancement, it resembles outcomes assessment by calling for institutions to provide evidence that the assessment is sustainable and becomes part of the feedback loop of the open systems model to the planning process (see Figure 1.1).

The typical characterization of the quality assurance system for higher education encompasses six aspects:

1. *Student flow*: the number of students in the program, the graduation and transfer rates, the length of time it takes students to complete the program, and so on.

2. *Teaching faculty*: the number of teaching hours per faculty member, class size, and so on.

3. *Curriculum*: The extent to which the curriculum covers the discipline or profession, structure of the instructional process, teaching methods, examination procedures, methods of evaluation and determination of grades, extent to which programs of study are flexible (prescriptive) and guided by discipline or professional accreditation standards; and so on.

4. *Financial matters*: The allocation of funds to programs.

5. *Infrastructure and material facilities*: Adequacy of classrooms, including the availability of information technologies; and so on.

6. *Policy*: Evaluation systems for student satisfaction, management structure, how the curriculum (core and elective) has been set, structure of the faculty as an organization, and so on.[4]

It is most likely that judgments about the adequacy of universities for the six aspects are determined from the collection of outputs, such as student outcomes; however, universities need to collect and relate evidence about the sustainability of programs and document the return on investment or value for money, especially in those instances where higher education is being asked to do more with fewer resources. Outcomes assessment focuses on the outcomes of the educational process rather than on those inputs or outputs, or on the educational environment itself.

The first, third, and sixth aspect also relate "to the management and delivery of learning,"[5] and they involve internal and external perspectives. Feedback from students, employers, and others might be gathered and used to evaluate the effectiveness of programs, to redesign the curriculum, and to determine perceived satisfaction with the course of study. As Newby observes, "If the responsibility for quality does not lie with those responsible for the learning and if it is not continuously addressed by them, then there is a message that quality is felt to be unimportant."[6]

Newby believes that universities need to internalize quality assurance and "go beyond a quinquennial examination of practice and student achievement. It has to explore whether the purposes set out for the student learning experiences are appropriate and actually achieved—at both the level of the overall programme and the level of individual courses or modules."[7] In essence, he seems to be arguing for outcomes assessment and assessment of students based on their improvement as a result of completing the entire educational process—from the core curriculum through the set of elective courses. Quality assurance may intend to produce such an outcome; however, at present, such a clear and overarching focus does not exist.

Outcomes assessment determines the impact of a program of study and relevant institutional support services (e.g., the library) on making a difference in the lives of students—the extent to which the program or services, for instance, have an impact on their critical-thinking and problem-solving abilities. As a result, outcomes assessment appears at the course, program, and institutional levels. At the course level, the faculty set their expectations for student learning and develop methods to assess the extent to which students mastered (are able to apply) course content. At the program level, outcomes "communicate performance expectations to potential students, new faculty, and industry partners."[8] Program outcomes might be reviewed at the institutional level to identify any commonalities among different programs. Clearly, outcomes at all three levels examine performance expectations and capabilities of the students, and the evidence derived applies to readjusting expectations, developing new methods to improve learning, and challenging both the program and the learner. The intent of quality assurance, on the other hand, might be to:

- Maintain the market position of higher education—making higher education more competitive globally or improving the market share of a nation's appeal to the potential student population globally (Australia);
- Challenge higher education to demonstrate accountability (Australia, South Africa, and the United Kingdom) and also to show how it will achieve fitness-for-purposes with fewer funds coming from the national government (South Africa); and

• Improve accountability through the provision of output data (the United Kingdom) and the compilation of a general profile of university activity and health.

EXAMPLES

This section highlights three countries, Australia, South Africa, and the United Kingdom, while the next two chapters provide a different perspective from the UK and discuss quality assurance and outcomes assessment in Canada.

Australia

Because higher education in Australia "was under-resourced and staff were feeling the pressure of working longer hours and often dealing with students of varying ability," the country favored an approach to quality assurance that "would be cost effective, not unduly onerous on institutions being audited, have the support of government and the universities, and equally essential—conform to trends in the global community."[9] Under considerable "pressure" from international university quality assurance networks and supra-national organizations (e.g., UNESCO, the Organization for Economic Co-operation and Development, the World Bank, and the International Monetary Fund), Australia adopted quality assurance, but academic faculty, staff, and administrators viewed it as "just another imposition, foisted on them by a management impervious to the already stressful conditions engendered by endless bureaucratic red tape, large class sizes and pressures to frequently publish research results."[10]

Australia adapted a New Zealand framework, which "had dispensed with the highly contentious subject reviews which required the ranking of courses, the collection of exhaustive documentation, visits to institutions and the observation of teaching."[11] The institutional audits that replaced those subject reviews involve a detailed process in which institutions demonstrate the quality of their teaching and discuss the learning that the faculty think has occurred. New Zealand added transnational education and distance learning delivered electronically to the audit, and the Australian Universities Quality Agency (AUQA) accepted that addition.[12] Moreover, the New Zealand fitness-for-purpose framework "was cost effective, did not overtly intrude on the work of academics, was fairly highly regarded in the international arena and it offered an interpretation of QA [quality assurance] that was acceptable to politicians, bureaucrats and university administrators."[13]

This framework resisted any single definition of quality because the government's economic agenda imposed one on universities. Since 1996, with their reliance on public funding, the nation's universities had experienced funding cuts and had to realign their programs with the new fiscal realities. The government also favors quality assurance as a means for universities to identify their market position in global higher education.

Australian Universities Quality Agency (AUQA)

The AUQA, which was established by the Ministerial Council on Education, Training and Youth Affairs (MCEETYA) in March 2000, is an independent, not-for-profit national agency that promotes, audits, and reports on quality assurance in Australian higher education. The whole-of-institution audits are

> based on a self-assessment and a site visit. AUQA will investigate the extent to which the institutions are achieving their missions and objectives. They will assess the adequacy of the institution's quality assurance arrangements in the key areas of teaching and learning, research and management, including the institution's overseas activities. They will also assess the institution's success in maintaining standards consistent with university education in Australia.[14]

Most audits now involve multiple site visits to take account of onshore campuses and numerous offshore partnerships.

The AUQA has adopted the ADRI (approach, deployment, results, and improvement) system advanced by the Australian Business Excellence Framework, which was adopted in 1997 as framework for global excellence. With its emphasis on "strategy & planning," "leadership," "people," "success & sustainability," "customer & market focus," and "innovation, quality, & improvement," the ADRI forms the basis for auditing the nation's universities.[15]

Julie Hayford, the Quality Assurance Project Officer at the University of Adelaide, maintains that the framework that was adopted emphasizes processes and accountability. Still, she sees the challenges for AUQA as demonstrating the "link between fitness-for-purpose and quality improvement." She worries that higher education "will continue to suffer from diminishing quality in learning, teaching and research."[16] In essence, quality assurance resembles the type of audit review that colleges and universities in the United States prepared and were judged by prior to the current focus on student learning outcomes.

University Libraries

Regarding the inclusion of libraries at institutions of higher education in the review process, Martin Carroll of the Australian Quality Assurance Agency, Melbourne, underscores issues such as the increasing cost of library resources, the greater availability of electronic resources, and the need to support distance education programs and course offerings at multiple campuses. He sees the need for libraries to reposition themselves and to assume new roles and responsibilities—ones central to teaching, learning, research, and community engagement. University libraries, he believes, will continue to face new challenges and demands while experiencing a continual decline in resources (given zero growth or declining university budgets). University libraries need to design, prioritize, and provide resources and services in ways that best meet the institutional mission. In effect, library planning should be a part of institutional planning and should demonstrate the role of libraries as facilitators of "information-based learning." This is especially true when the Internet is challenging the "traditionally hallowed place" of libraries within higher education.[17]

Carroll also notes that it is insufficient to rely on a library representative to the academic board as the primary means for exercising the library's quality assurance contribution to teaching and course development. Libraries need to become institutional partners and leaders, as they focus on assisting the institution in achieving fitness-for-purpose and shift from merely providing information to being engaged in developing the information and technologically literate student. He encourages libraries to become much more involved in this transformation and in assisting faculty in developing course reading lists. He also favors libraries conducting satisfaction surveys but, when they use nationally developed instruments (e.g., that of the Rodski Behavioural Research Group, http://www.rodski.com.au/), they should contextualize the results when they want to use them for accountability purposes. Although not specifically mentioning the outcomes assessment movement in the United States, he seems to favor a similar partnership between the teaching faculty and university libraries in Australia, as both groups assess student learning outcomes and as libraries show how the statistics they gather have an impact on student learning.

Finally, it merits mention that the Council of Australian University Libraries (CAUL, http://www.caul.edu.au/), which was formed in 1975 to give the libraries a "common voice" on issues and a forum for a discussion of those issues, maintains a database for comparing outputs and satisfaction across libraries. CAUL defines the information literate person as possessing ten characteristics (e.g., "incorporate selected information into their knowledge base" and "recognise information literacy as a prerequisite for lifelong learning").[18] This characterization could be converted into the type of outcomes assessment in which many U.S. academic libraries need to engage. In effect, CAUL provides the type of foundation to achieve Carroll's vision of library involvement in information and technology literacy.

South Africa

The 1997 White Paper on Higher Education, issued by the Department of Education, called for a restructuring and transformation of higher education. It noted that in the past institutions of higher education lacked coordination and an articulation of a collective purpose in society. It also mentioned that higher education was marked by race separation—a separation of all races from each other—with institutions set aside to serve a particular race. Obviously some institutions were historically better funded than others. The White Paper pointed out that a democratic state should have a single coordinated structure for higher education to replace race-separated institutions. Since the adoption of the White Paper, the national government has expected higher education to meet internal pressures (i.e., increased public access to formal education, a redress of past wrongs [segregation by race], true equity in serving the public, and more responsiveness to helping the nation develop socially and economically) and external pressures to advance the knowledge economy and promote free trade.

The 1997 Higher Education Act established the Higher Education Quality Committee (HEQC), charged with promoting quality assurance in higher education, auditing the quality assurance mechanisms of higher education institutions, accrediting programs of higher education, and promoting quality. Accepting the White Paper, the Act also called for the HEQC to engage in program accreditation, to audit institutions, and to promote quality. Specifically, quality included the following components:

- Fitness-of-purpose (the framework is based on national goals, priorities, and targets, particularly in relation to redress and equity);
- Fitness-for-purpose (focus on a specified mission within a national framework that encompasses differentiation and diversity);
- Value for money to cover different purposes for higher education as set forth in the White Paper; and
- Transformation of learners (i.e., developing their capacity for personal enrichment, social development, and economic and employment growth).

For the period from 2004 to 2006, HEQC has three overarching areas of activity:

1. Conduct full-scale audits of all public and private institutions that have not merged (South Africa is currently consolidating the number of institutions of higher education).
2. Evaluate new programs that have requested accreditation. In general, HEQC does not evaluate existing professional programs by itself. It works with professional councils or other statutory bodies.
3. Conduct national reviews in selected programs or disciplinary areas.

From 2007 to 2009, HEQC will continue to audit institutions that are not affected by the mergers, accredit new programs, conduct national reviews as required, let institutions apply for self-accreditation, and re-accredit existing programs (that is, if an institution performs consistently poorly in seeking the accreditation of new programs and if audits and national reviews disclose significant problems).[19]

University Libraries

HEQC has developed audit criteria for teaching, learning, information technology infrastructure, and library resources. One criterion (number 4) applies to "academic support services (e.g., library and learning materials, computer support services, etc.) adequately supporting teaching and learning needs and help give effect to teaching and learning objectives." Another criterion (number 7) states:

> Suitable and sufficient venues, IT [information technology] infrastructure and library resources (which are integrated into the programme) are available for students and staff in the programme, providing favourable conditions for quality teaching and learning, research and student support. Policies ensure the proper management and maintenance of library resources, including support and access for students and staff.

The self-reports that institutions compile indicate the adequacy of library resources, as reflected in the part of the reports covering the library and in comments made to the on-site team when its members interview the library director and members of the faculty and administration. Those reports, for instance, cover the functionality of computer workstations and printers, software, and databases, and they indicate how students and staff receive proper training in the use of technology as required by individual programs.

HEQC realizes that the self-review does not focus sufficiently on the library and its contribution to higher education. As a result, it is now asking the library profession to develop a code of practice that reflects the library's role in (and contribution to) higher education. However, that code must contain national and comparable international benchmarks for libraries, include minimum standards for libraries, identify good practice guides, set forth the rights and responsibilities of students in relation to libraries, and show how the library aids in developing information literacy among students. The code must also address the following points specified in HEQC's audit criterion 19:

- "How frequently are user satisfaction surveys used to obtain feedback from the faculty and students regarding the quality of library services and how does the library use survey results for continuous quality improvement?"
- "How does the library use benchmarking to place its services in a comparative context and engage in continuous quality improvement?"
- "What process and procedures does the library use to review its services? How often are these reviews conducted and how do the results lead to improved service?"

- "How does the library determine its impact on the core functions of the institution (teaching, research and scholarship, and contribution to society and the economy)?"

HEQC is trying to change institutional and library cultures, and to move librarians away from the insular role that many of them have played in the past. HEQC envisions librarians as helping to improve the quality and delivery of teaching, learning, research, and community engagement. Furthermore, HEQC recognizes that change will take time and it is fully committed to requiring universities, including their libraries, to make that journey.

It might be hypothesized that, over time, outcomes assessment focusing on information literacy will become more of a central focus to the quality assurance movement in South Africa's higher education. HEQC sees the library as an institutional partner in helping students improve their information literacy skills and in developing materials-based modules that encourage independent learning. That partnership also extends to developing class and program reading lists, identifying materials for new and existing programs, helping programs and institutions prepare for audits and accreditation, helping institutions and faculty monitor the use of library resources, and engaging in self- and peer-assessment of the quality of library services.

These activities will present new challenges and opportunities for libraries. Compounding the difficulties, libraries (like their institutions) will be expected to do more with fewer resources, to serve multiple campuses (as institutions continue to merge), to deliver more resources and services to other campuses traditionally and digitally, to provide more information through library Web sites, and to cater to under-prepared students "by spoonfeeding them." As was explained to the author, students might go to one of the poorer (previously known as Black) universities directly from a rural community that has limited resources and probably no access to computers. Helping them succeed in obtaining a high-quality university education is not the sole responsibility of the teaching faculty. Librarians must assist the students in their adjustment—being able to use library resources and services and becoming an information and technologically literate person who is an independent learner.

Assessment relates to accountability and the development of South Africa as a knowledge economy. That country is in the process of creating an assessment culture for higher education that applies to teaching, learning, research and scholarship, and community engagement. That culture will involve an assessment of information and technology literacy and the extent to which students become effective independent learners over their professional careers. Such assessment will undoubtedly require the use of portfolios and other methods of direct and indirect assessment. Assessment will also involve the conduct of satisfaction and *service quality* surveys, the collection of outputs reflecting the extent of library use and the involvement of libraries in preparing guides, the conduct of usability studies reflecting the ease of navigation of library and university Web sites, and so forth.

United Kingdom

Similar to the other countries highlighted in this chapter and the previous volume, the United Kingdom does not equate quality assurance with the impact of learning on students. In fact, Steven Town of Cranfield University sees the national quality assurance movement in the UK as becoming less rigorous and relying more on the collection and reporting of outputs.[20] Ironically, a complication to the quality assessment movement is the fact that a prestigious university apparently does not concur with that focus and is refusing to participate. Nonetheless, he sees the measures collected as:

- Being in conformity with the requirements of the International Organization for Standardization (ISO), a "network of the national standards institutes of 146 countries,"[21] and the Quality Assurance Agency for Higher Education (QAA), which was established in 1977 "to safeguard the public interest in sound standards of higher education qualifications and to encourage continuous improvement in the management of the quality of higher education."[22]
- Reflecting a focus on value for money.
- Supporting the creation of a quality culture (e.g., total quality management).

The QAA, which has expressed interest in ascertaining the quality of the student learning experience, promotes best practice, and the development of codes of practice that govern academic quality and standards in higher education (e.g., for students with disabilities). It currently conducts institutional and subject reviews and examines the learning experience from the perspective of what teaching tries to accomplish as opposed to the impact of learning on the students.

University Libraries

The tendency of UK libraries is to equate impact with the volume of business accomplished (outputs) and to focus on objectives such as to:

- Measure the quantity and quality of services provided to users;
- Monitor the way in which money is spent;
- Monitor the usefulness of information sources purchased;
- Measure the kinds and amounts of work done by LIS staff;
- Monitor the usage of various LIS services;
- Assess LIS performance against published service standards;
- Compare the information services of one university to the services of other universities;
- Provide data for national surveys of university information service provision; and
- Use all these types of data to inform LIS management plans and decisions for future service provision.[23]

The universities cooperate with the Society of College, National & University Libraries (SCONUL), "which collates national data to allow service benchmarking and to demonstrate national trends in information provision to the British academic community." The types of data collected tend to focus on matters such as the:

- Number of monthly visits to the library;
- Number of visits to each campus library;
- Visits to campus libraries as percentage of total visits to the library system;
- Number of visits compared to the library's loan and return activity;
- Times of peak borrowing and return activity;
- Borrowing and return activity by day and campus library;
- Amount of photocopying in relation to the number of library visitors;
- Relative use of some Web information sources; and
- Number of monthly sessions on some Web information sources.[24]

In a report, *Information Support for eLearning: Principles and Practice*, issued in May 2004, SCONUL envisioned libraries playing an active and prominent role in fostering information literacy and advancing e-learning; however, it did not present e-learning in the context of student learning outcomes.[25]

Despite the picture presented in this section, there are some preliminary efforts to develop student learning outcomes and to apply them to UK universities (see the chapter twelve). The learning outcomes and assessment project conducted (from 2001 to 2004) at the Open University represents an initial effort to assess learning outcomes "with particular emphasis on the design and implementation of strategies and systems for the assessment of learning outcomes at [the] programme and course level to meet both institutional and QAA policy requirements."[26]

Illustrating the UK Literature

A cursory examination of the footnotes and bibliographies of writings on quality assurance discloses heavy reliance on the works produced in the UK and other countries. The writings examined do not make a connection to outcomes. A glaring example of a disregard of the developing, but rich, literature on outcomes assessment written from different institutional perspectives (e.g., university administrators, staff within departments or office of institutional research, faculty members, and librarians) is demonstrated in a ten library study in the United Kingdom, conducted under the auspices of the Library and Information Research Group and SCONUL, to "assess the impact of higher education libraries on learning, teaching, and research."

For one objective, improving "user skills to access e-resources," the study explored impact measurement and envisioned three e-measures:

1. Usage of user education services concerning e-resources:
2. Citations of purchased e-resources in student assessment; and
3. The number of modules or programs with information literacy skills as an explicit learning outcome.[27]

For the first two measures, the investigators studied the bibliographies of 20 percent of the dissertations completed in 2003, presumably from the ten institutions, and "counted the number of free and purchased e-resources cited." They planned to repeat data collection for "2004 dissertations to assess any changes in the amount of use of e-resources."

They also administered a self-assessment questionnaire, an indirect indicator of impact, on selected aspects of library skills (e.g., finding printed journals and using the Internet for academic studies) to students before their first library induction session and again at the beginning of the second semester. They also collected statistics about usage of educational sessions, an annual user satisfaction survey, and so on.[28]

A number of libraries and other organizations in different countries have adopted the balanced scorecard, which represents a matrix of measures that recount the performance of the organization from the perspective of its stakeholders and constituency groups. The balanced scorecard, which is essentially a tool for strategic management, encompasses five perspectives:

1. Financial;

2. Customer;

3. Process (the management of internal processes);

4. Staff development; and

5. Organizational learning and development.

Because those organizations are often part of a parent organization or institution, the scorecard must reflect a larger perspective. In the case of institutions of higher education, the library's balanced scorecard must also address institutional accountability, including the impact of the library in meeting the expectations of accrediting organizations, including those dealing with quality assurance or outcomes assessment. How do library collections and services make an impact on student learning outcomes related to information literacy and so on?

A PROPOSED COMPETITIVE FRAMEWORK

Traditionally institutions of higher education have tended to focus on teaching while downplaying learning, to view teaching from the perspective of student satisfaction as conveyed through teaching evaluations administrated at the end of the school term, and the collection of *input* measures (e.g., the number of students enrolled in the class and the number that the instructor teaches that term, the number enrolled compared to the number completing the course and the grades received, or the cost of teaching a particular course as reflected by a ratio that takes into account the number of students in the class and the salary of the faculty member for the school term) and *output* measures (e.g., the number of students starting and completing the course or program of study).

In the case of the United Kingdom and New Zealand, the Research Assessment Exercise (RAE) provides data on which higher education funding bodies "distribute public funds for research selectively on the basis of quality. Institutions conducting the best research receive a larger proportion of the available grant so that the infrastructure for the top level of research in the UK is protected and developed." Furthermore, RAE indicates "the relative quality and standing of UK academic research . . . the RAE provides benchmarks which are used by institutions in developing and managing their research strategies. Across the UK as a whole, research quality as measured by the RAE has improved dramatically over the last decade."[29]

The RAE audit of faculty focuses on outputs reflecting faculty productivity, which is defined in terms of the number of grants received, the number of scholarly papers accepted in peer-reviewed journal, the number of books published, the number of citations that faculty members receive, indicators of community engagement, and so on. National audits provide a means of comparing institutions, and, in the case of New Zealand, may result in setting government funding priorities for higher education.

Other pressures for change management in institutions of higher education might be decreased funding from the public purse, increased competition among institutions and programs, students and parents being more vocal in expecting value for money paid, and increased scrutiny from government and accrediting organizations over institutional claims of educational excellence. Clearly, higher education is not a protected sector in many countries, that is, it is not protected from public scrutiny and questions about the impact of its research and educational excellence on society.

CONCLUSION

When applied to teaching and learning, quality is an evolving concept. Yet, at this time, that concept does not institutionalize a culture of valuing student learning in higher education and lead to a universal commitment to continuous quality improvement. However, quality assurance agencies in Australia and South Africa are increasing their expectations of higher education, and they are now encouraging librarians to become more involved in assessing the impact of learning on students as they progress through their programs of study.

As Martin Carroll observes, on the surface, it may seem that quality audits such as those conducted in Australia

> may appear to focus on the process of teaching more than on the learning outcomes. The problem with such a view is that it ignores the funda-mental dilemma of fitness-for-purpose (as opposed to criterion-based) auditing. If the university itself still has a predominant focus on teaching and curriculum development rather than student learning outcomes, then the paucity of substance (e.g., student learning outcomes) for the panel to audit can leave it with nowhere to go, especially if it is to avoid the trap of succumbing to a desire to be prescriptive about what the university "should" be doing. In other words, the relatively light extent of comment on this matter by external quality assurance bodies can be more a reflection of the current state of play within universities rather than a lack of will and ability to audit it by the quality assurance body.[30]

As a consequence, any shift to outcomes assessment will be evolutionary as opposed to the situation in the United States whereby accrediting organizations expect institutions of higher education to embrace out-comes assessment. However, many countries are taking a long-term approach, one in which they guide institutions for subsequent audits. Outcomes assessment, on the other hand, requires a more rapid shift in organizational and institutional cultures.

South Africa is an example of a country in which the national gov-ernment has increased its expectations of higher education while si-multaneously telling the higher education community to improve its quality with a decrease in public funding. The problems facing that country are enormous and those problems are not confined to higher education. Because there is not enough money to solve or target all of the problems as the highest priority, the educational system must improve and the quality assurance agency is strongly nudging higher education to transform its culture and to make better use of dwindling resources. Codes of practice become a way to complement institutional audits and to get subgroups within higher education (e.g., librarians) to set the expectations of institutional quality for which the quality assurance agency can hold them accountable. Clearly, the goal of national quality assurance agencies is to change the existing culture of assessment and to involve the constituent groups in shaping and managing change. The concept of fitness-for-purpose is likely to undergo change in the coming years, and one of those changes might be embracing information and technology literacy, with accountability being defined through the outcomes that individual institutions set.

Notes

1. Peter Newby, "Culture and Quality in Higher Education," *Higher Education Policy* 12 (1999), 265.

2. Mien Sergers and Filip Dochy, "Quality Assurance in Higher Education: Theoretical Considerations and Empirical Evidence," *Studies in Educational Evaluation* 22, no. 2 (1996), 118.

3. Geoff Scott, "Change Matters: Making a Difference in Higher Education," keynote address at Leadership Forum (Dublin: European University Association, February 2004). Available at http://www.eua.be/eua/ (accessed November 29, 2004).

4. Newby, "Culture and Quality in Higher Education," 264.

5. Ibid.

6. Ibid.

7. Ibid.

8. Wisconsin Indianhead Technical College, "Program Outcomes/Assessment Plan 2002–2003" (Ashland, WI: Wisconsin Indianhead Technical College, 2002). Available at http://www.witc.edu/instruct/assess/pgmout03/10-196-1 (accessed November 19, 2004).

9. Julie Hayford, "Does Being Last Give You the Advantage?: Quality Assurance in Australian Higher Education," Proceedings of the Australian Universities Quality Forum 2003, AUQA Occasional Publication. Available at http://64.233.161.104/search?q=cache:KAxAneLcR58J:www.auqa.edu.au/auqf/2003/proceedings/AUQF2003_Proceedings.pdf+julie+hayford&hl=en (accessed November 29, 2004).

10. Ibid.

11. Ibid.

12. Ibid.

13. Ibid.

14. Australian Universities Quality Agency, "AUQA Information" (Melbourne, Australia: Australian Universities Quality Agency). Available at http://www.auqa.edu.au/aboutauqa/auqainfo/index.shtml (accessed November 26, 2004).

15. SAI Global Professional Services, "Australian Business Excellence Framework" (Sydney, Australia: SAI Global Professional Services, 2003).

Available at http://www.businessexcellenceaustralia.com.au/GROUPS/ABEF/ (accessed November 29, 2004). See also Felicity McGregor, "Excellent Libraries: A Quality Assurance Perspective," in *Advances in Librarianship*, vol. 28, edited by Danuta A. Nitecki (Amsterdam: Elsevier, 2004), 17–53.

16. Hayford, "Does Being Last Give You the Advantage?"

17. Insights for this section of the chapter were partially derived from the author's interaction with librarians and speakers attending the University of Stellenbosch Library, Seventh Annual Symposium, Stellenbosch, South Africa, October 28–29, 2004. Part of the section was taken from the address, "Quality Assurance in Australian University Libraries—Issues identified through institutional quality audit," given by Martin Carroll, Australian Quality Assurance Agency, Melbourne, Australia. Available at http://www.lib.sun.ac.za/sym2004/papers.htm (accessed November 27, 2004).

18. *Information Literacy Standards*, 1st ed. (Canberra, Australia: Council of Australian University Libraries, 2001), 1. Available at http://www.caul.edu.au/caul-doc/InfoLitStandards2001.doc (accessed December 15, 2004).

19. Insights for this section of the chapter were derived from the author's interaction with librarians and speakers attending the Seventh Annual Symposium, the University of Stellenbosch Library. Part of the section was taken from the address, "Partnering with Librarians for Improved Quality of Higher Education," given by Dr. Prem Naidoo, Director of Accreditation, HEQC. See http://www.lib.sun.ac.za/sym2004/papers.htm (accessed November 26, 2004).

20. See Stephen Town, "Compliance or Culture? Achieving Quality in Academic Library Service," Seventh Annual Symposium, the University of Stellenbosch Library. Available at http://www.lib.sun.ac.za/sym2004/papers.htm (accessed November 27, 2004). In January 2003, the UK issued a *White Paper on The Future of Higher Education*, which supports Town's characterization of quality assurance taking a step backward from focusing directly on student learning outcomes. See *White Paper on the Future of Higher Education* (London: Department of Education and Skills, January 2003). Available at http://www.dfes.gov.uk/hegateway/uploads/White%20Pape.pdf (accessed November 27, 2004). See also J. Stephen Town, "The SCONUL Task Force on Information Skills," in *Information and IT Literacy: Enabling Learning in the 21st Century*, edited by Allan Martin and Hannelore Rader (London: Facet, 2003), 53–65.

21. International Organization for Standardization, home page (Geneva, Switzerland: International Organization for Standardization). Available at http://www.iso.org/iso/en/ISOOnline.frontpage (accessed December 15, 2004).

22. Quality Assurance Agency for Higher Education, Home page (Gloucester, UK). Available at http://www.qaa.ac.uk/ (accessed December 15, 2004).

23. Napier University, "Statistics & Performance Indicators" (Edinburgh: Napier University, 2002). Available at http://nulis.napier.ac.uk/Statistics/Statistics.htm (accessed November 27, 2004).

24. Napier University, "Key Statistics for LIS Service Usage in SCONUL Years" (Edinburgh: Napier University, 2002). Available at http://nulis.napier.ac.uk/Statistics/Sconul.htm (accessed November 27, 2004).

25. Society of College, National, and University Libraries, *Information Support for eLearning: Principles and Practice* (London: Society of College, National, and University Libraries, 2004). Available at http://www.sconul.ac.uk/pubs_stats/ (accessed November 27, 2004).

26. Open University, Centre for Outcomes-based Education, "Current Projects: Assessment of Learning Outcomes" (London: The Open University, November 2004). Available at http://www.open.ac.uk/cobe/projects.html (accessed November 27, 2004).

27. Philip Payne, John Crawford, and Wendy Fiander, "Counting on Making a Difference: Assessing Our Impact," *Vine* (Southampton, England: Southampton University Library) 34, no. 4 (2004): 176–183. Available from Emerald Fulltext.

28. Ibid.

29. Higher Education & Research Opportunities, "RAE [Research Assessment Exercise]: What Is the RAE 2001?" (Newcastle upon Tyne, England: Higher Education & Research Opportunities, 2001). Available at http://www.hero.ac.uk/rae/AboutUs/ (accessed November 27, 2004).

30. E-mail correspondence from Martin Carroll (Audit Director and Business Development Manager, Australian Universities Quality Agency, Melbourne, Australia) to Peter Hernon (March 2, 2005).

CHAPTER 12

Standardized Learning Outcomes: Assessing and Recording Achievement in Non-Accredited Adult Education Courses

Jutta Austin

Traditionally, most courses offered by adult community colleges in the United Kingdom were non-accredited, without any formal assessment. In fact, many writers have provided evidence of a consensus among adult education providers and adult learners that formal assessment is at best irrelevant and at worst a disruptive factor in adult community learning.[1] However, adult community learning (ACL) providers have to satisfy national standards and funding bodies as well as their learners. With the advent of formula funding by the Learning and Skills Council (LSC) and the arrival of the Adult Learning Inspectorate (ALI) in whose inspection framework the first question is, "How well do learners achieve?," adult colleges now need to rethink fundamentally their approaches to assessing and recording student achievement in non-accredited courses.

Most assessment in the UK tends to take the form of tests and examinations, to be formal and summative, and to look at products rather than at the learning process. Recently, however, an awareness of flaws in the education system and new developments in curricula, as well as the desire to meet goals of equal opportunity and widening participation, have given rise to new theories and methods of assessment.[2] Psychologists and sociologists have become less concerned with the practice and consequence of selection of candidates by examination results and more interested in the impact of assessment on motivation and learning, and how that impact can be developed more positively.[3] In the context of assessment in adult community learning courses, both government agencies and individual colleges have acknowledged the unsuitability of existing methods. Searching for alternatives and more flexible methods of assessing and recording achievement, many agencies have turned to the use of learning outcomes as a possible approach to assess and record achievement.

In 1993, the Further Education Development Agency (FEDA) offered a seminar on "Assessing Outcomes in Adult Education." Many participating adult education providers then started their own development work. Although they used a number of different approaches, all colleges chose assessment that is criterion-based, rather than norm-based (as in schools in the UK), and, at least in part, process-oriented rather than product-oriented. They developed systems that accommodated individual students' needs, widely differing abilities, and the general desire for unobtrusive, informal assessment. However, the reported models have two limiting features in common:

1. They are concerned primarily with ways of recording achievement (that is, they offer various designs of forms); and
2. They do not look in depth at the substance of assessment; learning outcomes remained largely unexplored.

In these models, teachers and students are told what forms to fill in but not how to decide what should go on the forms. Subjectivity and personal judgment rule and render the resulting records of achievement a very dubious source of real information. However, although subjectivity is inherent to all assessment and unavoidable, it is possible, to some extent, to harness it by devising prescriptive though not restrictive systems of standardized learning outcomes. Such systems bridge the chasm between the government demand for formal assessment and the real needs of adult learners. Using standardized learning outcomes provides teachers with identifiable levels of attainment and helps learners choose suitable courses.

The concept of standardized learning outcomes should not be that of a straightjacket (as can be the case with some accreditation schemes), but that of a safety net which gives teachers and learners freedom and flexibility, but which still leads to formally recorded and clearly describing achievement. Moving from the total freedom of developing learning outcomes into a system based on structured selection enables teachers and students to gain flexibility in achieving unified recording of achievement that will satisfy funding bodies and inspection agencies and show clearly what learning has occurred. The crucial factor in this scenario is the nature of the learning outcomes. They must not simply be a finite list of what teachers would be likely or expected to want to assess. The system must be intrinsically hospitable (i.e., open-ended), flexible, comprehensive, and non-restrictive, but must at the same time promote consistency and order. One system which has these properties is faceted classification, which is a way of classifying subjects by listing their individual components and providing rules for bringing components together in consistent, predictable ways to express any subject. This model is the basis for the design of standardized learning outcomes for an outcome bank for adult education colleges in Essex, England.

A SYSTEM OF STANDARDIZED LEARNING OUTCOMES

To satisfy the approaching demands for assessment and achievement recording, the Essex Adult Community Learning Service established a preliminary system for recording achievement in 2000. Teachers designed their own learning outcomes for each course. These were recorded on a card and ticked, or dated when a student had achieved them. At the end of the course, ticks were counted, and an achievement of 70 percent of learning outcomes counted as a "pass," that is, having achieved the aim of the course. There was no control over the number, content, or wording of the outcomes. As a result, the outcomes were as varied in content and level as the students. Adult community colleges cater to all adults of at least sixteen years of age. Learners come in order to achieve qualifications, develop a career, learn more about a hobby, help their children with school work, have a social time, or escape loneliness. Their educational capabilities and backgrounds vary from minimal literacy to a university degree, and there are equally large differences in the time and inclination they have to work for their courses. With completely free choice as to learning outcomes, teachers could tailor them to individual student needs, but there was no consistency of objectives and levels and therefore no real proof of achievement.

Faced with the imminent demands of the new funding and inspection system, the adult community learning providers in Essex set up an Unaccredited Learning Working Group to develop a centralized outcome bank, a system of consistent, level-differentiated learning outcomes for the assessment of all non-accredited courses in the county. The purpose was not to design just another recording system, but to design one that would:

- Help teachers choose appropriate learning outcomes;
- Not drive teachers and students away (keeping in mind the special outlook on assessment common in adult education);
- Provide an adequate measure of quality assurance; and
- Satisfy the government's demands for valid and reliable assessment.

The system would have to be:

- Open-ended (hospitable): Allow for all present and future learning outcomes to be included;
- Flexible: Allow teachers to do what they had always done but in a more controlled environment;
- Easy to use: Add as little as possible to part-time teachers' workload;
- Unobtrusive: Not frighten the students away; and
- Self-consistent and transparent: Demonstrate achievement reliably.

DESIGN PROCEDURE

The first step in designing a comprehensive set of standardized learning outcomes within a given curriculum area is to study all relevant materials—universal and special classification systems, curricula, textbooks and reference books in the field, Internet materials, government-set outcomes and criteria, and non-standardized outcomes used previously. From these materials, all possible subject and skill components for the courses in the curriculum area are identified, and a classification system is designed for them. This classification system includes rules for how to combine different components in consistent ways.

All collected non-standardized outcomes, as well as standard outcomes from examinations and accreditation agencies, are classified in this system. The system is adjusted until there is at least (and only) one correct place for each outcome and each combination of outcome elements.

A code is then designed for the learning outcomes. The code always starts with two letters denoting the curriculum area, followed by a combination of numbers and letters that express categories and sub-categories, running numbers, and achievement levels. As these codes are expressive of content and level, their use in students' achievement records allows teachers to write abbreviated versions of the actual outcomes. Code assignment takes place as outcomes are written for all identified and classified subject and skill components of the curriculum area. Standardized wording is introduced and modified as appropriate during this process.

At all stages during this procedure, teachers teaching in the curriculum area concerned are kept informed and asked for feedback. The classification system for the outcomes in particular is discussed at length with teachers, and modifications are made as necessary before any learning outcomes are designed. Feedback is sought every time a major category of outcomes is completed. In this way, flaws, possibly caused by the project worker not being a subject specialist, are picked up and rectified early on in the process.

Modern Languages

The first curriculum area to be covered was languages. Nine skills-based main outcomes were designed for each level, using precise language to differentiate between them. The requirements for different levels are in accordance with national curriculum requirements for different stages of attainment. The next step involved developing subdivisions. For the four main skills (speaking, listening, reading, and writing), teachers can choose between skills-based subdivisions (e.g., for speaking: "ask a simple question") or topic-based subdivisions. The skills-based subdivisions are listed as standard outcomes, but topic selection is open-ended. Teachers can choose any topic area they wish and put it into the context of the main skills outcome they are using.

For example, to assess speaking through several topic areas, they might list "speaking: shopping," "speaking: travel," and so forth, and use speaking tasks within these topics to assess the students. These tasks reflect the level of competence expressed in the relevant main outcome. If, on the other hand, teachers want to assess speaking through specific speaking skills, they can list specific skill outcomes (e.g., "speaking: ask simple questions" and "speaking: give information in topics studied") and can assess learning using tasks reflecting the level of the outcomes.

Further main outcome categories in Modern Languages are pronunciation, foreign script or alphabet, grammar, literature, and culture. All of these have open-ended subdivisions to be chosen by teachers for groups of sounds or characters, grammatical features, or specific literary or cultural topics. In all these cases the main outcome clearly expresses the level on which such topical work or specific skills have to be assessed, so that the teacher can select any topic. The book of outcomes that was

Figure 12.1
Page from Outcome Book for Modern Languages

Learning Outcomes Grammar

Level 1 Year 1	Apply the basic grammar of nouns/pronouns, adjectives, selected particles and verbs to produce familiar structures
Level 1 Year 2	Apply the basic grammar of nouns/pronouns, adjectives, some particles and verbs (including past tense) to produce simple structures
Level 2 Year 1 (Year 3)	Apply the grammar of nouns/pronouns, adjectives, common particles and verbs (several tenses) to produce structures of one or two clauses
Level 2 Year 2 (Year 4)	Apply the grammar of nouns/pronouns, adjectives, all common particles and verbs (most tenses) to produce both simple and complex structures
Level 3	Produce a wide range of correct grammatical structures including the use of all tenses and less common particles
a) Subdivision by skill	NO subdivisions
b) Subdivision by grammar feature	Subdivide the main learning outcome by the elements of grammar you teach in your course
	Examples: Genders of nouns, Adjective endings, Comparison, Prepositions of position, The verb "to be," Past tense, Passive, Subjunctive
	Subdivisions may be used as Maintenance subdivisions using the following phrase:
	Demonstrate retained acquired competence to (e.g., "apply the subjunctive accurately")

Figure 12.2
Page from Outcome Book for Modern Languages

Level 1 Year 1 (Beginners)
Main outcomes and subdivisions

By the end of the course students will be able to:

ML11 use the active vocabulary and grammar presented during the course in comprehensible spoken sentences

a) Subdivision by skill:
1. give and respond to basic information on topics studied
2. communicate face to face in simple sentences on topics studied
3. use some basic expressions and conventions
4. ask simple questions and make simple requests

b) Subdivision by topic:
Subdivide the main learning outcome by the topics you are studying during your course. Assessment in topic learning outcomes always has to take place for the skill for which they are a subdivision (i.e., here for speaking).

Examples: "Personal Identification," "Hobbies," "Shopping," "Ordering meals," "Travel," "Directions," "Numbers"

ML12 understand short statements, questions, and requests containing the vocabulary and grammar presented during the course

a) Subdivision by skill:
1. understand the gist of basic information given
2. understand simple spoken sentences on topics studied
3. extract meaning from simple conventional expressions
4. understand simple questions and requests
5. recognize the most commonly used sounds of the foreign language

b) Subdivision by topic:
Subdivide the main learning outcome by the topics you are teaching during your course. Assessment in topic learning outcomes always has to take place for the skill for which they are a subdivision (i.e., here for listening).

Examples: "Talking about yourself," "Hotel and Accommodation," "Weather"

produced shows the system twice. The first section is organized by outcome, and under each outcome all of its levels are listed. The second section is organized by levels and constitutes the main tool for the teacher, who can go straight to the relevant level and find all the outcomes and outcome choices available for a specific course. Figures 12.1 and 12.2 show pages from both sections of the book.

Art and Design

The second curriculum area covered was art and design. This was more difficult, because art is a very varied curriculum area as compared to languages. In art, there are many elements (e.g., media, subject matter, techniques, and inherent features such as color, composition, and perspective), and each needs to be available to be combined with any other into a learning outcome that applies to, for example:

- Painting a still life in watercolor;
- Showing depth through shading; and
- Applying linear perspective to draw a building.

To satisfy the special demands for art outcomes, a kind of faceted system (A combines with B, and B combines with A) of outcome building blocks was chosen, where each element can become the main element to be subdivided by any other elements. The Dewey Decimal Classification, which public libraries use, provided inspiration. The resulting comprehensive system allows all teachers to build their own stock of learning outcomes. Standard phrasing for the three levels is prescribed, but the content of outcomes is open to choice within the system.

The system is divided into nine main categories. The first one covers inherent features (e.g., color, tone, and perspective) and takes priority over all other categories. That is to say, any outcome dealing with any inherent feature in any role will be found here. The second category, which covers subjects, is used for outcomes related to subjects of art where the medium used is irrelevant (e.g., outcomes about knowing the human anatomy). Categories three to eight cover the various arts (drawing, painting, print making, sculpture, photography, and architecture), and the final category covers art history.

Category one is subdivided into the different inherent features and category nine has no obligatory subdivisions, but has optional subdivisions addressing the art form. Art history of different artists, periods, and places is covered through optional elements within the individual outcomes. All other categories are subdivided into some or all of eight standard subdivisions (obligatory), which cover, for example, critical appraisal, apparatus and tools, materials, and techniques. Many outcomes have option elements, for example: "identify and distinguish between main types of [*surfaces*] used for [*optional: medium, for example oil*] painting." In this outcome, specific types of surface and specific

Figure 12.3
Page from Outcome Book for Art and Design

AD1 Inherent features

    Summary: AD1A Measurement
              AD1B Mark/Line
              AD1C Perspective
              AD1D Tonality
              AD1E Color
              AD1F Texture
              AD1G Form/Solidity/Volume
              AD1H Shape/Negative Shape
              AD1I Light/Shade
              AD1J Composition
              AD1K Style/Mood
              AD1L Movement

Note 1: All outcomes can be <u>extended</u> to cover specific subjects (including detail of subjects), media and/or techniques.
    Examples of phrasing:
        demonstrate basic/extended/advanced competence in . . . (*outcome*)
        in [*subject, e.g.,* still life]
        . . . (*outcome*) using [*medium, e.g.,* pencil]
        . . . (*outcome*) by [*specific techniques, e.g.,* hatching]

Note 2: When two or more inherent features are combined to an outcome where one feature affects the other(s) or is a tool for the other(s), use an outcome listed under the affected feature.
    Examples: use tone to show perspective—*belongs under perspective.*
              use line to express form—*belongs under form/solidity/volume.*
              use tone to express light and shade—*belongs under light/shade.*

Level 1: AD1-1(1) demonstrate a basic understanding of the principles of
Level 2: AD1-1(2) demonstrate an extended understanding of the principles of
Level 3: AD1-1(3) demonstrate an advanced understanding of the principles of
                                [art & design
                                drawing
                                painting
                                photography
                                etc: any main outcome category]

media may optionally be inserted, or, alternatively, the outcome can be used as a general outcome about knowledge of painting surfaces.

    In addition to optional elements stated within specific outcomes, notes in all categories and subdivisions list additional options for how one may tailor the outcomes to one's needs. Figures 12.3 through 12.5

Figure 12.4
Page from Outcome Book for Art and Design

AD3 Drawing

Summary: AD3   Drawing
         AD3A Drawing using pencil
         AD3B Drawing using charcoal
         AD3C Drawing using chalk, crayon, pastel
         AD3D Drawing using pen, ink
         AD3E Drawing using other media

         AD3.1 Philosophy, appreciation, critical appraisal
         AD3.2 Inherent features
         AD3.3 Apparatus, equipment, tools
         AD3.4 Materials, surfaces, supports
         AD3.5 Media, techniques, processes
         AD3.6 Subjects, style, mood, viewpoint
         AD3.7 Finishing the product, maintenance, repair
         AD3.8 History, biography

Note 1: Use this category also for outcomes covering both drawing and painting. Adjust phrasing accordingly.

Note 2: This category contains all drawing outcomes. Where use of a specific medium needs to be expressed in an outcome, add the extra letter to the code and use standard phrasing as shown in the example below.

Example: AD3.5-4(1) use hatching
         AD3A.5-1(1) distinguish between pencil grades

Level 1 AD3-1(1) demonstrate basic competence to creatively develop an idea for a drawing

Level 2 AD3-1(2) demonstrate extended competence to creatively develop an idea for a drawing

Level 3 AD3-1(3) demonstrate advanced competence to creatively develop an idea for a drawing

Level 1 AD3-2(1) demonstrate basic understanding of the principles of drawing

Level 2 AD3-2(2) demonstrate extended understanding of the principles of drawing

Level 3 AD3-2(3) demonstrate advanced understanding of the principles of drawing

Level 1 AD3-3(1) produce a simple [*medium, e.g.,* charcoal] drawing

show pages from the Art and Design outcome book. Although complex and comprehensive, the system has already been reported by art teachers (who started using it in September 2003) to be easy to use and helpful due to its self-consistency and transparency which, in line with

Figure 12.5
Page from Outcome Book for Art and Design

Level 1 AD7.4-4(1) demonstrate basic competence in using [*material, consumable, e.g.,* inks, *or* data cards]

Level 2 AD7.4-4(2) demonstrate extended competence in using [*material, consumable, e.g.,* inks, *or* data cards]

Level 3 AD7.4-4(3) demonstrate advanced competence in using [*material, consumables, e.g.,* inks, *or* data cards]

AD7.5   Media, techniques, processes

Note 1: Outcomes in AD7.1 can be <u>extended</u> to cover specific subjects.
     Example: apply filters [in scientific and technical photography]
          Code: AD7.5-7(2)

Note 2: Outcomes concerned with overall production of specific subject works
     (without reference to specific techniques) are found in group AD7.6
     Subjects.

Note 3: For outcomes indicating use of techniques in the services of specific
     inherent features, use main category AD1 Inherent features.
     Example: demonstrate basic competence in using aperture control to
          create movement
          Code: AD1K-2(1)

Level 1 AD7.5-1(1) focus a camera
Level 2 AD7.5-1(2) focus appropriately to subject matter
Level 3 AD7.5-1(3) focus in conjunction with aperture control

Level 1 AD7.5-2(1) demonstrate basic competence in exposure control
Level 2 AD7.5-2(2) control exposure for appropriate tonal range

Level 1 AD7.5-3(1) demonstrate basic competence in using the
               aperture control
Level 2 AD7.5-3(2) apply aperture to depth of field
Level 3 AD7.5-3(3) translate apertures into the stop system

Level 1 AD7.5-4(1) demonstrate basic understanding of shutter
               speed control
Level 2 AD7.5-4(2) use shutter speeds under various light conditions
Level 2 AD7.5-5(2) use shutter speeds to translate movement
Level 3 AD7.5-4(3) apply shutter speed creatively to subjects

Level 1 AD7.5-6(1) demonstrate basic understanding of focal length

classification theory, allows one and only one correct place for each outcome. The transparency and consistency also make the system a tool fit to satisfy course providers and funding bodies as to the quality of assessment and recording of achievement.

The system was developed in close cooperation with the art department teachers at the Adult Community College, Colchester. At all stages of the development, the system was tested by transposing previously used, non-standardized outcomes into the new system. No outcomes were found impossible to transpose. As an additional help, an alphabetical subject index was prepared following the PRECIS method.[4] PRECIS, which stands for PREserved Context Index System, uses syntax and a multi-position entry to display subject terms within the context in which they appear in the text. With this index, teachers can go directly to outcomes for any combination of subject/skill elements they might want. Figure 12.6 shows a page from this index. Finally, pages covering the various categories in the outcome books are color-coded, so that teachers can quickly find those pages that are relevant for choosing outcomes for a particular course.

Counseling

The third curriculum area to be dealt with was counseling, which is divided into five categories (the counseling arena, counseling theories and models, counseling skills and techniques, counselor self-awareness and self-development, and specific types of counseling [counseling modes and environments, types of clients, and specific issues]). The outcomes consist of standardized structures with option elements, for example:

- Demonstrate in-depth knowledge [or: understanding] of [counseling theory/model or: any part or feature of a counseling model] [optional: and its implementation in the counseling process]; and

- Demonstrate general understanding of the use and appropriateness/effectiveness of [specific counseling skill(s)] when counseling [specific types of clients, for example children.]

The counseling outcome book also has a PRECIS index. Figures 12.7 and 12.8 show a page of text and an index page.

Information and Communications Technologies (ICT) and Other Curriculum Areas

Outcomes for ICT, an extensive area, were initiated in spring 2004. This is a complex undertaking, as different kinds of outcomes are needed in

Figure 12.6
Index of Outcome Book for Art and Design

Art history (Sculpture, AD6.8) 42
Art history (Standard subdivisions, list in guidance notes, section 1.1.4) 2
Art history (Subjects, AD2.8) 20
Art photography (Photography, AD7.6) 46, 47
Artists (Art history, AD9)
   Critical appraisal of work 49
Assessment (Guidance notes, section 1.4) 6

Biography (Standard subdivisions, list in guidance notes, section 1.1.4) 2
Biography. Artists (Drawing, AD3.8) 28
Biography. Artists (Graphic art and Fine print making, AD5.8) 38
Biography. Artists (Painting, AD4.8) 34
Biography. Artists (Photography, AD7.8) 47
Biography. Artists (Sculpture, AD6.8) 42
Biography. Artists (Subjects, AD2.8) 20, 21
Blind embossing (Graphic art and Fine print making, AD5) 35, 37, 38
Block printing (Graphic art and Fine print making, AD5.5) 37, 38
Blocks (Graphic art and Fine print making, AD5.5) 37, 38
Brushes (Painting, AD4.5)
   Dry brush techniques 32
Brushes. Tools (Painting, AD4.5) 31
Buildings (Drawing, AD3.6) 27
Buildings (Painting, AD4.6) 33
Buildings (Subjects, AD2ARB) 19–21
Burnishing (Drawing, AD3.5) 25

Cameras (Photography, AD7.3) 44
Carving (Sculpture, AD6.5) 41
Casting (Sculpture, AD6.5) 41
Categories (Main categories in guidance notes, section 1.1.3) 2
Chalk (Drawing, AD3C) 22–28
Charcoal (Drawing, AD3B) 22–28
Chemicals (Photography, AD7.4) 44
Chine collé (Graphic art and Fine print making, AD5.5) 37
Choosing see Selection
Cityscapes (Drawing, AD3.6) 27
Cityscapes (Painting, AD4.6) 33
Cityscapes (Photography, AD7.6) 46, 47
Cityscapes (Subjects, AD2AR) 19–21
Civic landscape art (Main categories in guidance notes, section 1.1.3) 2
Civic landscape art (Main category, AD8) 48
Codes (Section 2.2) 8
Collograph (Intaglio) (Graphic art and Fine print making, AD5.5) 37, 38
Collograph (Relief) (Graphic art and Fine print making, AD5.5) 37, 38

Figure 12.7
Page from Outcome Book for Counseling

CL5C   Counselling for specific issues

> Note: Use these outcomes for issues causing a need for counselling, such as, for instance, personal family history, social phenomena and events, interpersonal relationship problems, life crises, stress, depression, loss and bereavement, substance abuse, disablement.

Level 1 CL5C-1(1)	demonstrate general understanding of the needs and issues pertaining to and surrounding counselling of clients for [specific issues causing a need for counselling, e.g., drug abuse] [or: specific]
Level 2 CL5C-1(2)	demonstrate comprehensive understanding of the needs and issues pertaining to and surrounding counselling clients for [specific issues causing a need for counselling, e.g., drug abuse] [or: specific]
Level 3 CL5C-1(3)	demonstrate in-depth understanding of the needs and issues pertaining to and surrounding counselling of clients for [specific issues causing a need for counselling, e.g., drug abuse] [or: specific]
Level 1 CL5C-2(1)	demonstrate basic competence in choosing appropriate structures for counselling clients for [specific issues causing a need for counselling, e.g., interpersonal relationship problems] [or: specific]
Level 2 CL5C-2(2)	demonstrate extended competence in choosing appropriate structures for counselling clients for [specific issues causing a need for counselling, e.g., interpersonal relationship problems] [or: specific]
Level 3 CL5C-2(3)	demonstrate advanced competence in choosing appropriate structures for counselling clients for [specific issues causing a need for counselling, e.g., interpersonal relationship problems] [or: specific]
Level 1 CL5C-3(1)	demonstrate basic competence in arranging a suitable setting for counselling clients for [specific issues causing a need for counselling, e.g., bereavement] [or: specific]
Level 2 CL5C-3(2)	demonstrate extended competence in arranging a suitable setting for counselling clients for [specific issues causing a need for counselling, e.g., bereavement] [or: specific]

Figure 12.8
Index of Outcome Book for Counseling

Boundaries. Ethical principles and procedures 14

British Association of Counselling and Psychotherapy
 Code of Practice for Counsellors 14
 Code of Practice for People using Counselling Skills 14

Career options. Counselling 11
Categories (Categories in guidance notes, section 1.1.4) 2, 3
Challenging. Counselling skills 22
Children. Specific types of clients 31–34
Choosing *see* **Selection**
Clarification. Client expectations
 By counsellors 25
Clarifying. Counselling skills 22
Class. Clients
 Social class 31–34
Classical conditioning. Examples of theories and models 17
Client issues
 Abuse 35–38
 Agencies engaged in counselling for specific issues 38
 Application of counselling theories and models 36, 37
 Bereavement 35–38
 Depression 35–38
 Disablement 35–38
 Ethical aspects 36
 Family history 35–38
 Interpersonal relationship problems 35–38
 Life crises 35–38
 Loss 35–38
 Psychological aspects 36
 Sexual identity 35–38
 Social phenomena and events 35–38
 Stress 35–38
 Substance abuses 35–38
 Use of counselling skills 37
Client issues (Subcategory, list in guidance notes, section 1.1.4) 3
Clients
 Abuse 35–38
 Age. Specific types of clients defined by age 31–34
 Bereavement 35–38
 Children 31–34
 Committing to agendas. Help by counsellors 22
 Cultural frames of reference. Specific types of clients
  defined by cultural frames of references 31–34
 Depression 35–38

different kinds of courses. Some comprehensive courses use individual outcomes (e.g., being able to work with Word and Excel), whereas short courses in specific software applications would require separate outcomes for individual skills (e.g., formatting, keying in, saving, and printing). Thus, there is need for outcomes on many different levels of specificity and for mechanisms for optionally combining outcome elements into any required new outcome.

The main categories are general ICT knowledge and auxiliary knowledge and skills (e.g., terminology, mathematics and machine logic, programming, keyboard skills, computer law, and data security); computer systems and general PC knowledge; creation, manipulation, and presentation of data and files; computer networks and electronic communication; and required subject knowledge for use of ICT in specific environments and subject fields.

Work on the ICT outcome collection ceased in summer 2004 following radical changes in government policy on the funding of adult education. These changes may require the bulk of courses to become either examination courses or accredited courses using a government-funded award framework and outcomes. However, the outcome collections already completed remain in use for the moment, and there is a possibility that work on the original goal of a county outcome bank may be continued after course provision has been adapted to work within the new funding parameters.

ASSESSMENT

Adult learners come to adult education with many different agendas. No standardized system of learning outcomes with outcomes chosen by the teacher for a whole class can adequately reflect this reality. Standard outcomes, which provide a clear picture of what a course will give students, are supplemented with individual learning outcomes. These are negotiated between teacher and individual student at any time during the course, including in retrospect at the end of the course, when a student might say, "I find my confidence has grown a lot." Individual learning outcomes are not tied to levels and can be anything at all.

The goal of including individual learning outcomes is to compensate for the restrictions inherent in any standard system, however open-ended and flexible it may be. At the same time, the standard outcome selection for individual students can be altered where necessary. For example, a student may be hard of hearing and may therefore be unable to achieve listening comprehension outcomes in a foreign language. For him or her, such outcomes would be replaced by, for example, more speaking or reading outcomes. In other cases, individual students need their outcomes level to be lowered or increased in order to reflect their competence adequately. By altering outcomes slowly and continually throughout the course, for individual students as appropriate (but always using standardized outcomes from the book), students' individual learning plans reflect a true record of what they have learned rather than a record of what they did not manage to learn.

Students' attitudes to the system will be influenced by how teachers present it. David Minton suggests that "within your teaching you can manage testing processes so that they are routes to learning rather than events to fear."[5] Assessment should be seen as an aid to learning and to understanding what the course is about, and it should encourage students by offering stages to pass on a road with a known destination or a road which is exciting in its own right. Several adult education providers that ran trials with non-standardized learning outcomes reported that a learning outcome skeleton helped students understand the structure and contents of their courses and thus led them toward greater participation and autonomy in what and how to learn.

Assessment is aimed at being informal and unobtrusive. Teachers should choose their learning outcomes to represent what they intend students to learn, and then should pick appropriate ordinary classroom tasks as assessment evidence. Outcomes are selective and only show part of what is being learned in a course. Minimum required and maximum allowed numbers of outcomes are stated in the system. The *representativeness* described in this chapter allows teachers to choose outcomes to fit in with the way they like to teach. Assessment practices are checked in conjunction with teacher observation. New teachers are individually trained in the system at the beginning of their employment.

EVALUATION

At the time of writing this chapter, the Adult Community College, Colchester, has used the standardized outcomes in Modern Languages and in Art and Design for one and a half years, and Counseling outcomes for half a year. At the end of the academic year 2003/2004, a questionnaire sent to language and art teachers obtained feedback on how they had found working with the new system after having been used to writing their own outcomes without any rules or restrictions.[6] The respondents reported satisfaction with the new system. They agreed with contents and level differentiation of the learning outcomes, and they found the system useful, helpful, and easy to access and use.

CONCLUSION

The strength of the new system lies in its flexibility and hospitality. In adult education, contents of non-accredited courses vary widely in a way that does not apply to examination-determined courses. Standard outcomes need to allow for more subject components and component combinations than would be possible to list. Providing structures of level-defined standardized wording with open-ended option slots promotes consistent assessment and achievement recording of whatever a teacher wants to teach. One curriculum area where this would be especially useful is craft. Should there be non-accredited craft courses in the future, and should funding be provided to develop standardized outcomes for these courses, a set of outcomes suitable for all the subjects in the extremely diverse collection of courses could be framed around categories of materials (e.g., outcomes for work with textiles and paper). For any one course, outcomes could then be chosen from all the relevant material categories. A similar approach could also be used for health and fitness courses. It remains to be seen whether funding will allow such courses to run, and whether funding will be given to continue the development of the outcome bank.

It is generally recognized (though not always admitted) that assessment is intrinsically subjective and can be a dubious measure of ability and achievement. Traditionally, assessment tries to eliminate subjectivity through a variety of control measures, but the project described here neither denies nor tries to eliminate subjectivity. This is a system with two faces: to teachers and learners it is open and flexible, allowing them to choose outcomes which reflect intended learning; to other stakeholders (i.e., colleges needing quality assurance and funding agencies requiring proof of achievement) it offers control, clearly differentiated levels, and consistency across teachers.

This chapter uses the word "achievement" in the way in which educationalists and bureaucrats tend to, hiding or ignoring the fact that there is no objective or precise definition of "achievement" other than perhaps the dictionary definition: "having brought something to a successful outcome."[7] But who determines what constitutes a successful outcome? Surely, the way to decide this is by relating undertakings to their goals. For many adult learners, the participation in a course is itself the goal, and so achievement ought to be measured as "successful participation" (i.e., happy and actively taking part). However, funders want measurable achievement to prove the worth of courses, and increasingly this measure relates to qualifications leading to employment. So the best we can achieve is an assessment system that can support happy and goal-free participation, as well as learning, as students achieve whatever goals they may have; a system that also satisfies quality assurance and funding demands in a world where little merit is assigned to just "being" or "doing."

Notes

1. Pablo Foster, Ursual Howard, and Arina Reisenberger, *A Sense of Achievement: Outcomes of Adult Learning* (London: Further Education Development Agency, 1997): 5; Pauline Nashashibi, *Learning in Progress: Recognising Achievement in Adult Learning* (London: Learning and Skills Development Agency, 2002): p. 3; Kathleen Watters, "Able to Learn 'Just for the Hell of It'," *Adults Learning* 13, no. 8 (2002): 10–11.

2. Maggie Greenwood and John Vorhaus, ed., *Recognising and Validating Outcomes of Non-accredited Learning: A Practical Approach* (London: Learning and Skills Development Agency, 2001); Christopher Pole, *Assessing and Recording Achievement* (Buckingham, UK: Open University Press, 1993).

3. H. Torrance, "Introduction," in Pole, *Assessing and Recording Achievement*, p. ix. See Greenwood and Vorhaus, *Recognising and Validating Outcomes of Non-accredited Learning*; Foster et al., *A Sense of Achievement*.

4. Derek Austin originally developed PRECIS for the British National Bibliography, and many agencies use it.

5. David Minton, *Teaching Skills in Further and Adult Education* (London: City and Guilds of London Institute,1997): 208.

6. Jutta Austin, *Use of the Learning Outcome Bank for Non-accredited Courses* (Colchester, UK: Adult Community College Colchester, 2004). (Unpublished internal report).

7. *Chambers Dictionary* (Edinburgh: Chambers Harrap, 1998), p. 12.

CHAPTER 13

Outcomes Assessment in Canadian Higher Education

Heidi Julien

O utcomes assessment in Canadian higher education is not yet wide-spread. However, concern for quality is evident. Calls for institutional accountability to stakeholders and the general public have been heard from several quarters for a number of years. The issue of how to measure the quality of higher education is still outstanding. For example, there is an ongoing debate about whether or not performance indicators are a possible or appropriate way to measure the quality of higher education, but actual assessments efforts have focused mainly on output measures. Over the past fifteen years, there has been much talk with little action; many different stakeholders have raised the need for better assessment measures in higher education but few institutions have responded with practical initiatives, programs, or policy changes.

GENERAL CALLS FOR QUALITY ASSESSMENT

In 1990, the Association of Universities and Colleges of Canada (AUCC) established the Commission of Inquiry on Canadian University Education to "review the educational function of Canadian universities and to find ways by which universities can ensure that their educational programs are of high quality."[1] The issues addressed by the Commission included concern for appropriate balance between teaching and research efforts, participation by marginalized groups in higher education, and coordination and cooperation with colleges. The Commission acknowledged that universities tended to view relevance issues with ambivalence, and found fundamental differences between stakeholder groups in their perspectives on higher education: students and the government believe the reason to attend university is to obtain a better job, whereas faculty believe the most important reason is for personal intellectual development. The Commission also reported that universities have no faith in employment projections and do not respond to them, and it recommended that all graduates should possess oral and written self-expression skills, although it is rare for those skills to be tested upon entry to or exit from institutions. The report noted that 42% of full-time students who had entered university in 1985 had not graduated with a degree within five years. Stuart L. Smith suggested that the high attrition rate was due to the inadequate quality of higher education, and concluded that the ongoing search for international performance indicators was futile. He recommended that the AUCC form an Academic Auditing Committee to gather and publish data, including surveys of graduates, surveys of employers, system-wide accounting of students (retention and attrition), results of standardized exit tests of writing ability, and information regarding teaching methods, class size, and professors. It is interesting to note that most of these are output, rather than outcome, measures.

The response of the AUCC to Smith's report focused on two themes: institutions need to increase their commitment to teaching and learning, and openness and accountability are vital. The AUCC stated that public accountability includes communicating what universities do, how well they do it, and how their performance is measured.[2] The AUCC suggested there was an urgent need to develop performance measures, institute teacher training programs, and make changes to the assessment and reward systems. Core competencies (written and verbal communication, leadership, management skills, and self-management) should be central to the curriculum. However, the AUCC disagreed with the Commissioner's recommendation for a minimum number of classroom hours, arguing that the quality of teaching cannot be assessed by the number of hours taught.

Interest in assessment issues continued, and three years later Gilles G. Nadeau summarized the results of a pan-Canadian project to identify and define criteria and indicators of quality and excellence for postsecondary institutions in six areas: students, programs, faculty, administrators, institutional environment, and institutional context variables.[3] Surveyed stakeholders, including governments, agencies, university boards, student union presidents, and business leaders, identified over

100 criteria. Nadeau suggested that universities evaluating quality levels in the six key areas could use these common criteria.

In 1996, the Ontario Undergraduate Student Alliance issued a report calling for increased accountability for higher education in Canada. The report's basic premise was that universities need to be more accountable to students, who are funding institutions through their tuition. The focus of concern was administrative, particularly financial matters, and outcomes assessment was not mentioned.[4]

In 1999, the Canadian Council of Ministers of Education issued a report on public expectations of higher education.[5] These expectations were divided into six key areas: quality, accessibility, mobility and portability, relevance and responsiveness, research and scholarship, and accountability. The Council favored actual student learning outcomes and other explicit outcomes to measure performance. The report explained that it is important to articulate expectations in order to implement them into policy and practice, supply a framework for accountability, and provide a basis for discussion and action across Canada. Expectations under each main area were divided into system-level expectations, institutional-level expectations, and individual-level expectations.

Critically examining various calls for accountability, William A. Bruneau and Donald C. Savage argued that performance indicators are not a means of measuring accountability. They asked, "How does one measure the intangibles of education—critical thinking, creativity, tolerance, wisdom?"[6] They further argued that the use of performance indicators imposes costly and "highly centralized bureaucracies" onto the university system.[7] Performance indicators are used to shift the blame for funding cuts from governments, which imposed these cuts onto university boards, and the cuts further undermine the balance between market demand and broader social objectives. Performance indicators are interventionist and relevant to market control, not to education. They make teaching and learning "commodities for sale."[8] Bruneau and Savage suggest a number of alternatives to performance indicators, including normative statistics, institutional quality assurance policies, and regular, publicized, departmental reviews focused on teaching, research, and service.

Recently, the Canadian Library Association sponsored a pre-conference workshop at its 2005 annual conference, titled "Creating an Environment of Continuous Assessment: Practical Approaches for Academic Libraries."[9] This suggests ongoing concern for quality assurance in the library sector of Canadian higher education.

Also recent, the Rae Review on Post-Secondary Education in Ontario, limited to one Canadian province, called for quality assurance efforts to establish quality standards assessed through qualitative and quantitative measures to ensure improvements to postsecondary education.[10] A specific recommendation was to establish learning outcomes for generic courses, such as first-year introductory courses, across the province. The report also suggested that each post-secondary institution develop multi-year plans to improve educational quality and to measure those outcomes. The degree to which these recommendations will be implemented remains to be seen.

ASSESSMENT EFFORTS

Parallel to these arguments for quality assurance in Canadian higher education, actual assessment efforts were undertaken. Paul Anisef and Etta Baichman reviewed several national graduating student surveys relating to higher education and jobs for graduates.[11] They found that selecting appropriate educational relevance indicators remained unresolved. Few research studies focused on employers' satisfaction with graduates' skills. However, the surveys revealed that there is clear support for the value of direct work experience. Institutions approved of assessing graduates and employers but less than one-third conducted their own surveys. Concern with monitoring employer and graduates' satisfaction varied by faculty, with the strongest concern in professional faculties. Respondents indicated that there is not enough funding, resources, or cooperation to complete employer or graduate satisfaction assessments. Anisef and Baichman recommended strategies for monitoring educational relevance, including the coordination of surveys with alumni associations, the establishment of employer advisory committees, and better use of existing surveys.

Mount Royal College in Calgary, Alberta, appears to be on the forefront of outcomes assessment in Canadian higher education.[12] The college initiated an outcomes-based approach to its curriculum in 1997, implementing an assessment plan policy shortly thereafter. Learning outcomes identified through a college-wide collaboration focus on communication, thinking, computer literacy, ethical reasoning, information retrieval and evaluation, and group effectiveness. These learning outcomes are intended to drive curriculum development. The goal of assessment is to ensure graduates have the knowledge, skills, and abilities needed for success in their vocations, citizenship, and lifelong learning.

Edudata Canada summarizes provincial government, institutional, and national graduate survey projects, most of which are designed to determine graduates' success in obtaining employment, unemployment rates, job satisfaction, and satisfaction with the education obtained.[13] Existing surveys include:

- Alberta University and University College Graduate Employment Outcomes Survey;
- Ontario University Graduate Survey;
- Maritime Provinces Higher Education Commission Report;
- British Columbia College and Institute Outcomes Project;
- National Graduate Surveys;
- Canadian Undergraduate Survey Consortium, which included twenty-six universities in 2001, and which collects data using questionnaires on a three-year cycle:
  - The Student Information Survey (plans, goals, finances, reaction to education experience);
  - Graduating Student Survey (satisfaction and perception of university experience); and
  - First Year Student Survey (demographics, reason for attending university, orientation reactions, transition process).

An ongoing National Survey of Student Engagement is one international attempt at quality assessment in which some Canadian institutions have participated.[14] The purpose of the survey is to gather information about participation in programs offered by academic institutions. The results are used to estimate how undergraduate students spend their time and what they gain by attending postsecondary institutions. It is expected that institutions will also use the results to identify areas that can be improved, in and outside the classroom. For the 2004 survey, 473 institutions participated. Canadian institutions participating in 2005 included: Carleton University, Concordia University, Trinity Western University, University of New Brunswick, University of Ottawa, University of Regina, University of Windsor, and York University. It should be noted that these are all medium-sized universities, focused on teaching.

The Pan-Canadian Education Indicators Program (PECIP) is an ongoing initiative of the Canadian Education Statistics Council, established to create a set of statistical measures for Canadian educational systems.[15] The program strives to provide accurate and reliable information on education to foster informed decision making, policy initiatives, and program development. The focus is on statistical output measures for postsecondary education (e.g., percent increases in enrollment, research and development statistics, graduation rates, correlations between earnings, and educational attainments). The Canadian Council of Ministers of Education is working on a set of PCEIP indicators. Draft indicators have been created for context (including demographics), features, and characteristics of systems in higher education (including student inputs, learner progress, human resources, technology, and post-school learning), and outputs and outcomes (including achievement and effectiveness, efficiency and productivity, responsiveness and relevance, and equity).

The Council of Ministers of Education also has made comparisons of Canadian higher education with other Organisation for Economic Cooperation and Development (OECD) countries.[16] The indicators used are all input and output measures, including measures of human and financial resources invested in education, how education systems are operating and evolving, and measures of returns on educational investments.

Assessment Efforts in Canadian Academic Libraries

A recent report by the Canadian Association of Research Libraries concluded that user surveys indicate that library users were generally satisfied with service quality but unsatisfied with the adequacy of collections and technology infrastructure.[17] The surveys analyzed did not address outcomes.

Specifically with respect to information literacy instruction, some Canadian university libraries have recently participated in Project SAILS (Standardized Assessment of Information Literacy Skills).[18] Operated by Kent State University Libraries and Media Services, this project was established because information literacy has become a focal point of many libraries' missions. Assessment is also increasingly recognized as a key initiative to improve programs and to meet the obligation of accountability. With those ideas in mind, the project's purpose is to develop a valid and credible instrument for programmatic level assessment of information literacy skills. Current Canadian participants include the University of Alberta, University of British Columbia, University of Calgary, University of Manitoba, University of New Brunswick, University of Western Ontario, and York University.

Individual libraries also have participated in other assessment efforts. For example, the University of Alberta Libraries has participated in the LibQUAL+ project, which surveys user perceptions about service quality related to libraries and their collections and services. This project does not deal with student learning outcomes.

There is an understanding of the need to demonstrate quality in Canadian higher education. Nevertheless, progress has been slow, and actual attempts continue to focus on quantitative input and output measures, or satisfaction ratings, rather than substantive outcomes assessment. There are exceptions to this general state of affairs, including one recent study of outcomes undertaken in Canadian academic libraries.

CASE STUDY OF OUTCOMES ASSESSMENT IN CANADIAN ACADEMIC LIBRARIES*

Introduction

One of the primary threads in a longitudinal analysis of information literacy (IL) instruction in Canadian academic libraries has focused on evaluation of that instruction. Recently, that research program focused on outcomes of IL instruction by testing information literacy skills and interviewing students to explore their experiences of information literacy instruction. Particular emphasis was given to investigating instructional effectiveness and assessing learning outcomes to identify those institutional and pedagogical factors that promote successful outcomes.

Providing effective access to information is essential to enable citizens to engage fully in private and public life. Numerous government initiatives have focused on both providing and maximizing access to

---

*This study was previously published as Heidi Julien and Stuart Boon, "Assessing Instructional Outcomes in Canadian Academic Libraries," *Library & Information Science Research* 26, no. 2 (2004), 121–139.

online information resources. In order to assure access to and effective use of global information resources, society must look further to the development of the necessary information skills. For current investments in information and communication technology to prove worthwhile, individuals must possess the skills to use those technologies; in other words, to determine their own information needs, to use a number of information retrieval tools efficiently, to evaluate the retrieved information, and to use that information to answer their needs. Taken together, these skills are commonly known as information literacy, and provide the basis for the effective use of information. The definition of information literacy used in this study is "a set of abilities requiring individuals to 'recognize when information is needed and have the ability to locate, evaluate, and use effectively the needed information.'"[19]

The past decade was marked by a serious decline in the resources available to academic libraries in Canada. This same decline was experienced in other locales. In Canada, however, the weak purchasing power of the Canadian dollar further worsened the situation, resulting in a budget loss of up to 33% for collections.[20] At the same time, the complement of full-time librarians steadily decreased with little renewal of the profession. David Holmes found that, on average, Canadian academic librarians had been at their institutions for sixteen years. Meanwhile, circulation was dropping, and interlibrary loan activity was increasing. A general state of underfunding and lack of resources, human and otherwise, was the practical context for this study, ironically occurring precisely when information literacy instruction was beginning to be seen as a necessity.[21]

Problem Statement

The evaluation of client instruction in general is greatly in need of improvement.[22] Not viewed by the majority of administrations as a funding priority, only a minority of libraries have formal instructional objectives. Library instruction is typically handled by a small dedicated staff, and the evaluation of client instruction is normally informal and formative.[23] A number of summative evaluations suggest that student grades and program completion rates for undergraduates are improved by client instruction.[24] These are indirect measures of student learning (i.e., they are gross indicators, but not direct evaluations), and are a valuable tool in assessing instructional outcomes.[25] In addition, more direct assessment done in specific contexts has found, for instance, that students who receive instruction increase their searching effectiveness and are able to select marginally more relevant information sources.[26] Researchers report that systematic assessment is helping to shape library services.[27] Further confirmation and extension of these outcomes is necessary; for example, can other short- and longer-term benefits resulting from effective instruction be determined? Such benefits might include specific search skills, improved cognitive understanding, and attitudinal changes (e.g., increased self-confidence) that promote more effective or efficient use of information resources. From the perspectives of both the institution and the client, information literacy instruction clearly results in positive outcomes.

This study investigated instructional effectiveness from a number of perspectives, extending earlier research into current practices of instruction in Canadian academic libraries.[28] The perspectives examined include those of academic librarians (instructors), undergraduate students (clients), and academic library managers. Furthermore, by measuring the students' success in achieving the learning objectives determined by instructors, an assessment of the learning outcomes was conducted.[29] This study identified those factors that, in concert, ensure that students obtaining information literacy instruction at Canadian colleges and universities receive sufficient skills to acquire and evaluate the information they need throughout their lives.

Theoretical Frameworks

The theoretical frameworks supporting this study included a phenomenological approach to exploring personal meanings of information literacy, and educational assessment theory, highlighting the importance of evaluating outcomes (summative) with the goal of instructional improvement (formative). Based on phenomenological research into learners' conceptions and experiences of information use, Christine S. Bruce offers a rich understanding of information literacy as experienced by learners that is applicable to this study.[30] The ways in which users relate to information (subject-object relations) vary greatly. Using information technology, finding information, executing a process (i.e., searching), controlling information, building personal knowledge bases, gaining novel insights by integrating knowledge with personal perspectives, and using information for others' benefit are all meanings attributed to information literacy.[31] Thus, the experience of information literacy is a highly personal one. As a result, the framework upon which conceptions of instructional effectiveness, from the learner's perspective, were explored in this study is clearly constructivist. There was, therefore, no assumption of particular outcomes of information literacy instruction. The actual outcomes first needed to be identified, and then assessed.

Assessment theory, referring specifically to student outcomes assessment, is reflected in the span and logical sequence of the study. Serbrenia J. Sims suggests a broad definition of assessment, drawn from Carol Boyer and Peter Ewell, as the gathering of evidence relating to the impact of instruction.[32] With the long-term intention of improving instruction (formative assessment), this definition emphasizes the importance of evaluating outcomes (summative evaluation). As the study necessitated the detailed analysis of three academic libraries as case studies and in order to achieve a rich pool of data from which to identify success factors, significant effort went into the triangulation of numerous avenues of data retrieval. As Sims notes, identifying key audiences and obtaining support for in-depth assessment is key to successful project completion; valid data are obtained by assessing output, rather than input measures; and outcomes appropriately assessed include cognitive (gains in knowledge), psychological (changes in attitudes or values), behavioral (changes in actions), and longer-term outcomes (program completion rates, changes in grades). According to Michael Q. Patton, two of the three primary uses of evaluation findings are to improve programs and to generate knowledge (e.g., about what works).[33] These uses of evaluation findings were core goals of this study.

Objectives

The objectives of the study were: (1) to identify the outcomes of information literacy instruction (including, for students, cognitive, behavioral, and affective outcomes; and for universities and colleges, higher student achievement and program completion rates); (2) to characterize "success" in achieving those outcomes from the viewpoints of instructional librarians and from the students' perspectives; and (3) to identify those institutional and pedagogical factors which promote successful outcomes. This study followed two national surveys of information literacy instruction in academic libraries and used a three-phase design to identify and assess student learning outcomes, and determine those pedagogical and institutional factors that support effective instruction.[34]

Methods

Two medium-sized universities and one medium-sized college/technical institute, all in different provinces, were visited. Altogether, three Canadian academic libraries were involved in the study. Both universities are research-oriented and offer a range of undergraduate, graduate, and professional programs. University 1 consists of six faculties and prides itself on providing innovative teaching to its 13,000 full-time and 7,500 part-time students. Four major campus libraries provide service to this university. University 2 consists of 16 faculties serving 30,000 students. Five main campus libraries serve the university's information needs. The college provides apprenticeship, certificate, and diploma programs to more than 32,000 students in a wide variety of fields. The college campus is served by one main library.

Interviews conducted on-site at these three Canadian academic libraries comprised the first phase of the study. In total, nineteen instructional librarians, seven senior library administrators, six instructional faculty who regularly take their classes for library instruction, and two former librarians recently involved in library instruction were interviewed. Interviews were semi-structured, and explored instructional goals, support for instruction, pedagogical practices, methods of evaluation for instruction, and challenges faced by instructors. The findings of the interviews closely matched data obtained in previous quantitative surveys and are reported elsewhere.[35] At each site, instructional documentation was also analyzed to provide context for instructional activities. A declared commitment to instruction was evidenced by the instructional documentation provided by the site libraries. Each of the libraries provided supporting materials for the students (handouts, workbooks, and assignments) and had constructed programs tailored to specific classes. Since teaching faculty who include information literacy instruction in their courses also incorporate library instruction assignments into their course marks for students, there is clear evidence of faculty participation in information literacy instruction. Such cooperation with faculty is critical for the success of information literacy instruction.[36]

No evaluation or quantitative measures of institutionally significant outcomes of information literacy instruction were available at any of the institutions. Instructional librarians, administrators, and teaching faculty provided anecdotal evidence to support positive learning outcomes. No one at the three participating institutions, however, was monitoring the outcomes of instructional efforts in any systematic fashion (e.g., by tracking changes to student grades or program completion rates). Phase One participants (instructor librarians) described informal, formative feedback of a positive nature, such as more sophisticated questions posed at the reference desk and improved student assignments. These determinants of "success" provided the basis for the belief, not confirmed by substantive evidence but held by most interview participants, that their library instruction is useful and makes students more self-sufficient in their research. For instance, there was no systematic, valid evidence that the instructional goals articulated by interview participants were being achieved. Those goals included (in rank order): teaching students to use search tools (e.g., databases) effectively so as to encourage self-reliance, affirming that the library is a friendly place, informing students that the library exists, and teaching critical thinking skills. The relative achievement of these goals at each site could not be determined in the absence of proper evaluation; thus, from the institutional perspective, it was not possible to characterize definitively instructional success.[37]

The second phase of the study focused on the pre- and post-testing of student learning in the instructional sessions conducted at the three academic libraries. In Phase Two, pre- and post-testing of learning was conducted using seven groups of students (two groups at University 1, three groups at University 2, and two groups at the college). The student groups received relatively short instructional sessions, ranging from fifty minutes to three hours in length (for one graduate-level class). Paper-and-pencil tests were constructed in cooperation with the instructional librarians to test learning of the specific learning objectives for each group involved. Following the normal practice of the librarian instructors, tests were designed without reference to any external standards, such as the standards established by the Association of College and Research Libraries.[38] This was appropriate, as the librarians used neither these standards nor any others as the basis for their instruction. In order for tests to be valid, they needed to be based on the individualistic learning objectives being used in each testing context. This means that the test results are not directly comparable, since the tests for each group were unique. All students were provided with detailed information sheets and consent forms for the study and given the option to participate. Individuals who chose to participate signed the provided consent forms. Participation rates varied from 12% to 81%, with a mean of 41%. The instructional librarians administered the tests at each site, with the pre-test being administered immediately prior to instruction, the first post-test being administered immediately following instruction (or one week following instruction in one case, noted below), and a post-post-test being administered three to four months following instruction. Tests typically focused on search strategies, reading catalog and database records, general understanding of source types, information evaluation criteria, and library policies. To encourage student participation and minimize testing time, all question items were constructed for quick response. Students typically took between five and fifteen minutes to complete the tests. Question items included multiple choice, true/false, and other short-answer types of questions. The first post-test was intended to assess short-term learning, while the second post-test was intended to assess longer-term retention of learning.

The third and final phase of the study involved interviewing individual students in each setting who participated in information literacy instruction in Phase Two. These interviews were conducted to access the perceptions of students about the outcomes of instruction. Students who indicated an interest in participating in an interview were contacted by telephone and invited to participate. Students who participated were paid $20 for their participation in the study. Interviews with consenting students occurred at each campus within two months of completing the final post-test. Ten students were interviewed from University 1, twelve students were interviewed at University 2, and six students were interviewed at the college. Interviews lasted from one-half hour to one hour in length. They were tape-recorded and transcribed by the interviewer within a few days. The interviews were semi-structured, and focused on the following questions:

- Please describe your experiences in instructional activities or programs in the library during your undergraduate program.
- How did your experiences change your understandings of information and its use?
- In what ways did you find the instruction to be valuable or not so valuable?
- How did the skills you learned during those activities contribute to your learning and educational success?
- Were your feelings of confidence or anxiety relating to information use affected by your instructional experiences?

Responses to the questions, and other comments made by participants during the interviews, were analyzed using content analysis, assisted by QSR NVivo software.

Pre-test and Post-test Results

Figure 13.1 shows the general pattern of test results for the seven participating groups. Statistically significant score increases were found in four of the groups (one from University 1, two from University 2, and 1 from the college) (see Table 13.1). Alternatively, a statistically significant *decrease* in test scores from the post-test to the post-post-test ($t = -2.75$, $df = 20$, $p < 0.05$) was demonstrated by one group from University 2. This sole group was comprised of graduate students while all others were undergraduates. Particular difficulties with identifying key concepts in a statement of information need, identifying synonyms for key concepts, articulating evaluation criteria for information, and Boolean logic were common to all groups. Following instruction, improvement in test scores was apparent, particularly for the ability to identify parts of catalog/ database records.

The four groups that demonstrated statistically significant increases in test scores were given particular analytical attention to investigate the

Figure 13.1
Changes in Average Student Test Scores for
Seven Participating Groups

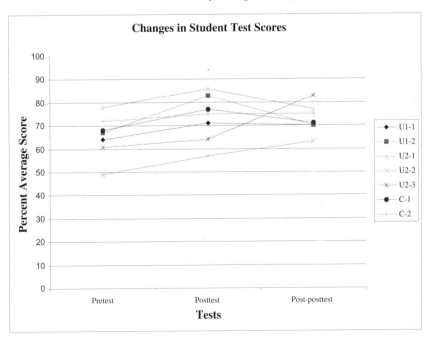

Table 13.1
Statistically Significant Increases to Test Scores

Group	Increase in scores	2-tailed t-test
University 1 (business students)	Pre-test to post-test	$t = -3.84$, df $= 158$, p < 0.001
	Pre-test to post-post-test	$t = -3.60$, df $= 141$, p < 0.001
University 2 (biology students)	Pre-test to post-test	$t = 2.75$, df $= 149$, p < 0.05
	Pre-test to post-post-test	$t = -9.01$, df $= 112$, p < 0.001
University 2 (communications students)	Pre-test to post-test	$t = -2.32$, df $= 97$, p < 0.05
	Pre-test to post-post-test	$t = -4.16$, df $= 100$, p < 0.0001
College (creative communications students)	Pre-test to post-test	$t = -2.82$, df $= 9$, p < 0.05

reasons for these significant results. The instructional librarian for the group of business students at University 1 felt that their success might be attributable to the fact that the students were encouraged to sign up for small-group consultations after the initial instructional lecture, in order to get hands-on experience with the material discussed in the instruction session. This librarian reported that the instructional "session was geared very closely to a specific and very challenging assignment ... [so] we had motivated learners" (personal communication). In addition, the librarian noted that most of the students did indeed voluntarily attend an additional session. This librarian had also worked closely with the faculty member teaching the business course: "I held several meetings during the summer to discuss the structure of the assignments and the actual content of the instruction session" (personal communication). The librarian provided reference materials (i.e., guidelines for evaluating electronic resources and other resource lists) in the student course packages and made print copies of instructional materials available on reserve in the library. Analysis of the Phase Three student interviews for that group shows that they spoke of increased understanding of how to do detailed searches, and how to evaluate information. They also expressed increased confidence in their own skills, and with asking for help in their research. Interestingly, these same students indicated that they did not feel that the information literacy skills they had learned were transferable outside the context of that particular business course.

Statistically significant increased test scores were demonstrated in two groups of students at University 2. At this institution, information literacy has recently been identified as an essential academic skill in a university document addressing cross-campus learning support. The institution's library has expressed interest in incorporating information literacy instruction into the undergraduate core curriculum. The instructional librarian for the biology students, one of the two "successful" groups at this institution, suggested the following reasons for their success:

> We [were] thinking that they may have retained what they learned because of the assignment that they had to do that was a part of that class. When the assignment is returned to them, they can keep it, and it becomes a bit of a guide to researching in the library. The class is also two hours long, and so students were more or less able to complete the whole assignment right after the teaching section, so that may have also allowed the concepts to cement. Also, there is at least one other lab session during that semester that requires students to find another reference in addition to their text or lab manual. The lab coordinator does have to stipulate that the reference is to be an article, and has to remind students that they did learn how to do that, but she reports that some students actually will find more than one article for that lab. So perhaps going over the whole process one other time helped refresh their memory as well.

The instructional librarian for the communications students, the second group whose test scores demonstrated that some learning had occurred, suggested that the increase in knowledge demonstrated at the point of the first post-test may be due to the fact that the students wrote that test a full week following instruction, "giving the content time to 'sink in'" (personal communication). Analysis of the student interviews within these groups indicates that the students believe that their ability to search databases efficiently and to evaluate Internet resources were improved through their information sessions. Several students spoke of increased confidence in using the library, in locating material in the collection, and in asking librarians for help when needed. In addition, several students recalled learning more efficient use of Boolean operators, despite the fact that this learning was not reflected in test scores.

Less clear are the reasons for the success of the creative communications class at the college. The instructional librarian had no comments to offer in light of the increase in test scores for this group. The student interviews suggest that the students in the session did not find it particularly interesting or engaging, in fact the opposite might be said. However, one point that each of the students interviewed made was that library staff were very approachable. One student did reveal that the session taught him an important lesson: "I never even knew that there was someone sitting at the front of the library that wanted you to go over there and interrupt them because they are bored. . . . I can just walk into the library and ask them to help me out and I never knew that was available." A particular strength in the college context is the impressive instructional documentation provided by the library. Students are provided with workbooks, which are carefully laid out, very thorough, detailed, and tailored specifically to the content of each course. In the interviews, it became clear that these instructional materials were highly appreciated by students. Indeed, these workbooks most certainly provide strong reinforcement for in-class instruction and could easily be used independently of instructional classes to teach information literacy concepts.

Results of Student Interviews

There were too few students in the interview pool from each specific instructional group to make comparisons between groups based on the interview data. Thus, these data should be considered as a general indication of the views of students who participated in the instructional sessions that were a part of this study.

Prior Instructional Experiences

Students were asked about their instructional experiences prior to participating in the instructional sessions involved in this study. The vast majority (n = 21) reported that they had had very little previous library instruction (either at the high school or postsecondary level), or none at all. Those who had little previous instruction uniformly reported that that instruction had been very general and not particularly helpful (especially in comparison with their most recent library instruction). The remainder of the sample reported some valuable previous instructional experience, but nearly all of these reported that they had learned something new from their most recent instructional experiences. Students who had received prior instruction were also quick to point out that these recent instructional sessions were highly effective at reinforcing lessons learned previously.

Lessons Learned

When queried about what they learned in instructional sessions, a range of the most salient lessons learned (i.e., those that were recalled first) were reported, including how to use the catalog (n = 5), how to use electronic databases (n = 5), and a variety of specific skills (e.g., using Boolean logic in searching) and generalities (e.g., how to research). All of the respondents were able to suggest at least one thing learned from the instructional session, even if the lesson was not new. This recall appears to be quite individual, reflecting individual needs and previous experience, although what students recall learning does bear a relationship with the stated learning objectives of the instructional session attended.

Changed Ideas about Information

When asked how their instructional experiences changed their ideas about information and its use, students provided a variety of responses. These responses suggest that the question was a challenging one for many of them. Six claimed that their instructional experiences had not changed their ideas, while the majority (n = 22) reported some changes. These changes were typically reported as an increase in knowledge about information (particularly how much exists and is available to students through the library) and how to access that information (by referring to specific searching skills learned). Increased comfort and confidence with researching information was also frequently reported as a response to this question. For instance, one student noted that her instructional experiences "made me more aware of what was out there and what I had access to." Another student said, "I feel a lot more comfortable now. Being first-year, everything was really overwhelming and I didn't know how to use a thing, but after that I just... number one, I just felt much more comfortable with asking for help, and number two, I didn't even feel I needed to because that [instruction]... pretty much gave me a good idea of how to use everything." Several students commented on their new independence in accessing information following their instruction.

Increased Confidence

Twenty-three (82.1%) of the students were able to respond positively to the question asking whether their confidence increased as a result of library instruction. This confidence was related to increases in students' knowledge and skills (n = 17), and to a new confidence in asking for help when it is needed (n = 1), or to both factors (n = 11). For instance, one student noted, "I gained more confidence and actually knew what I was doing. And I had way less anxiety, because I knew that they [library staff] would help me if I did in fact get stuck." Although students were not asked to comment on changes to their perceptions of librarians, eighteen of the twenty-eight participants made specific statements relating to this unintended outcome of instruction. Many of these comments noted that the expertise of individual librarians or of librarians in general was now apparent, and that the students now realized how helpful librarians can be.

How Instruction Improved Skills

Students were asked how the instruction they received improved their skills. In addition to general comments about better efficiency, and greater awareness of information resources, fourteen students noted that they had a greater awareness of databases and how to use them, thirteen students noted their improved searching skills, five respondents referred specifically to their new skills in using Boolean operators, seven respondents mentioned that they learned to search the library catalog more efficiently, and three respondents stated that they now know how to evaluate Web pages. These results are consistent with those found by Elizabeth Carter, who conducted focus groups following library instruction and learned that students' research skills had improved as a result.[39]

How Instruction Was Valuable

When asked to comment on the ways in which library instruction was valuable, twenty-six students responded positively. Most responses focused generally on the knowledge that students gained, particularly in terms of the volume of information available, and methods to access it. An example of this type of comment is, "They introduce all these new mediums of information to us, such that we were able ... now that we have all these resources and all these things, we can come in and use them." Some students referred specifically to their increased searching efficiency or to specific skills learned (as noted above).

How Instruction Was Not Valuable

Students' statements about what aspects of instruction were not so valuable were equally revealing. A sizeable minority of respondents (n = 12) provided responses to this question. For some students, particular skills or knowledge seemed to be lacking from the instruction they received. For instance, one student stated, "One thing I would have wanted was just how to search on the open... Internet.... Most of what we dealt with was what came off of electronic databases." Others commented that what they did learn was a little overwhelming, or that what they learned was insufficiently specific. One student referred to the instruction as being "rushed," while another felt that his instructional session took longer than it needed. Two students thought that their instructional session was repetitive, covering material already understood. Despite this "annoyance," the students who had been through more than one session seemed far more capable of remembering what was taught and discussed with greater clarity the way in which the information sessions were or were not of use to them. As with other things, reinforcement seems to play a big role in ideas sticking in the minds of students. Finally, two students suggested that in the absence of sufficient practice, most of what they had learned had been forgotten.

Contributions to Educational Success

The ways in which instruction contributed to students' overall educational success was also probed. While assessing learning outcomes in relation to previously established learning objectives is one useful method of evaluating library instruction, it is equally valuable to identify unintended learning outcomes. Table 13.2 shows the proportion of students who independently identified a variety of ways in which their library use instruction positively influenced their personal educational success. Participants were not provided with specific response categories from which to choose, with the exception of the particular question about changes in confidence. The outcomes noted by the participants were clustered according to theme, using content analysis. The most prominent outcomes relating to educational success that were identified by the participants were a feeling of increased confidence in using the library (separate from responses to the interview question that focused specifically on confidence) and more confidence in asking for help from library staff and in doing library research. Similarly, a large majority of participants noted that their information searching was more efficient as a result of instruction. More than half of the students believed that they receive higher grades as a direct result of their library instruction, particularly on assignments that called for library research.

Table 13.2
Ways in Which Students Believed That Instruction
Influenced Their Educational Success

Identified Benefit to Educational Success	Number of Students	Percentage of Total (n = 28)
Increased confidence about the library	22 U1 = 8; U2 = 9; C = 5*	78.6
Feel more comfortable asking the library staff for help	20 U1 = 7; U2 = 5; C = 8	71.4
Feel more confident when doing research	20 U1 = 8; U2 = 7; C = 5	71.4
More effective library use generally	20 U1 = 9; U2 = 7; C = 4	71.4
Know more about information sources	18 U1 = 8; U2 = 5; C = 5	64.3
Better understanding of where resources are located	18 U1 = 7; U2 = 5; C = 6	64.3
Research is now easier	16 U1 = 6; U2 = 4; C = 6	57.1
Better grades resulted	15 U1 = 7; U2 = 7; C = 1	57.1
Increased efficiency in library use	14 U1 = 4; U2 = 8; C = 2	53.6
Know how to use databases	14 U1 = 4; U2 = 6; C = 4	53.6
Increased understanding of information	12 U1 = 4; U2 = 5; C = 3	42.9
Easier to use catalog	10 U1 = 4; U2 = 4; C = 2	35.7
Able to find a greater variety of information	8 U1 = 1; U2 = 4; C = 3	28.6
Able to find more precise (relevant) information	8 U1 = 4; U2 = 2; C = 2	28.6
Get more information	7 U1 = 2; U2 = 4; C = 1	25.0
Do more searches	6 U1 = 2; U2 = 1; C = 3	21.4
Able to find more current information	4 U1 = 1; U2 = 2; C = 1	14.3
Find better quality information	4 U1 = 3; U2 = 0; C = 1	14.3

(*Continued*)

Table 13.2
Ways in Which Students Believed That Instruction
Influenced Their Educational Success (*Continued*)

Identified Benefit to Educational Success	Number of Students	Percentage of Total (n = 28)
Learned to cite sources appropriately	2 U1 = 0; U2 = 2; C = 0	7.1
Now use inter-library loan	2 U1 = 0; U2 = 2; C = 0	7.1

*Breakdown of students from each participating institution (U1 = university one; U2 = university two; C = college). The total number of students interviewed from each institution is: 10 (U1), 12 (U2), 6 (C).

Surely these outcomes, even if not explicitly identified by library instructors as learning objectives, are welcome results.

It is clear that the educational success outcomes noted by the participants are not mutually exclusive in their meaning. For instance, increased confidence is unquestionably related to students' increased ability to search databases or to use the library more efficiently. However, what is notable about this list of positive educational outcomes generated by the participants is its length and variety, in addition to the degree to which students agreed with one another about the specific outcomes that accrue from library instruction. Table 13.2 provides detail about the numbers of students from each participating institution that make particular claims about the ways in which instruction has contributed to their educational success.

Suggestions for Changes to Instruction
Sixteen students also provided useful feedback in the form of suggestions for various changes to instruction. Some of these suggestions focused on specific skills or databases for which they wanted more instruction. Others made logistical suggestions, such as suggesting that the instructional sessions should be voluntary rather than mandatory (to avoid redundancy for some students), or that all undergraduate students should be required to attend library instruction. Other ideas related to the teaching style of the librarians. For example, three students from the college specifically stated that instructors need to demonstrate more enthusiasm about the content of their instruction. As one student

noted, "[the instruction] could have been a little more exciting, but that's not a traditional library trait, I guess."

Statements about Teaching Methods

A majority (n = 20) of students made unsolicited comments relating to pedagogy (instructional methods) during the interviews; eleven of these were generally negative, while the remaining nine were generally positive. For example, some students whose instructional sessions did not include any active or hands-on learning, noted that continuous lecturing can be very dull. As one student noted, he "spent a lot of time counting tiles." Others felt that their session's instructor had tried to force too much content into the time available, which overwhelmed the students. On the other hand, positive comments noted the value of visual aids to learning, such as live demonstrations of catalog or database use. In addition, those students whose instruction included hands-on practice in a lab context clearly saw the value of that method. The overall demeanor of the instructor was also noted, so where the librarian instructors were viewed as friendly, students came away with a positive attitude about the session and its content. All these reflections about pedagogy indicate that the student respondents were relatively aware of effective teaching techniques.

Discussion

This study was limited in its scope, but provides some evidence for outcomes that may be applicable to a range of academic library contexts. From the testing phase of the study, the most obvious conclusion to be drawn is that student learning in a cognitive sense increases only in some contexts (i.e., for some instructional librarians in particular circumstances). To assume blindly that students are learning from the instruction being provided in many contexts is therefore inappropriate. Assumptions of any kind, drawn without any basis in systematically collected and verified data, whether direct (such as testing or observations of student behavior) or indirect (such as interviewing students about the outcomes of their instructional experiences), to illustrate instructional "success," are clearly unfounded. The results reported here, while offering no insight into other variables potentially influencing student learning (e.g., classroom atmosphere and instructors' pedagogical skills, which were not assessed directly), suggest that success (at least as measured by cognitive variables tested in the pre- and post-tests) appears to relate primarily to the following factor: opportunities for reinforcement of learning objectives, either by providing detailed and aesthetically appealing documentation to support learning, or through additional assignments requiring the application of concepts learned. At minimum, the testing results suggest that learning variables long understood by educationalists to be significant, such as appropriate reinforcement, ought to be considered by information literacy instructors. Indeed, the value of reinforcement has been shown to improve understanding of information literacy concepts.[40]

From the perspectives of the students, asking them directly about their instructional experiences enriches this picture of success. Students reported that they gained knowledge of what is in the library and where to find the materials they are looking for. In addition, one of the most promising outcomes apparent from the data gathered in this study is the increase in confidence, which was the most commonly reported attitudinal outcome relating to educational success. Increased confidence following instruction has been found previously.[41] Because confidence is related to self-efficacy, a concept increasingly recognized as central to success in information seeking in a variety of contexts, this result suggests an important success as a result of the instruction examined here.[42]

Of all the students' responses, the ones that seemed the surest, apart from their willingness to approach librarians, were those that indicated that students had learned a better appreciation for the variety of materials in the library and had learned where to find those materials. This is where there is a clear link between what the instructor-librarians had hoped to have achieved and the actual outcome of the library information session. Nearly all students mentioned in some way that they "knew more" about what was in the library or that they understood "how" to find things in the library. Even in the odd instances of individual students saying that they did not use the library, they still understood what was there and how to get it. The pattern of results suggests that the students are, to a significant extent, getting the message underlying the instructor-librarians' information sessions: that is, the library is a useful, comfortable place with a large amount of information available and helpful librarians. This finding is particularly relevant in light of recent reports that, over the past several years, students in general appear to be seeking less help from library staff.[43]

It may be surprising that students tended not to indicate specific concrete information literacy skills learned, or integrated into their long-term information-seeking behavior. Few students were taught and/or mentioned learning about proper citation style, for example. Considering the importance of developing a search statement and understanding Boolean logic, the number who mentioned it was significantly low and seems to have only really been successfully taught at University 2, where information literacy has been articulated as an essential academic skill. It is of interest to note that the library's section of the university's reporting documents does not include information literacy-related statistics or outcomes (since these were not collected). This brings into question the library's role in supporting the general university objectives at this institution. Nevertheless, students interviewed at that institution described, sometimes at length, their use of Boolean logic and constructing/changing search statements to find the information they need. The overall impression from that group was that the instructor-librarians had very much reinforced the importance of building effective search strategies, and the students definitely took that message home. Difficulties understanding Boolean logic have been identified by other studies.[44] Similarly, a surprisingly small set of students discussed now being able to find more "quality information" or described actual means or methods of improvement, but, at the same time, were quick to say that they were more "effective" and that research was "easier," without necessarily explaining why or how. In the end, they were less able to describe specific instances of using this or that skill, but rather commented on how they "felt" more capable.

Attempting to infer a generalizable "experience" of information literacy from the student interviews is tricky. Certainly, the positive outcomes described by most respondents reflect a new sense of control or personal mastery over their information research efforts and increased comfort level with using the library. This control, which apparently arises from new understandings of, and appreciation for, information and how to retrieve it effectively, would be related to the increased confidence the students noted. In addition, the data collected in the student interviews are consistent with several of Bruce's findings: that the experience of information literacy relates to using information technology, finding information, executing a process (i.e., searching), controlling information, and building personal knowledge bases.[45] One of the student respondents made a point about now being able to assist others, which is another of Bruce's primary findings.

CONCLUSION

Instruction contributed to students' overall educational success and the study identified factors that characterize success in achieving those outcomes from the viewpoints of instructional librarians and from the perspectives of students. These data provide a basis on which to advance instruction toward identifiable, positive outcomes for students in postsecondary institutions. An emphasis on program-long outcomes is essential if librarians are to justify devoting institutional resources to instructional activities. To remain content with positive anecdotal feedback about information literacy instruction, which is currently the usual practice, is both unsatisfactory and unprofessional. In order to substantiate instructional efforts, student learning outcomes must be assessed in a systematic and valid manner, with consideration for the whole context of learning and for the collaborative relationship with department faculty. Furthermore, because this research (both the testing and student interviews) shows so clearly the benefits of sound pedagogy, it is no longer tenable to send librarians or other library staff who lack pedagogical training into courses or workshops with the hope of achieving successful course outcomes for students. Once more, the call to library decisionmakers must go out: successful information literacy instruction requires resources and partnerships. The need for financial resources is obvious, and surely the benefits of skilled human resources are now well documented. If information literacy instruction is to fulfill its promise and is to thrive in Canadian academic institutions, library administrators are obligated to act accordingly.

Despite its small scale, this work demonstrated the value of applying a well-triangulated set of methods to a problem as complex as assessing instructional outcomes. Bringing together the perspectives of instructional librarians, library administrators, and students, with direct evidence of student success by testing, achieves a well-rounded picture of success in information literacy instruction—especially when the evidence ultimately extends for the duration of a student's program and involves the teaching faculty in setting and meeting stated outcomes. That success rests largely on sufficient resourcing of instruction, but also relates to the myriad positive outcomes experienced by the students. Those outcomes are cognitive (increased knowledge), behavioral (e.g., making use of library services and resources; more effective searching skills), and affective (decreased anxiety and increased confidence; greater personal mastery over the information universe). Without a doubt these outcomes present the strongest case for increasing libraries' efforts to bring the benefits of information literacy to their users.

ACKNOWLEDGMENTS

The author thanks the participants in the study—the academic libraries, librarians, library administrators, and students who gave of their time and energies so willingly; and research assistants Stuart Boon, Sandra Anderson, and Sandra Hart for their valuable assistance. The study was supported by a Standard Research Grant from the Social Sciences and Humanities Research Council of Canada (No. 410-2000-0250), to the author.

Notes

1. Stuart L. Smith, *Report: Commission of Inquiry on Canadian University Education* (Ottawa, ON: Association of Universities and Colleges of Canada, 1991), 1.

2. Association of Universities and Colleges of Canada Task Force on the Report of the Commission of Inquiry on Canadian University Education, *Report of the Association of Universities and Colleges of Canada Task Force on the Report of the Commission of Inquiry on Canadian University Education* (Ottawa, ON: Association of University and Colleges of Canada, 1992).

3. Gilles G. Nadeau, *Criteria and Indicators of Quality and Excellence in Colleges and Universities in Canada: Summary of the Three Phases of the Project*, (Winnipeg, MB: Centre for Higher Education Research and Development, University of Manitoba, 1995).

4. Ontario Undergraduate Student Alliance, *Improving Accountability at Canadian Universities: Presented to the Council of Ministers of Education of Canada, Second National Consultation on Education, Edmonton, Alberta, May 1996* (Toronto, ON: Ontario Undergraduate Student Alliance, 1996).

5. Council of Ministers of Education, Canada, *A Report on Public Expectations of Postsecondary Education in Canada* (Toronto, ON: Council of Ministers of Education, Canada, 1999. Available at http://www.cmec.ca/postsec/expectations.en.pdf (accessed November 16, 2004).

6. William A. Bruneau and Donald C. Savage, *Counting Out the Scholars: How Performance Indicators Undermine Universities and Colleges* (Toronto, ON: James Lorimer, 2002), 2.

7. Ibid., 3.

8. Ibid., 220.

9. Canadian Library Association, *Creating an Environment of Continuous Assessment: Practical Approaches for Academic Libraries* (Toronto, ON: Canadian Library Association, 2005). Available at http://www.cla.ca/conference/2005/p2.htm (accessed May 23, 2005).

10. Bob Rae, *Ontario: A Leader in Learning: Report and Recommendations* (Toronto, ON: Government of Ontario, 2005). Available at http://www.raereview.on.ca/en/pdf/finalReport.pdf (accessed April 25, 2005).

11. Paul Anisef and Etta Baichman, *Evaluating Canadian University Education through the Use of Graduate and Employer Surveys*. Research report (Ottawa, ON: Commission of Inquiry on Canadian University Education, 1991).

12. Mount Royal College Academic Development Centre, Curriculum Renewal (Calgary, AB: Mount Royal College Academic Development Centre, 2004). Available at http://www.mtroyal.ca/cr (accessed November 18, 2004).

13. See Edudata Canada home page (Vancouver, BC: University of British Columbia, Faculty of Education, 2004). Available at http://www.edudata.educ.ubc.ca (accessed November 16, 2004).

14. See National Survey of Student Engagement. *Quick Facts* (Bloomington, IN: National Survey of Student Engagement, the Indiana University Center for Postsecondary Research, 2004). Available at http://www.indiana.edu/~nsse/html/quick_facts.htm (accessed November 17, 2004).

15. Statistics Canada and the Council of Ministers of Education, Canada, *Education Indicators in Canada: Report of the Pan-Canadian Education Indicators Program 2003* (Ottawa, ON: Statistics Canada, 2003). Available at http://www.statcan.ca/english/freepub/81-582-XIE/2003001/highlights.htm (accessed April 26, 2005).

16. Council of Ministers of Education, Canada, *Education at a Glance: OECD Indicators: Country Profile for Canada*, 2004 (Toronto, ON: Council of Ministers of Education, Canada, 2004). Available at http://www.cmec.ca/stats/Profile2004.en.pdf (accessed April 26, 2005).

17. Canadian Association of Research Libraries, *The State of Canadian Research Libraries 2001–2002* (Ottawa, ON: Canadian Association of Research Libraries, University of Ottawa, 2003). Available at http://www.carl-abrc.ca/projects/state/state_2001_2002-e.html (accessed April 26, 2005).

18. See *Project SAILS—Project Description* (Kent, OH: Kent State University, Libraries and Media Services, 2004). Available at http://sails.lms.kent.edu/projdescription.html (accessed November 16, 2004).

19. See American Library Association, *Presidential Committee on Information Literacy. Final Report* (Chicago: American Library Association, 1989). Available at http://www.ala.org/ala/acrl/acrlpubs/whitepapers/presidential.htm (accessed May 23, 2005).

20. David Holmes, "Commentary on the 1998–1999 CARL Statistics: An Introduction and Retrospective Overview" (Ottawa, ON: Canadian Association of Research Libraries, University of Ottawa, 2000). Available at http://www.carl-abrc.ca/projects/stats/Commentary_Overview.htm (accessed November 30, 2001).

21. Ethel Auster and Shauna Taylor, *Downsizing in Academic Libraries: The Canadian Experience* (Toronto, ON: University of Toronto Press, 2004).

22. Linda G. Ackerson and Virginia E. Young, "Evaluating the Impact of Library Instruction Methods on the Quality of Student Research," *Research Strategies* 12 (1994): 132–144; Mignon S. Adams, "Evaluation," in *Sourcebook for Bibliographic Instruction*, edited by Katherine Branch and Carolyn Dusenbury (Chicago: Bibliographic Instruction Section, Association of College and Research Libraries, American Library Association, 1993), 45–57; Heidi Julien, "User Education in New Zealand Tertiary Libraries: An International Comparison," *The Journal of Academic Librarianship* 24 (1998): 301–310; Heidi Julien and Stuart Boon, "From the Front Line: Information Literacy Instruction in Canadian Academic Libraries," *Reference Services Review* 30 (2002): 143–149; Heidi Julien and Gloria J. Leckie, "Bibliographic Instruction Trends in Canadian Academic Libraries," *Canadian Journal of Information and Library Science* 22 (1997): 1–15; Nancy Thomas Totten, "Teaching Students to Evaluate Information," *RQ* 29 (1990): 348–354.

23. Julien, "User Education in New Zealand Tertiary Libraries"; Julien and Boon, "From the Front Line"; Julien and Leckie, "Bibliographic Instruction Trends in Canadian Academic Libraries"; Cheryl LaGuardia, *Teaching the New Library: A How-to-Do-It Manual for Planning and Designing Instructional Programs* (New York: Neal-Schuman, 1996); Diana D. Shonrock, *Evaluating Library Instruction: Sample Questions: Forms and Strategies for Practical Use* (Chicago: American Library Association, 1996).

24. Arlene Greer, Lee Weston, and Mary Alm, "Assessment of Learning Outcomes: A Measure of Progress in Library Literacy," *College & Research Libraries* 52 (1991): 549–557; Larry Hardesty, Nicholas P. Lovrich, and James Mannon, "Library-Use Instruction: Assessment of the Long-Term Effects," *College & Research Libraries* 43 (1982): 38–46; John Cornell Selegan, Martha Lou Thomas, and Marie Louise Richman, "Long-Range Effectiveness of Library Use Instruction," *College & Research Libraries* 44 (1983): 476–480.

25. Cecilia López, "Assessment of Student Learning: Challenges and Strategies," *The Journal of Academic Librarianship* 28 (2002): 356–367.

26. Mark Emmons and Wanda Martin, "Engaging Conversation: Evaluating the Contribution of Library Instruction to the Quality of Student Research," *College & Research Libraries* 63 (2002): 545–561.

27. Nancy H. Seamans, "Student Perceptions of Information Literacy: Insights for Librarians," *Reference Services Review* 30 (2002): 112–123.

28. Julien, "User Education in New Zealand Tertiary Libraries"; Julien and Leckie, "Bibliographic Instruction Trends in Canadian Academic Libraries."

29. Robert E. Dugan and Peter Hernon articulated the importance of assessing outcomes rather than outputs. Robert E. Dugan and Peter Hernon, "Outcomes Assessment: Not Synonymous with Inputs and Outputs," *The Journal of Academic Librarianship* 28 (2002): 376–380.

30. Christine Susan Bruce, *The Seven Faces of Information Literacy* (Adelaide, Australia: Auslib Press, 1997).

31. Ibid., 154.

32. Serbrenia J. Sims, *Student Outcomes Assessment: A Historical Review and Guide to Program Development* (New York: Greenwood Press, 1992); Carol M. Boyer and Peter T. Ewell, *State-Based Case Studies of Assessment Initiatives in Undergraduate Education: Chronology of Critical Points* (Denver, CO: Education Commission of the States, 1988).

33. Michael Quinn Patton, *Utilization-Focused Evaluation: The New Century Text*, 3rd ed. (Thousand Oaks, CA: Sage Publications, 1997).

34. Heidi Julien, "Information Literacy Instruction in Canadian Academic Libraries: Longitudinal Trends and International Comparisons," *College & Research Libraries* 61 (2000): 510–523; Julien and Leckie, "Bibliographic Instruction Trends in Canadian Academic Libraries."

35. Julien, "Information Literacy Instruction in Canadian Academic Libraries"; Julien and Boon, "From the Front Line"; Julien and Leckie, "Bibliographic Instruction Trends in Canadian Academic Libraries."

36. Evelyn B. Haynes, "Library-faculty Partnerships in Instruction," in *Advances in Librarianship*, edited by Irene Godden (Toronto, ON: Academic Press, 1996): 191–222; Patricia Iannuzzi, "Faculty Development and Information Literacy: Establishing Campus Partnerships," *Reference Services Review* 26 (1998): 97–116; Marian C. Winner, "Librarians as Partners in the Classroom: An Increasing Imperative," *Reference Services Review* 26 (1998): 25–30.

37. Julien and Boon, "From the Front Line."

38. American Library Association, Association of College & Research Libraries, *Information Literacy Standards for Higher Education* (Chicago: American Library Association, 2000).

39. Elizabeth W. Carter, "'Doing the Best You Can with What You Have': Lessons Learned from Outcomes Assessment," *The Journal of Academic Librarianship* 28 (2002): 36–41.

40. Lilith R. Kunkel, Susan M. Weaver, and Kim N. Cook, "What Do They Know? An Assessment of Undergraduate Library Skills," *The Journal of Academic Librarianship* 22 (1996): 430–434.

41. Bryn Geffert and Robert Bruce, "Whither BI? Assessing Perceptions of Research Skills over an Undergraduate Career," *RQ* 36 (1997): 409–417; David N. King and John C. Ory, "Effects of Library Instruction on Student Research: A Case Study," *College & Research Libraries* 42 (1981): 31–41; Diane Prorak, Tania Gottschalk, and Mike Pollastro, "Teaching Method and Psychological Type in Library Bibliographic Instruction: Effect on Student Learning and Confidence," *RQ* 33 (1994): 484–495.

42. Heidi Julien, "Barriers to Adolescents' Information Seeking for Career Decision Making," *Journal of the American Society for Information Science* 50 (1999): 38–48; Reijo Savolainen, "Network Competence and Information

Seeking on the Internet: From Definitions Towards a Social Cognitive Model," *Journal of Documentation* 58 (2002): 211–226; Thomas Daniel Wilson, "Human Information Behaviour," *Informing Science* 3 (2000): 49–56.

43. Ethelene Whitmire, "A Longitudinal Study of Undergraduates' Academic Library Experiences," *The Journal of Academic Librarianship* 27 (2001): 379–385.

44. Jill Coupe, "Undergraduate Library Skills: Two Surveys at Johns Hopkins University," *Research Strategies* 11 (1993): 188–201; Kunkel, Weaver, and Cook, "What Do They Know?"

45. Bruce, *The Seven Faces of Information Literacy.*

CHAPTER 14

Information Technology and Outcomes Assessment in Higher Education

Renée N. Jefferson

Information technology (IT) is a major factor driving changes in the way students, faculty, and most people communicate, learn, find, and use information.[1] Another major factor is outcomes assessment, whose purpose is to produce change in prescribed areas and to ensure that these changes are accomplished. Separately, the effect of each factor in the higher education environment is profound. Their interconnection further compounds the changes within higher education. IT has changed the faculty-student relationship—altering the ways in which many faculty members teach and the ways in which students learn—as well as the operation of academic support units. For example, with the availability of Web courseware systems (e.g., Blackboard and WebCT), course-related information is distributed directly to students digitally. Faculty may use a Web courseware product simply to post basic course information, or as a teaching platform for all course activities and interactions. Students' access and use of the information depends on faculty's use of the Web courseware product. IT has had an impact on daily operations and altered the focus of many academic support units. Its impact on the institution's academic library has been most profound, especially in the area of library instruction.

Traditionally, academic library instruction included classes on general orientation to library services and resources, and instruction on subject-specific resources. The majority of these resources were located in the library, requiring frequent negotiation of the physical library. Today, with a significant portion of an academic library's resources available online, library users can access library resources 24 hours a day, 7 days a week, 365 days a year from any location around the world. This digital environment knows no country boundaries and highlights the need for library instruction that focuses on issues of ethical use of information, access to information, evaluation of that information, and the conversion of that information into knowledge.

Like other academic support units, the library must incorporate information technology into its instructional goals. Measurement of these goals must evolve from basic outputs (e.g., the number of instructional sessions requested by faculty and the number of students attending these sessions) and basic inputs (e.g., types of resources used) to more complex user information (e.g., the occurrence, level, and impact of learning). The focus of library instruction—information literacy—is becoming learner-centered, focusing on the mastery of specific student learning outcomes shared by programs and the library. Against this background, this chapter examines the impact of IT and outcomes assessment within the higher education environment, with specific focus on the academic library.

INFORMATION TECHNOLOGY IN HIGHER EDUCATION

Higher education in developed countries is "characterized by the convergence of an information rich society, the rapid growth of information technology, and the emergence of learning themes which focus on the learner."[2] Examples of such learning themes include lifelong learning, independent learning, contextualized learning, customized learning, flexible learning, transformative learning, collaborative learning, situated and just-in-time learning.[3] Ross Todd suggests that IT is the key instrument in enabling the implementation of these learning themes.[4]

The focus on learner-centered themes, which requires higher education institutions to re-evaluate and redefine educational approaches, is based on the assumption that "traditional universities will have to change significantly in the direction of flexible delivery through information technology, or risk losing a share of their market to more innovative rivals in the public or private sector."[5] Traditionally, technology was regarded as a supplement to traditional education, rather than a means of transforming it.[6]

Miriam Drake, who discusses the transformative abilities of IT, defines information technology as information logistics, that is, the storage, transmission, receipt, retrieval, and manipulation of data in all forms, including voice, text, photographs, graphics, and multimedia.[7] Her perspective recognizes the availability of a variety of technological formats in which to store and transmit different types of information. Those various technological formats and information types affect all academic units involved in the learning process.

Within academic units, information technologies (e.g., computer and telecommunications) influence the dissemination of information between faculty and students. For example, faculty may rely on presentation software (e.g., PowerPoint) or Web courseware systems for their teaching. Students may submit course assignments using electronic mail or a Web courseware system. These technologies provide faculty and students with many options for facilitating the learning process.

INFORMATION TECHNOLOGY IN ACADEMIC LIBRARIES

Information technology has changed academic library services and processes in a number of ways. Examples include the development of national bibliographic utilities such as the Online Computer Library Center (OCLC) in the 1970s, the automation of card catalogs in the 1980s, and the creation of new forms of online publications in the 1990s.[8] These changes have been adaptive, rather than fundamental.[9] Processes and routines (e.g., online cataloging and online interlibrary loan) have been adapted without fundamentally changing the content of the work, the structure of the library organization, or the purpose of the library.[10] Departure from adaptation requires planning for the future.

As Jan A. Baltzer declares, "libraries need a new approach to information technology that can refocus staff...toward a vision of how technology can enable the library to provide newer, richer types of services to an increasingly diverse population."[11] To accomplish this task, academic libraries need to develop and implement technology plans. Having such plans assists libraries in aligning their goals with those of their institutions. The plan can help an academic library identify and prioritize needed technologies to support the teaching, learning, and research needs of its users, as well as library programs and services.[12]

Both strengths and weaknesses concerning technological implementations need to be identified.

Most important, a technology plan can assist libraries in measuring, evaluating, and assessing progress by helping to answer questions related to accountability. Such questions include

- Are the technologies effectively applied to meet the educational mission of the library and to enhance the competencies of students in using information and communication technologies?
- Are service and administrative operations improved through increased efficiencies and productivity?[13]

The question then focuses on the components of a technology plan which addresses user needs, rationale, the mission statement, key challenges, strategies, goals, objectives, implementation/action plan, and evaluation, measurements, and assessments.[14] The library's technology plan should supplement and/or complement the technology plans of other academic units and the institution.

In addition to the development of an information technology plan, the application of information technology in libraries has necessitated the development of library computer-use policies. Like the information technology plan, computer-use policies may supplement and/or complement those of other units, or the institution. Jason Vaughan proposes two primary reasons why an academic library should have its own policy.[15] A library computer-use policy adds visibility to whatever higher-level policy may be in place, and it reflects rules governing local library resources that are housed and managed by the library.[16] While broader university policies generally apply to all users of computing technology, local library policies can work to address all users of the library PCs, and make distinctions as to when, where, and what each group can use.[17]

The advancement of IT has often forged a union between academic computing services and the academic library. Both units support the mission of the institution by creating and implementing goals to meet the needs of the academic community. However, technological advances have enabled both units to examine their goals, and notice the similarities in those goals. Academic libraries and computing services are on a path toward functional convergence as they focus on "managing a diverse and rich body of information and making such information useful in research, teaching, and learning."[18]

OUTCOMES ASSESSMENT IN HIGHER EDUCATION

Accreditation organizations within higher education expect academic institutions to provide clear and unambiguous evidence of student learning. For more than a decade, these organizations have modified their requirement that institutions collect input and output measures related to faculty, courses, and books. They now embrace the idea that institutions should focus on outcome measures related to what students learn.[19] In 1998, Bonnie Gratch Lindauer reported that all seven regional accrediting organizations included in their standards or supplemental publications statements about the importance of student outcomes assessment.[20] It is evident that outcomes assessment has become a key component in demonstrating institutional effectiveness, efficiency, and quality.

Increasingly, institutional and program accrediting bodies expect colleges and universities to produce data-driven evidence of the achievement of intended outcomes to reflect and document institutional effectiveness.[21] Objective means of assessment are becoming more common as higher education institutions respond to requirements put forth by regional and program accrediting bodies.[22] These requirements include information on what students learn, how well they learn, measures and procedures used to determine program effectiveness, evidence that demonstrates effectiveness, and the use of the evidence to improve performance.[23] They require institutions and programs of study to consider multiple data collection methods to produce different, but complementary, evidence of student learning.

Academic support units are often held to similar or the same standards as their parent institutions. Outcomes assessment places responsibility on all institutional units to provide evidence of their contributions to meeting educational outcomes and to incorporate outcomes assessment in organizational planning and improvement.[24] Lindauer states that the teaching-learning role of academic libraries is well established, as are the expectations of accreditation organizations that libraries connect their evaluation of collections, resources, and services to educational outcomes.[25] In 2002, she conducted content analyses of the standards and pertinent supplemental documentation of eight higher education accrediting commissions.[26] Overall trends in accreditation that affect libraries and information resources were identified, and observations and recommendations for the library community were made.[27]

Important trends in the accreditation documents related to libraries include emphases on goal-based assessment using mission-driven standards to define educational quality, the assessment of student learning, and information literacy as a specific student learning outcome. A key observation and recommendation for libraries include the collaboration of librarians with faculty in teaching and evaluating information literacy skills.[28] These findings illustrate the importance of student learning outcomes in fulfilling the mission of academic institutions.

Outcomes

Higher education distinguishes between two types of outcomes: *student outcomes* and *student learning outcomes*. Student outcomes, which are really outputs, refer to aggregate statistics on groups of students (e.g., graduation rates, retention rates, and employment rates for a graduating class). Student learning outcomes encompass assorted attributes and abilities, both cognitive and affective, that reflect how the experiences at an institution supported student development as individuals. *Cognitive outcomes* include the demonstrable acquisition of specific knowledge and skills, while *affective outcomes* probe how the college experience influenced students' values, goals, attitudes, self-concepts, world views, and behaviors.[29]

Bruce T. Fraser, Charles R. McClure, and Emily H. Leahy found it important to distinguish between *outcomes of interest*, *desired outcomes*, and *actual outcomes*. Outcomes of interest are ones—relatively few in number—on which a particular college or university concentrates at a given time; the selection reflects the complex, ever-changing array of relevant, local values. For the outcomes of interest, desired outcomes are the aspirational levels of achievement or production that an institution sets in advance to determine whether it has attained future success on some important dimension of its operation. Actual outcomes are the real achievement or production levels for an outcome of interest as measured at a given time.[30]

In their review of different definitions of outcomes, John C. Bertot and McClure found common elements. In general, they believe that outcomes:

- "Include the notion of an impact, benefit, difference, or change in a user, group, or institution based on the use of or involvement with a library service or resource;

- Are predetermined based on a service/resource planning process in which the library engages to produce desired service/resource outcomes through the setting of service/resource goals and objectives; and

- Involve measuring and demonstrating the extent to which library services/resources meet the anticipated outcomes determined by the library or imposed by the community the library serves (e.g., academic institution, county, or city)."[31]

Student learning outcomes reflect how library users have changed as a result of their contact with the institution's library and its resources, services, and programs.[32] Each library must identify learning outcomes for its users, and assess the resources needed to meet the outcomes. In partnership with academic programs and the teaching faculty of those programs, librarians need to assess the impact of teaching on learning. Libraries that include outcomes assessment as a part of their instructional programs join with the teaching faculty to address issues such as whether the academic performance of students improve through their contact with the library, whether the library's bibliographic instruction program results in a high level of "information literacy" among students, and whether faculty members who collaborate with the library's staff are more likely to view the library collection as an integral part of stated outcomes.[33] To address these issues, libraries, often with cooperation from teaching faculty, choose appropriate direct and indirect methods for data collection. They also must decide how the results of the data collection will be used to improve learning as defined in student learning outcomes.

Elizabeth W. Carter notes that assessment takes time, effort, and planning. It requires buy-in and support of one's own department and department head, colleagues in other departments, and the administration.[34] This view is supported by Peter Hernon and Robert E. Dugan, who point out that outcomes assessment does not occur in a vacuum; it is interrelated to the accomplishment of an assessment plan.[35] Once the outcomes have been set, librarians and teaching faculty will need to establish a schedule for assessment (e.g., at the end of a specified semester, at the conclusion of a set of required courses, or upon graduation), determine who will be assessed (e.g., those in certain programs or departments, culturally diverse students, or students completing specific program requirements), determine who will do the assessment, and link the results back to the assessment plan.[36] These steps illustrate the cyclical nature of outcomes assessment (see Figure 1.1). An outcomes assessment plan is not static. It requires continual development, implementation, evaluation, and review.

INFORMATION TECHNOLOGY AND OUTCOMES ASSESSMENT IN ACADEMIC LIBRARIES

The academic library supports the instructional mission of its institution. Integral to this role is the assessment of information literacy skills. According to the *Information Literacy Competency Standards for Higher Education* that the Association of College and Research Libraries developed, information literacy includes the acquisition of information and communications technology (ICT) skills.[37] The information literate student "recognize[s] when information is needed and...[has] the ability to locate, evaluate, and use effectively the needed information."[38] ICT "skills enable [students] to use computers, software applications, databases, and other technologies to achieve a wide variety of academic, work-related, and personal goals."[39] There is a definite link between students' acquisition of information literacy and ICT skills.

The *Standards* serve as guidelines for faculty, librarians, and others in developing local methods for measuring student learning in the context of an institution's unique mission.[40] Outcomes related to ICT skills are included in the *Standards*. Academic librarians, as well as teaching faculty, should include these skills in their outcomes and assessment of information literacy. One assessment framework that will assist librarians in this endeavor is a scoring rubric. In educational settings, a rubric is a set of formal guidelines used to rate student work throughout a program of study; it measures their advancement to graduation.[41] Sandra Bloomberg and Melaine McDonald offer a rubric for assessing the increase in competency of students with technology, specifically their ability to use ICT proficiently and to access information ethically.[42]

In the context of using rubrics, data collection focuses on the extent to which the particular part of the rubric has been achieved. For example, the rubric for ICT might identify an "intermediate level" that students should attain. How well have they attained those particular expectations? What modifications in the learning process might be necessary? These are the types of questions that merit examination through the use of courseware and classroom performance system software (e.g., E-Instruction). To illustrate, a librarian can use a courseware system to administer pre- and post-tests. The pre-test is placed on the system, where students can access and take the pre-test. Information from the pre-test is used to create or modify the information literacy instruction session. The instruction session is conducted in person or virtually using features of the system such as video streaming, discussion forums, or chat rooms. The post-test is administered. Results show whether students learned the concepts presented during instruction, or whether additional instruction is necessary.

If modifications are required in the learning process, courseware systems may or may not permit their immediate identification. However, classroom performance systems are designed to provide instant feedback from students during instruction.[43] Feedback is provided using remote control devices such as "clickers" and a portable receiver.[44] The clickers communicate with receivers by infrared or radio signals which feed the results to the instructor's or librarian's computer. Classroom performance systems can be used to give quizzes or tests that can be graded automatically and immediately.[45] With this capability, a librarian will be able to gauge a student's comprehension of a concept and make changes during the instruction session.

Many academic libraries provide instruction classrooms with individual computer workstations for students and an instructor's workstation for the librarian. The availability of computer workstations makes it easy for librarians to create exercises for students to participate actively in the instruction session. When librarians use computers in the learning process, assumptions often are made about a student's computer technology skills. These assumptions include basic computer operation skills such as using a keyboard and mouse or downloading information to a file. Students who possess basic computer operation skills will be able to focus on the information literacy skills being taught during the instruction session. Those who do not possess these skills will be likely to focus on getting the computer to work at all.

The use of an instructor's workstation in classrooms with individual computer workstations may hinder communication between the librarian (or instructor) and students. For example, a librarian who is demonstrating the use of an online database will need to sit or stand at the computer workstation. This position may make it difficult to communicate visually with students. ICT may be used to facilitate interpersonal communication between the librarian (or instructor) and student. For example, SMART Boards (or interactive whiteboards) remove librarians from behind the instructor's workstation and permit them to maintain eye contact with students.[46] Tablet PCs (notebook computers that can permit access and use of online resources and computer applications) enable students to become active, mobile participants in the instruction session.[47] Using this technology, a librarian may create a performance-based exercise that requires a student to locate materials in different sections of the library. The student can take along a Tablet PC and be able to access the librarian (through email or chat) and the library's online resources while trying to locate the materials.

CONCLUSION

To keep abreast of technological advances, it is important for academic libraries to have technology plans that identify and prioritize needed technologies to support the teaching, learning, and research needs of faculty and students.[48] When developing or revising these plans, libraries need to consider and include the application of technology to the learning outcomes assessment process. Technology is a means to the end. It can assist in conducting outcomes assessment (e.g., placing student work in digital portfolios), and can be used to improve pedagogy (e.g., using SMART Boards and clickers which assist with content decision making during instruction). Too often technology plans discuss what is in the library's instruction room, but not how to use the technology to meet specific learning outcomes.

Higher education's focus on outcomes assessment asks for all institutional units, including the library, to provide evidence of their contributions to achieving desired educational outcomes. Academic libraries must link the evaluation of their collections, resources, and services to educational outcomes.[49] For example, how does collection development advance the accomplishment of stated outcomes? Outcomes assessment provides a mechanism by which all institutional units can plan, develop, implement, and evaluate student learning outcomes.

Notes

1. Miriam A. Drake, "Technological Innovation and Organizational Change," *Journal of Library Administration* 19, no. 3/4 (1993): 39–53.

2. Ross Todd, "WWW, Critical Literacies and Learning Outcomes," *Teacher Librarian* 26, no. 2 (1998), 16.

3. Ibid.

4. Ibid.

5. Jim Cleary, "Academic Libraries, Networking and Technology: Some Recent Developments," *The Australian Library Journal* 43 (1994), 236.

6. Ibid.

7. Drake, "Technological Innovation and Organizational Change," 39.

8. Susan Rosenblatt, "Information Technology Investments in Research Libraries," *Educom Review* 34, no. 4 (1999): 28–32.

9. Ibid.

10. Ibid.

11. Jan A. Baltzer, "Consider the Four-Legged Stool as You Plan for Information Technology," *Computers in Libraries* 40, no. 4 (2000), 42.

12. Robert E. Dugan, "Information Technology Plans," *The Journal of Academic Librarianship* 28 (2002): 152–156.

13. Ibid., 154–155.

14. Ibid.

15. Jason Vaughan, "Policies Governing Use of Computing Technology in Academic Libraries," *Information Technology and Libraries* 23, no. 4 (2004): 153–167.

16. Ibid., 153.

17. Ibid., 155.

18. Cleary, "Academic Libraries, Networking and Technology," 239.

19. Kenneth R. Smith, "New Roles and Responsibilities for the University Library: Advancing Student Learning Through Outcomes Assessment," *Journal of Library Administration* 35, no. 4 (2001): 29–36.

20. Bonnie Gratch Lindauer, "Defining and Measuring the Library's Impact on Campuswide Outcomes," *College & Research Libraries* 59 (1998), 549.

21. Ronald L. Baker, "Evaluating Quality and Effectiveness: Regional Accreditation Principles and Practices," *The Journal of Academic Librarianship* 28 (2002): 3–7.

22. Elizabeth Choinski, Amy E. Mark, and Missy Murphy, "Assessment with Rubrics: An Efficient and Objective Means of Assessing Student Outcomes in an Information Resources Class," *portal: Libraries and the Academy* 3 (2003): 563–575.

23. Peter Hernon and Robert E. Dugan, *An Action Plan for Outcomes Assessment in Your Library* (Chicago: American Library Association, 2002), 2.

24. Lindauer, "Defining and Measuring the Library's Impact on Campuswide Outcomes," 548.

25. Ibid., 549.

26. Bonnie Gratch Lindauer, "Comparing the Regional Accreditation Standards: Outcomes Assessment and Other Trends," *The Journal of Academic Librarianship* 28 (2002): 14–25.

27. Ibid., 14.

28. Ibid., 19–20.

29. Hernon and Dugan, *An Action Plan for Outcomes Assessment in Your Library*, 3.

30. Bruce T. Fraser, Charles R. McClure, and Emily H. Leahy, "Toward a Framework for Assessing Library and Institutional Outcomes," *portal: Libraries and the Academy* 2 (2002): 505–528.

31. John Carlo Bertot and Charles R. McClure, "Outcomes Assessment in the Networked Environment: Research Questions, Issues, Considerations, and Moving Forward," *Library Trends* 51 (2003), 594.

32. Hernon and Dugan, *An Action Plan for Outcomes Assessment in Your Library*, 31.

33. Ibid.

34. Elizabeth W. Carter, " 'Doing the Best You Can with What You Have': Lessons Learned from Outcomes Assessment," *The Journal of Academic Librarianship* 28 (2002): 36–41.

35. Hernon and Dugan, *An Action Plan for Outcomes Assessment in Your Library*, 77.

36. Ibid.

37. American Library Association. Association of College and Research Libraries, *Information Literacy Competency Standards for Higher Education* (Chicago: American Library Association, 2000), 5, 6.

38. American Library Association. "Presidential Committee on Information Literacy" (Chicago: American Library Association, 1989). Available at http://www.ala.org/acrl/legalis.html (accessed May 12, 2005).

39. American Library Association, Association of College and Research Libraries, *Information Literacy Competency Standards for Higher Education*, 3.

40. Ibid., 6.

41. Michael Simkins, "Designing Great Rubrics," *Technology & Learning* 20 (1999): 23–30.

42. Sandra Bloomberg and Melaine McDonald, "Assessment: A Case Study of Synergy," in *Outcomes Assessment in Higher Education: Views and Perspectives*, edited by Peter Hernon and Robert E. Dugan (Westport, CT: Libraries Unlimited, 2004), 259–289.

43. Center for Instructional Technologies, "Classroom Performance Systems Frequently Asked Questions" (Austin: University of Texas, n.d.). Available at http://www.utexas.edu/academic/cit/howto/labinstructions/cpsfaqs.html (accessed May 22, 2005).

44. Ibid., section 1, paragraph 2.

45. Elizabeth Zuckerman, "Interactive 'Clickers' Changing Classrooms," Associated Press, Domestic News Section, May 13, 2005. Available from Lexis/Nexis Academic (accessed June 24, 2005).

46. SMART Board is an interactive whiteboard that transforms a computer and a projector into a digital tool for whole-class teaching and learning.

Teachers and students can access any computer application, including the Internet and CD-ROMs, by touching the whiteboard's large, touch-sensitive surfaces. They can write over applications in digital ink and then edit, save, print, or post their notes online for future reference or absent students.

47. Norman Oder, "Tablet PCs Free Librarians," netConnect, Departments Briefings' Section, October 15, 2003. Available from Lexis/Nexis Academic (accessed June 24, 2005). Tablet PCs are notebook computers that are a little smaller than a legal pad. About one inch thick, the devices weigh only 3.2 pounds and can make use of wireless access.

48. Dugan, "Information Technology Plans," 152.

49. Lindauer, "Defining and Measuring the Library's Impact on Campuswide Outcomes," 548.

CHAPTER 15

Some Techniques for Outcomes Assessment

Gloriana St. Clair and Carole A. George

M any universities and colleges pride themselves on making decisions based on data. Scientific methods (i.e., observation, hypothesis testing, prediction, and experimentation leading to conclusion) that pervade many disciplines on campus also permeate administrative thinking. The standard for accepting the results of studies is high and credibility must be earned through well-designed, -executed, and -presented work. In some of these institutions, total quality management training was introduced throughout campus in the 1990s. While the trappings and vocabulary of that approach may no longer be evident, the core (basing decisions on data rather than intuition) remains. The current culture of assessment is consonant with a focus on the use of evidence that is not anecdotal. In this culture, university libraries must work with faculty and other campus colleagues to develop assessment measures on which to plan, implement, and evaluate their programs, services, and collections.

Of the many measurable aspects of learning, outcomes are the more difficult to assess when compared with metrics such as inputs and outputs. Many universities have long been focused on student learning as a goal. For instance, at Carnegie Mellon University, in 1939 to 1940, the Carnegie Plan articulated a commitment to empowering students to become lifelong learners. The university's adherence to that goal remains, as Vice Provost for Education Indira Nair notes, "Today, the educational mission of Carnegie Mellon remains 'to serve our students by teaching them leadership and problem-solving skills, and our values of quality, ethical behavior, responsibility to society and commitment to work.'"[1] More and more, in every college, this commitment to learning manifests itself in discussion of and allegiance to learning outcomes.

In western Pennsylvania, the focus on student learning outcomes has been sharpened by the decision of the region's accrediting organization, Middle States Commission on Higher Education, to begin to judge libraries on their partnerships with institutional faculty in addressing information literacy skills of students. This is a bold change in focus, and a number of smaller institutions in the region have had to move quickly to meet this new requirement. The purpose of this chapter is to explore and describe some assessment processes and techniques related to student learning outcomes, including planning and goal setting, information literacy, information behavior, continual review, graduate student interviews, and think-aloud protocols.

PLANNING AND GOAL-SETTING

Steve Hiller and Jim Self suggest the following reasons for developing a comprehensive assessment plan: accountability and justification, improvement of services, comparison with others, identifying changing patterns, identifying questionable services, and marketing and promotion.[2] They maintain that libraries can develop effective assessment measures by focusing on users, collecting measurable results, and using both quantitative and qualitative techniques.

Collecting measurable data over time provides a basis for comparison to determine the need for improvements and measure progress towards goals for services and collections. Collecting data in standard format among a group of libraries provides a basis for comparison of one library or library system with others that are similar. These comparisons provide a standard by which libraries can assess progress towards goals and strategically plan for the future. Many libraries have followed such a model: strategic planning to develop goals, and development of assessment measures to collect and evaluate information systematically.

Strategic planning and goal-setting begin with the institution's vision and mission, echoed by the library's vision and mission, which in turn direct decisions, strategies, and assessment measures. In many libraries the dean or director of libraries and a library governing body lead this process with input from library faculty and staff. For example, Carnegie

Mellon's library assessment activities are incorporated within each departmental program and activity.

With a focus on student learning through library experiences (both formal, structured activities and informal, as-needed activities) many libraries are beginning to develop assessment measures for student learning outcomes. The focus on outcomes of programs and services is a major element in a library's culture of assessment. While *inputs* describe the materials that libraries provide for their users (e.g., electronic and paper collections, services, equipment, and staff) and *outputs* measure the work that has been completed (e.g., the number of books that have been circulated or reference queries that have been answered), *outcomes* describe users and how they might be affected by or changed as a result of their experiences with the libraries.[3] Outcome measures might describe what users have learned and how their information literacy abilities have improved as a direct result of their experience with the library. Outcomes assessment transfers the focus from what and how library collections and services are used to how libraries have had an impact on student learning and supported students' artistic, research, and scholarly work—and what changes can be made to improve those efforts.

INFORMATION LITERACY

A library information literacy plan may have one or more drivers, such as faculty who continually lament their students' declining critical thinking and information literacy skills, or an accreditation program, with its required assessment standard of student learning outcomes. The plan must include defined learning objectives. To develop students' fluency in obtaining, evaluating, and using information in a manner that most effectively supports research and educational pursuits, the library must identify and recruit campus partners who can help plan and achieve well-rounded learning objectives. After all, information literacy is not the sole responsibility of the library. The plan therefore must lead to a partnership with the teaching faculty so that learning objectives applicable to *all* students can be achieved.

Both formal and informal assessment measures may be used to determine how the information literacy program has affected students' use of information in support of their research, as well as to document the effectiveness of the program, and to plan for future classes. Both librarians and teaching faculty should be involved in setting these measures and gathering, interpreting, and applying the results. An information literacy program should evolve through an ongoing deployment/assessment cycle that will change to meet the changing needs of students, technology, and education.

INFORMATION BEHAVIOR

Concern about students' ethical use of information is high on campuses nationally and surfaces in many different venues. For over a decade, students in higher education have been introduced to the information environment through a variety of methods. At Carnegie Mellon, this takes the form of a two-week mixed computer/peer student teacher program. The goal of this program and similar ones nationwide includes educating students about evaluating information sources and the ethical use of information. However, the easy availability of information sources and need for information quickly often results in students' misuse of information. This section examines the universities' efforts in guiding students in ethical and reliable information choices and the students' information behavior when using and choosing information, including illegally downloading music, plagiarism, and reliance on Google as the primary source for identifying information.

Colleges and universities are under strict scrutiny from the music industry, which believes that students are illegally downloading music files, and which often targets universities and prosecutes students. In April 2005, the Recording Industry Association of America (RIAA) sued 405 students at 18 colleges and universities for illegally distributing music and movies. Many colleges and universities generally limit the amount of bandwidth that students and faculty can use daily and may suspend students' network privileges if they are caught illegally downloading music.[4] It is difficult, of course, to distinguish between legal downloading, using a service such as iTunes, and illegal downloading, without violating student privacy. Some universities have responded by establishing licenses that allow legal access to music for their students.

Many universities, including Carnegie Mellon, spend "a great deal of effort in educating students about copyright law. Carnegie Mellon, for example, teaches an entire section of that in a course that every student is required to take."[5] It might be argued that the arrest for copyright violation of students who have taken such a course indicates that the learning outcome was not met, because the students did not act in accordance with the course's teachings. That would be a simplistic interpretation inasmuch as students are able to rationalize their behaviors around music downloading in terms of their own needs and desires even though they are aware that they may be breaking the law.

Computers do make all kinds of copying absurdly easy. Holders of intellectual property rights (e.g., RIAA, the movie industry, and publishers) have been quick to try to bar technologies such as videocassette recorders and TiVo. Both the music industry and the others involved continue to try to develop copyright protection technologies. Clearly, universities and libraries are responsible for teaching students the laws. Reasonable learning outcomes, though, should consider focusing on knowledge, rather than behavior, as an indicator of success.

In the case of plagiarism, many institutions are using software that identifies papers whose wording too closely matches that of Web sources. Some faculty urge students to run these programs themselves on their own work so that the students themselves can see whether they have used sources improperly. This creative approach engages students in the process of checking their own work and managing their use of source materials to conform to ethical standards.

College and university faculty want students to use more than Google to identify information for their assignments. They often report returning papers to students when they believe that all sources have been found on the Web, rather than in more reliable places. Engineering and science faculty have been particularly strident in their criticism of student use of Google when they should be using SciFinder Scholar and other science and engineering indices. Both discipline faculty and librarians must take responsibility for establishing learning outcomes that focus on students' use of appropriate information in their projects and papers. Accrediting organizations (e.g., the Middle States Commission on Higher Education) clearly believe that the task of ensuring that students understand copyright and other intellectual property laws belongs at least partially to the library. Examples of assessment criteria typically contain three main tasks: understanding the ethical, legal, and socioeconomic issues around information; following copyright and other intellectual property laws; and acknowledging use of information sources.[6] These issues should be part of every college and university's information literacy efforts as both departmental faculty and librarians examine how students' knowledge, skills, abilities, and ethics progress throughout their program of study. Progress is cast in terms of outcomes and scoring rubrics that offer benchmarks to show what students have mastered at different points of their program.

CONTINUAL REVIEW

Tracking, charting, counting, testing, and studying are meaningless without follow-up activities that provide insights, produce improvements, or support planning and decision making. For assessment measures to be used successfully, information must be collected and reviewed at regular intervals to evaluate progress towards goals and make changes if necessary. For example, at Carnegie Mellon University, review of assessment measures and planning and goal-setting is accomplished in the context of regular advisory board visits. Consistent with the university's assessment program, the library advisory board is composed of trustees and distinguished librarians. The advisory board reviews the library's goals and programs on a multi-year cycle. Formal and informal feedback from the advisory board is essential to establishing library goals. The advisory board recently suggested establishing a more open connection between assessment efforts and actions, repeating a standard evaluation instrument enabling national comparisons, and self-testing with an instrument that measures general student satisfaction.

With input from faculty and staff, results of assessment measures can inform the program planning phase in order to revise and make changes as needed to improve the program. In addition, libraries, working together with departmental faculty, need to know where to focus efforts; that is, what program of instruction or assistance has been most effective in improving student learning. Faculty and librarians need to know how to develop a total environment that supports student learning—what resources and services are highly desired by students. Only in partnership with faculty can information literacy across diverse disciplines be accomplished. Feedback from students provides insight. For example, at Carnegie Mellon, library staff conducted graduate student interviews and think-aloud protocols to generate feedback about students' information literacy skills as well as obstacles to learning, what resources students rely on, and what library efforts are most effective in improving students' skills. Information from these studies not only provides feedback on learning outcomes, but also on where and how to improve the program.

GRADUATE STUDENT INTERVIEWS

In an effort to gain insight into graduate students' information-seeking behavior and learning outcomes, the library has conducted over 100 graduate student interviews (one-to-one interviews with graduate students representing all campus departments), with a projected follow-up study via think-aloud protocols to observe student behavior directly as they complete a task related to information literacy and that requires use of library resources. These methods, discussed in the following sections, involve interaction with students and observation to gather feedback about their experiences as they seek information using library resources. Graduate student interviews and think-aloud protocols are reports and observations of students' experiences as they use the library to support their coursework and inquiry process. Students' explicit reports on how the library experience contributed to their learning provide a measure of outcomes (e.g., "Selects efficient and effective approaches for accessing the information needed from the investigative method of information retrieval system").[7]

Methodology

Using a qualitative research approach, the library designed face-to-face structured interviews—one student interviewed by one library interviewer. Qualitative methodology was chosen because it provides a deeper understanding of the issues and details, enabling insight into the process. Sharan B. Merriam asserts that "The key philosophical assumption . . . upon which all types of qualitative research are based is the view that reality is constructed by individuals interacting with social worlds."[8] She explains that interviewing is necessary when direct observation is not possible or reasonable, or when one is interested in "past events that are impossible to replicate."[9] In this case, the interview process was undertaken to gain understanding about the reality of students' information-seeking behavior over the course of their studies at university.

Procedure

The graduate students interviewed represented more than thirty university departments and seven colleges, varied as to gender, first language, years of study, and discipline. The interviews explored how graduate students seek and obtain information to support their research and studies with respect to their research process, methods of obtaining information, preferred sources, and their searching and obtaining procedures.[10] The research design was based on the belief that graduate students:

- Have no organized approach to seeking information to support their research and studies;
- Rely heavily on electronic materials, and selection of sources is influenced by convenience and speed, thereby eliminating much high quality information; and
- Have not yet developed personal resources and professional networks to support their research.

The study examined students' use of the Internet and other sources of information; the role of professors, advisors, peers, and outside contacts; and obstacles and influences (time, money, and convenience). The interviews measured student learning outcomes (e.g., "Uses various search systems to retrieve information in a variety of formats")[11] and provided insight into the roles that the library, librarians, and library resources play in students' search. In addition, student interviews revealed reasons why students might search outside of reliable library resources, problems they had using and finding library information, and ways that the library could accommodate students' research preferences.

A brief electronic survey helped to formulate the questions for subsequent one-on-one interviews. The Web-based survey, which included both closed- and open-ended items, was completed by graduate students (748) who responded to an e-mail invitation (3,012). Though no incentives were offered, the survey had a 25% response rate. Results of the online survey indicated that:

- The three most important features used to determine search strategy were quality of information (93%), convenience (67%), and speed (46%);
- When searching for information, students went first to an Internet search engine (80%), then to the library Web site (41%), then to professors, librarians, and classmates (38%), and only then to the paper library (33%);
- Consistent with their search pattern, when asked to rate *convenience of use*, students responded that online search engines (87%)

and the library Web site (41%) were convenient, and professors, librarians, and classmates (44%) were somewhat convenient; and

- Students did not make a distinction between searching and obtaining resources.

The interview design was based on previous research and the results of the online survey. The script included questions that would:

- Explore why students chose the Internet first, what information they found, and how they used it;
- Develop insight into students' searching procedures, which resources were used and which were reliable choices; and
- Determine what factors influenced students' research patterns and resource choices.

Results

Though the library is still in the process of completing its final analysis and report, an early look at the results indicates several influences on student learning as well as areas in which the library could improve collections and services.

Contributing Factors

Factors that influence student learning include convenience/inconvenience of information resources, knowledge/lack of knowledge, time constraints, and information overload. Convenience is the major reason that students turn first to the Internet, while perceived inconvenience influences students' nonuse of library resources and interlibrary loan services. Lack of knowledge about library databases, interlibrary loan services, and available libraries leads to nonuse of these services. Newer students, especially, reported that though they attend orientation sessions, they are either overwhelmed by the amount of information they receive or forget what is taught. One student said, "If you don't know what it is that you're supposed to be using to find something...if you don't know that tool already, you don't seem to ever use it."

The time that students have to complete a task also influences what resources are used. Students reported not using interlibrary loan because they always need material quickly. They bypass the library because parking, selecting books, or photocopying articles takes too much time. They avoid learning new tools because of lack of time.

Web Resources: Library and Non-library Internet

Results indicated that graduate students overwhelmingly prefer online, electronic, full-text resources. With time constraints caused by juggling school, work, and family, students turn to Web resources, accessing both library or non-library sites. One student said: "If I didn't have the Web then I probably wouldn't be . . . having enough time to do a job or something like that because I'd have to physically go to the library and do the research; the Web significantly cuts down the time."

Having a good understanding of how and why students use online resources can prepare libraries to make decisions regarding how and what services to offer on the Web, encouraging use of the library's reliable resources. Graduate students reported on their reasons for using various online resources:

- Online, full-text materials are fast; printouts are cheap (or free) and provide high-quality images; online information is easy to search and store; digital resources are available at all hours.

- Students search the non-library Web to get a general idea about their research area, find basic information, and explore search terms.

- Students use non-library Web resources such as Amazon.com and Google because they feel that these sites have superior search functionality to library search engines.

- Students in technical fields go to the non-library Web for current information, because authors in those disciplines often publish their own papers online. Other students rely heavily on library databases because they consider them to be reliable sources.

Improvements: Strengthening the Program

A major reason to assess student learning outcomes with respect to information literacy is to improve the ability of students to become information literate. The library needs to understand its role in this process. Getting a baseline picture of the use of resources and services puts the library in a good position to measure at a later time the effect of introducing planned change. In addition, the library needs to know what formal and informal, planned and as-needed instructional sessions have been viewed as beneficial by students and the faculty who teach them. Assessing student learning outcomes places the library in a better position to know where to focus efforts in strengthening the information literacy program. Insight gained from the interviews will be used during the planned process of program improvement.

Faculty input to the issue of student learning about discipline resources came from a number of ongoing partnerships. The library head discussed the issue with deans and department heads while the information literacy program leader listened to heads, liaison librarians, and other colleagues. A center for excellence in learning actively contributed to the program design.

The library gained more insight into how best to strengthen the information literacy program and where to focus efforts by examining the students' responses regarding the library's instructional sessions. Influences reported by students included structured library learning sessions and informal interactions provided on an as-needed basis. Orientation and tours, usually offered at the beginning of each semester, guide students through the library and introduce them to general resources. Students reported that these information sessions were helpful as an introduction to the library.

Discipline-specific, librarian-instructed classes help students learn about resources and databases in their field of study. Students reported that cheat sheets and worksheets from these classes were valuable and held their value over time. As some students explained, "We had a librarian come into one of our classes one time...for an hour. That's where I got that cheat sheet and that was so beneficial. And I started using the library after that."

Once the full report of the graduate student interviews is finalized, the types of themes noted in this section will be discussed with library employees and the faculty. The results will be included in planning and goal-setting to improve the learning environment, search skills, and learning of students. According to the Middle States Commission on Higher Education, identifying and measuring student learning outcomes is only part of the improvement process.[12] Discussing and analyzing results of outcomes measures with faculty, staff, and students informs the design of follow-up procedures, including future program planning and reassessment to measure improvement. For example, when graduate student interviews are completed, reassessment in the form of interviews will be conducted using a smaller sample of graduate students. Results of the follow-up interviews will be used to measure student progress and improvement in outcome measures in information literacy.

By understanding the factors that obstruct as well as contribute to students' learning, the libraries are better able to address these issues during the planning process. And by understanding how and which library-provided student learning sessions are most effective, the library is better able to focus or improve upon efforts designed to contribute to student learning.

THINK-ALOUD PROTOCOLS

The work of K. Anders Ericsson and Herbert A. Simon[13] on human cognition and information processing has often been cited as providing the theoretical framework for the think-aloud protocols.[14] In a later review of their early work, Ericsson explains that he and Simon argued "that the closest connection between thinking and verbal reports is found when subjects verbalize thoughts generated during task completion."[15] By observing participants during task completion, the need to rely on long-term memory is eliminated, thus limiting errors caused by recollection of behavior. The use of protocols will provide some insight into issues raised by the interviews.

To explore the information-seeking behavior of graduate students further, the library plans to conduct think-aloud protocols with about thirty-five students, again varying as to gender, first language, years of study, and discipline. Think-aloud protocols require that participants complete a task while talking about what they are doing and why. Tasks will require participants to use both print and electronic resources. Participants' behavior and verbalization will be observed and recorded by the researcher. Verbalization of thoughts provides a mental model of the participant's research process, thus enabling a better understanding of their behavior.

While the interviews asked students to recall their information-seeking behavior, think-aloud protocols will enable library faculty to observe behavior and capture information as students complete a set of related tasks. Direct observation will be an excellent method for assessing student learning as programs are put into place. The results of the current and future studies have already provided information about the research needs and habits of graduate students with respect to student learning outcomes related to information literacy, including information retrieval, search strategies, and information use. The American Library Association provides a list of information literacy outcomes standards, many of which can be observed during think-aloud protocols; for example, "Implements the search strategy in various information retrieval systems using different user interfaces and search engines, with different command languages, protocols, and search parameters," and "Selects efficient and effective approaches for accessing the information needed from the investigative method or information retrieval system."[16] These studies will be valuable in assessing students' information-seeking behavior and will inform the planning process for the information literacy program and student learning outcomes.

Usability Studies: Think-aloud Protocols

As the number and types of electronic resources increase, the focus of collections and services offered by any library has shifted from onsite access to online access. Students increasingly rely on and demand more electronic books, journals, and services. As libraries attempt to accommodate these changing needs, new challenges emerge. With the proliferation of information resources, selecting reliable sources becomes even more difficult for students. Adding to the problem are the convenience and familiarity of students with non-library Web-based resources. Google and Amazon.com search engines have become the standard of comparison—and, in this comparison, library search engines fail. Because they are fast, easy, and convenient, students often turn to non-library Web-based resources first despite the sometimes questionable worth of the source. For libraries to promote and develop students' use of reliable library Web resources, they need to know how students are using the interfaces, what problems they have, and what features are most important in order to design easily accessible and friendly library system interfaces. Usability testing with students is the key to gaining insight into these questions.

In usability testing, some libraries rely strongly on think-aloud protocols to gather feedback from students regarding their use of digital collections and interfaces. The main purpose is to determine strengths and weaknesses of an interface design in order to create a site that successfully enables users' access to information. Think-aloud protocols also provide an excellent opportunity to observe students' behavior as they navigate Web sites and to measure student learning outcomes, for example, "Implements the search strategy in various information retrieval systems using different user interfaces and search engines, with different command languages, protocols, and search parameters."[17]

Staff at libraries use think-aloud protocols to gather data on several digital interfaces and Web sites including the library's Web site, a site that supports digitized archival papers, a rare book Web site, and an image Web site.[18] Observations of students' actions and transcripts of their verbalizations provided rich data for analysis. Results from study of the library Web site[19] indicated several aspects of site design that affect student learning outcomes:

- Students navigate sites from top to bottom and left to right. Color and graphics attract attention;
- Font size, color, location, and spacing increase the visibility of important links;
- Breaking information into segments, leading with links or key-words, and limiting text increases readability and scanability;
- Consistency in page design, use of global headers and footers, and labels using common terminology increases usability and reduces the learning curve; and
- Global headers and footers provide a sense of place, offer consistent exits, and support navigation.

Obtaining student feedback with think-aloud protocols during the design process helps to insure user-centered interfaces. Think-aloud protocols also provide a measure of student learning outcomes related to information literacy. An example of an outcome measure is that students expressed dissatisfaction with the design of interfaces to Web resources. This outcome led to the redesign of tested Web sites and digital inter-faces, informed the design of subsequent interfaces, and increased the usability of the sites. Protocols also measured students' ability to interact successfully with Web interfaces. Student success and comfort with Web interfaces increases the likelihood that students will choose academic databases and resources rather that the less precise general Web search engines. Outcomes assessment using think-aloud protocols enables li-braries to provide user-friendly alternatives to non-library Web-based resources and to create an environment that is supportive of student learning. This encourages use of the preferred academic Web-based resources and leads to improved information literacy skills over time.

CONCLUSION

Assessing student learning outcomes is part of a total assessment plan that includes faculty consultation, program planning and goal-setting, developing assessment measures, program implementation, and review with planning for program improvement. Continual review at regular intervals contributes to an ongoing process of program improvement. By focusing on student learning outcomes and how interaction with the libraries improves student learning, academe is better able to determine the effect of libraries on student learning. By continuing to generate feedback from students and faculty, libraries are better able to determine where and how to focus efforts leading to improved learning skills in each of the disciplines. And by generating information to determine baselines, faculty and librarians are in a better position to measure growth in learning outcomes over time. Outcomes assessment is difficult for any college or university. However, the types of methods described here (graduate student interviews and think-aloud protocols) provide insight into the habits of technologically adept students, and enable libraries to accommodate changing information-seeking behaviors and focus on student learning outcomes.

ACKNOWLEDGMENT

The authors wish to thank Cindy Carroll for her help editing the manuscript.

Notes

1. Carnegie Mellon University, "Higher Education at Carnegie Mellon University: An Introduction by Vice Provost for Education Indira Nair" (Pittsburgh, PA: Carnegie Mellon University, 2005). Available at http://www .cmu.edu/home/education/education_intro.html (accessed July 29, 2005).

2. Steve Hiller and Jim Self, "Making Library Assessment Work," University of Washington and University of Virginia Association of Research Libraries, ARL 4th Human Resources Management Symposium, Washington, D.C. (November 9, 2004).

3. American Library Association, Association of College and Research Libraries, "Standards for Libraries in Higher Education" (Chicago: American Library Association, 2004). Available at http://www.ala.org/ala/acrl/acrlstan dards/standardslibraries.htm (accessed July 29, 2005).

4. Kim Leonard and Bill Zlatos, "Students Hit with Copyright Lawsuits," *Pittsburgh Tribune-Review* (April 14, 2005). Available at http://pittsburghlive.com/x/tribune-review/s_324000.html (accessed July 29, 2005).

5. Joel Smith, quoted by reporter Scott Mervis, "Carnegie Mellon, Pitt Students Targeted in Action against Illegal Music Swapping," *Pittsburgh Post Gazette* (April 13, 2005). Available at http://www.post-gazette.com/pg/05103/487349.stm (accessed July 29, 2005).

6. Middle States Commission on Higher Education, *Developing Research & Communication Skills: Guidelines for Information Literacy in the Curriculum* (Philadelphia, PA: Middle States Commission on Higher Education, 2003), 73.

7. American Library Association, Association of College and Research Libraries, *Information Literacy Competency Standards for Higher Education* (Chicago: Association of College and Research Libraries, 2000).

8. Sharan B. Merriam, *Qualitative Research and Case Study Applications in Education* (San Francisco: Jossey-Bass Publishers, 1998), 6.

9. Ibid., 72.

10. A study of graduate students' information-seeking behavior by Carnegie Mellon University Libraries' research team (Gloriana St. Clair, Carole A. George, Joan Stein, Alice Bright, and Terry Hurlbert).

11. American Library Association, Association of College and Research Libraries, *Information Literacy Competency Standards for Higher Education.*

12. Middle States Commission on Higher Education, *Developing Research & Communication Skills*, 66.

13. K. Anders Ericsson and Herbert A. Simon, *Protocol Analysis* (Cambridge, MA: MIT Press, 1984, 1993).

14. M. Ted Boren and Judith Ramey, "Thinking Aloud: Reconciling Theory and Practice," *IEEE Transactions on Professional Communication* 43 (2000): 261–278; K. Anders Ericsson, "Protocol Analysis and Verbal Reports on Thinking" (Tallahassee: Florida State University, 2002). Available at http://www.psy.fsu.edu/faculty/ericsson/ericsson.proto.thnk.html (accessed July 29, 2005).

15. Ibid.

16. American Library Association, Association of College and Research Libraries, *Information Literacy Competency Standards for Higher Education.*

17. Ibid.

18. User studies reports by Carole A. George. Unless noted otherwise, these are unpublished library reports and may be obtained by request to her. See "Carnegie Mellon University Libraries Mind Models Exhibit: User Studies." (Pittsburgh, PA: Carnegie Mellon University, 2005). Available at http://www.library.cmu.edu/Libraries/MindModelsUserStudiesRpt.pdf (accessed July 29, 2005).

19. Carole A. George, "Usability Testing and Design of a Library Web site: An Iterative Approach," *OCLC Systems and Services: International Digital Library Perspectives Journal* 21 (2005): 167–180.

CHAPTER 16

Collaborating on Information Literacy

Elizabeth Carter and Renée N. Jefferson

The American Library Association Presidential Committee on Information Literacy defines an information literate person as someone who can "recognize when information is needed and [has] the ability to locate, evaluate, and use effectively the needed information."[1] Students are more likely to become information literate when information literacy instruction is "integrated into courses, linked to an assignment, and designed cooperatively by librarian and course instructor."[2] Furthermore, that instruction continues beyond an individual course and advances student knowledge, skills, and abilities throughout an entire program of study. Effective collaboration occurs when people bring together their respective strengths and expertise for a common goal—developing the information literate graduate, with an end result more effective than each collaborator could achieve on his or her own.[3]

Effective collaborations require structure to assure that goals are met.[4] Structure for information literacy instruction involves the development and implementation of relevant student learning outcomes. It might also include joint planning of assignments and the design of the instruction class, designation of teaching responsibilities during the class, developing methods of assessing results, evaluating results, and using those results to improve the instruction and learning opportunities. In collaborative instruction, students see a team, comprised of discipline-based faculty as content experts and library faculty as procedural experts, thus making the interrelationship of these elements clearer to students.[5] It is in this environment of collaboration that "library instruction becomes relevant to assignments and classroom lectures, communicating the importance of research,"[6] enabling students to more effectively navigate the maze of available resources, increasing comfort level, and decreasing anxiety, all resulting in better quality work.

Fundamental to all information literacy programs is the desire to determine effectiveness of instruction or services, identify problematic areas, and make changes to programs, collections, or services based on data gathered from assessment. In this regard, participation by discipline-based faculty is essential because they have the students and they assign and grade the projects. These faculty collaborate with library faculty on assessment to develop the ability of students to locate, retrieve, evaluate, and use (properly, ethically, and legally) information relevant to the accomplishment of class assignments, as well as to function as independent learners upon graduation.

THE CITADEL

Daniel Library at The Citadel, the Military College of South Carolina, has established a history of serious and sustained outcomes assessment for library research instruction. The Citadel is a comprehensive, regional university with a resident, undergraduate Corps of Cadets of approximately 2,000 students and a graduate program offering masters and specialist degrees in 20 concentrations to approximately 1,300 students.

Until 2004, assessment focused on undergraduate classes, although research instruction for graduate students comprised approximately 15 percent of Daniel Library's instruction program. The library's long-standing relationship with the college's School of Education offered opportunities to expand assessment to this level. Two courses were selected for assessment in fall 2004: Education 512, "Data Collection and Assessment," and Education 549, "Applied Measurement Techniques." Both courses are required of all students in the Master of Education and Master of Arts in Teaching programs in education and school counseling, include a major research project, and are gateway courses to the rest of the graduate education degree. Students are encouraged to take these courses early in their program of study to establish good research skills early on. In all assessment programs, the key element is the collaboration between library and teaching faculty to determine instructional effectiveness.

Freshmen cadets are pre-tested and post-tested on their information literacy skills and asked to respond to a series of attitudinal and usage questions. Political science majors are pre-tested and then, after an eight-week-long intervention of resource-focused classes, post-tested on their knowledge of scholarly sources in the social sciences, developing search strategies, analyzing information in order to answer research questions related to class content, and documenting sources. History majors enrolled in a historiography class participate in end-of-term focus group sessions sharing information about their research experiences. Students from a cadet living group take part in a multi-year study to examine if and how student research needs, information-seeking behaviors, and library use change and evolve from freshman to senior years. Upper-level biology majors enrolled in a genetics course where science literature is used to enhance student understanding of the scientific method are assessed at the course level on successes of this method.

EVOLUTION OF THE INSTRUMENT

The current instrument used to measure information literacy evolved from a pre-test/post-test assessment using a free-response-key-concept methodology along with attitudinal and usage measures developed in the mid-1990s by one of the authors and a member of The Citadel's psychology department.[7] This assessment determined that research instruction for numerous sections of a core course, Psychology 209, "Psychology of Individual Behavior," was effective.

The free-response-key-concept method of assessment has been successfully implemented over the years. The method was adapted from David Barclay, who concluded that "testing is the only practical way for instruction librarians to collect hard evaluation data" and that a free-response question elicits the best indication of student knowledge because "the act of writing an answer to a free-response question . . . has more in common with the unstructured act of library research and so may be a better test of a student's ability to use a library."[8] His recommended method of scoring answers against a key or ideal response provided a layer of objectivity in scoring.

Following the success of the psychology assessment, the instrument was modified to measure learning in the library's instruction program for freshmen cadets, a required, one-time, two-hour class designed to introduce new college students to college-level library research.[9] For this application, the free-response question was changed to include two questions asking students to describe steps they would take to find a book

Figure 16.1
Information Literacy Assessment, Free Response Method

Library Survey Post Test

PLEASE USE NO. 2 PENCIL
RIGHT · ▬ ▬	WRONG ⊘ ⊖ ⊗ ⊜

M M D D Y Y   S.S #   Course #

Company:

Reg. Staff	1B Staff	2B Staff	3B Staff	4B Staff
A	B	BD	C	D	E
F	G	H	I	K	L
M	N	O	PB	R	T

During the Fall 2002 semester:

1. Did you receive instruction on how to use the Daniel Library?

Never   Once   2-5 times   More than 5 times

2. Did you use the Daniel Library to use or check out books, articles, or other material for your classes?

Never   Once   2-5 times   More than 5 times

3. Did you use resources from the Daniel Library to prepare a research paper or bibliography?

Never   Once   2-5 times   More than 5 times

4. Did you use the Internet or World Wide Web to prepare a research paper or bibliography?

Never   Once   2-5 times   More than 5 times

5. Did you use the library as a quiet place to read or study?

Never   Once   2-5 times   More than 5 times

6. Did you ask a librarian or staff member for help in finding information on a topic?

Never   Once   2-5 times   More than 5 times

7. Did you use a computerized index or database (of journal articles or books) to find information on a topic?

Never   Once   2-5 times   More than 5 times

Do you agree?

8. Do you agree with the statement, "Everything is on the web"?

Strongly Agree   Agree   Disagree   Strongly Disagree   Don't Know

9. A step in using web-based materials for research is to examine the web page for information about its author's qualifications and affiliation.

Strongly Agree   Agree   Disagree   Strongly Disagree   Don't Know

10. You must always document information found on the Internet.

Strongly Agree   Agree   Disagree   Strongly Disagree   Don't Know

Please answer the following questions about library computer services.

11. Do you feel that the computer services offered by the library are:

Very Satisfactory   Satisfactory   Unsatisfactory   Very Unsatisfactory

12. If unsatisfactory, why?

3. Do you have a personal PC on campus?   Yes   No

4. If yes, is it a: Laptop   Desktop

5. Which Internet browser do you prefer?   Netscape Navigator   Internet Explorer

Clearly list all of the steps you would go through in order to perform the following tasks.

6. Find a book in The Citadel Library on the subject of   *earthquakes.*

17. Find a journal or magazine article on the subject of   *earthquakes.*

and a journal article on a designated topic. The pre-test attitudinal and usage measurement asked students about their library experiences in high school, while the post-test measurement queried students about their first semester library experiences (see Figure 16.1). The pre-test was administered during Freshman Academic Orientation, and student academic leaders within student residences administered the post-test at semester's end. Library faculty continued to work toward developing information literacy skills in freshmen and to measure learning through this process until The Citadel inaugurated a first-year experience course in 2000.

A major course goal of the first-year experience course, Citadel 101, was to develop library research skills, and the goals, processes, and assessment methods from the freshman library instruction program were adapted to the new course. Library faculty worked closely with Citadel 101 faculty to develop a unit that was integral to the class, teaching students to narrow topics; develop search strategies; use a variety of sources; evaluate sources for accuracy, relevance, and appropriateness;

and document references to complete a graded assignment. Library faculty continued to assess effectiveness of instruction for first-year students using the free-response test with attitude and usage survey methodology, with modifications in wording, format, and questions as the instrument was refined.[10]

Library faculty were satisfied with the assessment instrument and confident in the reliability of data collected through this assessment method, using it to inform and enhance the library instruction program,[11] although the time required to score answers manually for a large number of participants was a drawback of the free-response method. Statisticians from the college's institutional research department were at this point "crunching the numbers" from pre-test and post-test scores and the attitudinal and usage survey, and they were amenable to helping develop and support a totally machine-readable instrument. The instrument used in these current studies was developed after critical examination of the scoring concern and collaboration between authors on how to retain valuable information gained from the free-response method while providing a more feasible method for scoring nearly one thousand pre-tests and post-tests each year. The authors sought a method that would enable students to explain how to search for specific information, yet couched in a format that could be scored electronically. Discussions within the college's scholarship of teaching and learning interest group, CASTLE: Citadel Academy for the Scholarship of Teaching, Learning and Evaluation,[12] suggested a method of reconciling these two requirements.

PROCEDURES

As it happened, the CASTLE group was on a similar quest, searching for a "critical thinking, multiple choice assessment" instrument.[13] A clinical vignette approach, used extensively in medical education,[14] provided a viable solution. This method presents students with problem-solving vignettes that simulate real situations followed by multiple choice questions designed to elicit "a logical, context-sensitive, reflective reasoning process."[15] This approach was adapted to assess student information literacy (see questions 10–13 in Figure 16.2). Instead of writing the steps one would follow to locate a book or a journal article on a given topic, students were presented with a research scenario and asked to select answers from a multiple choice list to describe the best search strategy and finding process. New to this iteration of the assessment instrument were questions

Figure 16.2
Information Literacy Assessment (Revised, 2004)

DANIEL LIBRARY
THE CITADEL
INFORMATION LITERACY
ASSESSMENT

PLEASE USE NO. 2 PENCIL

| RIGHT | WRONG |
- Use a No. 2 pencil only
- Fill in bubble completely

Your complete and honest answers will aid us in our development of instruction. Please complete the entire survey.

Please print and fill in your social security number:

1. Did you use the library this semester?

　　○ Yes (Go to next question)

　　○ No (Go to question 4)

2. How often did you use the library?

　　○ 1-2 times per week

　　○ 3-4 times per week

　　○ 5 or more times per week

3. For each catagory, select the reason(s) for using the library. Please select all that apply.

Locate materials:
　○ books
　○ articles
　○ videos/dvds
　○ music cds
　○ books on tape
　○ other, please specify _____

Access online information:
　○ database to locate articles
　○ Internet/World Wide Web
　○ other, please specify _____

Receive instruction:
　○ attend a library research instruction class
　○ receive assistance with an assignment
　○ other, please specify _____

Study:
　○ study alone
　○ study with a group

Socialize/relax:
　○ meet with friends/classmates
　○ browse newspapers/magazines
　○ other, please specify _____

4. How would you rate your skills in using the computer to locate information for a school assignment?

　　○ Excellent, can locate all required information for an assignment

　　○ Good, can locate most of the required information for an assignment

　　○ Poor, can locate only a little of the information required for an assignment

　　○ No skills, cannot locate any information required for an assignment

5. Has anyone taught you how to locate materials in the library?

　　○ Yes (Go to next question)

　　○ No (Go to question 7)

6. Which of the following person(s) assisted you in learning how to locate materials in the library? Please select all that apply.

　　○ Librarian
　　○ Teacher
　　○ Friend/relative
　　○ Other, please specify_____

(Continued)

Figure 16.2
Information Literacy Assessment
(Revised, 2004) (*Continued*)

7. Where did you access the Internet or World Wide Web? Please select all that apply.

   ○ Home

   ○ School

   ○ Public library

   ○ Friend or relative's home

   ○ Other, please specify _____

Use the Venn Diagrams below to answer questions 8 and 9:

Figure 1   Figure 2   Figure 3   Figure 4

---

8. Which Venn diagram above best represents information on "Stress" AND "School"?

   ○ Figure 1

   ○ Figure 2

   ○ Figure 3

   ○ Figure 4

9. Which Venn diagram above best represents information on "Stress" OR "School"?

   ○ Figure 1

   ○ Figure 2

   ○ Figure 3

   ○ Figure 4

You need to find information on the relationship between **sleep deprivation** and **academic achievement** for a research paper for one of your classes. Your professor has instructed the class to use scholarly books and journal articles as references. Answer questions 10-13 using this scenario.

---

10. Which is the best search to find a <u>book</u> on this topic?

    ○ Search the library catalog for sleep deprivation

    ○ Search the library catalog for sleep deprivation and academic achievement

    ○ Search the library catalog for sleep and academic achievement

    ○ Search Google for sleep and academic achievement

    ○ Search Google for sleep deprivation and academic achievement

    ○ Search Google for sleep deprivation

    ○ Search a database for sleep deprivation

    ○ Search a database for sleep deprivation and academic achievement

    ○ Search a database for sleep and academic achievement

(Continued)

> The following list describes steps involved in locating a <u>book</u> in the library.
> 1. Write down the call number
> 2. Identify the keywords in the topic
> 3. Search a database by keyword
> 4. Search the library catalog by keyword
> 5. Select the most appropriate book from the results list

11. Using the information above, which numerical order is the correct order for finding a <u>book</u> in the library?

       2,4,5,1

       2,3,5,1

       4,2,1,5

       4,2,5,1

       3,2,5,1

12. Which is the best search to find a <u>journal article</u> on this topic?

       Search the library catalog for sleep deprivation

       Search the library catalog for sleep deprivation and academic achievement

       Search the library catalog for sleep and academic achievement

       Search Google for sleep and academic achievement

       Search Google for sleep deprivation and academic achievement

       Search Google for sleep deprivation

       Search a database for sleep deprivation

       Search a database for sleep deprivation and academic achievement

       Search a database for sleep and academic achievement

> The following list describes steps involved in locating an <u>article</u> in the library.
> 1. Write down the citation to the article
> 2. Identify the keywords in the topic
> 3. Search a database by keyword
> 4. Search the library catalog by keyword
> 5. Select the most appropriate book from the results list

13. Using the information above, which numerical order is the correct order for finding an <u>article</u> in the library?

       2,4,5,1

       2,3,5,1

       3,2,1,5

       3,2,5,1

       4,2,5,1

(Continued)

311

Figure 16.2
Information Literacy Assessment
(Revised, 2004) (*Continued*)

> Wolfson, Amy R. and Carskadon, Mary A.
> Sleep Schedules and Daytime Functioning in Adolescents
> Child Development v69 n4 p875-87 Aug 1998
> 00093920
> English
> ERIC
> EJ572360
> http://search.epnet.com
> 1 Aug. 2004
> Linked Full Text

14. Which of the following would be a <u>correct</u> and <u>complete</u> citation for the above item in a bibliography or works cited list?

   ○   Wolfson, Amy R. and Mary A. Carskadon. "Sleep Schedules and Daytime Functioning in Adolescents." <u>Child Development</u> 69.4 (1998): 875-87. <u>ERIC</u>. 1 Aug. 2004 <http://search.epnet.com>.

   ○   Wolfson, Amy R. and Mary A. Carskadon. <u>Sleep Schedules and Daytime Functioning in Adolescents.</u> Child Development, vol. 69, no. 4, August 1998: 875-87. <u>ERIC</u>. 1 Aug. 2004 <http://search.epnet.com>.

   ○   Wolfson, Amy R. and Mary A. Carskadon. (EJ572360) "Sleep Schedules and Daytime Functioning in Adolescents." <u>Child Development</u> 69.4 (1998): 875-87.

   ○   Wolfson, Amy R. "Sleep Schedules and Daytime Functioning in Adolescents." <u>Child Development</u> 69(1998): 875:87. <u>ERIC</u>. 1 Aug. 2004 <http://search.epent.com>.

15. Please indicate how true each of the following statements are for you, on a scale of 1 to 5, where 1 is not at all true and 5 is very true.

	Not at all True				Very True
I feel comfortable in libraries	(1)	(2)	(3)	(4)	(5)
I am good with computers	(1)	(2)	(3)	(4)	(5)
I enjoy reading	(1)	(2)	(3)	(4)	(5)
I can usually find what I need at the library	(1)	(2)	(3)	(4)	(5)
I like puzzles and brain teasers	(1)	(2)	(3)	(4)	(5)
I probably do not spend enough time at the library	(1)	(2)	(3)	(4)	(5)
I like to do my studying at the library	(1)	(2)	(3)	(4)	(5)
I usually get the help I need at the library	(1)	(2)	(3)	(4)	(5)
I have learned a lot about research from libraries	(1)	(2)	(3)	(4)	(5)

measuring student understanding of Boolean operators (see questions 8 and 9, Figure 16.2) and documentation of sources (question 14, Figure 16.2). Questions 1 through 7 in Figure 16.2 identified library use patterns and question 15 measured attitudes toward libraries and research. Freshmen and graduate students took the same pre-test and post-test, with minor modifications for clarity. For example, freshmen were asked to identify a correct journal citation in MLA (Modern Language Association) style, while graduate students were asked to identify the correct APA (American Psychological Association) style.

The instructional objective for freshmen was based on the Citadel 101 course goal of developing library research skills, with learning outcomes measured by a student's ability to use Boolean logic in searching, to locate books and journal articles on a given topic, and to document sources correctly. The instructional objectives for graduate students were to describe the steps involved in carrying out a literature review and to apply the steps by conducting a review of the literature for an action research study assignment.

The pencil-and-paper test used the machine-readable data collection and assessment program, Scantron.[16] Freshmen were administered the pre-test in the library during Freshman Academic Orientation and post-tested in their respective Citadel 101 classes. Graduate students were given pre-tests in the library just prior to their scheduled research instruction class, and took their post-tests in class later in the semester.

RESULTS

Results are reported for freshman cadets and graduate students, and by comparative analysis. Sections on freshmen and graduate students present information on previous library or media center use, current use of the campus library, and performance on the Information Literacy Test. The comparative analysis section examines the similarities and differences in performance between the two student groups.

Freshman Cadets

Previous Library or Media Center Use

Some 519 freshman cadets responded to questions regarding previous library or media center use. A high percentage, 83%, reported using the

Figure 16.3
Previous Library or Media Center Use of Freshman Cadets

Freshman Cadets

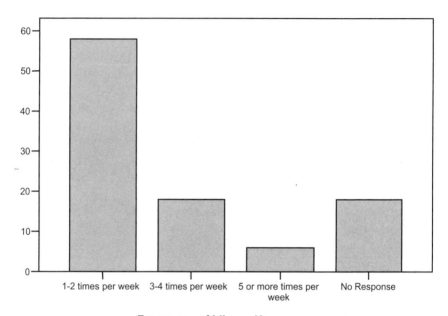

Frequency of Library Use

library or media center at their previous schools. Figure 16.3 shows the frequency of library use. Materials listed as primary reasons for library use were books (49%), articles (28%), and multimedia items (videos/ DVDs, music CDs, books on tape; 15%). When queried about online access, a majority of first-year students (62%) went to the library to gain access to the Internet, while 37% used databases to access articles. More than one-third (36%) attended a library research instruction class, and a majority (61%) received assistance with an assignment. Less than half browsed newspapers/magazines (47%) and met with friends/ classmates (48%). A majority studied alone (57%), while the remainder (43%) studied with a group.

Current Campus Library Use

A total of 347 freshman cadets answered questions about their current use of the campus library. Almost all of them (93%) used Daniel Library during the fall 2004 semester. Figure 16.4 shows the frequency of library use. Materials listed as primary reasons for library use were books (42%), articles (37%), and multimedia items (videos/DVDs, music CDs; 13%). Nearly half (49%) accessed the Internet and databases containing journal articles. A majority of freshmen (62%) attended a library research instruction class, and more than one-third (35%) received assistance with an assignment. Less than half (41%) browsed newspapers/magazines. A majority (63%) studied alone, while the remainder (37%) studied with a group. More than half (51%) used the library to meet with friends/classmates.

Information Literacy Test

Information literacy questions focused on three areas of competency: Boolean operators, search strategies, and bibliographic citation com-

Figure 16.4
Current Library or Media Center Use of Freshman Cadets

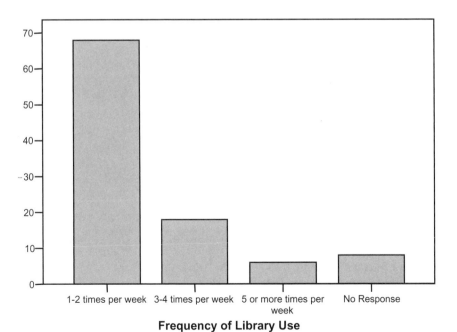

Freshman Cadets

Frequency of Library Use

ponents. Two hundred and four freshman cadets completed the pre-test and post-test information literacy questions. Of this number, 89% reported on the pre-test that their computer skills for locating information for a school assignment were "good" or "excellent." On the post-test, 96% reported having "good" or "excellent" computer skills.

Pictures of Venn diagrams were used to illustrate the correct use of AND and OR for Boolean operators. On the pre-test, 68% of freshmen answered the AND Boolean operator question correctly. However, only 62% answered the question correctly on the post-test. Similar results occurred with the OR Boolean operator question as 10% answered the question correctly on the pre-test, while 7% answered it correctly on the post-test.

Search strategy questions focused on locating a book and a journal article for a topic by asking subjects to identify steps to locate a book in the library, and steps for locating an article. The best strategy to find a book on the topic "stress" and "sleep deprivation" was identified correctly by 47% of freshmen on the pre-test, and 50% on the post-test. Forty-four percent identified the best strategy to find an article on the assigned topic on the pre-test, with 59% responding correctly on the post-test. On the pre-test, 49% of freshmen identified the correct order for finding a book in the library. The percentage increased on the post-test, with 61% identifying the correct order. Similar results occurred for identifying the correct order for finding a journal article in the library. On the pre-test, 50% responded correctly while 60% responded correctly on the post-test.

The bibliographic citation was taken from the Educational Resources Information Center (ERIC) database. Components of the citation included names of authors, title, journal name, volume, issue, pages, date, ERIC journal number, and other parts of a bibliographic database record. Freshmen were asked to identify the correct and complete citation required for a bibliography or works cited list. On the pre-test, 30% answered the question correctly, while the percentage answering correctly increased to 42% for the post-test.

To examine differences between pre-test and post-test performance, the Information Literacy Test items were placed into one of four categories: (1) Boolean operators, (2) search strategies for books, (3) search strategies for articles, and (4) bibliographic citations. Differences were based on the number of correct responses. A significant difference occurred for category 3, search strategies for articles ($\chi^2(1)$, $p < .05$). Significant differences were not found for the other three categories. However, significant differences were found among the four categories

Table 16.1
Freshman Cadet Feelings about Libraries and Other Related Activities (by Pre-test and Post-test)

Statement	Pre-test (%)	Post-test (%)
I feel comfortable in libraries	80	85
I am good with computers	67	82
I enjoy reading	36	45
I can usually find what I need at the library	57	74
I like puzzles and brain teasers	40	44
I probably do not spend enough time at the library	66	48
I like to do my studying at the library	36	32
I usually get the help I need at the library	59	74
I have learned a lot about research from libraries	45	66

based on pre-test performance ($\chi^2(3)$, p $<$ .05). Similar results were found for post-test performance ($\chi^2(3)$, p $<$ .01).

In addition to test items, freshmen were asked to respond to nine statements regarding their feelings about the library and other related activities on both the pre-test and post-test (see Table 16.1). The scale for each item ranged from 1 (*not true*) to 5 (*very true*). On the pre-test, a majority reported feeling comfortable in libraries (80%), finding what they needed at the library (57%), and receiving necessary help at the library (59%). While similar responses occurred on the post-test, the percentages did increase from pre-test to post-test. Responses were different for activities such as enjoying reading and liking puzzles and brain teasers, as the percentages of freshmen responding "true" and "very true" to these statements was less than 50% on both pre-test and post-test.

Graduate Students

Previous Library or Media Center Use

A total of fifty-two graduate education students answered questions about their previous library use. A large percentage (96%) had used the library at their previous academic institutions. Figure 16.5 shows frequency of use. Materials listed as primary reasons for library use were books and articles (49% each). These results were similar to the reasons

Figure 16.5
Previous Library Use of Graduate Students

Graduate Students

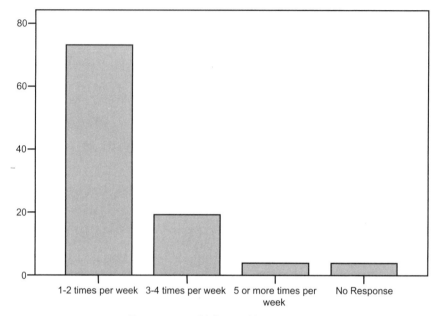

Frequency of Library Use

students listed regarding online access. Approximately 51% accessed the Internet, while 48% used databases to access articles. About one-third (32%) attended a library research instruction class. However, a majority (61%) received assistance with an assignment. Less than half (43%) browsed newspapers/magazines. A majority studied alone (51%) and the remainder (49%) studied with a group. Less than half (39%) met with friends/classmates.

Current Campus Library Use

Some forty-nine graduate education students answered questions about their current use of the campus library. Most of them (96%) used Daniel Library during the fall 2004 semester. Figure 16.6 shows frequency of

Figure 16.6
Current Library Use of Graduate Students

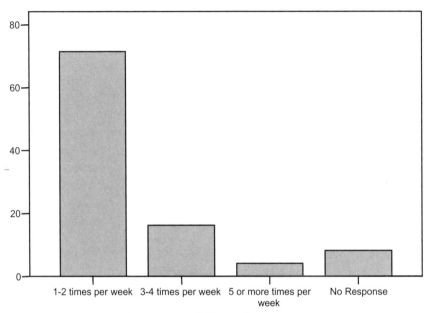

Graduate Students

use. Materials listed as primary reasons for library use were articles (50%) and books (31%). A majority of these graduate education students (59%) used the library to access the Internet, while 41% used databases to access articles. A majority (63%) attended a library research instruction class. However, approximately one-third received assistance with an assignment. Fifty percent browsed newspapers/magazines. A majority studied alone (59%), while 41% studied with a group. Less than half (42%) met with friends and classmates.

Information Literacy Test

Information literacy questions focused on the same three areas of competency: Boolean operators, search strategies, and bibliographic citation components. Of the fifteen graduate education students completing pretest and post-test information literacy questions, all of them reported on the pre-test and post-test that their skills in using a computer to locate information for a school assignment were either "good" or "excellent."

Pictures of Venn diagrams were used to illustrate the correct use of AND and OR for Boolean operators. On the pre-test, all graduate education students answered the AND Boolean operator question correctly; however, 93% answered the question correctly on the post-test. For the OR Boolean operator, all graduate education students answered the question correctly on both the pre-test and post-test.

Search strategy questions focused on locating a book and a journal article for a topic, identifying steps to locate a book in the library, and identifying steps for locating an article. The best strategy to find a book on stress and sleep deprivation was identified correctly by 40% of graduate education students on the pre-test, and 60% of them on the post-test. Seventy-three percent identified the best strategy to find an article on the assigned topic on the pre-test, and 87% responded correctly on the post-test. On the pre-test, 60% of graduate students identified the correct order of steps for finding a book in the library, and 67% identified the correct order on the post-test. Similar results were found when identifying the correct order for finding a journal article in the library. On the pre-test, 60% responded correctly, and 73% responded correctly on the post-test.

The chi-square test of independence revealed no significant differences between pre-test and post-test performance for the four categories. However, similar to the freshman group, significant differences were found among the four categories based on pre-test performance $(\chi^2(3), p < .05)$, and post-test performance $(\chi^2(3), p < .01)$.

Similar to the freshmen, the bibliographic citation was taken from the ERIC database. On the pre-test, 27% answered the question correctly, and for the post-test the number decreased to 13%. In addition to the test items, graduate education students were asked to respond to nine statements regarding their feelings toward the library and other related activities on both the pre-test and the post-test (see Table 16.2). The scale for each item ranged from 1 (not true) to 5 (very true). On the pre-test, a majority (80%) reported feeling comfortable in libraries, finding what they needed at the library (80%), and receiving necessary help at the library (74%). While similar responses occurred on the post-test, the percentages did increase from pre-test to post-test. Responses varied for activities such as enjoying reading and liking puzzles and brain teasers. A majority of graduate education students responded "true" and "very true" to enjoying reading on the pre-test

Table 16.2
Graduate Students' Feelings about Libraries and Other
Related Activities (by Pre-test and Post-test)

Statement	Pre-test (%)	Post-test (%)
I feel comfortable in libraries	80	87
I am good with computers	73	80
I enjoy reading	60	67
I can usually find what I need at the library	80	86
I like puzzles and brain teasers	47	47
I probably do not spend enough time at the library	66	67
I like to do my studying at the library	33	13
I usually get the help I need at the library	74	93
I have learned a lot about research from libraries	53	80

(60%) and the post-test (67%). Less than 50% reported liking puzzles and brain teasers on both the pre-test and the post-test.

Comparative Analysis

There are a number of differences between freshman cadets and graduate education students. The number of students responding to each section varied greatly. For the previous library or media center use section, responses were provided by 519 freshman cadets and 52 graduate education students. The current campus library use section received responses from 347 freshmen and 49 graduate education students. Additionally, the information literacy test section received responses from 204 freshmen and 15 graduate education students.

Differences varied regarding the primary reasons that freshmen and graduate education students used materials at their previous libraries. Freshmen reported that books, articles, and multimedia items were the primary reasons for using their previous library, while graduate education students reported only books and articles. Use of online access also varied between the two groups of students. More freshmen (62%) than graduate education students (51%) used the library or media center at their previous schools to access the Internet/World Wide Web. However, more graduate education students (48%) used their previous libraries to access bibliographic databases than freshmen (37%).

Similar results occurred for previous library use, assistance with instruction, and browsing. An overwhelming majority of freshmen (83%) and graduate education students (96%) reported previous library use. The same percentage (61%) of both groups used their previous libraries to receive assistance with an assignment. Similar percentages occurred for using libraries to browse newspapers/magazines: 47% for freshmen and 43% for graduate education students.

Almost all students reported using the Daniel Library at The Citadel during the fall 2004 semester: 93% of freshmen and 96% of graduate education students. Frequency of use was also similar, as 68% percent of freshmen and 71% of graduate education students used the library one to two times per week. Attendance at library instruction classes was similar, as 62% of freshmen and 63% of graduate education students attended a library research instruction class.

Performances on the Information Literacy Test were similar for both student groups. A majority of freshmen and graduate education students correctly answered the Boolean operator AND question, however, the percentage declined from pre-test to post-test for each group, from 68% to 62% for freshmen and from 100% to 93% for graduate education students. Opposite results occurred for questions on search strategies. The percentage of correct responses increased from pre-test to post-test for questions on locating books and articles on a specific topic. For locating books, the percentage increased from 47% to 50% for freshmen and from 40% to 60% for graduate education students. For locating articles, the percentage increased from 44% to 59% for freshmen and from 60% to 73% for graduate education students.

Responses were similar for identifying the correct order of steps to find a book and an article in the Daniel Library. For freshmen, the percentage of correct responses increased from 49% on the pre-test to 61% on the post-test. For graduate education students, the percentage increased from 60% to 67% from pre-test to post-test. However, responses were not similar for the bibliographic citation question. Freshmen had an overall increase of correct responses from pre-test (30%) to post-test (40%), while graduate education students decreased in correct responses (27% to 13%).

The chi-square test was used to examine differences between freshmen and graduate student pre-test performance for the four categories: (1) Boolean operators, (2) search strategies for books, (3) search strategies for articles, and (4) bibliographic citations. Significant differences between the pre-test performance for freshmen and graduate students were found for each category ($\chi^2(1)$, p < .01). Similar results were found for each category based upon post-test performance ($\chi^2(1)$, p < .01).

Responses to statements regarding students' feelings toward the library were similar on the pre-test and post-test for both groups. On the pre-test and post-test, a majority of freshmen and graduate education students reported feeling comfortable in libraries, finding what they needed at the library, and receiving help they needed. Percentages ranged from 57% to 80% on the pre-test and from 74% to 93% on the post-test. Responses to statements regarding other related activities varied from pre-test to post-test for both groups. On the pre-test and post-test, a majority (60% and 67%, respectively) of graduate education students reported that they enjoyed reading. For freshmen, less than 50% for the pre-test and post-test (36% and 45%, respectively) reported that they enjoyed reading. Less than 50% of both student groups reported liking puzzles and brain teasers: among freshmen (40%) and graduate education students (47%) for the pre-test; and among freshmen (44%) and graduate education students (47%) for the post-test reported to like puzzles and brain teasers.

RELATING THE FINDINGS TO STUDENT LEARNING OUTCOMES

Fundamental components of all assessment programs include a desire to determine the effectiveness of instruction and services, identify problematic areas, collect relevant information, and close the loop by making changes to programs, collections, or services based on data gathered for assessment. Effectiveness of instruction was determined using the Information Literacy Test as pre-test and post-test measures of first-year and graduate education students' information literacy skills. Freshmen and graduate education students experienced difficulty in meeting some of the instructional outcomes identified for the library instruction session. Of the four categories, significant changes in performance occurred for the "search strategies for articles" category for freshman cadets. For graduate students, significant differences were not found between any of the four pre-test and post-test measures. Both groups experience difficulty with Boolean operators and graduate students showed a slight decrease from pre-test to post-test in ability to identify a correct journal citation in APA style.

Test performances of freshmen and graduate education students identified areas for program changes. One area is test administration.

The test was administered using Scantron forms for both groups. During future test administrations, graduate education students will take the test electronically, while Scantron forms will continue to be used with freshmen due to the logistics of administering the test twice to more than six hundred students. A second area for program change is the population of graduate education students. The goal is to increase their participation in taking both the pre-test and post-test. Including the Information Literacy Test as part of course requirements may assist in increasing student participation. Finally, test items, especially those concerning use of Boolean operators and identifying correct journal article citations, will be reexamined to determine whether revision and/or additional instruction are needed. Anecdotal evidence exists for both possibilities. During freshman pre-testing (the authors did not administer the post-tests) students had questions about the Venn diagrams and many appeared puzzled by them, thus the possibility exists that they did not understand the diagrams and/or the concept was so new to them that Citadel 101 instruction needs more focus on this concept. While graduate student's ability to recognize a correct journal citation declined from pre-test to post-test, the low scores in both tests indicate a need to focus instruction in that area as well.

CONCLUSION

Instruction and assessment go hand-in-hand; assessment provides constructive feedback on the efficacy of instruction. Both should be integral to course and program goals and should be simple and focused. Through collaboration with faculty across disciplines, "the library can strengthen its assessment process by developing realistic measurement devices to determine consistently how well information competencies are vertically and horizontally integrated into (and aligned with) the curriculum,"[17] in order to achieve the information literacy goal of producing students, and citizens, "who have learned how to learn."[18]

Notes

1. American Library Association, Presidential Committee on Information Literacy, *Final Report* (Chicago: American Library Association, 1989). Avail-

able at http://www.ala.org/ala/acrl/acrlpubs/whitepapers/presidential.htm (accessed August 2, 2005).

2. Elizabeth W. Carter and Timothy K. Daugherty, "Library Instruction and Psychology: A Cooperative Effort," *Technical Services Quarterly* 16 (1998): 33.

3. Dick Raspa and Dane Ward, "Listening for Collaboration: Faculty and Librarians Working Together," in *The Collaborative Imperative: Librarians and Faculty Working Together in the Information Universe*, edited by Dick Raspa and Dane Ward (Chicago: Association of College and Research Libraries, 2000), 3.

4. Doug Cook, "Creating Connections: A Review of the Literature," in *The Collaborative Imperative*, 27.

5. Carter and Daugherty, "Library Instruction and Psychology," 34.

6. Ibid., 39–41.

7. Timothy K. Daugherty and Elizabeth W. Carter, "Assessment of Outcome-focused Library Instruction in Psychology," *Journal of Instructional Psychology* 24 (1997), 29–32.

8. Donald Barclay, "Evaluating Library Instruction: Doing the Best You Can with What You Have," *RQ* 33 (Winter 1993), 197–198.

9. Elizabeth W. Carter, "'Doing the Best You Can with What You Have': Lessons Learned from Outcomes Assessment," *The Journal of Academic Librarianship* 28 (2002), 37–38.

10. Ibid., 39–40.

11. Carter, "'Doing the Best You Can with What You Have,'" 40–41.

12. The Citadel, "Citadel Academy for the Scholarship of Teaching, Learning and Evaluation" (Charleston, SC: The Citadel, 2005). Available at http://faculty.citadel.edu/carnegie/index.htm (accessed May 9, 2005).

13. Kathy Van Eerden, "Using Critical Thinking Vignettes to Evaluate Student Learning," *Nursing and Health Care Perspectives* 22 (2001), 232.

14. Ibid., 231–234; J.P.C. Chau, A. M. Chang, I.F.K. Lee, W. Y. Ip, D.T.F. Lee, and Y. Wooten, "Effects of Using Videotaped Vignettes on Enhancing Student's Critical Thinking Ability in a Baccalaureate Nursing Programme," *Journal of Advanced Nursing* 36 (2001): 112–119.

15. Van Eerden, "Using Critical Thinking Vignettes to Evaluate Student Learning," 232.

16. Scantron Corporation, "The Bridge to Knowledge" (Irvine, CA: Scantron Corp., 2005). Available at http://www.scantron.com (accessed May 18, 2005).

17. Ilene F. Rockman, "The Importance of Assessment," *Reference Services Review* 30 (2002), 182.

18. American Library Association, Presidential Committee on Information Literacy, *Final Report*.

CHAPTER 17

Developing an Information Literacy Assessment Instrument

Terrence Mech

This chapter chronicles the development of a valid and reliable measure of students' information skills at King's College in Wilkes-Barre, Pennsylvania. The twenty-five-item multiple-choice assessment instrument uses the *Information Literacy Competency Standards for Higher Education* as its conceptual framework.[1] With an emphasis on higher-order skills and a range of difficulty, the instrument is designed for use by undergraduates at four-year institutions.

KING'S COLLEGE

King's College, founded in 1946 by the Congregation of Holy Cross from the University of Notre Dame, enrolls 2,200 full-time and part-time students in 34 undergraduate major programs as well as master's programs in education (reading), health care administration, and physician assistant studies. As an independent four-year college, King's prepares students for a purposeful life through a broadly based liberal arts curriculum.

More than 80 percent of King's first-year students return for their sophomore year, a percentage well above the national average. Sixty-one percent of King's first-year, full-time students graduate within four years; 69 percent do so within six years. Ninety-nine percent are employed or in graduate school within six months of graduation. King's is included in *Barron's Best Buys in College Education* and continues to place in the top tier of the *U.S. News & World Report's Best Colleges Guide*.[2] The college is one of sixteen institutions nationwide named to the American Association of Colleges and Universities' Greater Expectations Initiative.

In 1984, after two years of faculty discussion, King's College implemented a new core curriculum. In designing that curriculum as a plan for learning, the faculty identified several transferable skills necessary for a vibrant liberal education: critical thinking, effective writing, effective oral communication, quantitative reasoning, technology competence, information literacy, and moral reasoning.[3] These essential skills contribute to students' success in college and throughout their careers.

With the implementation of the core curriculum, the college initiated a comprehensive assessment program to improve teaching and student learning. The basic elements of the program consisted of pre- and post-tests in many core classes and in the major programs, the Sophomore-Junior Diagnostic Project, the Senior Integrated Assessment, Competency Growth Plans, and Goals for the Major. Primarily course embedded, the faculty's assessment program provides students with clear expectations. Assessment results are used to identify curricular, programmatic, pedagogical, and student strengths and weaknesses. As part of its assessment efforts, the college monitors institutional factors that support the curriculum and student learning outcomes such as the effectiveness of advisement and other services to students, quality of facilities and co-curricular activities, as well as the college's intellectual and social atmosphere.

LIBRARY AND INFORMATION LITERACY

In 1982, as part of the Core Curriculum discussions, librarians prepared a series of study guides and a hands-on introduction to the library. By 1984, all students in Core 110, Effective Writing (a required first-year course), were expected to complete a self-paced library workbook. The idea was to provide students with a common introduction to the library upon which faculty and librarians could build. Several years later in the evolution of the core curriculum, the self-paced library workbook morphed into a more flexible course-integrated exercise.[4]

Throughout the process, librarians and faculty were looking for indications that their efforts were making a difference in students' learning.

Evaluation of the workbook program used two types of assessments: an objective test that measured student improvement in selecting and interpreting tools and strategies, and a subjective questionnaire in which students rated their experiences with the workbook and their attitudes after completing it. Our experiences with the workbook pre- and post-test results were similar to those of other colleges at the time. For many students the learning appeared marginal at best. Although students' evaluations of the workbook were overwhelmingly positive, our experiences at the reference desk indicated that students did not transfer the information and skills acquired through the workbook exercises to actual research projects.[5] In retrospect the post-test was too close to the learning experience. Confronted with the gap between what students thought they knew and a new perception of their information skills, we realized a semester was not long enough for students to process the experience and adopt new behaviors. Anecdotal evidence suggested that this was a manifestation of first-year students' tendencies to compartmentalize what they learn, not applying that knowledge in a different situation or course.

Confounding our understanding of the situation was the wide variety of library and information-related experiences students brought with them to college, and the faculty's perception that students' information skills were better than they really were. These two factors led the library to explore various ways to identify just what information skills students bought to college and how students felt about their abilities to navigate a library and to complete a research project. The resulting research was used to inform the faculty that students' anxieties about libraries and research are very real, and that students' anxieties about libraries and information skills are unrelated to students' academic ability, as measured by scholastic aptitude test (SAT) scores.[6]

Selection of an appropriate instrument to measure students' information skills proved more difficult. In the mid-1980s, the library examined two instruments, *Minimum Library Use Skills* and the *Library Skills Test*.[7] Both instruments focused on traditional library skills: being able to interpret citations and information found in a catalog record or journal index, knowledge of Library of Congress subject headings, the Dewey Decimal classification system, indexes, parts of a book, and library terminology. *Minimum Library Use Skills* intended to measure the minimum skills college students should acquire by the end of their sophomore year. The *Library Skills Test* was designed for use with students in grades seven through twelve and college freshmen. Unlike *Minimum Library Use Skills*, the *Library Skills Test* provided norms for college freshmen, which made it possible to interpret results. However, in the late 1980s and early 1990s with the widespread introduction of online catalogs, CD-ROM-based periodical indexes, the Internet, Gopher, and the World Wide Web, these instruments were no longer seen as appropriate means to measures students' information skills.

With increased access to information, the problem most students faced was sorting through the volume of material. This challenge also signaled a shift in the library's mission. Previously, when students' biggest concern was finding material for their projects, the library focused on building a collection to meet student's needs. However, with access to materials less and less of a challenge for students, the level of students' information skills became a more glaring issue.

With the development of the Association of College and Research Libraries' (ACRL) *Information Literacy Competency Standards for Higher Education* in 2000 and the Middle States Commission on Higher Education's "new" *Characteristics of Excellence in Higher Education* in 2002, with its emphasis on student learning and assessment, the search for an appropriate way to measure students' information skills took on renewed interest.[8,9] In the review process of Middle States Commission's accrediting standards, it was readily apparent that the regional accrediting organization was more interested in how a library and its information resources contribute to a student's education rather than how many journals were available or the library's percentage of the institution's education and general expenditures. Previously, the regional accrediting standards, while not prescriptive, devoted a separate section to libraries and students' use of information resources. With the new Middle States standards there was no separate library section but rather a pronounced interest in a college's curriculum and knowing if students were graduating with essential college-level skills, including information literacy.[10]

At the time of Middle States' vetting process, virtual institutions (e.g., the University of Phoenix) were seeking regional accreditation. With the development and promise of electronic databases, as well as the practice of contracting for academic library services, a legitimate question was "In such a changing information and technological environment, is a physical library a prerequisite for any degree-granting institution of higher education?" What came out of the spirited Middle States Commission's discussions was the consensus that every institution of higher education, virtual or physical, should prepare students to be independent learners by requiring students to develop information skills (skills of inquiry, information management, and analysis).[11] This shift in focus which made students' information skills an explicit curricular expectation corresponded with Middle States' interest in the use of assessment results to document and improve student learning.

EVOLUTION OF THE INSTRUMENT

King's College has been collecting self-reported assessments of seniors' information skills since 1992 through its annual Program Evaluation Survey. Graduating seniors complete a brief survey which inquires about their satisfaction with selected aspects of their major program (quality of instruction and courses, variety of courses, availability of instructors, and academic and career advisement) and the college's contribution to selected learning outcomes (intellectual growth; aesthetic and cultural growth; critical thinking ability; writing; oral communication; ability to locate, evaluate, and select information; sensitivity to ethical decision making; and technology competence). Survey results are compiled, sorted by major, compared with previous years, and distributed by the institutional research office. Table 17.1 is an example of how students' satisfaction with their information skills is presented.

While the major programs use various criteria and different course-embedded methods to assess students' skills in senior capstone courses, this information was seldom systematically collected or shared outside of departments, and meaningful program-level comparisons were impossible. Knowing that students' self-reported data from the graduation survey did not always reconcile with the available anecdotal evidence, the library saw a need for a conceptually rigorous, quantitative, objective college-level assessment of students' information skills that provided for program-level comparisons. Ideally, the instrument would serve as a four-year pre-and post-test for use with students, and provide faculty with a tangible set of information literacy questions and concepts their students should be able to answer and demonstrate. The instrument was built around the question of what should a graduating senior know or be able to do. Although the instrument was to be more of a formative assessment to identify the strengths and weakness of a student cohort's information skills, it was important to construct an instrument that was difficult enough to differentiate among students' ability levels. A latent consequence of using the instrument with first-year students was that it communicated these expectations of skill proficiency to the students as well.

Table 17.1
Students' Self-Report of Information Skills

Ability to Locate, Evaluate, and Select Information						
	1992	1993	1994	1995	1996	Average
College Average	4.24	4.29	4.26	4.23	4.29	4.26
Accounting	3.92	4.16	4.26	4.13	4.05	4.10
Biology	4.25	4.55	3.80	4.11	4.43	4.23
Business Administration	4.09	4.17	4.27	4.18	4.40	4.22
Chemistry			5.00	4.67	5.00	4.89
Communications	4.48	4.42	4.35	4.54	4.28	4.41
Computer Science	4.00	4.00	3.75	4.20		3.99
Computers & Info. Systems	4.32	4.31	4.00	4.22	4.33	4.24
Criminal Justice	4.18	4.14	4.19	3.92	4.19	4.12
Elementary Education	4.29	4.13	4.23	4.29	4.41	4.27
English	4.29	4.61	4.48	4.68	4.48	4.51
Finance	4.27	4.36	4.50	4.00	3.86	4.20
Gerontology		4.40	4.67	4.25	4.25	4.39
Health Care Management	4.10	4.00		4.17	4.25	4.13
History	4.42	4.46	4.38	3.90	4.53	4.34
Human Resources Mgmt.	4.46	4.80	3.89	4.15	4.54	4.37
International Business	3.92	4.25	4.38	4.25	4.17	4.19
Marketing	4.50	3.92	4.43	4.20	4.06	4.22
Mathematics		4.00	4.00	4.20	3.00	3.80
Political Science	4.10	4.24	4.33	4.00	4.47	4.23
Psychology	4.33	4.36	4.33	4.50	4.22	4.35

Scale: 5 (excellent) 4 (good) 3 (average) 2 (below average) 1 (poor)

In fall 2000, Gene Berger, instructional/reference librarian, reviewed the literature on information skills–related test and assessment instruments. A number of the instruments examined contained measures of students' attitudes toward libraries and the research process, as well as questions about the nature and frequency of students' use of libraries and information resources. His search identified only a few potential instruments that focused exclusively on students' skills and that were modeled on ACRL's *Information Literacy Competency Standards for Higher Education*. With permission, a copy of Maryville College's *Information Literacy Competency Inventory (Pretest)* was borrowed and adapted.[12] The Maryville instrument contained twenty institution-specific questions relating to four of the five *Information Literacy Competency Standards for Higher Education*. Maryville College did not assess standard four (use information effectively to accomplish a purpose). No reliability or other psychometric information about the instrument was available.

Over time King's increased the number of questions to twenty-five with four possible responses. Questions were rewritten to make them generic, not specific to any particular institution, information tool, or discipline and reflective of all of the *Information Literacy Competency Standards*. Questions were written with an emphasis on higher-order skills, knowledge gained through experience rather than general understanding, and application rather than the recall of information. A number of the questions are interpretive exercises, which require individuals to read a passage or table and apply their knowledge to the situation. A reading comprehension question is also included.

Writing clear test questions with good alternative responses was a challenge made easier once we understood the science and finer points of test construction.[13] One of the first tasks was to construct an assessment matrix or test blueprint which identified the exact standard, performance indicator, and outcome we intended to measure and the corresponding question used to measure it. This allowed us to balance the distribution of questions among the five standards. Based upon a variety of analyses after each assessment survey, certain questions were eliminated, re-created, or reconstructed to ensure a fair question. Questions were revised to eliminate clues or responses that allowed students to make inferences or deductions and so increase their odds of guessing correctly. During the process, librarians, support staff, students, and selected faculty reviewed questions and responses for jargon, content, and fairness. The various perspectives were helpful in identifying potentially confusing language or instructions and for keeping the questions focused on the selected standard and objective. As of spring 2005 only four questions and some of their responses resemble the original items. Table 17.2 reflects some of the instrument's evolution.

In spring 2001, for purposes of developing the instrument, data was collected from 390 first-year students in three required first-year core courses. Not surprisingly, the initial results revealed significant differences among students in the different core courses. First-year students are assigned to a particular course based upon certain criteria including the results of their writing samples. The corresponding information

Table 17.2
Instrument Evolution

Information Literacy Competency Standard	Maryville College (Fall 2000)	King's College (Spring 2001)	King's College (Fall 2003)	King's College (Spring 2004)
Standard 1	5 questions	5 questions	5 questions	5 questions
Standard 2	11 questions	11 questions	5 questions	5 questions
Standard 3	2 questions	7 questions	5 questions	5 questions
Standard 4	No questions	No questions	4 questions	5 questions
Standard 5	2 questions	2 questions	6 questions	5 questions
	20 questions	25 questions	25 questions	25 questions

literacy results resonated with faculty familiar with the core course placement criteria. Based upon further analysis, revisions were made to the instrument. In fall 2001, three hundred first-year students were surveyed for purposes of refining the questions. The results were similar, honors students scored significantly better than other students. Based upon the subsequent analysis twelve questions were revised for fall 2002.

In fall 2002, the assessment results from 205 first-year students were shared with all faculty in an effort to develop a common understanding of entering students' information skills and to reinforce the importance of core and major programs in developing students' skills. With a composite score and sub-scores for each of the five *Competency Standards*, we were able to assist faculty in more accurately identifying particular gaps in

Table 17.3
Freshman Information Skills by Course (Fall 2002)

Course	N	Mean %	Standard Deviation	Range %
Core 99	26	48.77	10.55	24–64
Core 100	52	60.15[*]	17.03	4–100
Core 110	127	57.20[*]	12.48	12–80
Total	205	56.82	13.89	4–100

*Refers to comparisons within column where the mean scores of the group are significantly ($p \leq .05$) higher than the mean scores of the other group.

Table 17.4
Freshman Information Skills by Standards (Fall 2002)

Standard	N	Mean %	Standard Deviation	Range %
Standard 1	205	50.6	22.50	0–100
Standard 2	205	56.8	23.39	0–100
Standard 3	205	71.2	22.90	0–100
Standard 4	205	42.0	20.14	0–100
Standard 5	205	64.0	25.86	0–100

students' information skills (see Table 17.3 and 17.4). The results challenged some commonly held faculty assumptions and reinforced others about students' skill levels.

Having developed the instrument to the extent that it was fairly reliable with freshmen, it was time to test the instrument's suitability for seniors. In fall 2002, 150 seniors in capstone courses encompassing 8 major programs were assessed. The comparative data from freshmen and seniors allowed us to explore the instrument's ability to discern and measure differences in skill levels among different student cohorts. For seniors, significant differences were identified by major program. Details of the senior comparisons were shared with the participating instructors and department chairs. When the results were presented, the participating programs were only identified as major A, B, C, etc. In conversations with the instructors and department chairs, only the code for their major's results was revealed. This was done to promote discussions of improvement and to avoid any sense of punishment or embarrassment. Knowing the comparative location of their majors' information skills was all most departments wanted to know.

In spring 2003, to test the revisions from the fall's analysis, ninety-four seniors in a different mix of seven major programs were surveyed. Again, significant differences were identified by major and the assessment results were shared via e-mail with all faculty in participating departments to facilitate discussion (see Table 17.5).

In fall 2002, it was discovered that a few department chairs had not widely shared the assessment results of their senior majors' information skills with department faculty. These failures to disseminate the results lead to hallway "grumbling" by the uninformed faculty. Since faculty members are more likely to respond when information is presented in

Table 17.5
Seniors' Information Skills by Standard (Spring 2003)*

Major	N	Composite Scores	Standard 1	Standard 2	Standard 3	Standard 4	Standard 5
Seniors	94	55.83	57.66	49.79	66.81	45.21	68.72
Major A	15	46.40[b]	45.33	41.33	53.33	40.00	60.00[b]
Major B	14	49.43	60.00	45.71	57.14	42.86	50.00[b]
Major C	16	52.25	58.75	45.00	58.75	51.56	57.50[b]
Major D	15	55.47	64.00	44.00	73.33	41.67	62.67[b]
Major E	7	57.71	57.14	54.29	71.43	32.14	80.00
Major F	15	63.20	56.00	62.67	76.00	48.33	82.67
Major G	12	70.00[a]	63.33	60.00	83.33	54.17	100.00[a]

*Please note that in some cases the small group size and number of questions per standard may preclude more meaningful statistical comparisons.

[a,b]Refers to comparisons within column where the mean scores of group[a] are significantly ($p \leq .05$) higher than the mean scores of group[b].

terms of "their" major, sending the department's results to all department faculty was an effective way to get their attention. Once all of the participating departments' faculty knew which group code represented the results of their majors, the results were distributed to the college's entire faculty and staff.

By this time in the instrument's evolution we knew the development process was going to be a continuous incremental repetition of item review, revision, and testing. During summer 2003, analysis was conducted on the spring's results and changes were made to two questions. To solicit comments and partners in the development of comparative norms, the instrument was shared with a several other colleges. In fall 2003, King's College surveyed 200 freshmen and 132 seniors from 10 major programs for purposes of assessment and refining the instrument. That semester, Marywood University also used the instrument to assess the information skills of 165 first-year students. The freshman results were shared between the two institutions for the purpose of developing comparative norms and furthering conversations on each campus. In spring 2004, King's College assessed 134 seniors in eight major programs. Again, the appropriate information was shared with all faculty and staff.

In fall 2004, the instrument was used to assess the information skills of 256 first-year students and 142 seniors at King's College. Seeking to address their own institutional needs, two other area colleges volunteered to assess their students' information skills. Data on an additional 573 first-year, 217 senior, and 29 graduate students were collected. To further enhance the utility of the results, the instrument's 25 questions were also classified as knowledge (12) or application (13)

Table 17.6
Information Skill of Seniors and Graduate Students from Three Northeast Pennsylvania Colleges by Standard: Mean Scores/Percentage (Fall 2004)*

	N	Composite Scores	Standard 1	Standard 2	Standard 3	Standard 4	Standard 5
	388	57.22	61.24	54.54	55.31	58.04	56.96
College 1 (Seniors)	142	57.32	60.56	56.62	60.00	58.45	50.99[b]
College 2 (Graduate)	29	56.28	63.45	48.28	47.59	57.24	64.83[a]
College 3 (Seniors)	217	57.27	61.38	54.01	53.27	57.88	59.82[a]

	N	Composite Scores	Knowledge	Application
	388	57.22	58.93	55.63
College 1 (Seniors)	142	57.32	61.80	53.20
College 2 (Graduate)	29	56.28	57.18	55.44
College 3 (Seniors)	217	57.27	57.30	57.25

*Please note that in some cases the small group size and number of questions per standard may preclude more meaningful statistical comparisons.

[a,b]Refers to comparisons within column where the mean scores of group[a] are significantly ($p \leq .05$) higher than the mean scores of group[b].

Standard 1: Determine the extent of information needed
Standard 2: Access the needed information effectively and efficiently
Standard 3: Evaluate information and its sources critically
    Incorporate selected information into one's knowledge base
Standard 4: Use information effectively to accomplish a specific purpose
Standard 5: Understand the economic, legal, and social issues surrounding the use of information, and access and use information ethically and legally

Table 17.7
Percentiles—Seniors (Fall 2004)

Composite		Knowledge		Application	
Score	Percentile	Score	Percentile	Score	Percentile
24	1	17	2	15	1
28	3	25	6	23	5
32	4	33	11	31	10
36	9	42	22	38	20
40	14	50	40	46	34
44	20	58	56	54	52
48	28	67	73	62	72
52	41	75	87	69	88
56	51	83	96	77	96
60	62	92	99	85	99
64	73				
68	83				
72	90				
76	94				
80	97				
84	98				
88	99				

questions depending upon whether the question asked for advanced information based upon experience or whether it asked individuals to apply their knowledge. Assessment results are now presented in the form of a composite score and sub-scores for each of the five *Information Literacy Competency Standards for Higher Education*, as well as sub-scores for knowledge and application. Scores are expressed as a percentage based upon the number of questions answered correctly (see Table 17.6). With the data from the other two participating colleges, percentiles for the composite score and sub-scales were developed. These percentiles help to place an institution or department's scores in a larger perspective (see Table 17.7).

Psychometrics

Knowing that a common tactic of any individual or group that does not like the outcome of an assessment is to discredit the instrument or the methodology in order to avoid talking about the results, it was important to develop a conceptually and statistically sound assessment instrument that preempted that response. Using the *Information Literacy Competency Standards for Higher Education* as its conceptual framework, the spring 2005 version of the twenty-five-item instrument had a reliability (Cronbach's alpha) of .67. The instrument provides sub-scales for each of the five *Information Literacy Competency Standards* plus measures of knowledge and application.

Factor analysis was used to examine how well the instrument's theoretical construct held up under statistical scrutiny. The five *Information Literacy Competency Standards'* diverse range of overlapping performance indicators (22), outcomes (87), and objectives (138) did not contribute to a clean factor analysis. Although all of the instrument's questions eventually loaded, they did not all load along the lines of the conceptual framework. Researchers at Kent State's Project SAILS and James Madison University had similar experiences and used their factor analysis to identify twelve skill sets measured by their respective instruments.[14] In retrospect, this is not surprising since the committee that wrote *Information Literacy Competency Standards for Higher Education* clearly did not develop them with instructional design or test and measurement concerns in mind.

In working with a statistician, Daniel Ghezzi, assistant professor of mathematics, King's College, it became apparent that our desire for a relatively brief but rigorous instrument—twenty-five items—limited the upper range of the instrument's reliability. With an earlier reliability of .60 and all other factors remaining the same, doubling the number of questions to fifty would result in a projected alpha of .75; while sixty questions would achieve a projected alpha of .78. Although earlier versions of the instrument had higher reliability measures, the questions did not discriminate among students' abilities.

Adding additional items to the instrument to increase its reliability was not attractive because the increased length of the instrument could increase "fatigue" among students completing the assessment. This was borne out at Saint Francis University (Loretto, Pennsylvania), when in 2003 the length of an earlier version increased to fifty items to improve the internal validity, only to see a decrease in the number of questions students answered. Unlike the situation at James Madison University (Harrisonburg, Virginia), where students are required to pass the sixty-item *Information Literacy Test* by the end of their sophomore year, students at King's College and numerous other four-year institutions do not have the same incentive to take the test. When students have to pass such an examination their motivation is different because their individual test results affect their degree progress. In many situations where there are no graduation requirements for a passing score, the assessment methods used to sample a student cohort's information skills depend upon an instrument that is brief and discriminating, and does not induce "fatigue" in students. The trade-off between a higher reliability and avoiding test fatigue seemed reasonable in our environment.

Individual questions were examined and reexamined to obtain a true measure of students' skills. Early in the development process, predicted versus actual responses were used to identify the "easy" and "too difficult" questions (chi-square test of independence). Selected questions were examined to determine if it was the question's content, phrasing, structure, or possible responses that might be skewing results. Frequency distributions of responses for each question were analyzed to identify responses that were not sufficiently distracting or not seen as potentially viable. Eventually, item difficulty based upon the percentage of students who answered the question correctly was calculated for every item. In fall 2004, item difficulties ranged from 8.59 to 74.61 for freshmen and from 20.45 to 83.40 for seniors.

Corrected item total correlation and quartile analysis were used to identify a question's contribution to the instrument's internal consistency. A reliability analysis was performed with special attention to the corrected item total correlation. This measure for each question represents the correlation between the question and the total score calculated excluding the question. Low correlation coefficients indicate questions that may not be measuring the same trait or characteristics as the remainder of the instrument.

Following the corrected item total correlation analysis, we checked the instrument's ability to discriminate among students' skill levels. Using their composite scores, students were sorted into quartiles. The low-scoring quartile (Q1) formed the first group, with the next two quartiles (IQR) representing students with scores in the middle 50 percent. The third group (Q4) represents the high-scoring fourth-quartile students. Using chi-square procedures these groupings allowed us to examine each question's effectiveness in discerning and measuring students' skill levels. Ideally, for each question, the three groups' scores are clearly separated with the IQR group outperforming the Q1 group, and the Q4 group outperforming the IQR group. With a truly discriminating question, a smaller percentage of the Q1 group answered the question correctly, with an increasingly higher percentage of the IQR group and Q4 groups responding correctly.

Once the instrument's reliability coefficient consistently averaged .60 or above and the decision was made not to increase the length of the instrument, it was possible to begin developing norms for the instrument. Knowing first-year and senior students' scores is interesting, knowing how they varied by subscale is useful, and knowing how seniors' scores varied by major is constructive. Nonetheless, the absence of any external validation of the instrument with statistical norms was an issue that needed to be addressed. Through the cooperation of other institutions, as part of the larger context of outcomes assessment in higher education, it was possible to develop the first set of meaningful external comparisons for the instrument.

LARGER CONTEXT

Starting in the 1990s state and national calls for accountability and workforce readiness seemed to increase with the annual hikes in tuition. Coupled with these calls were significant expenditures for technology that accompanied technology's arrival on campuses in the form of personal computers and networks. In this environment colleges and departments were forced to do some introspective soul searching about the nature and purpose of higher education at the millennium and their role in it. Institutions that can document their effectiveness or contributions to students' learning are in better positions to support the rhetoric found in their catalogs and maintain the public's trust.

While the development of the King's College information literacy assessment instrument was a local response to a local need, it was actually part of a national effort to develop and assess students' information skills. At the millennium, several colleges and universities were searching for effective ways to measure students' information skills. In the state of Washington, a 2000 state legislative mandate charged the state's six public baccalaureate institutions with developing and implementing a program to assess information and technology literacy at the baccalaureate level.[15] House Bill 2375 was part of the state's larger assessment effort that included writing and quantitative reasoning skills. Washington's working group adopted ACRL's *Information Literacy Competency Standards for Higher Education* as the basis for a scoring rubric for use with samples of students' work. The assessment methodology called for a student reflective statement and required the training and "norming" of raters who would be scoring the samples of student work.

The labor-intensive methods and the relatively small number of samples that could be reviewed each year proved to be problematic and precluded meaningful generalizations and cross disciplinary and institutional comparisons.

Information literacy is an integral part of James Madison University's (Harrisonburg, VA) competency-based general education program.[16] Freshmen complete a locally developed Web-based tutorial on information skills, *Go for the Gold*, composed of eight self-paced instructional modules and exercises. At the end of the tutorial, students may then take or retake the university's *Information-Seeking Skills Test* (ISST). Students are required to pass the fifty-three-item, multiple-choice, Web-based ISST before registering for their sophomore year. Because James Madison University believes information skills are necessary for students' academic success, freshmen who do not pass the ISST have their registration held up until they pass the test. Seniors at James Madison take a major-specific information literacy test. Although seniors do not have to obtain a passing score, the assessment results are used for program evaluation purposes.

Capitalizing on their investment, librarians and assessment specialists at James Madison developed a generic version of their instrument for sale to other institutions through the university's Center for Assessment and Research Studies. This sixty-item multiple-choice Web-based test is known as the *Information Literacy Test* (ILT). The ILT, with a reliability of 0.88, measures all of the ACRL competencies except for standard four. Subscales are provided for knowledge and application as well.

In 1998, using item response theory, Kent State University librarians began developing an instrument to document claims that information skills contribute to students' academic success and retention. They sought to design an easily administered, valid, and reliable universal measure of students' information skills at the institutional level that provided internal and external benchmarking. With such an instrument, libraries could document students' information literacy levels, identify areas for improvement, and document the effectiveness of an institution's information literacy efforts.

Drawing upon the learning outcomes in ACRL's *Information Literacy Competency Standards for Higher Education*, testing of the instrument on Kent State students began in the fall of 2001, followed by testing at Oregon State University in the spring. In the fall of 2002, the Project for Standardized Assessment of Information Skills (Project SAILS) and Kent State University received a three-year grant ($252,418) from the

Institute of Museum and Library Services to support the continued development of the instrument and testing at other institutions. The grant also provided for the development of three discipline-specific assessment modules (standard four). During 2004–2005, in an effort to refine the instrument and develop the benchmarks for the twelve information skill sets measured, seventy-seven institutions administered the instrument to their students. Using a computer and Internet connection, students were presented with 45 randomly generated multiple-choice or multiple response questions from a test bank of 130 questions. Institutions involved in the testing surveyed two hundred to five hundred undergraduate students and paid $1,800 for the collection and analysis of the information.[17] During 2005, Project SAILS reviewed all of the data and examined validation issues before making a decision about the general release of the instrument in 2006.

The Bay Area Community Colleges Information Competency Assessment Project grew out of activities at Diablo Valley College, a San Francisco area community college, and California's state-wide initiative to make information competency a graduation requirement for associate degrees at all 108 California community colleges.[18] The State Chancellor's Office of the California Community Colleges identified information competency as a system-wide priority in 1996. In the fall of 1999, Diablo Valley College received a state grant to integrate information competency into the college's curriculum and to promote it to other educational institutions. A number of Bay Area community colleges and others joined Diablo Valley College to develop a challenge-out or credit-by-examination instrument for use or modification by community colleges that have an information competency requirement. Drawing upon ACRL's *Information Literacy Competency Standards for Higher Education*, the instrument consists of two sections; Part A is forty-seven items (multiple choice, matching, and short answer), and Part B is twelve performance-based multiple-part exercises. The instrument was only field tested once.

Reflective of its commitment to graduating four-year students who are information competent, the California State University (CSU) system conducted a multiyear multi-dimensional, qualitative and quantitative study of its students' information skills and behaviors.[19,20] Using the expertise of the Social and Behavioral Research Institute affiliated with CSU, San Marcos, 3,309 students from 21 campuses were surveyed to collect baseline data on students' information skills. Drawn from a random sample, students participated in a twenty-five-minute telephone survey that engaged them in a verbal demonstration and explanation of how they would solve common information problems. Students also answered a series of questions about their research processes. A year later in spring 2001, a random sample of seventy-six lower and upper division students engaged in a series of four open-ended activities designed to study students' information-seeking behaviors and their abilities to evaluate, analyze, and use information. Using ethnographic research techniques, focus groups were conducted and taped for analysis. Computer keystrokes were captured while students used the Internet and online information resources to complete open-ended assignments. Researchers observed and noted students' actions during the process. The results indicated that "students [were entering] the California State University system without core information literacy skills and abilities such as critical thinking, decision making, and self-directed learning." The CSU research also found that students rely heavily on Web-based information resources and sources found through search engines, as opposed to information in library catalogs and subscription databases. Students often do not distinguish between scholarly and popular materials and they "tend to embrace the World Wide Web over the traditional library because of convenience, flexibility, and access to what is perceived to be large amounts of current information."[21] Phase III of the California State University system's assessment strategy called for a multi-pronged study to include a number of potential items including "the development and testing of questions for an entrance/exit assessment."[22]

In fall 2004, Educational Testing Service (ETS), the world's largest private educational testing and measurement organization, launched *ICT* (Information and Communication Technology) *Literacy Assessment*, a simulation-based testing program that measures postsecondary students' ability to define, access, manage, integrate, evaluate, create, and communicate information in a technological environment.[23]

The *ICT Literacy Assessment* measures multiple aspects of ICT proficiency. Rather than posing multiple-choice questions, it requires test takers to use basic technology as a tool to arrive at solutions. The test requires that students use technology to perform information management tasks, such as extracting specific information from a database, developing a spreadsheet, or composing an e-mail message that summarizes research findings. Equipped with a computer in a proctored environment and pencil and paper for notes, students are challenged to respond to sixteen tasks over the course of the two-hour online test.

In developing this new test, ETS partnered with the California Community College System, California State University System, Miami Dade College, Oklahoma State University's College of Education, University of California at Los Angeles (UCLA), University of Louisville, University of Memphis, University of North Alabama, University of Texas System, and the University of Washington to develop the testing criteria for the *ICT Literacy Assessment*. In spring 2005, ETS and its partners worked with colleges and universities across the United States on the first large-scale test administration, the goal of which was to aggregate results for measuring the performance of particular groups. Aggregate score reports are available beginning in June 2005, and the instrument is expected to be available for general use in 2006.

According to ETS, maintaining a high level of proficiency in information and communication technology is critical for students' educational and professional advancement. The *ICT Literacy Assessment* will provide students with a gauge of how well they can use information and communication technology as a practical resource. The test will help two- and four-year colleges and universities focus on specific areas of student improvement and help schools provide documentation for accrediting organizations.

A number of other colleges and universities across the country are assessing their students' information skills. In fall 2000, Wartburg College (Waverly, Iowa) began collecting baseline information on entering students using a twenty-six-item *Information Literacy Pretest* as part of its Information Literacy Across the Curriculum effort.[24]

With several years of experience teaching information skills, the University of Mary Washington (Fredericksburg, Virginia) introduced a Web-based tutorial with assessments (TALON) in 2000. All entering freshmen, transfers, and graduate students must complete the tutorial and pass the assessment for each of the eight modules with a score of seventy-five or better in order to register for the next year's classes.[25] A growing number of colleges and universities (including the University of Wisconsin–Parkside, Minneapolis Community and Technical College, Florida Community College at Jacksonville, and University of South Dakota) have similar requirements that students successfully complete a required assessment of their information skills early in their progress toward achieving a degree.[26] Many of these institutions use this degree requirement as a way to guarantee that students have the skills they need for their academic coursework as well as their working careers.

OBSERVATIONS

While numerous American colleges and universities are striving to develop and assess their students' information skills, the particular flavor, form, and assessment processes vary according to each institution's pedagogical traditions. At King's College, the development of its information literacy assessment instrument was a local response to a national phenomenon. Use of the instrument provides faculty with comparative feedback on their seniors' information skills as well as baseline data on incoming students' skills. By sharing the data with all faculty members and staff, the library has been able to heighten faculty awareness gradually and to slowly warm the institutional and departmental waters of curricular and pedagogical change. In the absence of solid comparative assessment data, anecdotal evidence takes over, and faculty cannot effectively improve student learning. Providing standardized data on their seniors' information skills makes it possible for faculty to see "their students' faces" in the assessment results.

In only a few cases a department's initial reaction was to quibble with the results or the instrument's questions. After repeated assessments continued to confirm the relative ranking of their majors, the department moved on to the larger questions of how the department's curriculum, pedagogies, and expectations of students might have contributed to their students' information skills. In another case, all it took was the first set of results to confirm what department faculty had suspected; that their majors' skills were not as well developed as they would like. The comparison with other departments and the significant differences among them let faculty know that the issue was not just a universal concern, but rather a particular problem for their majors.

One department is frustrated with its results. Despite expressed interest in its students' information skills and renewed emphasis on the department's existing approach, students' skills have not changed significantly. However, a closer examination reveals that the department's efforts are largely compartmentalized in a first-year and senior-year course with little integration and sophisticated skill development in the intervening courses. For this department to be successful more of its faculty needs to see the connections among their actions and the department's expectations, curriculum, pedagogy, course structure, and their students' information skills.

In other departments the results are leading to quiet changes in expectations and assignments, as well as changes in the sophomore-junior diagnostic and senior capstone courses. A handful of departments are seeking to track their students' progression by capturing the data on students either as freshmen or as sophomores entering the major. This early capture of data will make meaningful comparisons possible when students are assessed again as seniors in their capstone course. In the college's cycle of program reviews, departments use the assessment results to demonstrate their effectiveness in enhancing student learning. Indeed, any successful effort to improve students' information skills must focus on how students are taught and how they learn.

CONCLUSION

Although it is early, the fact that other colleges are assessing their students' information skills may actually make it easier for King's College faculty to be comfortable in examining and improving the condition of their students' information skills. The context is no longer just "our" department or King's College, but rather academe-at-large. But more importantly, the use of assessment data has helped faculty to see a gap between what students know and what they should know. By focusing on what students are actually learning, faculty are confronted with the need to review the curriculum and draw upon a wider variety of pedagogical methods to help students develop their information skills.

Notes

1. American Library Association, Association of College and Research Libraries, *Information Literacy Competency Standards for Higher Education* (Chicago: Association of College and Research Libraries, 2000).

2. Donald W. Farmer, *Enhancing Student Learning: Emphasizing Essential Competencies in Academic Programs* (Wilkes-Barre, PA: King's College, 1988).

3. For additional background on the library's instructional program see Terrence F. Mech, "Working with Faculty in an Outcomes-Oriented Curriculum: Observations from the Library," in *The Librarian in the University: Essays on Membership in the Academic Community*, edited by H. Palmer Hall and Caroline Byrd (Metuchen, NJ: Scarecrow Press, 1990): 72–91; Judith Tierney, "Information Literacy and a College Library: A Continuing Experiment," in

Information Literacy Developing Students as Independent Learners, edited by Donald W. Farmer and Terrence Mech (Jossey-Bass *New Directions for Higher Education*), number 78 (summer 1992): 63–71.

4. Judith Tierney, "Information Literacy and a College Library," 65.

5. Terrence F. Mech and Charles I. Brooks, "Library Anxiety among College Students: An Exploratory Study," in *Continuity & Transformation: The Promise of Confluence*, edited by Richard AmRhien (Chicago: Association of College and Research Libraries, 1995), 173–179; Terrence F. Mech and Charles I. Brooks, "Anxiety and Confidence in Using a Library by College Freshmen and Seniors," *Psychological Report* 81 (1997): 929–930.

6. Wisconsin Association of Academic Librarians, *Minimum Library Use Skills: Standards Test, and Bibliography* (Madison: Wisconsin Association of Academic Librarians, 1984).

7. Illinois Association of College and Research Libraries, *Library Skills Test* (Bensenville, IL: Scholastic Testing Service, 1981).

8. American Library Association, Association of College and Research Libraries, *Information Literacy Competency Standards for Higher Education.*

9. Middle States Commission on Higher Education, *Characteristics of Excellence in Higher Education: Eligibility Requirements and Standards for Accreditation* (Philadelphia, PA: Middle States Commission on Higher Education, 2002).

10. Ibid., Standard 11, 31–39.

11. Oswald Ratteray, *A Survey of Librarians in the Middle States Region on the Role of the Library, Electronic Resources, and Information Literacy Training in Higher Education* (Philadelphia, PA: Middle States Commission on Higher Education, 1999).

12. Maryville College, *Information Literacy Competency Inventory (Pretest)* (Maryville, TN: Maryville College, 2000).

13. Helpful books include John C. Ory and Katherine E. Ryan, *Tips for Improving Testing and Grading* (Newbury Park, CA: Sage Publication, 1993); Linda Suskie, *Assessing Student Learning: A Common Sense Guide* (Bolton, MA: Anker Publishing, 2004).

14. *Project SAILS—Skill Sets* (Kent, OH: Kent State University, Libraries and Media Services, 2004). Available at http://www.projectsails.org/plans/skillsets.html#obj (accessed March 28, 2005); Julie Gedeon, Carolyn Radcliff, and Lisa O'Connor, Presentation: "Project SAILS: Facing the Challenges of Information Literacy Assessment," American Association for Higher Education Assessment Conference, June 14, 2004, Denver. Available at http://www.projectsails.org/publications/aahe_files/frame.htm (accessed March 28, 2005); Steve Wise and Katie Morrow, "Assessing Collegiate Student Information Literacy Skills with the Information Literacy Test," American Association for Higher Education Assessment Conference June 14, 2004, Denver. Available

at http://www.projectsails.org/publications/aahe_files/frame.htm (accessed March 28, 2005).

15. University of Washington, "Assessment of Information Technology Literacy" (Seattle, WA: University of Washington). Available at http://depts .washington.edu/infolitr (accessed March 28, 2005).

16. For information and history of James Madison University's information literacy and assessment efforts see, Lynn Cameron, "Assessing Information Literacy," in *Integrating Information Literacy into the Higher Education Curriculum: Practical Models for Transformation*, edited by Ilene F. Rockman and Associates (San Francisco: Jossey-Bass, 2004), 207–236; Christine E. DeMars, Lynn Cameron, and T. Dary Erwin, "Information Literacy as Foundational: Determining Competence," *The Journal of General Education* 52 (2003): 253–265.

17. *Project SAILS* (Kent, OH: Kent State University, Libraries and Media Services, 2004). Available at http://www.ProjectSails.org (accessed March 28, 2005); Lisa G. O'Connor, Carolyn J. Radcliff, and Julie A. Gedeon, "Applying Systems Design and Item Response Theory to the Problem of Measuring Information Literacy Skills," *College & Research Libraries* 63, no. 6 (2002): 528–543; Lisa G. O'Connor, Carolyn J. Radcliff, and Julie A. Gedeon, "Assessing Information Literacy Skills: Developing a Standardized Instrument for Institutional and Longitudinal Measurement," in *Crossing the Divide: Proceedings of the Tenth National Conference of the Association of College and Research Libraries*, edited by H. A. Thompson (Chicago: Association of College and Research Libraries, 2001), 163–174.

18. For details see Bonnie Gratch Lindauer and Amelie Brown, "Developing a Tool to Assess Community College Students," in *Integrating Information Literacy into the Higher Education Curriculum: Practical Models for Transformation*, edited by Ilene F. Rockman and Associates (San Francisco: Jossey-Bass, 2004), 165–206; and Bay Area Community Colleges Information Competency Assessment Project, home page (San Francisco, CA: City College of San Francisco, 2005). Available at http://topsy.org/ICAP/ICAPProject.html (accessed July 29, 2005).

19. California State University, "Information Competence in the CSU: A Report" (n.p.: California State University, 1995). Available at http://www. calstate.edu/LS/FinalRpt_95.doc (accessed March 28, 2005).

20. California State University, "Information Competence Assessment Phase Two Summary Report" (Pomona, CA: California State University, 2002). Available at http://www.csupomona.edu/~kkdunn/Icassess/phase2summary.htm (accessed July 29, 2005).

21. Ilene F. Rockman and Associates, *Integrating Information Literacy into the Higher Education Curriculum: Practical Models for Transformation* (San Francisco: Jossey-Bass, 2004), 14–15.

22. Kathleen Dunn, "Assessing Information Literacy Skills in the California State University: A Progress Report," *The Journal of Academic Librarianship* 28 (2002): 26–35.

23. Educational Testing Service, *ICT Literacy Assessment* (Princeton, NJ: Educational Testing Service, 2004–2005). Available at www.ets.org/ictliteracy (accessed November 8, 2004). Educational Testing Service, "ETS Launches ICT Literacy Assessment" (Princeton, NJ: Educational Testing Service, November 8, 2004). Available at http://www.ets.org/news/04110801.html (accessed August 2, 2005).

24. Wartburg College, "Information Literacy at Vogel Library" (Waverly, IA: Wartburg College, 2005). Available at http://public.wartburg.edu/library/infolit/ (accessed on March 28, 2005).

25. University of Mary Washington, "Information and Technology Proficiency at the University of Mary Washington—Library and Information Literacy" (Fredericksburg, VA: University of Mary Washington). Available at www.library.umw.edu/infoliteracy.html (accessed March 28, 2005).

26. University of Wisconsin–Parkside, "UW–Parkside Information Literacy Tutor" (Kenosha, WI: University of Wisconsin–Parkside, 2004). Available at http://www.uwp.edu/departments/library/infolit/intro (accessed March 21, 2005); Minneapolis Community and Technical College, "Minneapolis Community and Technical College—2004–2005 College Catalog—Information Literacy." Available at http://www.minneapolis.edu/academicAffairs/collegeCatalog/liberal_arts.cfm (accessed March 21, 2005); Florida Community College at Jacksonville, "Assessment and Certification" (Jacksonville: Florida Community College, 2005). Available at http://www.fccj.edu/campuses/kent/assessment/info_literacy.html (accessed March 21, 2005); University of South Dakota, "Information Technology Literacy Requirement" (Vermillion: University of South Dakota, 2000). Available at http://www.usd.edu/library/assessment_gateway/assessment/Literacy_Initiative/page1.htm (accessed March 21, 2005).

CHAPTER 18

Service Quality: A Perceived Outcome for Libraries

Martha Kyrillidou

Library service quality has been a concept that has been intensively researched and applied in libraries for more than a decade. Since 2000, there has been a collective effort to assess library service quality across institutions. Twelve institutions, members of the Association of Research Libraries (ARL), applied the same protocol in evaluating library service quality based on earlier work with SERVQUAL and using a Web-based survey framework. This effort led to LibQUAL+™, which, as of 2005, has been applied to more than seven hundred libraries. It has gained international significance as libraries from the United Kingdom and other European countries, as well as some institutions in Australia, Africa, and Asia are collaborating across borders.

Over the five-year period of the application of LibQUAL+™ as of the writing of this chapter, data have been collected from more than 400,000 library users regarding their perceptions of service quality. This kind of emphasis on library service quality issues within such a short time frame in a way that libraries can start benchmarking across time and across institutions was never imagined before to the extent and scale that it has taken place. Yet, where does all this intensive work on library service quality leave us? Can we start talking of service quality as a perceived *outcome* for libraries and library users? And, if yes, what are the trends and the short-term indicators that might be pointing to the possibility of conceptualizing library service quality as an outcome?

Clearly, there are different types of outcomes. The other chapters have viewed outcomes in the context of their impact of student learning.

As this chapter indicates, the challenge for the library community will be to show a connection between an outcome for service quality—the expectations of library users as they visit the library directly or through the Web—and impact of service expectations on student performance. It may well be that service quality and student satisfaction with library services produce a positive impact on students' learning. Thus, for the library community, it might pursue both types of outcomes and their connection. Still, service quality and satisfaction are not a substitute for the issues discussed in previous chapters.

In the context of the ARL New Measures Initiatives, an effort to measure information literacy skills known as Standardized Assessment of Information Literacy Skills (SAILS) has also provided opportunities for librarians to collaborate with faculty to understand students' levels of information literacy skills and how programmatic assessment of such efforts might be pursued. SAILS, which has been applied to more than seventy libraries, provides insights to institutions as to how their instructional programs are enhancing student learning. Other efforts sponsored by the Educational Testing Service (ETS) and California State University system are also aimed at developing standardized assessments of information literacy and may be used by institutions to better modify their programs to enhance student learning.

BACKGROUND

The landmark publication and 1999 Highsmith Award Winner titled *Assessing Service Quality: Satisfying the Expectations of Library Customers* by Peter Hernon and Ellen Altman, provided a thorough overview of library service quality issues, both theoretical and practical.[1] Library service quality came into the librarianship as part of the move toward total quality management which, from a product manufacturing perspective, transformed itself into the marketing services field. The realization that service is a performance that is perceived and that these perceptions are worthy of a systematic assessment seeped through the service industries, banking, and hotel services, and did not escape the attention of the library profession. Understanding perceptions is the first step in the successful management of these perceptions.

As Hernon and Altman explain, the "collective opinion of customers creates the library's reputation for service quality... Service quality is both individual and collective. The collective assessment of service quality creates the library's reputation in the community and for the administrators who fund the library."[2] Danuta Nitecki and Toni Olshen, who developed the ARL Online Lyceum of Measuring Library Service Quality in 2000, remind us that quality, much like beauty, is in the eye of the beholder. It is a highly individualized perspective shaped by prior experiences as well as current expectations of library users regarding the services they receive. The delivery of the service and rules of engagement that organizations define through mission statements, goals, and policies are important elements in shaping the received experience, but the ultimate defining point of the quality of the experience is shaped in the receiving end as "only customers judge quality, all other judgments are essentially irrelevant."[3]

In assessing library service quality, Hernon and Altman identify eleven questions that may be answered: (e.g., how much?, how many?, how valuable?, and how satisfied?). They urge libraries to focus on the customer-related indicators that provide insights into effectiveness, satisfaction, perceptions, expectations, and other concepts.[4] Complementary to the Hernon and Altman work is a rich literature on library service quality. It is worth highlighting three reviews of the topic, one written by Danuta Nitecki, another co-authored by Nitecki and Brinley Franklin as part of the New Measures Initiative, and a third one written by Fred Heath and Colleen Cook.[5] Nitecki reviews the quality movement starting from the changing perspectives in acceptable management approaches that influence the approaches a library takes to pursue excellence and assess quality. She views service quality criteria as being developed by both service providers and customers and the interaction and congruence between the criteria of service providers and those of customers are important elements for the successful delivery of services. In discussing issues related to the measurement of service quality, she points out the importance of establishing a clear purpose; the fit of the process of data gathering to the situation and need for data; the need to focus the assessment on learning rather than on keeping score; the importance of selecting methods that are appropriate for the information needed; and the importance of analyzing the data and acting on them. She concludes with the following observations:

> As we shift the role of the library away from being primarily a depository and caretaker of collections and cultural artifacts to being an active partner in the fulfillment of academic (community or corporate) missions, an assessment of the organization's activities and its relationship to

its customers will not be enough. The story of how libraries make a difference and are valued by communities served will need to go beyond measures of how well they function and how well they reflect the expectations of their customers. Quality may become a measure of distinction and a tool for improvement. The need to assess value gained by achievement of quality will be the next major challenge in gathering data in the quest for accountability and advocacy.[6]

Nitecki and Franklin focus on issues related to the difference between service quality and satisfaction, explore the need for the focus on these concepts in libraries, summarize existing practices for data gathering, pose questions for further research, and suggest next steps for ARL. In identifying questions for further research, they articulate the question of whether user satisfaction and user-based judgments of library service quality contribute to our understanding of library impact and value. "Are there libraries that are particularly successful either overall or in specific activities or with particular constituencies? If there are examples of successful libraries, are there best practices that can be identified as directly correlated to high levels of user satisfaction?"[7] They conclude with a call for a symposium to take place that would identify what libraries are doing in assessing user satisfaction and service quality, to what extent conclusions drawn from local user satisfaction studies are applicable across libraries, and what collaboration and support would be helpful to have in this area.

Heath and Cook emphasize the long-standing ties to work in the marketing services field in which Parasuraman, Zeithaml, and Berry developed the services gap model and the SERVQUAL instrument that focuses on measuring service quality as the gap between customer expectations and perceptions. As Heath and Cook note, research in marketing now explores issues related to expectations and perceptions of electronic service quality. They also describe how SERVQUAL work has led to the development of LibQUAL+™ and to a reduction in the number of dimensions that describe service quality.[8] Subsequent research in 2003 and 2004 has brought to the surface three more dimensions: affect of service, library as place, and information control.[9]

What can be said about LibQUAL+™ now? Is service quality measurement leading to a better understanding of the value of the library and does it constitute an outcome in and of itself? To answer this question we explore the interpretation of service quality as an outcome within the positive organizational change framework with emphasis on the appreciative inquiry method and the library summit concept; and we review the literature showing the relationship between service quality and measures of indirect outcomes as articulated in questions included in the LibQUAL+™ protocol.

SERVICE QUALITY AS A POSITIVE ORGANIZATIONAL CHANGE OUTCOME

Are customer-related indicators such as service quality and satisfaction library outcomes? If users experience either a positive or negative service transaction, might they change their perceptions of library service quality? Do they have elevated feelings of happiness or frustration, and how do these affective states relate to learning? Does this change of the affective state of users comprise a library outcome, and what meaningful interpretation might we assign to such experiences? Let us say, for example, that someone checking out a book from a library experiences a service failure at the circulation desk. As that person walks to the circulation desk to check out a book, he or she discovers that the circulation desk closes fifteen minutes prior to the library closing and, thus, the staff cannot check out the book. The user has the option of placing the book on reserve until the following day when he or she can return to check it out, but becomes frustrated with this experience. The result is that the user's level of satisfaction with library services diminishes. This specific user may or may not decide to come back the next day to check out the book. One can argue that this negative outcome is the result of a negative affective state that led the user to act, or interact in this case, in ways that he was not expecting. Can we characterize the affective state as an outcome, or is the outcome realized only when action takes place? The cumulative effect of positive or negative experiences that affect users' satisfaction levels creates a longer-lasting impression about the quality of services in a specific organization. Are those service quality perceptions outcomes in their own right?

The link between affective states and actions may be more or less loosely linked for different people depending on personality characteristics and other environmental factors. However, the cumulative effect of positive or negative affective states is an outcome in itself as it may be an inextricable link in a series of events ranging from the ability of the user to finish a paper, to study for an examination, to cite an article, to transform the way he or she feels, and ultimately to transform the way he or she thinks and acts. For many people outcomes are defined primarily as visible, actionable, and tangible benefits, or the lack thereof. Still, we may argue that much like quality is in the eye of the beholder, in the information age, the affective experience of using the library may be an outcome in and of itself even though it may be more closely linked to the user's subjective state of mind rather than to actions he or she may or may not take. Affective states of mind will eventually influence immediate or long-term action, or inaction. Affective states of mind may contribute to the realization of short-term outcomes but they will also invariably influence outcomes that require longer time frames to be realized.

If we focus on aspects of positive organizational thinking as recent literature points out, we are more likely to accept service quality issues as outcomes in and of themselves. According to positive organizational psychology and positive organizational management theories, the way we think affects the way we act. Therefore, thinking positively, having a high opinion of the library, and believing that using the library leads to beneficial outcomes indeed realizes these beneficial outcomes.

Appreciative Inquiry

Part of the positive organizational scholarship includes a school of thought and practice known as appreciative inquiry (AI).[10] AI is a methodology that helps leaders focus on the positive instead of the negative; rather than concentrating on problems the focus is on solutions. In the AI school of thought, an organization is a mystery to be embraced, whereas in the traditional problem-solving model, organizational problems are challenges to be solved through the process of identifying the issues, analyzing the causes, brainstorming solutions, and developing action plans. AI, on the other hand, includes steps such as appreciating what an organization is, envisioning what it might be, discussing what it should be, and innovating by focusing on what it will be and acting on that vision positively.

AI includes a four-step inquiry model (the four-D model): dream, design, destiny, and discovery. In the dream stage participants are asked to dream of a vision and a purpose, whereas in the design stage they explore the relationships and the organizational structures they enjoy. In the destiny stage they are asked to commit to a structure and work on its implementation, and in the discovery stage they are asked to influence and participate in the strategic context and maintain the positive core of the activities of an organization. AI is a way of focusing on the questions and understanding that it is the way we ask questions that determines the answers to a large extent. By focusing our questions on what works rather than on what does not work within an organization, we are magnifying something that is worthy of mention. Our attention should be focused on these issues that are worthy. So, instead of asking what the biggest problem is, we can focus on what the possibilities are, what the smallest change is that we can make that would have the biggest impact.

The basic elements of an AI question focus on describing a peak experience or a high point, things that are valued most about an experience, the conceptualization and formation of a desired future. AI uses positive language by focusing our attention to positive things, creates energy to answer questions and opportunities to think creatively, breaks automatic thinking about problems, includes an interplay on dialogue and storytelling, and works on defining a specific positive future. It is an interactive process that takes time to be implemented as it always stretches, challenges, and innovates. It is grounded in examples that bridge the best of what is with the best of what might be. And, it needs to be stated in bold, affirmative steps. The provocative proposition of appreciative inquiry is our ability to move from individual will to group will to realize something that is more powerful that the sum of the individuals.

AI is a transformative process because it helps us derive the future from reality. We can see it, we know what it feels like, and we move to a collective, collaborative view of where we are going. Unlike other methodologies that can be recipes, the results are invented with experience that leads to innovation and to action.

As part of trying to understand how the measurement of library service quality as done with LibQUAL+™ can lead to more positive outcomes, and to obtain experience with appreciative inquiry approaches, we worked on developing questions that focus on those aspects of appreciative inquiry that make the questions more positive. Figure 18.1 contains a list of questions that participants in a recent conference on positive organizational scholarship discussed. Three questions focus on a more descriptive and analytical approach, whereas the other three are framed within the more appreciative and innovative framework. The questions were tested with conference participants who had to choose one from the descriptive and analytical framework and discuss it for ten

Figure 18.1
Exploring Appreciative Inquiry as a Framework for Following Up on Your LibQUAL+™ Data*

"Descriptive and Analytical"

LibQUAL+™ result notebooks present "gap" analysis of your users' perceptions of library service quality for three dimensions of library service quality (a) affect of service, (b) library as place, and (c) information control. LibQUAL+™ shows the gap between users' minimum and desired expectations. Institutions tend to be descriptive and analytical when they are approaching the interpretation of their LibQUAL+™ results.

The following questions are offered as examples of describing the library services in descriptive and analytical terms:

Affect of Service

Describe an incident where a patron in your library received "bad" service and an incident where a patron received "exceptional" service. Identify an incident that demonstrates the interaction of library staff with patrons and shows lack or presence of empathy, reliability, trusted relationships.

Library as Place

Describe the physical facility of your library. What works and what doesn't? Identify how the facility meets the needs of undergraduates, graduate students, and faculty.

Information Control

Describe an incident where a patron in your library has identified the information he/she wanted and another incident where a patron has failed to identify the information they needed. Identify an incident that demonstrates the ability of patrons to find, or not, information in a self-sufficient way.

"Appreciative and Innovative"

The following questions are offered as examples of questions that are formulated along the lines of the appreciative inquiry (AI) framework as appreciative and innovative:

Affect of Service

1. Our goal is to provide exceptional service to you, our users. Describe an incident (it doesn't have to be library-related) when you received exceptional service.
   - What made this experience memorable to you?
   - What were the key elements that made this a positive experience?
   - What other factors would have enhanced the experience?

Library as Place

2. Imagine that you walk into the library and find it transformed.
   - What do you see in this image?
   - How does this transformed library feel to you?
   - What elements of your vision would help us achieve it?

Information Control

3. Imagine a time that you were looking for information. You were immediately successful in your quest. You found exactly what you wanted quickly and you received it in a format that was most useful to you.
   - What did your information quest look like?
   - What were the elements that made your search efficient and thorough?
   - Looking to the future, how would you enhance this experience?

Source: Joan Cheverie and Martha Kyrillidou, presentation at ARL/ OLMS Conference on Positive Organizational Scholarship, Washington, D.C., November 8–9, 2004.

minutes and then another one from the appreciative inquiry framework. Conference participants attending our session and participating in this exercise indicated that the appreciative and innovative framework of asking questions did indeed lead to a different discussion that focused on more positive, innovative, and effective outcomes.

Measuring library service quality can provide the basis for asking the right questions that can lead to positive, innovative, and effective outcomes. AI presents one framework that libraries can use to influence the outcomes from a service quality measurement exercise to focus on the more positive aspects of organizational development.

Library Summit

The library summit exercise is another approach that falls within the positive organizational framework scholarship. Clemson University and the University of Texas implemented the exercise as a follow-up activity to their LibQUAL+™ survey. The summit gathered people who have a stake in the future of university libraries to discuss LibQUAL+™ results, thereby adding depth and context to the survey numbers and generating fresh solutions and suggestions for service improvements.[11] Figure 18.2 highlights the benefits of the summit, which include the creation of goodwill, a follow-up activity that closes the information loop in the LibQUAL+™ assessment exercise, the attempt for the library to market and outreach, the generation of original ideas, and additional data for planning, as well as the creation of a collective will that fosters positive climate for change.

Figure 18.2
The Benefits of a Library Summit*

Goodwill. An organization that makes its weaknesses public and asks for advice and help gains positive regard. Participants and library staff also appreciate having their opinions taken seriously.

"Closing the loop." Library plans based on LibQUAL+™ survey results and Summit discussions provide good structure for showcasing positive outcomes in assessment.

Personal investment. Participants tend to take ownership of their ideas and may stay more involved and connected with the library to see if their suggestions are implemented.

Outreach. Everyone involved in a Library Summit learns something about library resources and services.

Original ideas. Library "outsiders" provide fresh interpretations and insights that might not be generated internally.

More data. Input from Library Summit participants provides richer and more detailed data for LibQUAL+™ survey items.

Buy-in. The Summit process is inclusive, so it reduces internal and external disagreements about priorities and decisions.

Climate change. Administrative, faculty, staff, and student endorsement of a Summit sets the tone for campus-wide collaboration in library success.

Source: Joseph Boykin, Jan Comfort, and Peg Tyler at Clemson University; Fred Heath, Damon Jaggars, and Jocelyn Duffy, "LibQUAL+™ and Decision Making: The Library Summit," flier prepared by Clemson University, University of Texas, and ARL (June 4, 2004).

Satisfaction, Service Quality, and Perceived Outcomes

The LibQUAL+™ survey itself asks a few questions regarding perceived outcomes. These questions and their relationship to service quality and general satisfaction questions were explored in a recent study investigating the validity of LibQUAL+™ scores, and specifically how total and subscale LibQUAL+™ scores are associated with self-reported, library-related satisfaction and perceived outcomes scores.[12] Participants included 88,664 students and faculty who completed the American English ($n_{AE} = 69,494$) or the British English ($n_{BE} = 19,170$) LibQUAL+™ language versions in the 2004 data collection cycle.

Results suggest that LibQUAL+™ scores primarily measure satisfaction rather than outcomes.

This research study explored the following questions: to what extent do LibQUAL+™ scores measure user satisfaction with the library and/or outcomes the library is perceived to facilitate for users? And, to what extent do the three LibQUAL+™ scale scores (i.e., service affect, library as place, and information control) correlate with user satisfaction with the library and/or outcomes the library is perceived to facilitate for users? "The outcomes questions focus on personal benefits to the user, such as the role of the library in facilitating academic advancement or staying abreast of developments in the field. These outcome items reflect issues of perceived value, as related to academic pursuits."[13] The results suggested that service quality scores primarily relate to satisfaction rather than perceived outcomes. "This result does *not* mean that LibQUAL+™ scores are uncorrelated with perceived outcomes. However, LibQUAL+™ scores are better correlated with satisfaction than with outcomes, and the relationship of outcome scores with LibQUAL+™ scores overlaps with or is common to the larger correlations of LibQUAL+™ scores with satisfaction. In other words, the outcomes in terms of perceived value in accomplishing academic pursuits are subsumed within the larger construct of general satisfaction."[14]

> As educational institutions increasingly view outcomes from different perspectives, the issue of whether outcomes measures should be strictly limited to productivity issues is a challenge to be resolved. It seems reasonable to argue that outcomes measures ought to encompass concerns about satisfaction that reflect perceived value-added contributions of library services to productivity. And in any case, users have a clear self-interest in helping us provide the services that they believe will make them more productive or efficient in their academic pursuits.[15]

LibQUAL+™ might be more of a satisfaction than an outcomes measure. Affective states of mind such as satisfaction are important and influence both perceptions of service quality and the realization of tangible outcomes. This finding is sensible as it relates to and confirms the theoretical basis of positive organizational scholarship discussed earlier. It also confirms once more that "LibQUAL+™ seems to behave in a theoretically intuitive manner as regards satisfaction versus academic outcomes."[16]

Information Literacy

Student learning has become central in the academic enterprise and libraries are refocusing their mission toward instructional partnerships. Teaching is gradually moving away from the mechanical to the conceptual and many libraries have recognized that information competencies need to be integrated strategically across the curriculum. An information literate person is someone who can locate, access, use, and evaluate information efficiently and effectively. Information literacy has been articulated through a variety of groups within the American Library Association, including the American Association of School Librarians and the Association of College and Research Libraries. Building on these perspectives, a research team from Kent State University secured an IMLS grant and partnered with ARL to develop a standardized tool known as SAILS for measuring information literacy outcomes. SAILS attempts to measure whether students gain information literacy skills through their academic experience and whether information literacy makes a difference to student success.[17]

In addition to the ARL SAILS New Measures work, the Educational Testing Service has been developing a new Information and Communication Technology (ICT) Literacy Assessment. The ETS ICT tool is a simulation-based testing program that measures postsecondary students' abilities to define, access, manage, integrate, evaluate, create, and communicate information in a technological environment. It is a tool that integrates and tests both cognitive and technological competencies.[18]

The National Survey of Student Engagement (NSSE)[19] is another instrument that libraries have examined to determine its relationship to the information literacy outcomes in which libraries are interested. This annual survey measures undergraduate "participation in programs and activities that institutions provide for their learning and personal development." At least one study that NSSE as an excellent diagnostic fit with the Information Literacy Competency Standards developed by ACRL as learning outcomes are correlated with student engagement. Case studies from the University of Mississippi and Indiana University–Purdue University Indianapolis demonstrate how librarians can apply NSSE results for the purposes of assessment.[20]

All these efforts are clearly pointing to the need for continued work in developing programs within the academic enterprise that define the information competencies of students in terms of specific information outcomes. They also demonstrate a variety of different perspectives of how information literacy may be defined, but the link between library service quality and direct outcome measures still needs to be established through systematic and controlled investigation. Academic libraries should continue to study the indirect impact of satisfaction and service quality measures on learning, but ultimately we need to understand the direct impact of these affective states on learning and research. There are studies now looking into measuring information literacy outcomes in a more direct way, but there has been no study attempting to look at the relationship between assessment of information literacy skills and service quality indicators. For example, in the context of the ARL New Measures Initiatives, it would be intriguing to study how SAILS and LibQUAL+™ have been applied across libraries and what the relation of these two is in different library settings.

A VIEW FROM THE TRENCHES: UNIVERSAL LIBRARY SERVICE PROVISION

Preliminary analysis of actions taken by libraries based on the results of the intensive and extensive assessment that the LibQUAL+™ protocol performs indicate that libraries are using library service quality to effect positive organizational change. This is clear both in reports published in the library and information science literature and on the Web pages libraries have created for further dissemination.[21] Both the AI framework and the library summit concept have the potential to serve as examples of how theory and practice can merge together to start creating positive outcomes from service quality assessment results.

Users' perceptions of their own personal outcomes related to improved productivity and success are linked to positive feelings regarding both service quality and satisfaction with library services. Whether all these indicators are sufficient to lead to richer understanding and enhanced impact of library services on the processes of teaching, learning, research, and community service is still an unanswered question, as the value of these processes is being challenged by public accountability pressures and technological change. Can librarians be perceived as true partners in the teaching and research process, and thereby integrate their assessment efforts with other institutional assessment efforts led by faculty?

It appears that libraries are rising to Rowena Cullen's challenge urging them to use the results of library service quality assessment to effect change.[22] Yet, whether these actions are sufficient to ensure thriving, creative, and innovative libraries that will withstand the increasing competition for attention still remains an unanswered question. The positive outcomes described in this chapter, and the unleashing of creative and innovative positive actions in libraries, underscore the urgency of not only internal improvement of service quality, but also effective and forceful external marketing of the library. Ultimately the best marketing is word of mouth from satisfied customers. Can libraries enlist faculty and students as partners and collaborators to work together with librarians to study the links between libraries and learning outcomes?

CONCLUSION

A massive exercise of assessing library service quality can lead not only to local improvements but also to regional, national, and international marketing efforts to unleash the creativity of librarians worldwide, joined by students, authors, teachers, and other partners. The challenge is to view as a professional obligation the need to act positively for fulfilling the information needs of library users all over the globe. The student of one institution today is the professor at the next institution tomorrow, the high school teacher in one country is the graduate student of an online university in yet another country, the elementary school student in Maryland is the summer school day camp student in Thessaloniki, Greece.[23]

Adopting *universal library service provision* as a vision may be bold enough but academic libraries still need to play a significant, partnership role in educating students and helping them change (improve their critical thinking, problem-solving, technological, communication, and other abilities) as they progress through their education. The challenge for those supporting the service quality and satisfaction movements in academic libraries will be to develop ways to connect these significant efforts to outcomes assessment as described by stakeholders such as regional and program accreditation organizations. Organizational effectiveness ensures that the library and other academic units support the institutional mission and engage in assessment for learning—"a systematic and systemic process of inquiry into what and how students learn over the progression of their studies . . . driven by intellectual curiosity about the efficacy of collective educational practices."[24] This is the next great leap forward for the service quality movement practiced in libraries.

Notes

1. Peter Hernon and Ellen Altman, *Assessing Service Quality: Satisfying the Expectations of Library Customers* (Chicago: American Library Association, 1998).

2. Ibid., 15.

3. Valarie A. Zeithaml, A. Parasuraman, and Leonard L. Berry, *Delivering Quality Service: Balancing Customer Perceptions and Expectations* (New York: The Free Press, 1990), 16.

4. Hernon and Altman, *Assessing Service Quality*, 51–58.

5. Danuta Nitecki, "Quality Assessment Measures in Libraries," *Advances in Librarianship* 25 (2001): 133–162; Danuta Nitecki and Brinley Franklin, "New Measures for Research Libraries," *The Journal of Academic Librarianship* 25 (1999): 484–487; Fred Heath and Colleen Cook, "SERVQUAL: Service Quality Assessment in Libraries," *Encyclopedia of Library and Information Science*, 2nd ed., vol. 4, edited by Miriam A. Drake (New York: Marcel Dekker, 2003), 2613–2635.

6. Nitecki, "Quality Assessment Measures in Libraries," 158.

7. Nitecki and Franklin, "New Measures for Research Libraries," 487.

8. Heath and Cook, "SERVQUAL." See also Colleen Cook and Fred M. Heath, "Users' Perceptions of Library Service Quality: A LibQUAL+™ Qualitative Study," *Library Trends* 49 (Spring 2001): 548–584; Colleen Cook and Bruce Thompson, "Psychometric Properties of Scores from the Web-based LibQUAL+ Study of Perceptions of Library Service Quality," *Library Trends* 49 (Spring 2001): 585–604.

9. With subsequent research three dimensions have emerged. These include affect of service, library as place, and information control, which subsumed the earlier dimensions of access to information and personal control.

10. David L. Cooperrider, Diana Whitney, and Jacqueline M. Stavros, *Appreciative Inquiry Handbook* (Bedford Heights, OH: Lakeshore Communications, Inc., 2003).

11. Joseph F. Boykin, "LibQUAL+™ as a Confirming Resource," *Performance Measurement and Metrics* 3, no. 2 (2002): 74–77. See also http://www.libqual.org and click on "Publications."

12. Bruce Thompson, Colleen Cook, and Martha Kyrillidou, "Concurrent Validity of LibQUAL+™ Scores: What Do LibQUAL+™ Scores Measure?" *Journal of Academic Librarianship* 31, forthcoming.

13. Ibid.

14. Ibid.

15. Ibid.

16. Ibid.

17. Lisa G. O'Connor, Carolyn J. Radcliff, and Julie A. Gedeon, "Applying Systems Design and Item Response Theory to the Problem of Measuring

Information Literacy Skills" *College & Research Libraries* 63, no. 6 (2002): 528–543; Lisa G. O'Connor, Carolyn J. Radcliff, and Julie A. Gedeon, "Assessing Information Literacy Skills: Developing a Standardized Instrument for Institutional and Longitudinal Measurement," in *Crossing the Divide: Proceedings of the Tenth National Conference of the Association of College and Research Libraries*, edited by H. A. Thompson (Chicago: Association of College and Research Libraries, 2001), 163–174.

18. Educational Testing Service, *ICT Literacy Assessment* (Princeton, NJ: Educational Testing Service, 2004–2005). Available at http://www.ets.org/ictliteracy (accessed August 1, 2005).

19. National Survey of Student Engagement (Bloomington: National Survey of Student Engagement, the Indiana University Center for Postsecondary Research, January 20, 2005). Available at http://www.indiana.edu/~nsse/ (accessed August 1, 2005).

20. Amy E. Mark and Polly D. Boruff-Jones, "Information Literacy and Student Engagement: What the National Survey of Student Engagement Reveals about Your Campus," *College & Research Libraries* 64, no. 6 (2003): 480–493.

21. Colleen Cook, ed., "The Maturation of Assessment in Academic Libraries: The Role of LibQUAL+™," *Performance Measurement and Metrics* 3, no. 2 (2002): 34–108; Fred M. Heath, Martha Kyrillidou, and Consuella A. Askew, eds., "Libraries Act on their LibQUAL+™ Findings: From Data to Action," *Journal of Library Administration* 40, no. 3 and 4 (2004): 1–240.

22. Rowena Cullen, "Perspectives on User Satisfaction Surveys," *Library Trends* 49 (Spring 2001): 662–686.

23. The last specific example draws on the personal experience of the author's children. The other possible roles described are also drawn from real life examples of the author's friends and family who are crossing international boundaries to fulfill their educational and information needs.

24. Peggy L. Maki, *Assessing for Learning: Building a Sustainable Commitment across the Institution* (Sterling, VA: Stylus Publishing, 2004), xvii.

CHAPTER 19

Future Directions in Outcomes Assessment

Peter Hernon and Robert E. Dugan

A recurring question is, "What is the proper balance among teaching, research/scholarship, and service for any faculty member seeking promotion and tenure?" Presumably those faculty members at the rank of full professor have answered that question, probably by tipping the balance toward research and publication. Promotion and tenure policies and committees tend to favor these categories, especially with publications appearing in peer-reviewed journals with high impact factors and outstanding national and international reputations. An underlying question is, "How do institutions recognize and reward excellent teachers?" David G. Evans, professor of hydrogeology and chair of the Department of Geology at California State University at Sacramento, calls for "a teaching Hall of Fame that included all excellent teachers willing to have their instruction reviewed and evaluated by their peers."[1] Still, the question remains, "What is the proper balance among teaching, research/publication, and service for junior faculty members trying to earn tenure?"

When promotion and tenure committees (as well as many faculty members) look for evidence of excellence in teaching/learning, they tend to see teaching through the eyes of the instructor, not the recipient of that instruction—the learner. On the other hand, when outcomes assessment concentrates on student learning outcomes, there is an expectation that faculty and administrators will align learning with the institutional mission statement and develop (and achieve) a characterization of program graduates—one supported with actual evidence, where that evidence is actually used to improve learning. As both this book and its companion, *Outcomes Assessment in Higher Education*, emphasize, more and more academic institutions are accepting the value of setting student learning outcomes. Stakeholders (e.g., state governments, regional accrediting organizations, and program accrediting bodies) support this alignment of programs of study to institutional mission statements. Stakeholders, including the federal government, expect academic institutions to produce and report aggregate student outcomes. Together, student learning outcomes and student outcomes form a basis for institutional accountability for learning that occurs at both the undergraduate and graduate levels.

Given this situation and the change in culture that it imposes on academic institutions, this chapter goes beyond current developments. It examines the direction that outcomes assessment is likely to take—both horizontally and vertically; offers a research agenda, one that funding agencies, it is hoped, might support; and discusses a government report. It also offers the perspectives of some of the recognized leaders of outcomes assessment in the United States and quality assurance elsewhere about critical issues that outcomes assessment may face in the near future.

DISCIPLINE-BASED OUTCOMES IN A FRAMEWORK FOR OUTCOMES PROCESSES

A strategic direction for outcomes assessment is the increasing realization of the importance of and need for the creation and assessment of discipline-based learning outcomes as well as broader institutional outcomes. While accreditation by the regional accrediting organizations will remain critical for higher education institutions, especially for meeting requirements to receive federal funds, accreditation for academic programs and disciplines is increasingly important in demonstrating educational effectiveness and accountability to internal and external stakeholders, and in defining a role for academic institutions in contributing to post-graduation careers.

As introduced in chapter one, institutions deploy a systematic, interactive, and integrated horizontal and vertical framework to gather, analyze, and report information as part of their efforts to demonstrate accountability through assessment planning processes within the institutional environment. However, regional and specialized program/discipline accreditors want institutions to evolve beyond planning for assessment to providing evidence that the process is actually used to compile and analyze student learning outcomes, and that the analysis is used to consider, plan, and implement changes in educational objectives and pedagogy in a continuous effort to improve learning.

Applying the framework for outcomes processes model advanced in Figure 1.2, learning outcomes are captured at the course level, and then compiled and reported to the department and disciplines levels. At that level the information is analyzed and combined with information from peer disciplines, and then reported upwards to the college or school level (e.g., school of arts and sciences). This horizontal level may aggregate analyses and outcomes from their respective departments and programs for upwards communication to the institution for summary reporting, inclusive of all schools, to stakeholders. As a result, the institutional framework to assess learning outcomes is increasingly dependent upon its vertical structures to collect and report evidence of student learning outcomes and its subsequent application of systematic changes to institutional and program educational objectives in order to improve student learning. The effort to measure outcomes through the institution's disciplines and courses is intended to provide the evidence sought by accreditors and to address the other stakeholders' demands for accountability and effectiveness.

Some examples illustrate this strategic direction. Faculty at Alverno College in Milwaukee, Wisconsin, have created a core curriculum (a horizontal structure in terms of Figure 1.1) that requires all students to demonstrate eight abilities:

1. Communications;
2. Analysis;
3. Problem solving;
4. Valuing in decision making;
5. Social interaction;
6. Developing a global perspective;
7. Effective citizenship; and
8. Aesthetic engagement.[2]

Faculty then integrate these abilities as appropriate into the design of their courses within their respective disciplinary contexts,[3] as they address the following questions:

- What should students be able to do and how should they be able to think as a result of study in a discipline?
- What does learning in the disciplines look like at different developmental levels?
- How do faculty design learning and assessment in the disciplines?
- How do faculty approach study of their disciplines with student learning as their primary focus?
- What institutional structures and processes can assist faculty to engage and teach their disciplines as frameworks for student learning?[4]

However, the faculty do not function exclusively within their own specific discipline. Alverno College has established an integrating horizontal framework of teaching, learning, and assessment by creating eight departments based on the eight identified abilities, and faculty represent their disciplines as members of these abilities-based departments.[5] This approach therefore integrates the vertical disciplines with the cross-disciplinary horizontal structure of the abilities.

Another application of the assessment of learning outcomes in the vertical institutional structure involves academic program/discipline accreditors. As an example of discipline accrediting organizations, the Council of Higher Education Accreditation (CHEA) recognizes AACSB International—the Association to Advance Collegiate Schools of Business (AACSB)—as the accrediting authority for collegiate institutions granting degrees in business administration and/or accounting. AACSB's published accreditation standards include the identification of learning experiences in general knowledge and skills in the undergraduate degree program related to:

- Communication abilities;
- Ethical understanding and reasoning abilities;
- Analytic skills;
- Use of information technology;
- Multicultural and diversity understanding; and
- Reflective thinking skills.[6]

This accrediting organization then identifies learning experiences in management-specific knowledge and skills areas for undergraduate and master's level general management degree programs, which include:

- Ethical and legal responsibilities in organizations and society;
- Financial theories, analysis, reporting, and markets;
- Creation of value through the integrated production and distribution of goods, services, and information;
- Group and individual dynamics in organizations;
- Statistical data analysis and management science as they support decision-making processes throughout an organization;
- Information technologies as they influence the structure and processes of organizations and economies, and as they influence the roles and techniques of management;
- Domestic and global economic environments of organizations; and
- Other management-specific knowledge and abilities as identified by the school.[7]

The seven general and knowledge skills would be applicable to many undergraduate programs (and are therefore horizontal), whereas the management-specific knowledge and skills areas represent the specific needs of the business discipline as a vertical structure.

The AACSB procedures and standards state that the assurance of learning standards evaluates how well a school accomplishes the educational aims of its activities. Every school must develop and make known its educational goals, and measure its accomplishments to demonstrate accountability so as to inform interested stakeholders of achievements compared against the stated goals. Another identified function of the learning standards is to assist the school and faculty in improving programs and services.

The AACSB requires schools to specify learning goals for each degree program (e.g., Bachelor of Science in Business Administration [BSBA], Bachelor of Science in Management Information Systems [BSMIS], and Bachelor of Arts in International Management [BAIM]); however, a set of learning goals for each major within a degree (e.g., BSBA degree with defined majors in finance, marketing, human resource management, operations management, and general management) would not require distinct learning goals for accrediting purposes.

The faculty in aggregate (in total or by some representative unit) is responsible for or otherwise involved in identifying and defining the school's learning goals. The learning goals are therefore integrated and support both horizontal (degree) and vertical structures (majors within each degree) within the vertically structured school (business program) within the institution (the ultimate horizontal level).

Lastly, AACSB states that schools must demonstrate that learning occurs for each of the learning goals the school has identified for its programs. Approaches identified include the criteria for selection of students through the admission process into the program, course-embedded measurements, and demonstration through stand-alone testing or performance. No single approach to assurance of learning is required, but AACSB seeks the application of direct over indirect outcomes measures.

A third example reviews the evolution of standards focused on the institutional level to that of the disciplines. In 2000, the Association of College and Research Libraries, a division of the American Library Association, published *Information Literacy Competency Standards for Higher Education*.[8] The standards were intended to be used in the context of the entire institution and do not specify any academic discipline. One regional accrediting organization, the Middle States Commission on Higher Education, has applied these institutional-based standards within its published guidelines.[9]

In 2004, the Science and Technology Section (STS) of the Association of College and Research Libraries approved a draft of *Information Literacy Standards for Science and Technology* intended to be used by "science and technology educators, in the context of their institution's mission, to help guide their information literacy–related instruction and to assess student progress."[10] This framework model, which applies to the entire institution, functions on the horizontal level, although the educational objectives and outcomes are likely to be planned and implemented by the academic library as a vertical entity with the involvement of interested academic departments (also in vertical structures to that of the institution). However, the model would be applied vertically from the institution to the science program (its horizontal peers would be likely to include humanities, social sciences, and so on) where the science departments would undertake a cross-departmental, horizontal planning process to identify shared educational outcomes and objectives. In turn, these educational objectives would be implemented, measured, and analyzed through specific, and vertical, discipline-based courses. Outcomes data compiled from the discipline-based courses would then be reported back to the horizontal level (the science program) for analysis and summary reporting to the other horizontal levels—the school in which the science program resides, and the institution.

The *Information Literacy Standards for Science and Technology* could also be applied to assist an academic program in demonstrating compliance with the accreditation standards as promulgated by its program accreditors. For example, CHEA recognizes ABET, Inc. as the organization responsible for the accreditation of education programs leading to degrees in engineering, engineering technology, computing, and applied science. ABET uses accreditation criteria to evaluate compliance with its four academic programs areas. Included in those criteria are requirements for programs to create educational objectives and outcomes, and to undertake an assessment process to demonstrate student attainment.[11] Performance indicators and outcomes specified by the *Information Literacy Standards for Science and Technology* fit well with the skills and abilities required to be demonstrated by students in academic programs seeking one or more of ABET's program accreditations.

In context, the *Information Literacy Standards for Science and Technology* is a strategic direction to provide guidelines to a vertical framework supporting program-specific standards. As a result, the information literacy guidelines for the science disciplines clarify and strengthen, without weakening, the institution's information literacy standards. Discipline-specific educational outcomes and objectives in the sciences will be identified, measured, analyzed, and reported. Additional information literacy guidelines may be created in the future to support and strengthen the learning outcomes assessment efforts for other vertical disciplines such as the humanities and social sciences, and in the professional programs such as business.

RESEARCH AGENDA

The research agenda is suggestive, rather than comprehensive. The intent is to illustrate that there is still much to learn about outcomes assessment and its practice, both within the United States and elsewhere. Questions on the agenda ask:

- How can academe promote student learning outcomes to policy-makers and other stakeholders who are accustomed to relying on aggregate student outcomes (e.g., graduation rate)? Why do employers value learning outcomes more than aggregate student outcomes? Can both parties be brought together?

- For master's programs that are one or two years in duration and in which students do not automatically progress from the collective set of core or required courses to completion of the elective portion, what are the alternatives to developing a scoring rubric that progresses from novice to intermediate and advanced (or graduate)?

- How well do the stated outcomes align (map) to the curriculum and educational practices?

- How common are faculty outcomes at those institutions engaged in the use of student learning outcomes? Faculty outcomes focus on the degree to which student learning outcomes affect the perceptions, values, skills, and teaching pedagogies of faculty. In those instances where institutions and programs have faculty self-evaluations, do faculty outcomes appear in those documents? How have those outcomes impacted student learning? Do such outcomes change classroom dynamics?

- What, if any differences, are there between public and private academic institutions in assessment, in particular student learning outcomes?

- How might student learning outcomes be more discipline focused?

- Do student learning outcomes engage students more in the life of the institution and program of study?

- Are there ways to gather and examine team and self-study reports of regional and program accreditation organizations across institutions and over time? The purpose would be to search for patterns and the evolution of outcomes assessment.

- Which program-accrediting bodies assess student learning outcomes and are there differences between their assessment processes?

- How has assessment changed institutional and program cultures? Where have the changes been successful and why?

- How valid are the tasks that reflect the accomplishment of particular learning outcomes?

- How well do special populations (e.g., international students with poor language and written communication skills, students with cognitive or physical challenges, and entering freshmen who need remedial assistance) master student learning outcomes? If problems exist, how are they resolved?

DEVELOPING A SET OF COMPREHENSIVE INDICATORS

Countries such as Australia, Canada, the United Kingdom, and the United States have extensive and broad statistical systems that have captured a substantial amount of highly specialized activity for years. There is a concerted effort in these countries to develop comprehensive key indicator systems that cast these activities in a broader framework to aid policymakers, researchers, and others in gaining a broader perspective. They should also be able to "clarify problems and opportunities, and track progress towards achieving results."[12] As the Government Accountability Office (GAO), formerly the General Accounting Office, noted in a major report titled *Informing Our Nation*,

> To be a leading democracy in the information age may very well mean producing unique public sources of objective, independent, scientifically grounded, and widely shared quality information so that we know where the United States stands now and how we are trending, on both an absolute and relative basis—including comparisons with other nations. By ensuring that the best facts are made more accessible and usable by the many different members of our society, we increase the probability of well-framed problems good decisions, and effective solutions.[13]

Those comprehensive key indicator systems might cover the *economy* (consumers and employment, transportation and infrastructure, finance and money, business and markets, government, and the world economy), the *environment* (the earth and its ecosystems, land, water, life, air, and national resources), and *society and culture* (health and housing; communities and citizenship; education and innovation; security and safety; crime and justice; children, families and aging; democracy and governance; and values and culture).

The GAO defines an indicator as "a quantitative measure that describes an economic, environmental, social or cultural condition over time. The unemployment rate, infant mortality rates, and air quality indexes are a few examples." The GAO then defines an indicator system as "an organized effort to assemble and disseminate a group of indicators that together tell a story about the position and progress of a jurisdiction or jurisdictions, such as the City of Boston, the State of Oregon, or the United States of America." These "systems collect information from suppliers (individuals who respond to surveys or institutions that provide data they have collected), which providers (e.g., the Census Bureau) then package into products and services for the benefit of users..."[14] Furthermore, indicator systems might be topical (cover, e.g., health, education, or public safety) or comprehensive ("pull together only the most essential indicators on a range of economic, environmental, and social and cultural issues").

Healthy People, an initiative of the Department of Health and Human Services started in 1979, highlights ten health indicators (e.g., physical activity, overweight and obesity) that are collected every ten years, and it provides national health objectives and indicators to measure progress, which are revisited every ten years.[15] It seems that "comprehensive key indicator systems are primarily but not exclusively, either learning-oriented or outcome-oriented.... The term outcome-oriented refers to a general concern with impact on the conditions of society."[16] Furthermore, "these indicator systems are used to monitor and encourage progress toward a vision for the future—or in some cases a specific set of goals—which have been established by the people and institutions within a jurisdiction."[17]

Although the report does not address outcomes—either student outcomes or student learning outcomes—a comprehensive indicator system might apply to the *condition of higher education* and reflect areas such as cost, student health, safety, and learning. The goals of stakeholders and those individuals paying for their own education or that of their dependents are to ensure that anyone seeking further education—be it vocational or other—has the opportunity to attend college or university and to do so at an affordable cost. Although issues related to quality become secondary, they are not unimportant, especially when stakeholders raise questions about value for money.

We are not convinced that there will be a comprehensive indicator system that reflects the condition of higher education or if there is that it will include matters relating to quality. However, if there is an attempt to develop such a system, quality should not be ignored. Which indicators best capture educational excellence and the above-mentioned areas? If other segments of society engage in developing comprehensive indicator systems, academe would undoubtedly want to link outcomes assessment with student outcomes and other measures to provide a way to determine on a periodic basis the condition of higher education nationally and perhaps by census regions and districts. The issue centers on which indicators to include and how to shift attention from teaching to learning, and how to represent Figure 1.2 in that depiction.

PERSPECTIVES ON FUTURE DIRECTIONS

The editors selected six individuals in different positions and who are well acquainted with outcomes assessment or quality assurance, and asked them to identify briefly some critical issues affecting the future of outcomes assessment.

Peggy L. Maki, Higher Education Consultant

Historically driven by external forces, such as accreditors, assessment of student learning has focused on documenting that students learn. As a result, colleges and universities design or use assessment methods primarily to demonstrate their program- and institution-level effectiveness. There is a far more compelling reason to engage in assessment of student learning beyond a documentary reason: to build knowledge across colleges and universities about *how* and *how well* students learn along the continuum of their studies at both the undergraduate and graduate levels. Similar to other professions that evolve their practices based on research in their fields, the challenge our colleges and universities face is purposefully to enter the territory of research on student learning. Movement into this territory will greatly influence the design of chronological educational practices that promote students' abilities to transfer, integrate, synthesize, apply, re-use, and even re-position their learning as they progress across their courses and educational experiences.

Inquiry into how and how well students develop and deepen their learning over time, as opposed to how or how well students learn in a course or module, is now the critical issue that colleges and universities face as they educate an increasingly diverse student population. Focus on learning as a continuum means that institutions may choose to enter the territory of research in one of two ways:

1. Conducting research on how students learn within the context of well-documented educational practices; and

2. Drawing on the results of research that others conduct and integrating that new knowledge into the design of teaching and learning: pedagogy, curricular and co-curricular design, instructional design, the use or integration of technology, and the nature and timing of educational experiences.

There are numerous exploratory avenues that a research-based commitment might take. Some of the possible research foci that are particularly relevant to teaching and learning include chronologically exploring, for example:

- How well students transfer, integrate, apply and re-use their learning across a field of study or profession within the context of intentional educational practices that span over students' entire program of study;
- How well students' approaches to learning inhibit or promote learning as they advance in a field of study or profession;
- How well visual, verbal, and other sensory methods of learning, as well as combinations of these methods, deepen students' conceptual knowledge; and
- How well students develop not only knowledge and understanding but also ways of knowing, habits of mind, and dispositions characteristic of a discipline, a field of study, or even of an institution's philosophy of general education.

Along with this commitment to research on learning or adapting the results of research conducted by others, such as is frequently reported by the National Research Council, there should be a concurrent commitment to build expanded learning communities across our colleges and universities. The purpose of these expanded communities would be to build upon and share new knowledge about the efficacy of educational practices. Thus, I envision the creation of local, regional, and national learning communities that will conduct and share results of their research or report on the efficacy of adapting research results into educational practices. For example, disciplinary faculty across colleges and universities in a state might meet periodically to learn about research in their field and its implications for teaching and learning. Or, disciplinary faculty from a multi-campus system might meet periodically to share results of adapting a new pedagogical approach to learning based on research about that approach across the system. Or, an institution or department within a regionally based consortium that decides to focus on pedagogy within a field or discipline might share its research or adaptations of research to advance educators' learning across the member institutions in that consortium. More public sharing of research on learning or use of research results to foster innovations or developments in teaching and learning will continually channel currency into the profession.

Engaging in research, sharing research, or adapting results of research will position higher education institutions to examine how well their educational practices contribute to students' abilities to transfer, integrate, apply, synthesize, reuse, and re-position their learning. Any profession advances when it explores the efficacy of its practices, verifying ones that continue to prove useful and those that do not. As a profession, teaching will benefit from research on how and how well students learn, not just in one course but across their program of study. Without new knowledge, the profession runs the risk of settling into practices that may not advance students' long-term learning. A commitment to research on learning or using that research becomes higher education's means of advancing or improving itself. Assessment, then, will move beyond an act of compliance to a process of inquiry. The results of this inquiry will promote new approaches to and principles of curricular design, pedagogy, instruction, use of technology or other educational tools, and educational experiences. Establishing channels of communication to share knowledge across institutional boundaries will assure that inquiry into how students learn will become a valued professional pursuit. Surely, building on knowledge and using new knowledge suits the purposes of higher education.

Sandra Bloomberg, Dean of the College of Professional Studies, New Jersey City University

Since at least the "fabulous fifties" of the last century, education of the populace was seen as the key to a prosperous and secure United States. President Eisenhower promoted and triumphantly signed the National Defense Education Act in part as a response to the perceptible challenge of the Soviet Union and as insurance that trained scientists and educated businesspeople would be available to the nation. These were the days of explosive growth in the economy and in academe. Not since the hectic period immediately following the Second World War had colleges and universities, struggling to educate the millions of returning servicemen and women availing themselves of the education benefits of the GI Bill, experienced such enrollment pressure.

Now, as the baby boom generation begins to welcome its grandchildren to its alma maters, it appears that some of our nation's faith in the probity of education has been lost. Certainly this is in part due to the absence of a security threat from a technologically advanced adversary. The replacement of the Soviet Union by Russia and other diminished states led to a "Peace Dividend" euphoria that could be described as delusional. In addition, the advent of technically accomplished, educated populations in Europe and Asia has made well prepared staff available for all manner of business, government, and even some military work at great savings. This has all had a dampening effect on modern academe.

Today, as never before in our experience, the foundations of modern academic principles are being called into scrutiny. With our society's focus on short-term results, obsession with immediate return on investment, and inability to tolerate abstraction, we are well advised to devise methods and techniques which demonstrate the efficacy of our efforts. One valuable approach we have employed is outcomes assessment. By this means, we have endeavored to offer practical means of assessing student learning. We have set goals for our students and ourselves and have attempted to quantify their impact. These steps were undertaken, at least in part, in response to feedback from stakeholders about incomplete or inadequate preparation of our graduates.

In certain segments of our country, ideologies have assumed the mantle of dogma and the resultant shift in national priorities is now the single greatest threat to an educated, globally competitive American society. The persistent drive to reduce the tax obligation of our wealthiest citizens, begun during the Reagan administration and perfected under the current administration has reduced already scarce resources available for educational research and innovation. If we wish to insure a well-educated and highly prepared citizenry, we must recast the priorities which motivate our business and, by extension, our civic and political communities. As long as the short-sighted priorities of business and amassing individual and corporate wealth supercede the value placed on the right of every individual in this country to a fundamentally sound education, it will be difficult, if not impossible, to realize even a modest national vision for educational fulfillment.

Other competing priorities include: mounting financial burdens resulting from national and international defense operations, a problematic social security system, and a dysfunctional health care system woefully inadequate to meet national needs.

Aside from these overarching issues are concerns about national educational leadership. For example, what entity or entities will fill the void left by the now defunct American Association for Higher Education

(AHHE)? For decades AAHE played a major role in higher education in general and specifically in researching and promoting assessment as central to teaching and learning. Although the body of work and research resides in thousands of faculty at institutions large and small throughout the country, the focus and momentum that are provided by a national organization have been lost.

Leadership at the state level is also of great concern. Poorly funded offices of higher education in some states have left a void in helpful guidance for colleges and universities, administrations and faculty. Strong state offices serve as valuable resources and clearinghouses for datum generated as the result of state and intra-state initiatives. Funding for these offices has been reduced and, in some states, restricted because of the drive to cut taxes.

Only strong leadership and serious financial commitments from presidents and provosts will make it possible for assessment initiatives to succeed. These leaders must help create a positive climate for staff and faculty eager to pursue the improved educational results assessment can provide their students and institutions. Sadly, there are often many reasons why even the most positively motivated institutional leaders are unable to achieve substantial levels of support for these initiatives. Among these may be finance, labor agreements, tenure, and poor resources.

Deans who value the opportunity assessment provides to strengthen students, faculty, and education; who are able to model good practice; and who possess perseverance, creativity, and a long-term vision are the cornerstone of successful assessment programs. These individuals are the primary sources of motivation, mid-level leadership, and resources for their faculty. However, there are numerous challenges at this level as well. In addition to those noted above, the typical obstacles that plague middle-managers in any organization exist.

Finally, most fundamental and critical to the successful institutionalization of student and program outcomes assessment are enlightened, committed faculty who view outcomes assessment as a means to enhance their efforts to support student learning and, thus, their professional practice. These dedicated individuals daily face obstacles which have daunted those seeking to innovate in less critical settings. Inertia, customary practice, peer pressure, and misinformation are all obstacles to be overcome. Indeed, there are thousands of such disciplinary experts who view the outcomes of their students' learning as central to how they define their success as teachers. These professionals are providing the basis for a committed core of motivated practitioners. Leaders in administration and faculty must continue to cooperate to create a "critical mass" of so inclined colleagues. Together they will be able to craft solutions to the unique obstacles encountered in their institutions.

Martin Carroll, Audit Director and Business Development Manager, Australian Universities Quality Agency

Before outlining the current state of systems in place for promoting student learning outcomes in Australian universities, it is necessary to provide a brief description of the Australian higher education sector, since its quality assurance framework is unique among comparable countries. An institution must meet stringent state-based accreditation criteria in order to achieve legal permission to operate and promote as a university. Evidence of the stringency is found in the relatively limited number of universities (forty) and the infrequency with which new universities are approved. Once accredited, universities in Australia are entitled to approve their own degree programs without requiring further external institutional or program accreditation (except for professional recognition purposes, such as in law or medicine). As such, there is little by way of national regulation with which to strategically direct androgogic developments. However, all universities are subject, approximately every five years, to an external audit of their quality assurance systems by the Australian Universities Quality Agency (AUQA). The reports of these audits are made public (http://www.auqa.edu.au/qualityaudit/). This has proven to be an effective mechanism in enhancing the universities' efforts to maintain world-class teaching and research.

Independent reviews of twenty-five Australian universities have been published by the AUQA since October 2002. The reviews address, *inter alia*, the effectiveness of quality assurance arrangements for teaching and learning, the teaching-research nexus, research, research training, and community engagement. As such, AUQA is now in an informed position to begin commenting on themes in the ongoing development of androgogic practice.

There are some clearly discernible themes in Australia at present. Most importantly, there is a renewed emphasis on androgogy. (I prefer this term over pedagogy because it acknowledges the wider spread of maturity among higher education students and the consequential implications for the learning and teaching relationship.) This emphasis is evident both within institutions and at national levels. Within higher education institutions, and particularly universities, there are a number of changes that have catalyzed this renewed emphasis. Some of these are (in no particular order) as follows.

Australia has experienced, and continues to project, massive growth in international student enrollments, both in Australia and in other countries. Indeed, Australia is experiencing the fastest growth among OECD (Organisation for Economic Cooperation and Development) countries. This phenomenon has placed the culturally relative nature of higher education back on the academic agenda. Examples of issues which give rise to this include content relevance, cross-cultural communication mores, English language competency, and student difficulties transitioning from their home country secondary schooling to Australian higher education systems.

Partly coincidental with the growth in international student enrollments is an increase in teaching through partnerships and part-time staff. Audited evidence shows that this can raise particular challenges for the quality assurance of teaching, as shall be discussed later.

A third major and ongoing change is the rise in use of technology-enabled learning management systems (e.g., WebCT/Vista and Blackboard). While the early focus of online learning systems tended to be on distance education, it now forms an integral part of all teaching and learning modes. Early uptake of such technology was criticized for focusing unduly on content provision at the expense of the teaching and learning interaction. Use of the systems has progressed beyond such concerns, and the focus is now clearly on facilitating student learning.

Lastly (for the purposes of this discussion), Australian higher education institutions are experiencing greater accountability for student learning outcomes. This most notably takes the form of tagged government funding schemes and public institutional audits by AUQA.

These are not minor changes. A significant re-emphasis on teaching and learning is required. This re-emphasis starts with the senior leadership within universities. Indeed, arising from its audits AUQA has found it necessary, on occasion, to call upon academic senates/boards (the academic governing bodies within universities) to exert greater leadership in this area.

Few universities in Australia promote a standardized androgogy such as outcomes based education (OBE). Indeed, a standardized androgogy would, in many cases, be seen as a backward step, given the recognition that different disciplines lend themselves to different methods of teaching and learning. However, there are some common developments evident. Within institutions the most obvious is the strategy of fostering explicit *graduate attributes* (also known by such other terms as *generic attributes* or *core student outcomes*). This general strategy, although currently being pursued in most Australian universities, is the responsibility of individual institutions. Therefore, precise implementation plans vary. Yet most tend to follow a similar pattern:

- Identifying the attributes at both generic and subject-specific levels;
- Mapping them against extant curricula and addressing any gaps;
- Considering how they may be addressed through teaching methods; and
- Establishing methods for assessing student development/uptake of the attributes.

Developing Graduate Attributes

Generic graduate attributes (GAs) are those qualities that all students of the university ought to have developed during their studies. Typical lists include (and are not limited to), in brief, such attributes as an aptitude and capacity for lifelong learning, teamwork skills, information literacy, independent research abilities, leadership qualities, high-level oral and written skills, cultural understanding, practice of ethical standards, and critical analysis and creativity. Interestingly, these lists are not significantly different from those put forward by champions of OBE.

Increasingly, universities are also establishing separate sets of attributes for postgraduate students. Such attributes typically include (and are not limited to) professional integrity, ability to make significant contributions to knowledge, awareness of interdisciplinary possibilities, and international academic fluency.

The process of agreeing on a core set of attributes goes right to the heart of higher education. In some universities this process alone has taken several years and involved discussions with faculty, student representatives, and external stakeholders (e.g., employers and industry partners). The result has been profound, for such exercises have perhaps had the consequence of forever repealing the sacredly held view that universities educate for life, whereas vocational education educates for jobs. There is little doubt now that, in Australia at least, government, public, and even academic stakeholders see graduate employment rates as a measure of success for a university.

The challenge of establishing GAs is compounded by a desire to agree on a set that is not only appropriate, but also *distinctive* to that university. Australian universities are experimenting with using GAs as a marketing tool for gaining competitive edge. It is too early to assess whether this strategy is having a discernible impact above, for example, choice of programs on offer, location, or traditional reputations based on other factors.

In most cases, these generic attributes are augmented by subject-specific learning objectives. Such learning objectives have been in place in Australian universities for much longer than generic graduate attributes. It is common practice for them to be set out in *subject outlines*, which also include a basic plan for the subject, details of the assessment schedule, timetabling, and other logistical details. Subject outlines are made available to students either before a subject commences, or at least before the date by which students can withdraw from a subject without academic or financial penalty. To some people, these are considered to be a form of contract between the university and the students for that particular subject although, in Australia, they have not yet been legally tested as such.

Graduate Attributes and Curriculum

Having determined a set of GAs, the next step generally followed is to determine the extent to which extant curricula are likely to facilitate their uptake by students. (For the purposes of this discussion, assume a *program* of study leads, if passed, to the conferment of a degree or diploma, and that a program is made up of numerous *subjects*.) One common practice is for universities to determine the extent to which each subject addresses the institutional GAs as well as its own discipline-specific learning objectives. Then, GAs are *mapped* against the overall program using a matrix-type approach. Mapping enables the identification of gaps (or, conversely, excessive redundancy/duplication), which may then be addressed through curriculum development processes. In many universities, requests to a faculty board or academic senate for new subject approvals (or major amendments to existing subjects) now need to incorporate evidence of which GAs will be supported by the subject and the method by which this will occur. This process requirement has certainly sharpened the attention of faculty.

Teaching for Graduate Attributes

It is axiomatic from a simple review of typical lists of GAs that relying only on curricula to ensure student uptake of GAs is not sufficient. Teaching design and practice are also germane.

This is resulting in a re-thinking of some long-standing quality assurance practices, such as teacher evaluations. Student evaluations of teaching are conducted in almost every Australian university and are compulsory in many cases. These surveys of student perception have been in place for several decades, and there may be an opportunity now to recast the issues they seek comment on in light of the GAs.

Student feedback considered thus far, along with the growing emphasis on higher education teaching as a professional activity, is resulting in changes to professional development for university teachers. AUQA has observed significant growth in the number of universities that now require new academic staff to complete a compulsory higher education teaching qualification (often a graduate certificate).

Most Australian universities have a professional development unit for academic staff (variably named). These usually provide the leadership for androgogic developments within the institution. Much of the emphasis of these units is on ensuring that staff are able to apply sound androgogic principles across the ever-increasingly flexible array of teaching methods. However, AUQA has sometimes found that such leadership is not well integrated into the program nor into subject accreditation/approval and review mechanisms. There is an opportunity within universities to better align the developmental aspect of the new androgogy with the regulatory processes.

AUQA has also identified systematic limitations to the ability of teaching staff to assist students with the uptake of GAs. Financial pressures have resulted in an increased use of part-time/sessional teaching staff. In most cases, such staff are not included within the professional development and performance management processes of the university. Nor are they necessarily well incorporated into the informal discussions by which academic staff explore teaching issues with peers.

The increase in teaching partnerships within Australia and transnationally has also presented particular challenges. AUQA reports that many universities rely on common curricula and assessment moderation as sufficient for academic quality assurance purposes. Sometimes this is augmented with a check on the resumes of academic staff engaged by the partner organization to undertake teaching duties. In its visits to these partner organizations, AUQA finds that it is rare for partner teaching staff to participate in any discussions with the university staff about teaching practice and the potential impact of different teaching methods on student learning outcomes.

Teaching responsibility for assisting students with the uptake of GAs is not limited to academic staff. For example, library and information technology staff are playing a central role in teaching students information literacy skills. Also, various student learning support services contribute through dedicated programs, sometimes developed as a result of benchmarking against international strategies (such as the peer-assisted study sessions, practiced in several Australian universities and adapted from work instigated by Deanna Martin of the University of Missouri). Demonstrable successes in enhancing student learning outcomes through such contributions have been the subject of numerous commendations from AUQA. The inevitable conclusion is that student learning is enhanced through the total university environment, and is not the sole domain of the classroom.

Assessing Graduate Attributes

The international concern with assessing student learning outcomes is shared in Australian higher education. Assessment policies and practices have been constantly evolving, especially as the range of learning media has expanded. Much of the emphasis over the past few years has been on monitoring the equivalence of student learning management (if not student learning itself) across multiple locations and modes. As a consequence, assessment methods themselves have been subject to considerable review and improvement. Leading academics, such as Geoff Scott,[18] have long advocated a system of matching the most appropriate assessment tools to each learning objective. However, it is still the case that the extent to which assessment methods provide an indication of student learning is partly a product of the student learning, but also partly a product of any limitations inherent in the design of the assessment method.

This comes into stark relief as the sector tries to develop assessment methods for newly explicated GAs which have previously been taken as fundamentally inherent in the teaching and learning interaction. A number of the GAs, such as the acquisition of life-long learning skills, may require longitudinal forms of assessment not currently developed.

National Developments

In addition to institutional developments, there have also been national developments aimed at facilitating student learning outcomes. Given that the Australian universities have a large degree of autonomy, it is sensible to augment this with national coordinating systems which can identify or develop good practice and make it more widely available. Two recent initiatives are particularly worth noting.

The Australian government has recently established the Carrick Institute for Learning and Teaching in Higher Education (http://www .carrickinstitute.edu.au/carrick/go). The Carrick Institute is charged with the mission of promoting and advancing learning and teaching in Australian higher education. Guaranteed funding of Aus$24 million per year from 2006 will help ensure that research into student learning can be fostered and the results made widely available.

AUQA is also responding to emerging androgogic practices by identifying, through the audit process, examples of good practice and making them publicly available through the AUQA "Good Practice Database" (http://www.auqa.edu.au/gp/). Since its launch in November 2003, good practices in the database have been accessed over 16,500 times. This indicates a strong desire for such information and is suggestive of a dynamic, active higher education sector.

Conclusion

After two decades dominated by institutional mergers, massive growth, implementation of new technologies, and responding to increased public accountability systems, the emphasis in Australian higher education seems to be refocusing on student learning. However, an unbalanced emphasis on reporting student learning outcomes may lead to undesirable consequences. It is essential that the sector maintains a balanced focus on learning objectives, curriculum development, teaching practice, and appropriate assessment of student learning. Independent and public audits of Australian universities suggest that awareness of a general framework for achieving such a focus is now endemic and progress towards its implementation is gaining momentum.

Central to this journey is a culture of self-reflection. The Australian higher education quality assurance framework includes a system of *fitness for purpose* audits, conducted by external peers and based upon each institution's own processes of self review of, particularly, programs and schools. Of course, these internal reviews are not navel-gazing exercises and do make use of external involvement and benchmark information.

Indeed, references to AUQA identifying issues are usually better interpreted as AUQA aggregating and reflecting issues identified by universities themselves. However, AUQA has, from time to time, found it necessary to emphasise that it is not adequate simply to *undertake* reviews. The *method* of review must, in keeping with the current themes, explicitly address student learning outcomes. Findings must be systematically incorporated into improvement planning processes. In that way, we can truly achieve the goal of a student-focused, learning university.

Oswald M. T. Ratteray, Associate Director, Middle States Commission on Higher Education

Faculty members in each discipline, staff, and administrators at colleges and universities tend to be quite clear about what their institution's specific learning outcomes should be and how those outcomes relate to the institution's mission. The academic enterprise at many institutions is further driven by large undergraduate class sizes and the relentless pressure to ensure that courses "cover" the required material in a specific time period. Thus, faculty, in many instances, are prevented from focusing on the individual learning strategies that will help students more efficiently manage the learning process and achieve the institution's goals more effectively.

During a course of study, however, students are bombarded with new information from a variety of sources. This onslaught starts with the college catalog from which the student selects courses to study. It is amplified on the first days of class when the faculty member outlines in detail what students need to know and, at least in broad terms, how and where they might or even should acquire that information. The intellectual nourishment that students gather may be found in the honeycomb of textbooks, library books, and other archival material, the massaging of raw data from seminal inquiry, and online or in-person exchanges with peers or expert practitioners in the same or related fields. Students then engage in a process of self-examination about the nature of truth, what it may mean to their prior understanding of reality, and ultimately what they specifically are going to do about the discovery—either in a particular course, in their subsequent college experience, or for the rest of their lives.

Between the initiation of inquiry and the terminal individual and institutional achievements, there is an enormous chasm. Some students negotiate it well on their own initiative, some require extensive support from faculty and staff, and others fall by the wayside. How to help bridge this gap is the challenge confronting many faculty in higher education.

For example, how can teachers best help art, architecture, or dance students manage the application of new information in the creative process; or seminarians resolve how to apply their own revelations in the context of faith and decisions about ministry; or clinical practitioners evaluate patient information in diagnosis and care; or players in sports programs identify and critique information to make strategic and winning field decisions?

Some faculty members are in the unique position—or, as some would say, have the luxury, especially with large classes—of actually being able to provide students with hands-on guidance toward understanding. However, this type of student support is one of the critical aspects of information literacy, and it represents the "keys to the kingdom" in the achievement of student learning outcomes.

Faculty intervention in information processing deserves further exploration with the goal of distilling cross-disciplinary or even discipline-specific principles that may help students, faculty, staff, and institutions reach their objectives. The ability to improve student learning outcomes also will help to satisfy the requirements of accrediting organizations, which ask institutions not only to define their learning outcomes but to assess mastery of those outcomes and to use the data to help improve teaching and learning.

Kathleen Dunn, Librarian Emerita, University Library, California State Polytechnic University

Will we still be talking about outcomes assessment in five years? In my 40+ years in academic libraries, I have seen many educational fads come and go. Outcomes assessment, which implies the measurement of learning over time with resulting improvements in the quality and content of student learning experiences, will stick only if librarians and library administrators commit to a culture of assessment. This is one of the most critical issues facing its application to information literacy in the next five years.

Measurements of learning have always been an integral and required part of the work of teachers and the experience of students at all levels. Whatever the label, there has always been a culture of assessment and measurement for teachers and students. One of the challenges of outcomes assessment agendas for teaching faculty has been to acknowledge that something they have long done could benefit from new approaches and a different emphasis.

However, the situation with libraries in educational settings has been different. While surveys and assessments of services and teaching programs have long been reported in the literature and discussed at conferences, there has never been a universally accepted requirement for assessment of any service including library instruction, unless the library offers courses that students take for credit. Good management practices and strategic planning activities have dictated periodic assessments of collections and services, but more often than not library staff perceive that they are just too busy providing services to put the time and energy required into designing and carrying out ongoing assessments of their programs and services. My experience with assessment suggests that even the practical issues can be daunting—establishing clear goals for the assessment, securing funding and staff to make it happen, identifying appropriate methodology and selecting representative student samples, and finding willing partners. Furthermore, in many academic libraries, library literacy instruction consists of fifty-minute sessions and tours, and there is little perceived need for assessment.

Yet, we seem to be moving in the right direction. There is now a stronger push for across-the-board assessment in academic libraries, inspired by limited funding and accountability issues. Some libraries and library systems have already adopted a culture of assessment. Standardized, Web-based assessment instruments, such as the Association of Research Libraries' LibQUAL+™, serve not only to make the process easier for libraries, but also encourage a culture of assessment. Outcomes assessment initiatives among teaching faculty are increasingly widespread and are having the effect of encouraging librarians to take more seriously the need for outcomes assessment of their information literacy programs. If these trends continue over the next few years, then the ongoing assessment of all library programs and services may become endemic in academic libraries of all sizes, just part of what is necessary to meet students' needs with effective and adaptable programs. After all, outcomes assessment can take many forms and a specific assessment does not have to be elaborate, time-consuming, and expensive. I am optimistic that librarians have the creativity to do literacy assessment in libraries large and small, and on a scale that makes sense in their individual library environments.

Bonnie Gratch Lindauer, Coordinator of Library Instructional Services at the Rosenberg Library, City College of San Francisco

Based on my direct experiences over the past two years as one of two faculty members leading my college's accreditation self-study planning and report, and as a member of a WASC (Western Association of Schools and Colleges) visiting team for another community college's self-study, I strongly believe that outcomes assessment has a solid future and is generally well accepted, although not fully applied, in higher education. My readings and experiences suggest that while most institutions have taken steps to identify critical student learning outcomes and other institutional outcomes and have provided forums for engaging the campus community in dialogues about outcomes assessment, not as many have progressed to the stage of having an institutional culture of outcomes assessment and an integrated system of assessment strategies at the course, program, and institutional levels. Still fewer have reached the point where they are using the findings from a regular schedule of assessing outcomes in their strategic planning and evaluation systems so that the feedback loop driving institutional improvements is established. A good number of institutions have been innovators and pioneers in this area for some time, but most colleges and universities have addressed the challenges and opportunities afforded by outcomes assessment in response to the emphasis placed on outcomes assessment in the standards of regional accrediting associations. In this setting, then, how are libraries progressing with outcomes assessment?

Academic libraries' involvement and experiences using outcomes assessment parallel those of other academic programs, demonstrating a good deal of variety in the extent to which outcomes assessment has been applied. Thanks to the publication of standards for information literacy and other assessment projects initiated by the Association of College and Research Libraries (ACRL), the Association of Research Libraries (ARL), Educational Testing Services (ETS), and others, there has been a lot of activity, publications, Web sites and conference programming in the past five years dedicated to outcomes assessment. Perhaps because information literacy has been well established and lends itself to measurable student learning outcomes, this area of academic library services has been more fully developed vis-à-vis outcomes assessment. Regarding other types of services and information resources, most libraries are still experimenting with identifying the "best" approaches for assessing the impact of their contributions and services for students and for their institutions. What, then, are the critical issues facing the application of outcomes assessment to information literacy for the next five years? I see three major issues which in some respects are interrelated:

1. A need for more research to add to a growing knowledge base; specifically, research is needed to address such questions as:
   - What classroom and co-curricular behaviors and activities support specific information literacy outcomes, such as critically evaluating information? In effect, what are the enabling behaviors that students engage in that contribute to the development of certain information literacy competencies?
   - What methods, materials, and modes of instruction are more effective in particular learning environments?
   - What are the best instruments, including standardized ones, to assess specific information literacy competencies?

   Of course, good research designs using multiple measures and longitudinal and replicated studies are important in truly adding value to the knowledge base. The development of standardized instruments such as ETS's Information & Communications Technology exam and the SAILS test for information literacy is a significant advance, and research reporting the findings of using these instruments is awaited. Current work to include information literacy–related items on the National Survey of Student Engagement (NSSE) should also be useful in furthering our understanding of behaviors that contribute to information literacy competencies.

   As a sub-issue, there is a need for more collaboration in doing research with faculty and administrators in other academic and student services programs. Outreach to other institutional divisions/programs and collaboration with faculty have been on the increase with many positive results. Indeed, information literacy standards and library instructional program change in response to using the standards have often been the driving motivation for collaboration and outreach. Planning and doing research about student learning outcomes with discipline-based faculty and student services professionals are critical components of sharing the responsibility for teaching information literacy and being responsive to ways to improve learning.

2. Development of a culture of outcomes assessment throughout the library so that the feedback loop from planning to assessment to making improvements is institutionalized. Progress related to this issue depends on library administrators and staff at all levels. Having more staff that are informed about and/or trained in conducting outcomes assessment is a necessary step, in conjunction with the commitment to broadening the focus of the library's mission to include institutional reflection and change based on research findings. Thus, a sub-issue is having both library support and access to institutional professional development resources to help librarians and other library staff develop their evaluation and assessment skills.

3. Coordination of academic professional association efforts to focus on fostering the research and dissemination of findings to inform best practices. To really advance the knowledge base of how outcomes assessment has been, and can be, applied to information literacy, it is imperative that there be a coordinated effort among the key professional associations to make this a priority.

Outcomes assessment does not appear to be a passing fad, if for no other reason than the continued existence of requirements in regional and professional associations' standards and some governmental agencies providing grants. Outcomes assessment is more than a tool; it has redefined how academic libraries view their role and relate to their institutions. It is a wonderful opportunity for librarians to connect with their colleagues in other institutional units/programs to help shape the future of teaching and learning in higher education.

CONCLUSION

With different stakeholders concerned about the cost of higher education and that students receive quality, or value for money, attention will continue to shift to the issue of quality. Quality relates to program content as demonstrated through faculty teaching and research. However, another dimension—one of increasing importance—relates to the learning, maturity, knowledge, skills, and abilities that students have directly gained from their program of study. As institutions continue to stake out their individual identities and to market the image of caring and nurturing learning organizations, student learning outcomes, together with student outcomes, become a way to demonstrate what institutions and particular programs stand for and what their graduates will know and be able to do. Student learning outcomes become a way not only to focus attention on what students learn both horizontally and vertically within the institution, but also to distinguish programs and institutions from their competitors. In effect, programs and institutions say "we stand for this" and "we have evidence that supports our claim" as well as "we also use that evidence for continuous quality improvement." Clearly, student learning outcomes have value to faculty, students, administrators, and all stakeholders. It is up to all of us to demonstrate this value and to refocus national discussion around it.

Notes

1. David G. Evans, "Point of View: How Not to Reward Outstanding Teachers," *The Chronicle of Higher Education* (May 20, 2005): B20.

2. Tim Riordan, "Introduction," in *Disciplines as Frameworks for Student Learning: Teaching the Practice of the Disciplines*, edited by Tim Riordan and James Roth (Sterling, VA: Stylus Publishing, LLC, 2005), xvi–xvii.

3. Ibid., xvii.

4. Ibid., xii–xiii.

5. Ibid., xvii.

6. AACSB International (The Association to Advance Collegiate Schools of Business), *Eligibility Procedures and Accreditation Standards for Business Accreditation* (Tampa, FL: AACSB International, 2005), 15.

7. Ibid., 15–16.

8. American Library Association, Association of College and Research Libraries, *Information Literacy Competency Standards for Higher Education* (Chicago: Association of College & Research Libraries, 2000).

9. Middle States Commission on Higher Education, *Developing Research & Communication Skills: Guidelines for Information Literacy in the Curriculum* (Philadelphia, PA: Middle States Commission on Higher Education, 2003).

10. American Library Association, Association of College and Research Libraries. Science and Technology Section (STS) Task Force on Information Literacy for Science and Technology, "Information Literacy Standards for Science and Technology: A Draft," *College & Research Libraries News* 66 (May 2005): 381.

Appendix: Web Resources

Candy Schwartz

Directories and Resource Collections

Assessing Student Learning: Available Resources
http://www.ala.org/ala/acrl/acrlpubs/crlnews/backissues2004/may04/stu
dentlearning.htm
Amy E. Mark prepared this guide to resources for *C&RL News* (vol. 65, no. 5, May 2004), a publication of the Association of College & Research Libraries (ACRL). Mark lists meta sites, student learning outcomes and assessment, library-oriented sources, electronic lists, journals, and corporate and fee-based solutions.

Central Queensland University, Assessment in Higher Education
http://ahe.cqu.edu.au/
Two staff members of the Faculty of Informatics and Communication at Central Queensland University, Australia, built and maintain this very rich guide to online and print resources, including articles, books, journals, listserv lists, conferences resources, associations, and Web sites. Updated every few months.

Educator's Reference Desk
http://www.eduref.org/
From the Information Institute of Syracuse, the Educator's Reference Desk brings together materials from the ERIC database, archived As-kERIC questions and responses, the Gateway to Educational Materials (GEM), and other sources. The Evaluation resource guide, linked on the opening page, covers alternative assessment, standards, research methods, and testing.

Florida Atlantic University, Assessment Resources
http://iea.fau.edu/pusateri/assess/
Resources collected to support assessment activities at Florida Atlantic University. Divided into sections which include student learning; teaching pedagogies; students skills, knowledge, and values; resources by discipline (i.e., FAU departments and programs); and resources for administration/support (often neglected).

North Carolina State University, Internet Resources for Higher Education Outcomes Assessment
http://www2.acs.ncsu.edu/UPA/assmt/resource.htm
In support of its well-documented assessment program (http://www2 .acs.ncsu.edu/UPA/assmt/), North Carolina State University maintains a vast and frequently updated collection. Annotated links to hundreds of online sites are divided into general resources, guides and handbooks, assessment of specific areas, individual institution assessment pages, accrediting agencies, and assessment by students.

University of Northern Colorado, Online Assessment Resources
http://www.unco.edu/assessment/tools/extern_resource.htm
The University of Northern Colorado's Office of University Assessment maintains a well-organized list of external resources in categories which go beyond the usual to include commercial resources, benchmarking, and software.

Organizations and Initiatives

American Educational Research Association (AERA)
http://www.aera.net/
AERA's Division D, Measurement and Research Methodology (http:// www.aera.net/divisions/?id=546), makes its newsletter available online, and sponsors a listserv list, AERA-D.

Association of American Colleges and Universities (AAC&U)
http://www.aacu-edu.org/
The AAC&U Web site has a section on assessment which links to its own publications and initiatives in the area and also includes almost a dozen separate Web pages which each present annotated resource lists

in key areas such as critical thinking, ethical behavior, capstones, and portfolios.

Association of College and Research Libraries (ACRL)
http://www.acrl.org/
A division of the American Library Association (ALA), ACRL has been a leader in the area of information literacy, and has an excellent collection of resources around its *Information Literacy Competency Standards for Higher Education* (http://www.ala.org/ala/acrl/acrlstandards/information literacycompetency.htm).

Baldridge National Quality Program (BNQP)
http://www.quality.nist.gov/Education_Criteria.htm
The 2005 edition of *Education Criteria for Performance Excellence* (http://www.quality.nist.gov/Education_Criteria.htm) forms the basis for the Malcolm Baldridge National Quality Award. The site includes a self-analysis worksheet which can be used to identify strengths and opportunities.

Bay Area Community Colleges Information Competency Assessment Project (ICAP)
http://www.topsy.org/ICAP/ICAProject.html
San Francisco area faculty librarians collaborated to develop a literacy competency instrument which was outcomes-based, referenced to national standards, and applicable to community colleges. The final report was published in 2003, and the Web site contains all the necessary materials for using the instrument.

Centre for Outcomes-Based Education (COBE)
http://www.open.ac.uk/cobe/
COBE is an advisory and research and development group within the UK's Open University. The site includes access to a newsletter and more than twenty reports and papers.

Council for Higher Education Accreditation (CHEA)
http://www.chea.org/
CHEA is a private nonprofit agency which coordinates U.S. accreditation activity, advocates for voluntary accreditation at national levels, and represents the U.S. accreditation community internationally.

EDUCAUSE

http://www.educause.edu/

Recent interest areas of the EDUCAUSE Learning Initiative (http://www.educause.edu/content.asp?section_id=86) have included learner-centered concepts, e-portfolios, and transformative assessment. The EDUCAUSE Center for Applied Research (ECAR: http://www.educause.edu/ecar/) makes a variety of its research publications available, some of which deal with outcomes assessment related to technology.

eVALUEd

http://www.evalued.uce.ac.uk/

The University of Central England, with assistance from the Higher Education Funding Council for England (HEFCE), has developed a toolkit to support evidence-based evaluation of electronic information services. The site includes a guide, an archive of tools, a means for creating custom tools, case studies, annotated links to other similar resources, and a searchable outcomes database (http://www.evalued.uce.ac.uk/outcomes/).

Institute of Museum and Library Services (IMLS)

http://www.imls.gov/

IMLS is an independent federal agency that provides services and funding to museums, libraries, and archives. Grantwinners must attend a two-day workshop on outcome-based evaluation (OBE). IMLS provides a good explanation of the basics and a collection of annotated links on its Web page about OBE (http://www.imls.gov/grants/current/crnt_obebasics.htm).

National Association of Independent Colleges and Universities (NAICU)

http://www.naicu.edu/

The NAICU Web site includes sections on accountability and assessment.

National Commission on Accountability in Higher Education

http://www.sheeo.org/account/comm-home.htm

This is an initiative of the State Higher Education Executive Officers (SHEEO) national association, with funding from the Ford Foundation. The Commission considers the state of higher education performance and accountability, holds meetings, gathers data and testimonies, and publishes reports.

Quality Assurance Agency for Higher Education (UK) (QAA)
http://www.qaa.ac.uk/
Founded in 1990, QAA is an independent organization that works with higher education institutions in the UK to both define academic standards and then review institutions against those standards.

U.S. Regional Accrediting Organizations

[Middle States Association of Colleges and Schools] Middle States Commission on Higher Education (MSCHE)
http://www.msche.org/
The Middle States Association of Colleges and Schools includes institutions in Delaware, the District of Columbia, Maryland, New Jersey, New York, Pennsylvania, Puerto Rico, the U.S. Virgin Islands, and several other overseas locations. In addition to directories, policy documents, and other local information, the site provides very valuable collections of guidelines and best practices.

[New England Association of Schools and College (NEASC)] Commission on Institutions of Higher Education (CIHE) and Commission on Technical and Career Institutions (CTCI)
http://www.neasc.org/
NEASC, the nation's oldest accrediting association, serves members in Connecticut, Maine, Massachusetts, New Hampshire, Rhode Island, and Vermont, and also accredits a number of American/international schools.

[North Central Association of Colleges and Schools] Higher Learning Commission (HLC)
http://www.ncahigherlearningcommission.org/
The HLC, founded in 1895, covers institutions in the states of Arkansas, Arizona, Colorado, Iowa, Illinois, Indiana, Kansas, Michigan, Minnesota, Missouri, North Dakota, Nebraska, Ohio, Oklahoma, New Mexico, South Dakota, Wisconsin, West Virginia, and Wyoming.

Northwest Commission on Colleges and Universities (NWCCU)
http://www.nwccu.org/
NWCCU accredits higher education institutions in Alaska, Idaho, Montana, Nevada, Oregon, Utah, and Washington.

[**Southern Association of Colleges and Schools**] **Commission on Colleges (COC)**
http://www.sacscoc.org/   .
COC accrediting activities serve institutions in Alabama, Florida, Georgia, Kentucky, Louisiana, Mississippi, North Carolina, South Carolina, Tennessee, Texas, and Virginia, and also some schools in Latin America.

[**Western Association of Schools and College**] **Accrediting Commission for Community and Junior Colleges (ACCJC) and Accrediting Commission for Senior Colleges and Universities (ACSCU)**
http://www.wascweb.org/
The Western Association of Schools and Colleges is responsible for California, Hawaii, and various territories or individual institutions in the Pacific Rim and East Asia, such as Guam and American Samoa.

Bibliography

Articles

Ackerson, Linda G., and Virginia E. Young. "Evaluating the Impact of Library Instruction Methods on the Quality of Student Research," *Research Strategies* 12 (1994): 132–144.

American Accounting Association. Teaching and Curriculum Section. Outcomes Assessment Committee. "Summary of 'Outcomes Assessment,'" *Journal of Accounting Education* 12 (1994): 105–114.

Angelo, Thomas A. "Reassessing (and Defining) Assessment," *AAHE* [The American Association for Higher Education] *Bulletin* 48, no. 3 (November 1995): 7–9.

Arnone, Michael. "New Commission Debates Accountability," *The Chronicle of Higher Education* 50 (May 21, 2004): A26.

Austin, Alexander W. "Point of View: To Use Graduation Rates to Measure Excellence, You Have to Do Your Homework," *The Chronicle of Higher Education* 51 (October 23, 2004): B20.

Baker, Ronald L. "Evaluating Quality and Effectiveness: Regional Accreditation Principles and Practices," *The Journal of Academic Librarianship* 28 (2002): 3–7.

Baltzer, Jan A. "Consider the Four-Legged Stool as You Plan for Information Technology," *Computers in Libraries* 40, no. 4 (2000): 42–45.

Barclay, Donald. "Evaluating Library Instruction: Doing the Best You Can with What You Have," *RQ* 33 (Winter 1993): 195–202.

Bertot, John Carlo, and Charles R. McClure. "Outcomes Assessment in the Networked Environment: Research Questions, Issues, Considerations, and Moving Forward," *Library Trends* 51 (2003): 590–613.

Boren, M. Ted, and Judith Ramey. "Thinking Aloud: Reconciling Theory and Practice," *IEEE Transactions on Professional Communication* 43 (2000): 261–278.

Boykin, Joseph F. "LibQUAL+™ as a Confirming Resource," *Performance Measurement and Metrics* 3, no. 2 (2002): 74–77.

Burd, Stephen. "Will Congress Require Colleges to Grade Themselves?," *The Chronicle of Higher Education* 49 (April 4, 2003): A27.

403

Burke, Joseph C. "How Can Colleges Prove They're Doing Their Jobs?," *The Chronicle of Higher Education* 51 (September 3, 2004): B6–B10.

———. "Trends in Higher Education Performance," *Spectrum: Journal of State Government* 76 (Spring 2003): 23–24.

Carter, Elizabeth W. " 'Doing the Best You Can with What You Have': Lessons Learned from Outcomes Assessment," *The Journal of Academic Librarianship* 28 (2002): 36–41.

Carter, Elizabeth W., and Timothy K. Daugherty. "Library Instruction and Psychology: A Cooperative Effort," *Technical Services Quarterly* 16 (1998): 33–41.

Chau, J.P.C., A. M. Chang, I.F.K. Lee, W. Y. Ip, D.T.F. Lee, and Y. Wooten. "Effects of Using Videotaped Vignettes on Enhancing Student's Critical Thinking Ability in a Baccalaureate Nursing Programme," *Journal of Advanced Nursing* 36 (2001): 112–119.

Choinski, Elizabeth, Amy E. Mark, and Missy Murphy. "Assessment with Rubrics: An Efficient and Objective Means of Assessing Student Outcomes in an Information Resources Class," *portal: Libraries and the Academy* 3 (2003): 563–575.

Christ, Carol T. "How Can Colleges Prove They're Doing Their Jobs?," *The Chronicle of Higher Education* 51 (September 3, 2004): B6–B10.

Cleary, Jim. "Academic Libraries, Networking and Technology: Some Recent Developments," *The Australian Library Journal* 43 (1994): 235–256.

Coble, Ran. "Trends in Higher Education: Changes in Governance," *Spectrum: The Journal of State Government* 74 (Spring 2001): 16–18.

Condon, William, and Diane Kelly-Riley. "Assessing and Teaching What We Value: The Relationship between College-Level Writing and Critical Thinking Abilities," *Assessing Writing* 9 (2004): 56–75.

Conklin, Kristin, and Travis Reindl. "To Keep America Competitive, States and Colleges Must Work Together," *The Chronicle of Higher Education* 50 (February 13, 2004): B20.

Cook, Colleen, ed. "The Maturation of Assessment in Academic Libraries: The Role of LibQUAL+™," *Performance Measurement and Metrics* 3, no. 2 (2002): 34–108.

Cook, Colleen, and Fred M. Heath. "Users' Perceptions of Library Service Quality: A LibQUAL+™ Qualitative Study," *Library Trends* 49 (Spring 2001): 548–584.

Cook, Colleen, and Bruce Thompson. "Psychometric Properties of Scores from the Web-based LibQUAL+ Study of Perceptions of Library Service Quality," *Library Trends* 49 (Spring 2001): 585–604.

Coupe, Jill. "Undergraduate Library Skills: Two Surveys at Johns Hopkins University," *Research Strategies* 11 (1993): 188–201.

Cullen, Rowena. "Perspectives on User Satisfaction Surveys," *Library Trends* 49 (Spring 2001): 662–686.

Daugherty, Timothy K., and Elizabeth W. Carter. "Assessment of Outcome-focused Library Instruction in Psychology," *Journal of Instructional Psychology* 24 (1997): 29–53.

DeMars, Christine E., Lynn Cameron, and T. Dary Erwin. "Information Literacy as Foundational: Determining Competence," *The Journal of General Education* 52 (2003): 253–265.

Drake, Miriam A. "Technological Innovation and Organizational Change," *Journal of Library Administration* 19, no. 3/4 (1993): 39–53.

Dugan, Robert E. "Information Technology Plans," *The Journal of Academic Librarianship* 28 (2002): 152–156.

Dugan, Robert E., and Peter Hernon. "Outcomes Assessment: Not Synonymous with Inputs and Outputs," *The Journal of Academic Librarianship* 28 (2002): 376–380.

Dunn, Delmer D. "Accountability, Democratic Theory, and Higher Education," *Educational Policy* 17 (January/March 2003): 60–79.

Dunn, Kathleen. "Assessing Information Literacy Skills in the California State University: A Progress Report," *The Journal of Academic Librarianship* 28 (2002): 26–35.

Eck, James C., and John W. Harris. "AALE Viability Indicators: Warning Lights on the Institutional Dashboard," *Assessment Update* 12, no. 4 (July–August 2000): 1–2, 14–15.

Emmons, Mark, and Wanda Martin. "Engaging Conversation: Evaluating the Contribution of Library Instruction to the Quality of Student Research," *College & Research Libraries* 63 (2002): 545–561.

Engelkemeyer, Susan W. "Institutional Performance Measures," *AAHE Bulletin* 51, no. 4 (December 1998): 3–6.

Evans, David G. "Point of View: How Not to Reward Outstanding Teachers," *The Chronicle of Higher Education* (May 20, 2005): B20.

Fraser, Bruce T., Charles R. McClure, and Emily H. Leahy. "Toward a Framework for Assessing Library and Institutional Outcomes," *portal: Libraries and the Academy* 2 (2002): 505–528.

Gathercoal, Paul, Douglas Love, Beverly Byrde, and Gerry McKean. "Web-based Electronic Portfolios," *EDUCAUSE Quarterly* 25, no. 2 (2002): 29–37.

Geffert, Bryn, and Robert Bruce. "Whither BI? Assessing Perceptions of Research Skills over an Undergraduate Career," *RQ* 36 (1997): 409–417.

George, Carole A. "Usability Testing and Design of a Library Web Site: An Iterative Approach," *OCLC Systems and Services: International Digital Library Perspectives Journal*, forthcoming.

Gittell, Marilyn, and Neil Scott Kleiman. "The Political Context of Higher Education," *American Behavioral Scientist* 43 (April 2000): 1058–1091.

Greer, Arlene, Lee Weston, and Mary Alm. "Assessment of Learning Outcomes: A Measure of Progress in Library Literacy," *College & Research Libraries* 52 (1991): 549–557.

Hardesty, Larry, Nicholas P. Lovrich, and James Mannon. "Library-Use Instruction: Assessment of the Long-Term Effects," *College & Research Libraries* 43 (1982): 38–46.

Harwell, Michael R. "Choosing between Parametric and Nonparametric Tests," *Journal of Counseling and Development* 67 (September 1988): 35–38.

Hearn, James C., and Janet M. Holdsworth. "Influences of State-Level Policies and Practices on College Students' Learning," *Peabody Journal of Education* 77, no. 3 (2002): 6–39.

Heath, Fred M., Martha Kyrillidou, and Consuella A. Askew, eds. "Libraries Act on their LibQUAL+™ Findings: From Data to Action," *Journal of Library Administration* 40, no. 3 and 4 (2004): 1–240.

Honan, James. "Monitoring Institutional Performance," *AGB Priorities* 5 (Fall 1995) (entire issue).

Iannuzzi, Patricia. "Faculty Development and Information Literacy: Establishing Campus Partnerships," *Reference Services Review* 26 (1998): 97–116.

Johnston, Brenda. "Summative Assessment of Portfolios: An Examination of Different Approaches to Agreement over Outcomes," *Studies in Higher Education* 29, no. 3 (June 2004): 395–412.

Julien, Heidi. "Barriers to Adolescents' Information Seeking for Career Decision Making," *Journal of the American Society for Information Science* 50 (1999): 38–48.

———. "Information Literacy Instruction in Canadian Academic Libraries: Longitudinal Trends and International Comparisons," *College & Research Libraries* 61 (2000): 510–523.

———. "User Education in New Zealand Tertiary Libraries: An International Comparison," *The Journal of Academic Librarianship* 24 (1998): 301–310.

Julien, Heidi, and Stuart Boon. "Assessing Instructional Outcomes in Canadian Academic Libraries," *Library & Information Science Research* 26, no. 2 (2004): 121–139.

———. "From the Front Line: Information Literacy Instruction in Canadian Academic Libraries," *Reference Services Review* 30 (2002): 143–149.

Julien, Heidi, and Gloria J. Leckie. "Bibliographic Instruction Trends in Canadian Academic Libraries," *Canadian Journal of Information and Library Science* 22 (1997): 1–15.

Kaplan, Robert, and David Norton. "Using the Balanced Scorecard as a Strategic Management System," *Harvard Business Review* 74 (January/February 1996): 75–85.

Ketcheson, Kathi A. "Public Accountability and Reporting: What Should Be the Public Part of Accreditation?," *New Directions for Higher Education* 113 (Spring 2001): 83–93.

King, David N., and John C. Ory. "Effects of Library Instruction on Student Research: A Case Study," *College & Research Libraries* 42 (1981): 31–41.

Kunkel, Lilith R., Susan M. Weaver, and Kim N. Cook. "What Do They Know? An Assessment of Undergraduate Library Skills," *The Journal of Academic Librarianship* 22 (1996): 430–434.

Lakos, Amos, and Shelly Phipps. "Creating a Culture of Assessment: A Catalyst for Organizational Change," *portal: Libraries and the Academy* 4 (2004): 345–361.

Layzell, Daniel T. "Linking Performance to Funding Outcomes at the State Level for Public Institutions of Higher Education: Past, Present, and Future," *Research in Higher Education* 40 (April 1999): 233–246.

Layzell, Thomas D. "How Can Colleges Prove They're Doing Their Jobs?," *The Chronicle of Higher Education* 51 (September 3, 2004): B6–B10.

Lindauer, Bonnie Gratch. "Comparing the Regional Accreditation Standards: Outcomes Assessment and Other Trends," *The Journal of Academic Librarianship* 28 (2002): 14–25.

———. "Defining and Measuring the Library's Impact on Campuswide Outcomes," *College & Research Libraries* 59 (1998): 546–570.

López, Cecilia. "Assessment of Student Learning: Challenges and Strategies," *The Journal of Academic Librarianship* 28 (2002): 356–367.

Lovett, Clara M., and Robert T. Mundhenk. "How Can Colleges Prove They're Doing Their Jobs?," *The Chronicle of Higher Education* 51 (September 3, 2004): B6–B10.

Lubinescu, Edward S., James L. Ratcliff, and Maureen A. Gaffney. "Two Continuums Collide: Accreditation and Assessment," *New Directions for Higher Education* 113 (Spring 2001): 5–21.

Mark, Amy E., and Polly D. Boruff-Jones. "Information Literacy and Student Engagement: What the National Survey of Student Engagement Reveals about Your Campus," *College & Research Libraries* 64, no. 6 (2003): 480–493.

Mech, Terrence F., and Charles I. Brooks. "Anxiety and Confidence in Using a Library by College Freshmen and Seniors," *Psychological Report* 81 (1997): 929–930.

Newby, Peter. "Culture and Quality in Higher Education," *Higher Education Policy* 12 (1999): 261–275.

Nitecki, Danuta. "Quality Assessment Measures in Libraries," *Advances in Librarianship* 25 (2001): 133–162.

Nitecki, Danuta, and Brinley Franklin. "New Measures for Research Libraries," *The Journal of Academic Librarianship* 25 (1999): 484–487.

O'Connor, Lisa G., Carolyn J. Radcliff, and Julie A. Gedeon. "Applying Systems Design and Item Response Theory to the Problem of Measuring

Information Literacy Skills," *College & Research Libraries* 63, no. 6 (2002): 528–543.

Prorak, Diane, Tania Gottschalk, and Mike Pollastro. "Teaching Method and Psychological Type in Library Bibliographic Instruction: Effect on Student Learning and Confidence," *RQ* 33 (1994): 484–495.

Pulley, John. "Crumbling Support for Colleges," *The Chronicle of Higher Education* 48, no. 29 (March 29, 2002): A28.

Reed, Charles B., and Edward B. Rust Jr. "How Can Colleges Prove They're Doing Their Jobs?," *The Chronicle of Higher Education* 51 (September 3, 2004): B6–B10.

———. "A More Systematic Approach," *The Chronicle of Higher Education* 51 (September 3, 2004): B7–B8.

Rockman, Ilene F. "The Importance of Assessment," *Reference Services Review* 30 (2002): 181–182.

Rodriquez, Raul O., Mark T. Green, and Malcolm James Ree. "Leading Generation X: Do the Old Rules Apply?," *Journal of Leadership & Organizational Studies* 9 (Spring 2003): 67–75.

Rooney, James J., and Lee N. Vanden Heuvel. "Root Cause Analysis for Beginners," *Quality Progress* 37, no. 7 (July 2004): 45–53.

Rosenblatt, Susan. "Information Technology Investments in Research Libraries," *Educom Review* 34, no. 4 (1999): 28–32.

Rybacki, Donald, and Dan Lattimore. "Assessment of Undergraduate and Graduate Programs," *Public Relations Review* 25 (Spring 1999): 65–75.

Savolainen, Reijo. "Network Competence and Information Seeking on the Internet: From Definitions Towards a Social Cognitive Model," *Journal of Documentation* 58 (2002): 211–226.

Seamans, Nancy H. "Student Perceptions of Information Literacy: Insights for Librarians," *Reference Services Review* 30 (2002): 112–123.

Selegan, John Cornell, Martha Lou Thomas, and Marie Louise Richman. "Long-Range Effectiveness of Library Use Instruction," *College & Research Libraries* 44 (1983): 476–480.

Sergers, Mien, and Filip Dochy. "Quality Assurance in Higher Education: Theoretical Considerations and Empirical Evidence," *Studies in Educational Evaluation* 22, no. 2 (1996): 115–137.

Shirley, R. C., and J. F. Volkwein. "Establishing Academic Program Priorities," *Journal of Higher Education* 49 (1978): 472–488.

Shulock, Nancy. "How Can Colleges Prove They're Doing Their Jobs?," *The Chronicle of Higher Education* 51 (September 3, 2004): B6–B10.

Simkins, Michael. "Designing Great Rubrics," *Technology & Learning* 20 (1999): 23–30.

Skolnik, Michael L. "Higher Education in the 21st Century: Perspectives on an Emerging Body of Literature," *Futures* 30 (1998): 635–650.

Smith, Kari, and Harm Tillema. "Clarifying Different Types of Portfolio Use," *Assessment & Evaluation in Higher Education* 28, no. 6 (December 2003): 625–648.

Smith, Kenneth R. "New Roles and Responsibilities for the University Library: Advancing Student Learning through Outcomes Assessment," *Journal of Library Administration* 35, no. 4 (2001): 29–36.

Steen, Lynn A. "20 Questions That Deans Should Ask Their Mathematics Departments (or, That a Sharp Department Will Ask Itself)," *AAHE Bulletin* 44, no. 9 (May 1992): 3–6.

Sullivan, Margaret M., and Peggy C. Wilds. "Institutional Effectiveness: More Than Measuring Objectives, More Than Student Assessment," *Assessment Update* 13 (September–October 2001): 4–5, 13.

Thompson, Bruce, Colleen Cook, and Martha Kyrillidou. "Concurrent Validity of LibQUAL+™ Scores: What Do LibQUAL+™ Scores Measure?," *Journal of Academic Librarianship* 31, forthcoming.

Tierney, Judith. "Information Literacy and a College Library: A Continuing Experiment," in *Information Literacy Developing Students as Independent Learners*, edited by Donald W. Farmer and Terrence Mech (Jossey-Bass New Directions for Higher Education), number 78 (summer 1992): 63–71.

Todd, Ross. "WWW, Critical Literacies and Learning Outcomes," *Teacher Librarian* 26, no. 2 (1998): 16–21.

Totten, Nancy Thomas. "Teaching Students to Evaluate Information," *RQ* 29 (1990): 348–354.

Van Eerden, Kathy. "Using Critical Thinking Vignettes to Evaluate Student Learning," *Nursing and Health Care Perspectives* 22 (2001): 231–234.

Vaughan, Jason. "Policies Governing Use of Computing Technology in Academic Libraries," *Information Technology and Libraries* 23, no. 4 (2004): 153–167.

Vos, Henk. "How to Assess for Improvement of Learning," *European Journal of Engineering Education* 25 (2000): 227–233.

Wagenaar, T. C. "The Capstone Course," *Teaching Sociology* 21 (July 1993): 209–214.

Watters, Kathleen. "Able to Learn 'Just for the Hell of It,'" *Adults Learning* 13, no. 8 (2002): 9–11.

Wellman, Jane V. "Assessing State Accountability Systems," *Change* 33 (March 2001): 46–52.

Whitmire, Ethelene. "A Longitudinal Study of Undergraduates' Academic Library Experiences," *The Journal of Academic Librarianship* 27 (2001): 379–385.

Wilson, Thomas Daniel. "Human Information Behaviour," *Informing Science* 3 (2000): 49–56.

Winner, Marian C. "Librarians as Partners in the Classroom: An Increasing Imperative," *Reference Services Review* 26 (1998): 25–30.

Zernike, Kate. "Tests Are Not Just for Kids," *New York Times Education Life Supplement*, section 4A (August 4, 2002): 26–30.

Books

Ary, Donald L., C. Jacobs, and A. Razavich. *Introduction to Research in Education*, 3rd ed. New York: Holt, Rinehart and Winston, 1985.

Association of American Colleges & Universities. *Our Students' Best Work: A Framework for Accountability Worthy of Our Mission*. Washington, D.C.: Association of American Colleges & Universities, 2004.

Auster, Ethel, and Shauna Taylor. *Downsizing in Academic Libraries: The Canadian Experience*. Toronto, ON: University of Toronto Press, 2004.

Behn, Robert D. *Rethinking Democratic Accountability*. Washington, D.C.: Brookings Institution Press, 2001.

Boyer, Carol M., and Peter T. Ewell. *State-Based Case Studies of Assessment Initiatives in Undergraduate Education: Chronology of Critical Points*. Denver, CO: Education Commission of the States, 1988.

Bruce, Christine Susan. *The Seven Faces of Information Literacy*. Adelaide, Australia: Auslib Press, 1997.

Bruneau, William A., and Donald C. Savage. *Counting Out the Scholars: How Performance Indicators Undermine Universities and Colleges*. Toronto, ON: James Lorimer, 2002.

Business-Higher Education Forum. *Public Accountability for Student Learning in Higher Education: Issues and Options*. Washington, D.C.: American Council for Education, April 2004.

Chambers Dictionary. Edinburgh: Chambers Harrap, 1998.

Cleveland, William S. *The Elements of Graphing Data*. Monterey, CA: Wadsworth Advanced Books and Software, 1985.

Committee on the Foundations of Assessment. *Knowing What Students Know: The Science and Design of Educational Assessment*, edited by James W. Pellegrino, Naomi Chudowsky, and Robert Glaser. Washington, D.C.: The National Academies Press, 2001.

Cooperrider, David L., Diana Whitney, and Jacqueline M. Stavros. *Appreciative Inquiry Handbook*. Bedford Heights, OH: Lakeshore Communications, Inc., 2003.

Deming, W. Edwards. *Out of the Crisis*. Cambridge, MA: Massachusetts Institute of Technology, 1987.

Ericsson, K. Anders, and Herbert A. Simon. *Protocol Analysis*. Cambridge, MA: MIT Press, 1984, 1993.

Farmer, Donald W. *Enhancing Student Learning: Emphasizing Essential Competencies in Academic Programs*. Wilkes-Barre, PA: King's College, 1988.

Fink, L. Dee. *Creating Significant Learning Experiences*. San Francisco: Jossey-Bass, 2003.

Foster, Pablo, Ursual Howard, and Arina Reisenberger. *A Sense of Achievement: Outcomes of Adult Learning*. London: Further Education Development Agency, 1997.

Glaser, Barney G., and Anselm L. Strauss. *The Discovery of Grounded Theory: Strategies for Qualitative Research*. New York: Aldine de Gruyter, 1967.

Glazier, Jack D., and Ronald R. Powell. *Qualitative Research in Information Management*. Englewood, CO: Libraries Unlimited, 1992.

Greenwood, Maggie, and John Vorhaus, eds. *Recognising and Validating Outcomes of Non-accredited Learning: A Practical Approach*. London: Learning and Skills Development Agency, 2001.

Hernon, Peter, and Ellen Altman. *Assessing Service Quality: Satisfying the Expectations of Library Customers*. Chicago: American Library Association, 1998.

Hernon, Peter, and Robert E. Dugan. *An Action Plan for Outcomes Assessment in Your Library*. Chicago: American Library Association, 2002.

Illinois Association of College and Research Libraries. *Library Skills Test*. Bensenville, IL: Scholastic Testing Service, 1981.

Institute for Education Best Practices. *Measuring Institutional Performance Outcomes: Consortium Benchmarking Study: Best-in-class Report*. Houston, TX: American Productivity & Quality Center, 1998.

Jaeger, Richard M. *Statistics: A Spectator Sport*. Beverly Hills, CA: Sage, 1983.

Kotter, John P. *Leading Change*. Boston: Harvard Business School Press, 1996.

LaGuardia, Cheryl. *Teaching the New Library: A How-to-Do-It Manual for Planning and Designing Instructional Programs*. New York: Neal-Schuman, 1996.

Livingston, Samuel A., and Michael J. Zieky. *Passing Scores: A Manual for Setting Standards on Performance on Educational and Occupational Tests*. Princeton, NJ: Educational Testing Service, 1982.

Lucas, Ann F. *Leading Academic Change: Essential Roles for Department Chairs*. San Francisco: Jossey-Bass, 2000.

Maki, Peggy L. *Assessing for Learning: Building a Sustainable Commitment across the Institution*. Sterling, VA: Stylus Publishing, 2004.

Merriam, Sharan B. *Qualitative Research and Case Study Applications in Education*. San Francisco: Jossey-Bass Publishers, 1998.

Middle States Commission on Higher Education. *Developing Research & Communication Skills: Guidelines for Information Literacy in the Curriculum*. Philadelphia, PA: Middle States Commission on Higher Education, 2003.

———. *Student Learning Assessment: Options and Resources*. Philadelphia, PA: Middle States Commission on Higher Education, 2003.

Minton, David. *Teaching Skills in Further and Adult Education*. London: City and Guilds of London Institute, 1997.

Nashashibi, P. *Learning in Progress: Recognising Achievement in Adult Learning.* London: Learning and Skills Development Agency, 2002.

National Commission on Accountability in Higher Education. *Accountability for Better Results: A National Imperative for Higher Education.* Denver, CO: State Higher Education Executive Officers, 2005.

Ory, John C., and Katherine E. Ryan. *Tips for Improving Testing and Grading.* Newbury Park, CA: Sage Publication, 1993.

Patton, Michael Quinn. *Utilization-Focused Evaluation: The New Century Text,* 3rd ed. Thousand Oaks, CA: Sage Publications, 1997.

Pole, Christopher. *Assessing and Recording Achievement.* Buckingham, UK: Open University Press, 1993.

Powell, Ronald R., and Lynn Silipigni Connaway. *Basic Research Methods for Librarians,* 4th ed. Westport, CT: Libraries Unlimited, 2004.

Rockman, Irene, and Associates. *Integrating Information Literacy into the Higher Education Curriculum: Practical Models for Transformation.* San Francisco: Jossey-Bass, 2004.

Ruben, Brent D. *Toward a Balanced Scorecard for Higher Education: Rethinking the College and University Excellence Indicators Framework.* New Brunswick, NJ: Rutgers University, Center for Organizational Development and Leadership, 1999.

Scott, Geoff. *Change Matters: Making a Difference in Education and Training.* Sydney, Australia: Allen & Unwin, 1999.

Senge, Peter, Art Kleiner, Charlotte Roberts, Richard Ross, George Roth, and Bryan Smith. *The Dance of Change: The Challenges of Sustaining Momentum in Learning Organizations.* New York: Currency/Doubleday, 1999.

Shewhart, Walter A. *Statistical Method from the Viewpoint of Quality Control.* New York: Dover Publications, 1939, 1986.

Shonrock, Diana D. *Evaluating Library Instruction: Sample Questions: Forms and Strategies for Practical Use.* Chicago: American Library Association, 1996.

Siegel, Sidney, and John Castellan Jr. *Nonparametric Statistics for the Behavioral Sciences.* New York: McGraw-Hill, 1988.

Sims, Serbrenia J. *Student Outcomes Assessment: A Historical Review and Guide to Program Development.* New York: Greenwood Press, 1992.

Spence, Robert. *Information Visualization.* Boston: Addison-Wesley, 2001.

Strauss, Anselm L., and Juliet Corbin. *Basics of Qualitative Research: Grounded Theory Procedures and Techniques.* Newbury Park, CA: Sage Publications, 1990.

Suskie, Linda. *Assessing Student Learning: A Common Sense Guide.* Bolton, MA: Anker Publishing, 2004.

Walvoord, Barbara E., and Virginia Johnson Anderson. *Effective Grading: A Tool for Learning and Assessment.* San Francisco: Jossey-Bass, 1998.

Webster's II New College Dictionary. Boston: Houghton Mifflin, 2001.

White, Jan V. *Using Charts and Graphs: 1000 Ideas for Visual Persuasion.* New York: Bowker, 1984.

Wisconsin Association of Academic Librarians. *Minimum Library Use Skills: Standards Test, and Bibliography.* Madison: Wisconsin Association of Academic Librarians, 1984.

Zeithaml, Valarie A., A. Parasuraman, and Leonard L. Berry. *Delivering Quality Service: Balancing Customer Perceptions and Expectations.* New York: The Free Press, 1990.

Book Chapters

Adams, Mignon S. "Evaluation," in *Sourcebook for Bibliographic Instruction,* edited by Katherine Branch and Carolyn Dusenbury (pp. 45–57). Chicago: Bibliographic Instruction Section, Association of College and Research Libraries, American Library Association, 1993.

Banta, Trudy W., and V.M.H. Borden. "Performance Indicators for Accountability and Improvement," in *Using Performance Indicators to Guide Strategic Decision Making,* edited by V.M.H. Borden and Trudy W. Banta (pp. 96–106). (New Directions for Institutional Research, No. 82). San Francisco: Jossey-Bass, 1994.

Bennion, Donald, and Michael Harris. "Developing a Culture of Assessment at Eastern Michigan University," in *A Collection of Papers on Self-Study and Institutional Improvement, 2004. Volume 3: Assessment of Student Learning* (pp. 29–31). Chicago: The Higher Learning Commission, 2004.

Bloomberg, Sandra, and Melaine McDonald. "Assessment: A Case Study in Synergy," in *Outcomes Assessment in Higher Education,* edited by Peter Hernon and Robert E. Dugan (pp. 259–289). Westport, CT: Libraries Unlimited, 2004.

Borden, V.M.H. "A Few Good Measures: The Impossible Dream?," in *Assessment to Promote Deep Learning: Insight from AAHE's 2000 and 1999 Assessment Conferences,* edited by Linda Suskie (pp. 31–40). Washington, D.C.: American Association for Higher Education, 2001.

Burke, Joseph C. "The Many Faces of Accountability," in *Achieving Accountability in Higher Education: Balancing Public, Academic, and Market Demands,* edited by Joseph C. Burke (pp. 1–24). San Francisco: Jossey-Bass, 2005.

———. "Preface," in *Achieving Accountability in Higher Education: Balancing Public, Academic, and Market Demands,* edited by Joseph C. Burke (pp. ix–xix). San Francisco: Jossey-Bass, 2005.

———. "Reinventing Accountability: From Bureaucratic Rules to Performance Results," in *Achieving Accountability in Higher Education: Balancing*

Public, Academic, and Market Demands, edited by Joseph C. Burke (pp. 216–245). San Francisco: Jossey-Bass, 2005.

Callan, Patrick M., and Joni E. Finney. "State-by-state Report Cards: Public Purposes and Accountability for a New Century," in *Achieving Accountability in Higher Education: Balancing Public, Academic, and Market Demands*, edited by Joseph C. Burke (pp. 198–215). San Francisco: Jossey-Bass, 2005.

Cameron, Lynn. "Assessing Information Literacy," in *Integrating Information Literacy into the Higher Education Curriculum: Practical Models for Transformation*, edited by Ilene F. Rockman and Associates (pp. 207–236). San Francisco: Jossey-Bass, 2004.

Collins, Janice, and Josh Bullock. "Evaluating Assessment: Turbulent Flight in the Life of an Assessment Evaluation Pilot Process," in *A Collection of Papers on Self-Study and Institutional Improvement, 2003. Volume 3: Promoting Student Learning and Effective Teaching* (pp. 61–63). Chicago: The Higher Learning Commission, 2003.

Cook, Doug. "Creating Connections: A Review of the Literature," in *The Collaborative Imperative: Librarians and Faculty Working Together in the Information Universe*, edited by Dick Raspa and Dane Ward (pp. 19–38). Chicago: Association of College and Research Libraries, 2000.

Dolence, Michael G., and Donald M. Norris. "Using Key Performance Indicators to Drive Strategic Decision Making," in *Using Performance Indicators to Guide Strategic Decision Making*, edited by V.M.H. Borden and Trudy W. Banta (pp. 63–80). (New Directions for Institutional Research, No. 82). San Francisco: Jossey-Bass, 1994.

Dugan, Robert E. "A Local Institutional Assessment Plan," in *Outcomes Assessment in Higher Education: Views and Perspectives*, edited by Peter Hernon and Robert E. Dugan (pp. 103–134). Westport, CT: Libraries Unlimited, 2004.

Ewell, Peter T. "Can Assessment Serve Accountability? It Depends on the Question," in *Achieving Accountability in Higher Education: Balancing Public, Academic, and Market Demands*, edited by Joseph C. Burke (pp. 104–124). San Francisco: Jossey-Bass, 2005.

———. "Developing Statewide Performance Indicators for Higher Education," in *Charting Higher Education Accountability: A Sourcebook on State-level Performance Indicators*, edited by S. S. Ruppert (pp. 147–166). Denver, CO: Education Commission of the States, 1994.

Greene, Andrea, Gail Mee, and Gayla Preisser. "Ensuring the Assessment Investment Pays Off: A Case Study," in *A Collection of Papers on Self-Study and Institutional Improvement, 2004. Volume 3: Assessment of Student Learning* (pp. 51–57). Chicago: The Higher Learning Commission, 2004.

Haynes, Evelyn B. "Library-faculty Partnerships in Instruction," in *Advances in Librarianship*, edited by Irene Godden (pp. 191–222). Toronto, ON: Academic Press, 1996.

Heath, Fred, and Colleen Cook. "SERVQUAL: Service Quality Assessment in Libraries," *Encyclopedia of Library and Information Science*, 2nd ed., vol. 4, edited by Miriam A. Drake (pp. 2613–2635). New York: Marcel Dekker, 2003.

Hernon, Peter. "Selecting from the Assessment Tool Chest," in *Outcomes Assessment in Higher Education*, edited by Peter Hernon and Robert E. Dugan (pp. 149–173). Westport, CT: Libraries Unlimited, 2004.

Hernon, Peter, and Robert E. Dugan. "Institutional Example: Academic Librarians and Faculty: Information Literacy," in *Assessing for Learning: Building a Sustainable Commitment across the Institution*, edited by Peggy L. Maki (pp. 108–110). Sterling, VA: Stylus Publishing, 2004.

Johnson, Jessica, Julie Wallin, and Karla Sanders. "Assessing an Institution's Outcomes Assessment Efforts: The Application of the Higher Learning Commission Assessment Matrix by Three Institutions," in *A Collection of Papers on Self-Study and Institutional Improvement, 2004. Volume 3: Assessment of Student Learning* (pp. 51–57). Chicago: The Higher Learning Commission, 2004.

Lindauer, Bonnie Gratch, and Amelie Brown. "Developing a Tool to Assess Community College Students," in *Integrating Information Literacy into the Higher Education Curriculum: Practical Models for Transformation*, edited by Ilene F. Rockman and Associates (pp. 165–206). San Francisco: Jossey-Bass, 2004.

Loacker, Georgine, and Maria Mentkowski. "Creating a Culture Where Assessment Improves Learning," in *Making a Difference*, edited by Trudy W. Banta (pp. 5–24). San Francisco: Jossey-Bass, 1993.

Maki, Peggy L. "Developing an Assessment Plan to Learn about Student Learning," in *Outcomes Assessment in Higher Education: Views and Perspectives*, edited by Peter Hernon and Robert E. Dugan (pp. 89–101). Westport, CT: Libraries Unlimited, 2004.

Massy, William F. "Academic Audit for Accountability and Improvement," in *Achieving Accountability in Higher Education: Balancing Public, Academic, and Market Demands*, edited by Joseph C. Burke (pp. 173–197). San Francisco: Jossey-Bass, 2005.

McGregor, Felicity. "Excellent Libraries: A Quality Assurance Perspective," in *Advances in Librarianship*, vol. 28, edited by Danuta A. Nitecki (pp. 17–53). Amsterdam: Elsevier, 2004.

Mech, Terrence F. "Working with Faculty in an Outcomes-Oriented Curriculum: Observations from the Library," in *The Librarian in the University: Essays on Membership in the Academic Community*, edited by H. Palmer

Hall and Caroline Byrd (pp. 72–91). Metuchen, NJ: Scarecrow Press, 1990.

Mech, Terrence F., and Charles I. Brooks. "Library Anxiety among College Students: An Exploratory Study," in *Continuity & Transformation: The Promise of Confluence*, edited by Richard AmRhien (pp. 173–179). Chicago: Association of College and Research Libraries, 1995.

North Central Association of Colleges and Schools, the Higher Learning Commission. *Handbook of Accreditation*, 2nd ed. (pp. 32–43). Chicago, IL: North Central Association of Colleges and Schools, 1997.

O'Connor, Lisa G., Carolyn J. Radcliff, and Julie A. Gedeon. "Assessing Information Literacy Skills: Developing a Standardized Instrument for Institutional and Longitudinal Measurement," in *Crossing the Divide: Proceedings of the Tenth National Conference of the Association of College and Research Libraries*, edited by H. A. Thompson (pp. 163–174). Chicago: Association of College and Research Libraries, 2001.

Raspa, Dick, and Dane Ward. "Listening for Collaboration: Faculty and Librarians Working Together," in *The Collaborative Imperative: Librarians and Faculty Working Together in the Information Universe*, edited by Dick Raspa and Dane Ward (pp. 1–18). Chicago: Association of College and Research Libraries, 2000.

Riordan, Catherine A., Jennifer J. Fager, and Timothy S. Hartshorne. "Strategies for Building a Culture of Assessment in Decentralized Institutions," in *A Collection of Papers on Self-Study and Institutional Improvement, 2004. Volume 3: Assessment of Student Learning* (pp. 35–40). Chicago: The Higher Learning Commission, 2004.

Riordan, Tim. "Introduction," in *Disciplines as Frameworks for Student Learning: Teaching the Practice of the Disciplines*, edited by Tim Riordan and James Roth (pp. xi–xix). Sterling, VA: Stylus Publishing, LLC, 2005.

Rogers, Gloria M. "Assessing Student Learning: Elegance in Simplicity," in *A Collection of Papers on Self-Study and Institutional Improvement, 2003. Volume 3: Promoting Student Learning and Effective Teaching* (pp. 55–57). Chicago: The Higher Learning Commission, 2003.

Torrance, H. "Introduction," in *Assessing and Recording Achievement*, by Christopher Pole (pp. 1–8). Buckingham, UK: Open University Press, 1993.

Town, J. Stephen. "The SCONUL Task Force on Information Skills," in *Information and IT Literacy: Enabling Learning in the 21st Century*, edited by Allan Martin and Hannelore Rader (pp. 53–65). London: Facet, 2003.

Wolff, Ralph A. "Accountability and Accreditation: Can Reforms Match Increasing Demands?," in *Achieving Accountability in Higher Education: Balancing Public, Academic, and Market Demands*, edited by Joseph C. Burke (pp. 78–103). San Francisco: Jossey-Bass, 2005.

Zumeta, William. "Accountability: Challenges for Higher Education," in *The NEA 2000 Almanac of Higher Education* (pp. 57–71). Washington, D.C.: NEA Communications Services, 2000.

Guidelines, Standards, and Accreditation Documentation

AACSB International (The Association to Advance Collegiate Schools of Business). *Eligibility Procedures and Accreditation Standards for Business Accreditation.* Tampa, FL: AACSB International, 2005.

ABET, Inc. *Criteria for Accrediting Engineering Programs.* Baltimore, MD: ABET–Engineering Accreditation Commission, 2004.

American Library Association. Association of College and Research Libraries. *Information Literacy Competency Standards for Higher Education.* Chicago: Association of College and Research Libraries, 2000.

———. *Information Literacy Standards for Higher Education.* Chicago: American Library Association, 2000.

———. *Objectives for Information Literacy Instruction: A Model Statement for Academic Librarians.* Chicago: Association of College and Research Libraries, 2001.

———. Science and Technology Section (STS) Task Force on Information Literacy for Science and Technology. "Information Literacy Standards for Science and Technology: A Draft," *College & Research Libraries News* 66 (May 2005): 381–388.

CHEA Institute for Research and Study of Accreditation and Quality Assurance. *Statement of Mutual Responsibilities for Student Learning Outcomes: Accreditation, Institutions, and Programs.* Washington, D.C.: Council for Higher Education Accreditation, September 2003.

Commission on Colleges of the Southern Association of Colleges and Schools. *Principles of Accreditation: Foundations for Quality Enhancement.* Atlanta, GA: Commission on Colleges of the Southern Association of Colleges and Schools, 2004.

Middle States Commission on Higher Education. *Characteristics of Excellence in Higher Education: Eligibility Requirements and Standards for Accreditation.* Philadelphia, PA: Middle States Commission on Higher Education, 2002.

———. *Characteristics of Excellence in Higher Education: Eligibility Requirements and Standards for Accreditation,* 12th ed. Philadelphia, PA: Middle States Commission on Higher Education, in press.

North Central Association of Colleges and Schools. The Higher Learning Commission. *Handbook of Accreditation*, 2nd ed. Chicago, IL: North Central Association of Colleges and Schools, 1997.
———. *Handbook of Accreditation*, 3rd ed. Chicago, IL: North Central Association of Colleges and Schools, 2003.

Government Publications

Organisation for Economic Co-operation and Development. *Education at a Glance: OECD Indicators*. Paris: Organisation for Economic Co-operation and Development, 2003.
United States Government Accountability Office. *Informing Our Nation: Improving How to Understand and Assess the USA's Position and Progress*, GAO-05-1. Washington, D.C.: Government Accountability Office, November 2004.

Reports

Anisef, Paul, and Etta Baichman. *Evaluating Canadian University Education through the Use of Graduate and Employer Surveys*. Research report. Ottawa, ON: Commission of Inquiry on Canadian University Education, 1991.
Association of Universities and Colleges of Canada Task Force on the Report of the Commission of Inquiry on Canadian University Education. *Report of the Association of Universities and Colleges of Canada Task Force on the Report of the Commission of Inquiry on Canadian University Education*. Ottawa, ON: Association of University and Colleges of Canada, 1992.
Boykin, Joseph, Jan Comfort, Peg Tyler, Fred Heath, Damon Jaggars, and Jocelyn Duffy. "LibQUAL+™ and Decision Making: The Library Summit." Flier prepared by Clemson University, University of Texas, and ARL (June 4, 2004).
Cambridge, Barbara L., Susan Kahn, Daniel P. Tompkins, and Kathleen B. Yancey. *Electronic Portfolios: Emerging Practices in Student, Faculty and Institutional Learning*. Washington, D.C.: American Association for Higher Education, 2001.
Council of Ministers of Education, Canada. *A Report on Public Expectations of Postsecondary Education in Canada*. Toronto, ON: Council of Ministers of Education, Canada, 1999. Available at http://www.cmec.ca/postsec/expectations.en.pdf (accessed November 16, 2004).

Maryville College. *Information Literacy Competency Inventory (Pretest)*. Maryville, TN: Maryville College, 2000.

Nadeau, Gilles G. *Criteria and Indicators of Quality and Excellence in Colleges and Universities in Canada: Summary of the Three Phases of the Project*. Winnipeg, MB: Centre for Higher Education Research and Development, University of Manitoba, 1995.

National Association of Independent Colleges and Universities. *Task Force Report on Appropriate Accountability: Regulations, the Responsibilities of Independence: Appropriate Accountability through Self-regulation*. Washington, D.C.: National Association of Independent Colleges and Universities, 1994.

Ontario Undergraduate Student Alliance. *Improving Accountability at Canadian Universities: Presented to the Council of Ministers of Education of Canada, Second National Consultation on Education, Edmonton, Alberta, May 1996*. Toronto, ON: Ontario Undergraduate Student Alliance, 1996.

Ratteray, Oswald. *A Survey of Librarians in the Middle States Region on the Role of the Library, Electronic Resources, and Information Literacy Training in Higher Education*. Philadelphia, PA: Middle States Commission on Higher Education, 1999.

Smith, Stuart L. *Report: Commission of Inquiry on Canadian University Education*. Ottawa, ON: Association of Universities and Colleges of Canada, 1991.

Web Resources

Acker, Stephen. "Overcoming Obstacles to Authentic ePortfolio Assessment," *Campus Technology* (2005). Available at http://www.campus-technology.com/news_article.asp?id=10788 (accessed July 31, 2005).

Adler, Karen. "Texas Universities to Be Tested: Accountability System for Higher Education Is Approved," *San Antonio Express News* (October 29, 2004): 7B. Available at LexisNexis Academic (accessed on November 2, 2004).

Allen, Mary. "Student Learning Outcomes in the CSU: Using Scoring Rubrics." Long Beach: The California State University. Available at http://www.calstate.edu/AcadAff/SLOA/links/using_rubrics.shtml (accessed May 7, 2005).

Alverno College. "Institutional and Program Assessment." Milwaukee, WI: Alverno College, n.d. Available at http://depts.alverno.edu/ere/ipa/ipa.html (accessed February 3, 2005).

American Library Association. "Presidential Committee on Information Literacy." Chicago: American Library Association, 1989. Available at http://www.ala.org/acrl/legalis.html (accessed May 12, 2005).

American Library Association. Association of College and Research Libraries. "Standards for Libraries in Higher Education." Chicago: American Library Association, 2004. Available at http://www.ala.org/ala/acrl/acrl standards/standardslibraries.htm (accessed July 29, 2005).

American Library Association. Presidential Committee on Information Literacy. *Final Report*. Chicago: American Library Association, 1989. Available at http://www.ala.org/ala/acrl/acrlpubs/whitepapers/presidential.htm (accessed May 23, 2005; August 2, 2005).

"Assessment of Student Academic Achievement: Assessment Culture Matrix," in *Restructured Expectations: A Transitional Workbook* (pp. 71–79). Chicago, IL: Higher Learning Commission, 2003. Available at http://www.ncahigherlearningcommission.org/resources/assessment/Assess Matrix03.pdf (assessed February 22, 2005).

Australian Information and Communications Technology in Education Committee (AICTEC). *e-Portfolio*. Sydney, Australia: Australian Information and Communications Technology in Education Committee. Available at http://standards.edna.edu.au/standards/e-portfolio.html (accessed July 31, 2005).

Australian Universities Quality Agency. "AUQA Information." Melbourne, Australia: Australian Universities Quality Agency. Available at http://www.auqa.edu.au/aboutauqa/auqainfo/index.shtml (accessed November 26, 2004).

———. "Good Practice Database." Melbourne, Australia: Australian Universities Quality Agency. Available at http://www.auqa.edu.au/gp/ (accessed July 29, 2005).

Baldrige National Quality Program. *2005 Education Criteria for Performance Excellence*. Washington, D.C.: Baldrige National Quality Program, 2005. Available at http://www.quality.nist.gov/PDF_files/2005_Education_Criteria.pdf (accessed July 1, 2005).

Barrett, Helen. *Pedagogical Issues in Electronic Portfolio Development* (2002). Available at http://www.electronicportfolios.com/EPpedissues.pdf (accessed July 31, 2005).

Barrett, Helen C., and Judy Wilkerson. *Conflicting Paradigms in Electronic Portfolio Approaches: Choosing an Electronic Portfolio Strategy That Matches Your Conceptual Framework*. Available at http://www.electronic portfolios.com/systems/paradigms.html (accessed July 31, 2005).

Batson, Trent. "The Electronic Portfolio Boom: What's It All About?," *Syllabus* (December 2002). Available at http://www.campus-technology.com/article.asp?id=6984 (accessed July 31, 2005).

Bay Area Community Colleges Information Competency Assessment Project. Home page. San Francisco, CA: City College of San Francisco, 2005. Available at http://www.topsy.org/ICAP/ICAProject.html (accessed July 29, 2005).

Bresciani, Marilee J. "Undergraduate Assessment at North Carolina State University: A Collaborative Effort." Raleigh: North Carolina State University, n.d. Available at http://www.ncsu.edu/provost/academic_programs/uapr/ assess/sacs_report.html (accessed February 3, 2005).

California State University. "Information Competence Assessment Phase Two Summary Report. Pomona: California State University, 2002. Available at http://www.csupomona.edu/~kkdunn/Icassess/phase2summary .htm (accessed July 29, 2005).

———. "Information Competence in the CSU: A Report." N.p.: California State University, 1995. Available at http://www.calstate.edu/LS/Final Rpt_95.doc (accessed July 29, 2005).

Canadian Association of Research Libraries. *The State of Canadian Research Libraries 2001–2002*. Ottawa: Canadian Association of Research Libraries, University of Ottawa, 2003. Available at http://www.carl-abrc.ca/ projects/state/state_2001_2002-e.html (accessed April 26, 2005).

Canadian Library Association. *Creating an Environment of Continuous Assessment: Practical Approaches for Academic Libraries*. Toronto, ON: Canadian Library Association, 2005. Available at http://www.cla.ca/conference/ 2005/p2.htm (accessed May 23, 2005).

Cape Fear Community College, Institutional Effectiveness/Planning and Research Office. *All about Institutional Effectiveness*. Wilmington, NC: Cape Fear Community College, n.d. Available at http://cfcc.edu/ie/allabout.htm (accessed March 4, 2005).

Carnegie Mellon University. "Higher Education at Carnegie Mellon University: An Introduction by Vice Provost for Education Indira Nair." Pittsburgh, PA: Carnegie Mellon University, 2005. Available at http:// www.cmu.edu/home/education/education_intro.html (accessed July 29, 2005).

Carroll, Martin. "Quality Assurance in Australian University Libraries—Issues Identified Through Institutional Quality Audit." Address given at the University of Stellenbosch Library. Seventh Annual Symposium. Stellenbosch, South Africa: University of Stellenbosch, October 28–29, 2004. Available at http://www.lib.sun.ac.za/sym2004/papers.htm (accessed November 27, 2004).

Center for Instructional Technologies. "Classroom Performance Systems Frequently Asked Questions." Austin: University of Texas, n.d. Available at http://www.utexas.edu/academic/cit/howto/labinstructions/cpsfaqs.html (accessed May 22, 2005).

The Citadel. "Citadel Academy for the Scholarship of Teaching, Learning and Evaluation." Charleston, SC: The Citadel, 2005. Available at http:// faculty.citadel.edu/carnegie/index.htm (accessed May 9, 2005).

Council of Ministers of Education, Canada. *Education at a Glance: OECD Indicators: Country Profile for Canada* (Toronto, ON: Council of Ministers of Education, Canada, 2004. Available at http://www.cmec.ca/ stats/Profile2004.en.pdf (accessed April 26, 2005).

Educational Testing Service. "Employees and Information Proficiency." Princeton, NJ: Educational Testing Service, February 22, 2005. Available at http://www.ets.org/ictliteracy/employer.html (accessed March 5, 2005).

———. "ETS Launches ICT Literacy Assessment." Princeton, NJ: Educational Testing Service, November 8, 2004. Available at http://www.ets.org/news/04110801.html (accessed March 5, 2005; August 2, 2004).

———. *ICT Literacy Assessment*. Princeton, NJ: Educational Testing Service, 2004–2005. Available at http://www.ets.org/ictliteracy (accessed November 8, 2004; August 1, 2005).

———. "Using Scores." Princeton, NJ: Educational Testing Service, February 21, 2005. Available at http://www.ets.org/ictliteracy/scores.html (accessed March 5, 2005).

Edudata Canada home page. Vancouver, BC: University of British Columbia, Faculty of Education, 2004. Available at http://www.edudata.educ.ubc.ca (accessed November 16, 2004).

ePortfolio.org. *About ePortfolio.org*. Newington, CT: Connecticut Distance Learning Consortium, 2005. Available at http://www.eportfolio.org/about.cfm (accessed July 31, 2005).

Ericsson, K. Anders. "Protocol Analysis and Verbal Reports on Thinking." Tallahassee: Florida State University, 2002. Available at http://www.psy.fsu.edu/faculty/ericsson/ericsson.proto.thnk.html (accessed July 29, 2005).

European Institute for E-Learning, *ePortfolio 2005*. Champlost, France: European Institute for E-Learning, 2005. Available at http://www.eife-l.org/portfolio/ep2005/ (accessed July 31, 2005).

Florida Community College at Jacksonville. "Assessment and Certification." Jacksonville: Florida Community College, 2005. Available at http://www.fccj.edu/campuses/kent/assessment/info_literacy.html (accessed March 21, 2005).

Frey, Richard. "Assessment, Accountability, and Student Learning Outcomes." Bellingham, WA: Western Washington University, Office of Institutional Assessment and Testing, n.d. Available at http://www.ac.wwu.edu/~dialogue/issue2.html (accessed February 3, 2005).

Gedeon, Julie, Carolyn Radcliff, and Lisa O'Connor. Presentation: "Project SAILS: Facing the Challenges of Information Literacy Assessment," American Association for Higher Education Assessment Conference, June 14, 2004, Denver. Available at http://www.projectsails.org/publications/aahe_files/frame.htm (accessed March 28, 2005).

George, Carole A. "Carnegie Mellon University Libraries Mind Models Exhibit—User Studies." Pittsburgh, PA: Carnegie Mellon University, 2005. Available at http://www.library.cmu.edu/Libraries/MindModels UserStudiesRpt.pdf (accessed July 29, 2005).

Gibson, David, and Helen Barrett. "Directions in Electronic Portfolio Development." *Contemporary Issues in Technology and Teacher Education* 2, no. 4 (2003): 559–576. Available at http://www.citejournal.org/vol2/iss4/general/article3.cfm (accessed July 31, 2005).

Greenberg, Gary. "The Digital Convergence: Extending the Portfolio Model," *EDUCAUSE Review* 39, no. 4 (July/August 2004): 28–36. Available at http://www.educause.edu/ir/library/pdf/ERM0441.pdf (accessed July 31, 2005).

Hayford, Julie. "Does Being Last Give You the Advantage?: Quality Assurance in Australian Higher Education," Proceedings of the Australian Universities Quality Forum 2003, AUQA Occasional Publication. Available at http://64.233.161.104/search?q=cache:KAxAneLcR58J:www.auqa.edu.au/auqf/2003/proceedings/AUQF2003_Proceedings.pdf+julie+hayford&hl=en (accessed November 29, 2004).

Higher Education & Research Opportunities. "RAE [Research Assessment Exercise]: What Is the RAE 2001?" Newcastle upon Tyne, England: Higher Education & Research Opportunities, 2001. Available at http://www.hero.ac.uk/rae/AboutUs/ (accessed November 27, 2004).

Holmes, David. "Commentary on the 1998–1999 CARL Statistics: An Introduction and Retrospective Overview." Ottawa, ON: Canadian Association of Research Libraries, University of Ottawa, 2000. Available at http://www.carl-abrc.ca/projects/stats/Commentary_Overview.htm (accessed November 30, 2001).

Hunt, James B., Jr., and Garrey Carruthers. "Foreword." San Jose, CA: The National Center for Public Policy and Higher Education, n.d. Available at http://measuringup.highereducation.org/foreward.cfm (accessed February 21, 2005).

IMS Global Learning Consortium, Inc. *IMS ePortfolio Specification*. Burlington, MA: IMS Global Learning Consortium, Inc., 2005. Available at http://www.imsglobal.org/ep/ (accessed July 31, 2005).

Information Literacy Standards, 1st ed. Canberra, Australia: Council of Australian University Libraries, 2001. Available at http://www.caul.edu.au/caul-doc/InfoLitStandards2001.doc (accessed December 15, 2004).

International Organization for Standardization. Home page. Geneva, Switzerland: International Organization for Standardization. Available at http://www.iso.org/iso/en/ISOOnline.frontpage (accessed December 15, 2004).

Jafari, Ali. "The 'Sticky' ePortfolio System: Tackling Challenges and Identifying Attributes," *EDUCAUSE Review* 39, no. 4 (July/August 2004): 48–49. Available at http://www.educause.edu/ir/library/pdf/erm0442.pdf (accessed July 31, 2005).

Kleniewski, Nancy. "Program Review as a Win-win Opportunity," AAHE Bulletin.com (May 2003). Available at http://www.webs.uidaho.edu/ipb/pdf_files/Win-Win.pdf (accessed July 29, 2005).

Leonard, Kim, and Bill Zlatos. "Students Hit with Copyright Lawsuits." *Pittsburgh Tribune-Review* (April 14, 2005). Available at http://pittsburghlive.com/x/tribune-review/s_324000.html (accessed July 29, 2005).

"Levels of Implementation and the Patterns of Characteristics Analysis Worksheet." Chicago, IL: The Higher Learning Commission, March 2002. Available at http://www.ncahigherlearningcommission.org/resources/assessment/02-AnlysWksht.pdf (accessed February 19, 2005).

Lewis, Karron G. "Evaluation of Teaching: Self-evaluation Techniques." Austin: University of Texas at Austin, Center for Teaching Effectiveness, n.d. Available at http://www.utexas.edu/academic/cte/sourcebook/evaluation2.pdf (accessed December 2, 2004).

López, Cecilia L. "Assessing Student Learning: Using the Commission's *Levels of Implementation*," 105th Annual Meeting of the North Central Association of Colleges and Schools, Commission on Institutions of Higher Education (Chicago, IL, April 2000). Available at http://www.ncahigherlearningcommission.org/resources/assessment/Lopez_Levels_2000.pdf (accessed February 19, 2005).

———. "Assessment of Student Learning," *Liberal Education* 84 (Summer 1998): 36–44. Available from EBSCOhost (Academic Search Premier; accessed February 27, 2005).

Lorenzo, George, and John Ittelson. *An Overview of E-portfolios*. Washington, D.C.: EDUCAUSE, 2005. Available at http://www.educause.edu/ir/library/pdf/ELI3001.pdf (accessed July 31, 2005).

Love, Douglas, Gerry McKean, and Paul Gathercoal. "Portfolios to Webfolios and Beyond: Levels of Maturation," *EDUCAUSE Quarterly* 27, no. 2 (2004): 24–37. Available at http://www.educause.edu/ir/library/pdf/EQM0423.pdf (accessed July 31, 2005).

McCloud, Robert. *Using ePortfolios for Engaged Learning: A Handbook for www.ePortfolio.org*. Newington: Connecticut Distance Learning Consortium, 2004. Available at http://www.eportfolio.org/EngagedLearning2.pdf (accessed July 31, 2005).

Mervis, Scott. "Carnegie Mellon, Pitt Students Targeted in Action against Illegal Music Swapping," *Pittsburgh Post Gazette* (April 13, 2005). Available at http://www.post-gazette.com/pg/05103/487349.stm (accessed July 29, 2005).

Metropolitan Community College. *Effectiveness Reviews*. Omaha, NE: Metropolitan Community College, January 12, 2004. Available at http://metroweb.mccneb.edu/institutionaleffectiveness/reviews.htm (accessed March 4, 2005).

Minneapolis Community and Technical College. "Minneapolis Community and Technical College—2004–2005 College Catalog—Information Literacy." Available at http://www.minneapolis.edu/academicAffairs/collegeCatalog/liberal_arts.cfm (accessed March 21, 2005).

Mount Royal College Academic Development Centre, Curriculum Renewal. Calgary, AB: Mount Royal College Academic Development Centre, 2004. Available at http://www.mtroyal.ca/cr (accessed November 18, 2004).

Naidoo, Prem. "Partnering with Librarians for Improved Quality of Higher Education." Address given at the University of Stellenbosch Library. Seventh Annual Symposium. Stellenbosch, South Africa: University of Stellenbosch, October 28–29, 2004. Available at http://www.lib.sun.ac.za/sym2004/papers.htm (accessed November 26, 2004).

Napier University. "Key Statistics for LIS Service Usage in SCONUL Years." Edinburgh: Napier University, 2002. Available at http://nulis.napier.ac.uk/Statistics/Sconul.htm (accessed November 27, 2004).

———. "Statistics & Performance Indicators." Edinburgh: Napier University, 2002. Available at http://nulis.napier.ac.uk/Statistics/Statistics.htm (accessed November 27, 2004).

Nasseh, Bizhan. "Internet-Generation & Adult Learners Will Create Major Challenges for Higher Education Institutions in the 21st Century." Muncie, IN: Ball State University, n.d. Available at http://www.bsu.edu/classes/nasseh/study/learners.html (accessed January 4, 2005).

National Academies Press. "Knowing What Students Know: The Science and Design of Educat..." Washington, D.C.: The National Academies Press, 2001. Available at http://www.nap.edu/books/0309072727/html/1.html (accessed May 17, 2005).

The National Center for Public Policy and Higher Education. *About Measuring Up: Questions and Answers about Measuring Up 2004.* San Jose, CA: The National Center for Public Policy and Higher Education, n.d. Available at http://measuringup.highereducation.org/qa.cfm (accessed February 21, 2005).

———. *Measuring Up 2004.* San Jose, CA: The National Center for Public Policy and Higher Education, n.d. Available at http://measuringup.higher education.org/default.cfm (accessed February 21, 2005).

National Institute of Standards and Technology. "Frequently Asked Questions about the Malcolm Baldrige National Quality Award." Washington, D.C.: National Institute of Standards and Technology, 2004. Available at http://www.nist.gov/public_affairs/factsheet/baldfaqs.htm (accessed June 3, 2005).

National Survey of Student Engagement. Bloomington: National Survey of Student Engagement, the Indiana University Center for Postsecondary Research, January 20, 2005. Available at http://www.indiana.edu/~nsse/ (accessed August 1, 2005).

———. "National Survey of Student Engagement: Quick Facts." Bloomington: National Survey of Student Engagement, the Indiana University Center for Postsecondary Research, January 20, 2005. Available at http://www.iub.edu/~nsse/html/quick_facts.htm (accessed February 21, 2005).

———. *Quick Facts.* Bloomington: National Survey of Student Engagement, the Indiana University Center for Postsecondary Research, 2004. Available at http://www.indiana.edu/~nsse/html/quick_facts.htm (accessed November 17, 2004).

North Carolina State University. "Active and Cooperative Learning." Raleigh: North Carolina State University, 2005. Available at http://www.ncsu.edu/felder-public/Cooperative_Learning, html (accessed May 7, 2005).

North Carolina State University. University Planning & Analysis. "Internet Resources for Higher Education Outcomes Assessment." Raleigh: North Carolina State University, n.d. Available at http://www2.acs.ncsu.edu/UPA/assmt/resource.htm (accessed December 5, 2004).

North Central Association of Colleges and Schools. "Assessment of Student Academic Achievement: Levels of Implementation." Addendum to the *Handbook of Accreditation*, second edition (pp. 6–13). Chicago, IL: Commission on Institutions of Higher Education, 2000. Available at www.ncacihe.org/aice/assessment/index.html (accessed February 21, 2005).

Oder, Norman. "Tablet PCs Free Librarians," netConnect, Departments Briefings' Section, October 15, 2003. Available from Lexis/Nexis Academic (accessed June 24, 2005).

Open Source Portfolio Initiative. *About OSPI*. Minneapolis, MN: Open Source Portfolio Initiative, 2005. Available at http://www.theospi.org/modules/cjaycontent/index.php?id=3 (accessed July 31, 2005).

Open University. Centre for Outcomes-based Education. "Current Projects: Assessment of Learning Outcomes." London: The Open University, November 2004. Available at http://www.open.ac.uk/cobe/projects.html (accessed November 27, 2004).

Payne, Philip, John Crawford, and Wendy Fiander. "Counting on Making a Difference: Assessing Our Impact," *Vine* (Southampton, England, Southampton University Library) 34, no. 4 (2004): 176–183. Available from Emerald Fulltext.

Peer Review of Teaching Project. "The Peer Review Process: Benchmark Portfolio." Lincoln: University of Nebraska, n.d. Available at http://www.unl.edu/peerrev/process.html#benchmark (accessed December 3, 2004).

———. "The Peer Review Process: Inquiry Portfolio." Lincoln: University of Nebraska, n.d. Available at http://www.unl.edu/peerrev/process.html#inquiry (accessed December 3, 2004).

Pennsylvania State System of Higher Education. *PASSHE Measures Performance and Rewards Success*. Harrisburg: Pennsylvania State System of Higher Education, 2005. Available at http://www.passhe.edu/content/?/performance (accessed June 10, 2005).

Petrides, Lisa, and Thad Nodine. "Accountability and Information Practices in the California Community Colleges: Toward Effective Use of Information in Decision Making," *iJournal: Insight into Student Services* (Issue No. 10) (Spring 2005). Available at http://www.ijournal.us/issue_10/print_version/ij_issue10prt_07.htm (accessed July 1, 2005).

Pew Forum. *IUPUI, The Urban Universities Portfolio Project: Assuring Quality for Multiple Publics.* Washington, D.C.: Pew Forum, undated. Available at http://pewundergradforum.org/project11.htm (accessed July 1, 2005).

Project SAILS. Kent, OH: Kent State University, Libraries and Media Services, 2004. Available at http://www.ProjectSails.org (accessed March 28, 2005).

Project SAILS—Project Description. Kent, OH: Kent State University, Libraries and Media Services, 2004. Available at http://sails.lms.kent.edu/proj description.html (accessed November 16, 2004).

Project SAILS—Skill Sets. Kent, OH: Kent State University, Libraries and Media Services, 2004. Available at http://www.projectsails.org/plans/skillsets.html#obj (accessed March 28, 2005).

Quality Assurance Agency for Higher Education. Home page. Gloucester, UK. Available at http://www.qaa.ac.uk/ (accessed December 15, 2004).

Rae, Bob. *Ontario: A Leader in Learning: Report and Recommendations.* Toronto: Government of Ontario, 2005. Available at http://www.raereview.on.ca/en/pdf/finalReport.pdf (accessed April 25, 2005).

Rodrigues, Raymond. "Want Campus Buy-In for Your Assessment Efforts?" Washington, D.C.: American Association for Higher Education, n.d. Available at http://aahebulletin.com/member/articles/2002-10-feature02_pf.asp? (accessed March 7, 2005).

SAI Global Professional Services. "Australian Business Excellence Framework." Sydney, Australia: SAI Global Professional Services, 2003. Available at http://www.businessexcellenceaustralia.com.au/GROUPS/ABEF/ (accessed November 29, 2004).

Scantron Corporation. "The Bridge to Knowledge." Irvine, CA: Scantron Corp., 2005. Available at http://www.scantron.com (accessed May 18, 2005).

Schrock, Kathy. "Assessment & Rubric Information." *Kathy Schrock's Guide for Educators.* Available at http://school.discovery.com/schrockguide/assess.html (accessed July 31, 2005).

Scott, Geoff. "Change Matters: Making a Difference in Higher Education," keynote address at Leadership Forum. Dublin: European University Association, February 2004. Available at http://www.eua.be/eua/ (accessed November 29, 2004).

Selingo, Jeffrey. "President Plans No Price Controls or Strict Accountability Rules for Colleges, New Education Secretary Says in Interview," *The Chronicle of Higher Education* (February 7, 2005). Available at http://chronicle.com/daily/2005/02/2005020701n.htm (accessed on February 12, 2005); *The Chronicle of Higher Education: Today's News* (February 7, 2005). Available at http://chronicle.com/temp/email.php?id=ipm3fvtra5chlr4ewbs4fserlyxt2ali (accessed February 8, 2005).

Shavelson, R. "Assessing Student Learning: The Quest to Hold Higher Education Accountable." Seminar presented at the Center for Advanced Study in the Behavioral Sciences Seminar, Stanford University (2000). Available at http://www.stanford.edu/dept/SUSE/SEAL/Presentation/Presentation%20PDF/Assessing%20student%20CASBS%20Seminar%202000.pdf (accessed May 31, 2005).

Shepherd University. Center for Teaching and Learning. Home page. Shepherdstown, WV: Shepherd University. Available at http://www.shepherd.edu/ctl/ (accessed July 28, 2005).

Siemens, George. *ePortfolios* (December 16, 2004). Available at http://www.elearnspace.org/Articles/eportfolios.htm (accessed July 31, 2005).

Smith, Brian. "Managing Generation X," *USA Today (Magazine)* 129 (November 2000). Available from Infotrac (accessed July 28, 2004).

Society of College, National, and University Libraries. *Information Support for eLearning: Principles and Practice.* London: Society of College, National, and University Libraries, 2004. Available at http://www.sconul.ac.uk/pubs_stats/ (accessed November 27, 2004).

Statistics Canada and the Council of Ministers of Education, Canada. *Education Indicators in Canada: Report of the Pan-Canadian Education Indicators Program* 2003. Ottawa, ON: Statistics Canada, 2003. Available at http://www.statcan.ca/english/freepub/81-582-XIE/2003001/highlights.htm (accessed April 26, 2005).

Stewart, Donald. "Considering the Public Interest," edited by Donald Stewart and Arthur W. Chickering, *Liberal Education* 81 (Spring 1995): 12+. Available from EBSCOhost Academic Search Premier (accessed November 14, 2004).

Texas Women's University. Office of Institutional Research and Planning. "Appropriate Outcome Measures of Student Learning," *Institutional Effectiveness Handbook* 9. Denton, TX: Office of Institutional Research and Planning, June 2003. Available at http://www.twu.edu/iep/Iehandbook.pdf (accessed March 3, 2005).

———. "Institutional Effectiveness Management Plan for Academic Programs," *Institutional Effectiveness Handbook.* Denton, TX: Office of Institutional Research and Planning, June 2003. Available at http://www.twu.edu/iep/IEhandbook.pdf (accessed March 3, 2005).

Town, Stephen. "Compliance or Culture?: Achieving Quality in Academic Library Service." Address given at the University of Stellenbosch Library. Seventh Annual Symposium. Stellenbosch, South Africa: University of Stellenbosch, October 28–29, 2004. Available at http://www.lib.sun.ac.za/sym2004/papers.htm (accessed November 27, 2004).

Training Resources and Data Exchange Performance-Based Management Special Interest Group. *How to Measure Performance: A Handbook of Techniques and Tools.* Oak Ridge, TN: Oak Ridge Associated Universities,

2005. Available at http://www.orau.gov/pbm/handbook/ (accessed June 15, 2005).

Treuer, Paul, and Jill D. Jenson. "Electronic Portfolios Need Standards to Thrive," *EDUCAUSE Quarterly* 26, no. 2 (2003): 34–42. Available at http://www.educause.edu/ir/library/pdf/EQM0324.pdf (accessed July 31, 2005).

United Kingdom. *The Future of Higher Education.* London: Department of Education and Skills, January 2003. Available at http://www.dfes.gov.uk/hegateway/uploads/White%20Pape.pdf (accessed November 27, 2004).

United Kingdom. Quality Assurance Agency for Higher Education. Home page. Gloucester, UK. Available at http://www.qaa.ac.uk/ (accessed December 15, 2004).

University of Alaska, Fairbanks. Office of the Provost. "Student Learning Outcomes Assessment." Fairbanks: University of Alaska, Fairbanks, n.d. Available at http://www.uaf.edu/provost.outcomes/ (accessed February 3, 2005).

———. "Student Learning Outcomes Assessment: A Step by Step Guide to Preparing an Outcomes Assessment Plan." Fairbanks: University of Alaska, Fairbanks, n.d. Available at http://www.uaf.edu/provost/out comes/StepByStep.html (accessed February 3, 2005).

University of Mary Washington. "Information and Technology Proficiency at the University of Mary Washington—Library and Information Literacy." Fredericksburg, VA: University of Mary Washington. Available at www.library.umw.edu/infoliteracy.html (accessed March 28, 2005).

University of South Dakota. "Information Technology Literacy Requirement." Vermillion: University of South Dakota, 2000. Available at http://www.usd .edu/library/assessment_gateway/assessment/Literacy_Initiative/page1.htm (accessed March 21, 2005).

University of Washington. "Assessment of Information Technology Literacy." Seattle: University of Washington. Available at http://depts.washing ton.edu/infolitr (accessed March 28, 2005).

University of Wisconsin–Parkside. "UW–Parkside Information Literacy Tutor." Kenosha: University of Wisconsin–Parkside, 2004. Available at http:// www.uwp.edu/departments/library/infolit/intro/ (accessed March 21, 2005).

U.S. Department of Education, National Center for Education Statistics. *The NPEC Sourcebook on Assessment.* Volume 2: *Selected Institutions Utilizing Assessment Results,* NCES 2000-172. Washington, D.C.: U.S. Government Printing Office, 2000. Available at http://www.nces.ed.gov/ pubs2000/2000196.pdf (accessed March 5, 2005).

Vandervelde, Joan. *Rubric for Electronic Portfolio (E-portfolio).* Menomonie: University of Wisconsin–Stout, 2005. Available at http://www.uwstout .edu/soe/profdev/eportfoliorubric.html (accessed July 31, 2005).

Wartburg College. "Information Literacy at Vogel Library." Waverly, IA: Wartburg College, 2005. Available at http://public.wartburg.edu/library/infolit/ (accessed March 28, 2005).

Weiss, Gregory L. *Institutional Effectiveness and Assessment for Academic Majors and Programs at Roanoke College*. Salem, VA: Roanoke College, May 2002. Available at http://www2.roanoke.edu/inst-res/assessment/Acad Man.htm (accessed March 4, 2005).

White Paper on the Future of Higher Education. London: Department of Education and Skills, January 2003. Available at http://www.dfes.gov.uk/hegateway/uploads/White%20Pape.pdf (accessed November 27, 2004).

Wisconsin Indianhead Technical College. "Program Outcomes/Assessment Plan 2002–2003." Ashland: Wisconsin Indianhead Technical College, 2002. Available at http://www.witc.edu/instruct/assess/pgmout03/10-196-1 (accessed November 19, 2004).

Wise, Steve, and Katie Morrow. "Assessing Collegiate Student Information Literacy Skills with the Information Literacy Test," American Association for Higher Education Assessment Conference, June 14, 2004, Denver. Available at http://www.projectsails.org/publications/aahe_files/frame.htm (accessed March 28, 2005).

Zuckerman, Elizabeth. "Interactive 'Clickers' Changing Classrooms." Associated Press, Domestic News Section, May 13, 2005. Available from Lexis/Nexis Academic (accessed June 24, 2005).

Unpublished Works

Austin, Jutta. *Use of the Learning Outcome Bank for Non-accredited Courses*. Colchester, UK: Adult Community College Colchester, 2004. Unpublished internal report.

Batson, Trent, Kim Chambers, and Eileen Palenchar. *Who's Doing What? ePortfolio in New England*. Unpublished presentation at NERCOMP 2005, Worcester, MA, March 7, 2005.

Carrigan, Sarah, Jeremy Fisher, and Philip Handwerk. "The Effectiveness of Institutional Effectiveness: Doing an Institutional Effectiveness Survey on the Web." Unpublished paper presented at the annual forum of the Association for Institutional Research, Cincinnati, OH, 2000.

Cheverie, Joan, and Martha Kyrillidou. Presentation at ARL/OLMS Conference on Positive Organizational Scholarship, Washington, D.C., November 8–9, 2004.

Gabriner, Robert. "The Significance of the New WASC Accreditation Standards for the California Community Colleges." Unpublished address to the State Academic Senate for California Community Colleges, San Francisco, April 15, 2004.

Hiller, Steve, and Jim Self. "Making Library Assessment Work." University of Washington and University of Virginia Association of Research Libraries, ARL 4th Human Resources Management Symposium, Washington, D.C., November 9, 2004.

López, Cecilia L. "What We Are Learning: Assessment Strategies from the Trenches." Unpublished PowerPoint presentation at the 107th Annual Meeting of the Higher Learning Commission. Chicago: The Higher Learning Commission, 2002.

Oehler, David C. "Creating and Using a 'Dashboard' to Monitor Institutional Performance." Unpublished paper presented at the American Association for Higher Education Assessment Conference, Denver, CO, 2003.

University of Stellenbosch Library. Seventh Annual Symposium. Stellenbosch, South Africa: University of Stellenbosch, October 28–29, 2004. Available at http://www.lib.sun.ac.za/sym2004/papers.htm (accessed November 27, 2004).

Index

AACSB. *See* Association to Advance Collegiate Schools of Business

Academic library, 273; accrediting organization for, 270, 277; assessment plan for, 279–280; of Canada, 246–247; focus on program outcomes of, 289; graduate student interviews on, 293–298; for IL at King's College, 328–331; information literacy plan of, 289, 297; inputs/outputs in, 274; IT in, 275–276; Lindauer on, 392–393; pretest/posttest on, 281; rubrics for, 280; student learning outcomes in, 278–280, 363; teaching/learning role of, 277; technology plans of, 282; Web courseware systems for, 281

Accountability: accrediting organization in, 102; assessment strategies for, 97–112, 369; in Australian higher education, 205; in Canadian higher education, 243; educational quality in, 2–3, 394–395; effectiveness in, 105; evidence for, 30, 31, 39–41, 136–142, 149, 367; goals for, 17–22, 98; in higher education, 32; for institution improvement, 29–31; institution measures for, 99–100; measures for, 98–103; performance measures for, 111; policy instruments for system of, 98; provision of support for, 21; quality demonstration in, 14, 17, 199; reasons to focus on, 15–16; stakeholders for, 44–45, 97; standards of AACSB for, 371; state government interest in, 52–53; state government monitoring of, 53, 98–103; understanding of, 13–14. *See also* Evidence, for accountability/quality improvement; Goals, for accountability/quality improvement

Accreditation process, 58; for course evaluation, 138; elements of, 24; evaluation of input measures in, 49; for federal funds, 368; goal evaluation in, 23–24; regional, 49, 368–369; self-regulatory system in, 49–50; self-study report for, 97; student learning outcomes in, 49

Accrediting organization, 111, 149, 216, 277, 288; AACSB International as, 370; for academic library, 270, 277; as accountability requirements source, 102; CHEA as, 370; electronic portfolio of, 154; ICT *Literacy Assessment* for, 344–345; for King's College, 330; regional, 368–369; as stakeholder, 48–50, 364, 368, 376, 394; student learning outcomes by, 102

ACRL. *See* Association of College and Research Libraries

ACT. *See* American College Testing

AI. *See* Appreciative inquiry, for positive organizational change

Allocation, of funding resources: stakeholders on, 41, 48, 54, 55; from student learning outcomes, 101, 102, 106, 108, 202

Alverno College, 168; agent of change in, 166; e-portfolio program of, 160; horizontal structural curriculum of, 369–370

American College Testing (ACT), 101, 109; as outcomes assessment, 99

Analysis of Variance (ANOVA): hypothesis testing in, 126, 127; as inferential statistic, 126–127; interval measurement scale as, 127; mean in, 126, 127; nominal measurement scale in, 127; parametric procedure in, 126; random sample in, 127; ratio measurement scale in, 127; sampling in, 127; Type I error in, 126

Appreciative inquiry (AI), for positive organizational change, 356–359; LibQUAL+ for, 357–359; model for, 356–357

Assessing Service Quality: Satisfying the Expectations of Library Customers (Hernon/Altmon), 352

Assessment: academic decision makers in, 66; in Canada, 244–246; Canadian Academic Libraries efforts for, 246–247; educational quality in, 2–3; free-response-key-concept method of, 305–308; as institutional accountability measures, 99; measurement quality in, 2; plan for academic library, 279–280; plan for institution, 103–108; of program outcome, 143, 144, 145; resistance to, 167; of student learning, 10–11, 24–25, 66,

98, 136, 137, 289; of teaching/learning, 136; in United Kingdom, 221–222, 236–237. *See also* Outcomes assessment; Outcomes assessment, in Canadian Academic Libraries

Assessment, horizontal/vertical levels of: by accrediting organization, 370; framework for, 7, 368; horizontal level of, 369–370, 372; key indicators development for, 375–377; research agenda for, 373–374; from standards, 372; vertical level of, 370–371

Assessment matrix, 63–84, 87–96; analysis worksheet for, 65; BCC use of, 75–76; benchmark indicators in, 64, 84; of CMU, 74–75; Doane College use of, 78; DU use of, 78; efficacy of, 64, 81–82, 96; EIU use of, 83; EMU use of, 81; of GSLIS, 184; implementation/progress levels in, 63–65; institutional culture pattern in, 64, 76, 88, 89; institutional support pattern in, 64, 76, 93, 94–95; Jamestown College use of, 77–78; level characteristics for plan of action, 70–73; MCC use of, 83–84; Moraine Park Technical College use of, 74; OSU use of, 82–83; patterns within, 63, 65, 66–67; program survey in, 73–74; progress measurement in, 69; research basis for, 67–69; RHIT use of, 79; shared responsibility pattern in, 64, 75, 78, 80, 81, 90, 91, 92; SLCC use of, 76–77; SMSU use of, 79–80; student learning effectiveness in, 70, 77; tool for accredited institution in, 63, 69, 84; tool for HLC/NCA peer reviewers, 63; UNL use of, 81–82; uses for, 69–74

Assessment process, of Kotter for creating major change, 168–175; anchoring new approaches in culture in, 175; broad-based action empowerment in, 173–174; communication of change vision in, 172–173; establishment of sense of urgency in, 168–170; guiding coalition creation in, 170; producing more change by, 175; short-term wins in, 174; vision/strategy development in, 170–171

Assessment process, of Shepherd University, 165–179; accreditation in, 168; Assessment Task Force in, 170, 171, 172; Center for Teaching and Learning development in, 175; change by shared learning, 167; communication forums for, 172–173; cultural shift indicators in, 175–179; *The Dance of Change* on, 166; new approaches in, 175; Office for Assessment of Student Learning in, 171, 172; student learning in, 170–172; use of Kotter's process for creating major change, 168–175

Assessment strategies, for accountability, 97–112, 369; benchmark indicators in, 108; direct/indirect methods of measurement, 106; findings on, 108–110; ICT as, 107–108; institutional effectiveness in, 103–108; outcomes prioritization/analysis in, 106; planning/implementation as, 103–108; portfolio use in, 106–107; proactive system of, 103–108; scope of participation in, 106; student testing as, 107–108

Association of College and Research Libraries (ACRL), 148, 280, 330, 372, 392; information literacy outcomes in, 362; LibQUAL+ measurement instrument by, 31, 247, 350, 351, 354, 355, 357–359, 360–361, 363, 391; New Measures Initiative by, 352, 353, 363; protocol for library service quality, 351; SERVQUAL measurement instrument of, 351, 354

Association to Advance Collegiate Schools of Business (AACSB), 370; accountability standards of, 371

AUQA. *See* Australian Universities Quality Agency

Australia: accountability in, 205; AUQA in, 204, 205, 388; fitness-for-purpose outcome assessment in, 205; higher education in, 204–207; OECD and, 383; quality assurance in, 204–207, 216; quality improvement in, 206; university libraries in, 206–207

Australian Universities Quality Agency (AUQA), 204, 205, 388; Carroll on, 382, 386

Autonomy: in higher education institution, 47, 48, 55, 56, 101, 237, 388; loss of, 56

Baldrige National Quality Program, 26–27; Baldrige Award of, 26, 199

Banta, Trudy W., 14, 16, 22

BCC. *See* Butler Community College

Bloomberg, Susan, 181, 184, 190, 200; on outcomes assessment, 379–382

Boolean operators: in information literacy, 148, 256, 259, 313, 316, 317, 319, 322, 323, 324

Borden, Victor M.H., 14, 16, 22

Business-Higher Education Forum, 15, 18, 28, 111

Butler Community College (BCC): assessment matrix use by, 75–76; shared responsibility pattern in, 75

Canada: academic library in, 246–247, 252, 254–257; assessment in, 244–246; higher education in, 241–267; NSSE in, 246; quality assurance in, 241–244
Canadian higher education: accountability in, 243; institutional collaboration in, 152, 161; outcomes assessment in, 241–267; performance measures in, 242; qualitative/quantitative research method in, 244; stakeholder in, 242; student learning outcomes in, 250, 266
Carnegie Mellon University: assessment measure review of, 292; copyright law education of, 290–291; graduate student interviews by, 292; student learning commitment of, 287; think-aloud protocols at, 298, 300
Carroll, Martin, 206, 216; on AUQA, 382, 386; on graduate attributes development, 384–387; on IT, 383; on outcomes assessment, 382–389
Central Michigan University (CMU): assessment matrix use by, 74–75
CHEA. See Council for Higher Education Accreditation
CHEA Institute for Research and Study of Accreditation and Quality Assurance, 15, 18, 24
The Citadel: outcomes assessment for, 304. See also Information literacy, at The Citadel
CMU. See Central Michigan University
Cost-effectiveness: in program reviews, 25–26; of tools/measures, 22–23

Council for Higher Education Accreditation (CHEA), 15, 49, 111
Course evaluation: accreditation process for, 138; example of, 139–140; by faculty self-evaluation, 141; methods of, 138; peer review for, 138; role of libraries in, 148; by video/audiotape, 141

The Dance of Change (Senge/Kleiner/ Roberts/Roth/Smith): on learning institution, 167; on Shepherd University assessment process, 166
Data: analysis in outcomes assessment, 287; collection methods, 135–149, 149; driven decision making, 1, 117; driven evidence, 277; research outcomes collection of, 14; rubrics for collection of, 280
Deming, W. Edwards, 17
Descriptive statistics, 124, 132; frequency distribution in, 121; graphic depiction in, 122–123; measures of central tendency in, 121–122; measures of variability in, 122
Doane College: assessment matrix use by, 78; peer review team of, 78
Drury University (DU): assessment matrix use by, 78–79; assessment review council of, 78; shared responsibility pattern in, 78
Dunn, Kathleen, 44; on information literacy, 390–392; on LibQUAL+, 391; on outcomes assessment, 390–392

Eastern Illinois University (EIU): assessment matrix use by, 83; feedback loop of, 83
Eastern Michigan University (EMU): assessment matrix use by, 81; peer

review team of, 81; shared
responsibility pattern in, 81
Educational Testing Service (ETS),
197, 352, 392; ICT in, 107, 197,
344, 362
Effectiveness, for student learning,
14, 97, 98, 106, 141, 195, 200, 246,
347, 382; for accountability, 105;
accrediting organization on, 24, 98;
in assessment matrix, 70, 77; of
cost, 22–23, 25–26; of curriculum,
3, 108, 202, 232, 244, 328;
definition of, 103; for funding
resources, 99; in information
literacy, 247, 250, 289, 304, 342; by
instruction, 304, 308, 323, 324;
library service quality in, 206–207,
355, 364; Maki on, 377; measures
of outcome for, 102, 117, 368;
Measuring Up in, 100; stakeholders
on, 39, 40, 42, 52, 54, 368, 369.
See also Institutional effectiveness;
Student learning
EIU. *See* Eastern Illinois University
Electronic portfolio (e-portfolio):
accrediting organization for, 154;
Alverno College program for, 160;
assessment use of, 153–154, 156;
benefits of, 158; conference for,
159–160; consideration by GSLIS,
190; content of, 154–155; goals/use
of, 153–154; LaGuardia
Community College program
for, 160–161; management of,
151–161; planning importance in,
152–153; problems of, 159;
program reviews by, 158; rubrics
for, 156, 157, 158; self-study report
for, 158; software for, 156–158;
student learning outcomes for, 154
EMU. *See* Eastern Michigan
University
E-portfolio. *See* Electronic portfolio

ETS. *See* Educational Testing Service
Evidence, for accountability/quality
improvement, 149; as basis for
important decisions, 30; ethical/
responsible use of, 31; framework
for, 136–142; for learning, 367;
punitive use of, 31; recognition of
efforts to improve, 31; stakeholders
desire for, 39–41
Ewell, Peter, 14, 16, 27, 250
Experimental designs, selection of,
117–118

Factor analysis: as inferential statistic,
127–128
Federal government: on accessibility/
affordability of higher education,
51; allocation of funding by, 51;
CHEA and, 51; as stakeholder,
51–52
Feedback loop, 80, 392, 394;
definition of, 3; of EIU, 83; in
GSLIS, 189; of open-systems
model, 3, 132, 202
Fitness-for-purpose, in outcome
assessment, 199, 203; in Australia,
205; international perspective on,
199; New-Zealand framework for,
205; role of library in, 206–207; in
South Africa, 208

GA. *See* Graduate attributes
General Accountability Office (GAO):
definition of key indicators by,
375–376
Goal evaluation, 22–29; accreditation
process in, 23–24; assessments of
student learning in, 24–25; Baldrige
National Quality Program in,
26–27; for institution improvement,
29–31; online institutional
portfolios for, 29, 79, 107;
performance indicators for, 27–28;

Goal evaluation (*continued*)
program reviews in, 25–26; quality
improvement tools for, 29; surveys
in, 28, 245; tools/measures for,
22–23. *See also* Course evaluation

Goals, for accountability/quality
improvement, 17–22; ends not
means of, 18–20; e-portfolio in,
153–154; in higher education,
17–18; from institutional mission,
17–18, 367; program planning/
implementation of, 21–22;
Shewhart/Deming model for,
17–22; of state government, 98;
targets for, 20–21

Government: higher institution
tension with, 50–51, 55–57, 101;
as stakeholder, 50–57

Graduate attributes (GA), 384–387;
Carroll on, 384–387

Graduate records examination (GRE),
as outcomes assessment, 99

Graduate School of Library and
Information Science (GSLIS), 129;
course description template by, 184,
186; course proposal form of, 188;
course syllabi by, 187; curriculum
review of, 189; existing assessment
at, 193–194; feedback loop in,
189; organization cluster in, 187;
outcomes assessment measures of,
182–183, 191–192, 195; self-study
report of, 183; of Simmons College,
181; student learning outcomes of,
183, 185, 196–197; summative
assessment by, 189

Graduate student interviews, for
learning outcomes: by Carnegie
Mellon University, 292; measurement in, 294; procedure for, 293;
qualitative method for, 293;
think-aloud protocols for, 298–299;
Web resources for, 296

Graphic depiction, in descriptive
statistics, 122–123

GRE. *See* Graduate records
examination, as outcomes
assessment

GSLIS. *See* Graduate School of
Library and Information Science

HEQC. *See* Higher Education Quality
Committee

Higher education: accountability/
quality improvement in, 32;
assessibility/affordability in, 41, 51;
in Australia, 204–207; in Canada,
241–267; college completion rate
in, 15; cost increase for, 15;
economic development contribution
from, 46; foundation support of, 16;
goals in, 17–18; IT in, 274–275;
selection of, 43–44; in South Africa,
207–211; stakeholders in, 39; state
boards support of, 54; student
learning outcomes in, 1, 18; in
United Kingdom, 211–214

Higher Education Act, 49;
amendments to, 51

Higher education association: Career
College Association, 43–44;
institutional report card support by,
44; performance-based information
support by, 43–44; as stakeholder,
43–45; standardization of
curriculum by, 44

Higher education consumer: cost
information for, 45–46;
performance standards for, 45;
return on investment in, 46; as
stakeholder, 45–46

Higher education institution:
autonomy in, 47, 48, 55, 56,
101, 237, 388; faculty within as
stakeholders, 47; priorities of, 48;
as stakeholder, 47–48

Higher Education Quality Committee (HEQC): of South Africa, 207

Higher Learning Commission of the North Central America (HLC/NCA), 63, 67, 75, 81; assessment process description, 68; Jamestown College and, 77; MCC and, 83

Hypothesis testing, 287; ANOVA and, 126, 127; null, 125, 126

ICT. *See* Information and Communication Technology

ICT *Literacy Assessment*, 197, 344–345; for accrediting organization documentation, 345

IL. *See* Information literacy

Inferential statistics, 124–128, 130, 132; ANOVA as, 126–127; factor analysis in, 127–128; Mann-Whitney U test, 127; sampling in, 124; t-test, 126

Information and Communication Technology (ICT), 107; as assessment strategy for account-ability, 107–108; exam of, 393; IL skills in, 280, 288, 362; librarian interpersonal communication in, 281; *Literacy Assessment* by, 197, 344–345; standardized learning outcomes for UK in, 232, 236

Information literacy (IL), 1, 278, 279, 288; Boolean operators for, 148, 256, 259, 313, 316, 317, 319, 322, 323, 324; ethical behavior in, 290–292; ICT *Literacy Assessment* for, 344–345; ICT skills in, 280, 288, 362; learning objectives in, 289; plagiarism in, 291; planning process for, 299; pre-test/post-test in, 304–305, 323; SAILS skills measurement for, 352; student learning outcomes in, 296; university systems for, 342–345

Information literacy (IL), at The Citadel: campus library use, 318; collaboration on, 303–325; comparative analysis in, 321–323; faculty/library in, 304; free-response assessment method for, 305–308; on freshman cadets, 313–317; on graduate students, 318, 324; Military College of South Carolina, 304–30; pretest/posttest in, 316, 318; procedure for, 308–313; program for assessment measures in, 289; student learning outcomes in, 323–324

Information literacy (IL), at King's College: academic library in, 328–331; assessment instrument development in, 327–347; assessment instrument evolution in, 331–341, 334; Freshman information skills in, 334–334; *Library Skills Test* in, 329; *Minimum Library Use Skills* in, 329; observations on, 346–347; pretest/posttest for, 329; self-reported assessments of, 331–332; Senior/graduate students information skills, 337; Senior information skills, 336–337

Information Literacy Competency Standards for Higher Education (*Standards*), 148, 280, 327, 330, 341, 342, 372; guidelines of, 280; for ICT skills outcomes, 280; and King's College, 332, 333, 338, 339

Information Literacy Standards for Science and Technology, 372; vertical level of assessment of, 373

Information technology (IT), 273–282; in academic library, 275–276; Carroll on, 383; in higher

Information technology (*continued*)
education, 274–275; IL in, 274;
library computer-use policies for,
276; outcomes assessment in,
277–280; student learning outcomes
in, 278–280; technology plan for,
275, 276
Inputs, 41, 55, 214, 246; in academic
library, 274; in assessment plan,
105; definition of, 99, 289;
examples of, 3; in framework model
for outcome processes, 5; as
institutional accountability
measures, 99; in open-system
model, 3
Institute for Education Best Practices:
performance measures in, 22, 23
Institutional audit, in United
Kingdom, 215
Institutional collaboration, 1, 393; AI
in, 357; in assessment, 2; in
Canadian higher education, 152,
161; on IL, 303; on IL at The
Citadel, 303–325; of librarians with
faculty, 278, 304, 325; for library
success, 36–, 354; Lindauer on, 393
Institutional effectiveness, 7, 18, 27,
32, 103–108, 105, 109, 112, 144,
145, 277, 341; based on statement
of purpose, 103
Institutional goals: educational
quality/outcomes, 26; public
priorities responsiveness to, 26;
resources/efficiency stewardship
of, 26
Institutional mission: crafting of, 68;
goals from, 17–18; learning goals
from, 367; for library service quality,
353; standards in, 24; statement in,
5, 7, 77, 104
International perspective, on outcome
assessment, 199–217; fitness-for-
purpose in, 199

Interval measurement scale, 125;
ANOVA and, 127
IT. *See* Information technology

Jamestown College: assessment
handbook of, 78; assessment matrix
use by, 77–78; HLC/NCA and, 77;
peer review team of, 77

King's College: accrediting
organization for, 330; rubrics at,
341. *See also* Information literacy, at
King's College
Kotter, John, 168, 169, 173; creation
of change process by, 168–175

Leading Change (Kotter): on process
for creating major change, 169
LibQUAL+, 31, 247, 350, 351, 354,
355, 357, 363, 391; Dunn on, 391;
perceived outcomes in, 360–361
Library service quality, 351–364;
ACRL protocol for, 351;
information literacy in, 362–363;
institutional mission for, 353;
LibQUAL+ evaluation for, 351;
measurement for, 353, 359; as
outcome, 351–352; perceived
outcomes for, 360–361; as positive
organizational change outcome,
355–363; student learning
effectiveness in, 206–207; user
satisfaction in, 361
Lindauer, Bonnie Gratch, 277; on
academic libraries, 392–393; on
collaboration, 393; on outcomes
assessment, 392–394; on SAILS,
393

Maki, Peggy, 4, 135, 143, 145, 183,
192; on outcomes assessment,
377–379; on student learning
effectiveness, 377

Mann-Whitney U Test: as inferential statistic, 127

Mass media, 58, 59; higher education information compilation by, 42; higher education reporting in, 42; as stakeholder, 42–43

MCC. *See* Mesa Community College

Mean, 121, 122, 123, 124, 126, 127, 252; in ANOVA, 126, 127; standard deviation in, 123; in Z-score, 124

Measurement: in assessment, 24; error, 118; in framework model for outcome processes, 7; scale of, 125

Measures, for accountability, 98–103. *See also* Performance measures

Measures, of central tendency: as descriptive statistics, 121–122; mean, 121, 122, 123, 124, 126, 127, 252; median, 121, 122, 182; mode, 121; normal curve, 123

Measures, of outcome: in assessment plan, 105; definition of, 289; effectiveness in, 102, 117, 368; program improvement in, 109

Measures, of variability: as descriptive statistic, 122; standard deviation in, 122

Measuring Up: The National Report Card on Higher Education, 42, 57; effectiveness in, 100

Mesa Community College (MCC): assessment matrix use by, 83–84

Middle States Commission on Higher Education, 23, 24, 118, 128, 131, 200, 288, 291, 297, 330; institutional based standards of, 372; Ratteray as associate director of, 389; on reliability/validity, 129

National Center for Public Policy and Higher Education, 100; *Measuring Up: The National Report Card on Higher Education* by, 44–45, 58

National Commission on Accountability in Higher Education, 16, 18, 21, 32

National Survey of Student Engagement (NSSE), 45, 393; in Canada, 246; for information literacy outcomes, 362

Nominal measurement scale, 125; ANOVA and, 127

Normal curve, 125; for measures of central tendency, 123; standard deviation in, 123

NSSE. *See* National Survey of Student Engagement

OECD. *See* Organisation for Economic Co-operation and Development

Oklahoma State University (OSU): assessment matrix use by, 82–83; peer review team of, 82–83

Online survey: for graduate student interviews, 294–295; RHIT use of, 79

The Open Source Portfolio Initiative (OSPI), 157–158

Open-system model, of planning process, 10, 131; audit trail in, 4; feedback loop in, 3, 132, 202; identification of outcomes in, 3–4; inputs in, 3; throughputs in, 3

Organisation for Economic Co-operation and Development (OECD), 15, 246; Australia and, 383

OSPI. *See* The Open Source Portfolio Initiative

OSU. *See* Oklahoma State University

Outcomes assessment: ACT as, 99; Bloomberg on, 379–382; in Canadian higher education, 241–267; Carroll on, 382–389; at The Citadel, 304; continual review

Outcomes assessment (*continued*) for, 292; at course level, 136, 203; data analysis in, 287; definition of, 100; Dunn on, 390–392; example of, 129–131; focus on student learning in, 1, 137; framework model for process of, 4–8; future directions in, 367–395; global perspective on, 199–217; goal-setting for, 288–289; GRE as, 99; GSLIS on measures of, 182–183, 191–192, 195; information behavior in, 290–292; as institutional accountability measure, 100; at institutional level, 23; IT on, 277–280; for Jamestown College, 77; Lindauer on, 392–394; Maki on, 377–379; planning process for, 3–4, 288–289; at program level, 136, 203; Ratteray on, 389–390; SAT as, 99; student grades in, 131–132; student learning in, 200; techniques for, 287–301; think-aloud protocols for, 300; of UNL, 82

Outcomes assessment, in Canadian Academic Libraries: discussion on, 263–265; IL analysis of, 247; methods in, 251–254; objectives of study in, 250; pre-test/post-test in, 252, 254–257; student interviews in, 253, 257–263; summative evaluations in, 248; theoretical frameworks for, 249–250

Outputs, 41, 55, 246; in academic library, 274; in assessment plan, 105; definition of, 100, 289; efficiency measures as, 41, 105; in framework model for outcome processes, 5; as institutional accountability measures, 100; student learning outcomes as, 278

Parametric procedure: ANOVA as, 126; t-test as, 126

Peer review, 140–141; of accrediting organization, 24; for course evaluation, 138; inquiry portfolio in, 138; team for Doane College, 78; team for EMU, 81; team for Jamestown College, 77; team for OSU, 82–83; team for SMSU, 80

Performance measures, 27, 30, 55, 57, 101; accountability in, 111; in Canadian higher education, 242; in education associations, 44; for GSLIS, 190; of Institute for Education Best Practices, 22, 23; stakeholder involvement in, 41, 42, 43, 112

Planning process, for assessment, 2; assessment cycle in, 4; open-system model of, 3–4

Policy instruments, for accountability system: capacity-building, 98; inducements, 98; mandates, 98; system-changing, 98

Positive organizational change outcome: AI in, 356–359; external marketing of library, 364; information literacy in, 362–363; library summit for, 359–360; satisfaction/perceived outcomes for, 360–361; universal library service provision, 363–364

Pre-test/post-test, 137; in Canadian Academic Libraries, 252, 254–257; for IL at The Citadel, 316–318; for IL at King's College, 329; IL in, 304–305, 323

The Princeton Review: *The Best 357 Colleges*, 43

Program reviews: cost-effectiveness in, 25–26; by e-portfolio, 158; quality/need in, 25

Qualitative research method, 106; in Canadian higher education, 244; reliability in, 128; for student learning outcomes, 146; of study, 120

Quality assurance: aspects of, 202; by AUQA, 205–206; in Australia, 204–207, 216; in Canada, 241–244; curriculum for, 202; in financial matters, 202; in infrastructure/material facilities, 202; intent of, 203–204; in South Africa, 207–211; in United Kingdom, 211–214

Quality improvement: in Australia, 206; in college completion rate, 15; goal articulation in, 17; higher education concerns in, 16; for institution, 29–31; link to accountability in, 199; in low-income student success rates, 15; provision of support for, 2; reasons to focus on, 15–16; understanding of, 13. *See also* Evidence, for accountability/quality improvement; Goals, for accountability/quality improvement

Quantitative research method, 106, 146; in Canadian higher education, 244; reliability in, 128; for student learning outcomes, 146; of study, 120

Random sample, 130; ANOVA and, 127; Mann-Whitney U test and, 127

Ratio measurement scale, 125; ANOVA and, 127

Ratteray, Oswald M.T.: on outcomes assessment, 389–390

Reliability, 118, 339; consistency in, 128; in qualitative/quantitative research method, 128; in research design, 128

Research outcomes, 149; data collection in, 14; inquiry process in, 146; international perspective of, 201; Maki on need for, 377–379; quality indicators in, 146; report writing skills in, 146

Rose-Hulman Institute of Technology (RHIT): assessment matrix use by, 79

Rubrics, 374; for academic librarians, 280; as assessment measure, 75, 191, 280, 292; BCC and, 75; benchmarks of, 292; for data collection, 280; for e-portfolio, 156, 157, 158; in frequency distribution, 121; for GSLIS, 193, 196; at King's College, 341; to provide formative feedback, 8; of SMSU, 80; in student learning outcomes, 8, 9, 146, 190

SAILS. *See* Standardized Assessment of Information Literacy Skills

Sampling: ANOVA in, 127; example of, 119; in inferential statistics, 124; probability/nonprobablility, 119; simple random, 119; in statistical inference, 118; stratified random, 120

Scholastic Aptitude Test (SAT), 329; as outcomes assessment, 99

SD. *See* Standard deviation

Self-study report: for accreditation, 97; for assessment, 77; of Doane College, 78; e-portfolio and, 158; for institution audits, 205; of MCC, 83; of Simmons College, 183; in South Africa, 209

Shewhart, Walter A., 17

Simmons College: description of, 12; GSLIS in, 182; self-study report of, 183

SLCC. *See* St. Louis Community College

SMSU. *See* Southeast Missouri State University

Software, for e-portfolio, 156–158; IMS Global Learning Consortium, 157; The Open Source Portfolio Initiative (OSPI), 157–158

South Africa: fitness-for-purpose outcome assessment in, 208; HEQC of, 207; higher education in, 207–211; quality assurance in, 207–211; self-study report in, 209; university libraries in, 209–21, 216

Southeast Missouri State University (SMSU): assessment matrix use by, 79–80; peer review team of, 80; shared responsibility pattern in, 80

Stakeholder, 1, 2, 5, 8, 27, 29, 32, 111, 112, 149, 152, 200, 201, 369; accountability for, 8, 15, 29, 39–41, 97, 98, 101, 103, 105, 110, 241, 371; accrediting organization as, 48–50; on allocation of funding resources, 41, 48, 54, 55; business/ employer as, 46–47; in Canadian higher education, 242; common values of, 40, 41; definition of, 39; federal government as, 51–52; on higher education accessibility/ affordability, 40; higher education association as, 43–45; higher education consumer as, 45–46; of higher education institutional accountability, 39–59; higher education institution as, 47–48; internal/external, 7, 8, 104, 384; mass media as, 42; performance expectations of, 97, 214; perspectives of, 40, 242; state government as, 52–58, 97; student learning support by, 368, 380, 395; summary outcomes report to, 8

Standard deviation (SD), 127, 130; mean in, 123; in measures of variability, 122; Z-score in, 124

Standardized Assessment of Information Literacy Skills (SAILS), 247, 339, 340, 343, 352, 363, 393; for information literacy outcomes, 362

Standardized learning outcomes, for United Kingdom: in adult education courses, 221–239; art/design curriculum in, 228–232, 233, 237, 238; as assessment approach, 222; counseling curriculum in, 232, 234–235, 237; design procedure in, 224–225; ICT curriculum in, 236; ICT in, 232; modern language curriculum in, 225–227; system for recording achievement, 223–224

Standards. See Information Literacy Competency Standards for Higher Education

State government: accountability in, 52–53, 98–103; Boards of Higher Education, 54, 56; capacity-building of, 98; executives/ lawmakers in, 52; governors/state legislatures, 53; imposed measures for accountability by, 98–103; inducements of, 98; mandates of, 98, 109; performance reporting/ budgeting, 54–55, 98, 101; as stakeholder, 52–58, 97; system-changing policy instrument by, 98; target attainment for funding, 100

Statistical test, nonparametric/ parametric, 126

Statistics. *See* Descriptive statistics; Inferential statistics

St. Louis Community College (SLCC): assessment matrix use by, 76–77; institutional culture pattern in, 76; institutional support pattern in, 76

Student learning, 41, 132, 277; active, 8; assessment for, 10–11, 24–25, 66, 98, 136, 137, 289; assessment matrix for, 70, 77; assessment process of Shepherd University for, 170–172; Carnegie Mellon University commitment to, 287; conceptual level of, 135; contributing factors for, 295–296; cooperative, 8; deep, 8; direct evidence of, 24, 27; faculty/librarian support for, 292; as goal, 135, 287; goal evaluation in, 24–25; HLC/NCA commitment to, 68; indirect evidence of, 24; libraries and, 362; Maki on, 378–379; as mission of higher education, 18; outcomes in assessment plan, 15–106, 130; service, 8; skills level of, 135; student performance examination of, 24. *See also* Effectiveness, for student learning

Student Learning Assessment, 128, 131, 144

Student learning outcomes, 149, 278, 288; in academic library, 278–280, 363; in accreditation process, 49; by accrediting organization, 102; allocation of funding resources from, 101, 102, 106, 108, 202; assessment for, 367; in Canadian higher education, 250, 266; direct measures in, 146; educational goals connection to, 2; educational program application to, 181–197; e-portfolio for, 154; experimental designs for, 118; by GSLIS, 183, 185, 196–197; higher education commitment to, 1, 18; IL in, 296; indirect measures in, 146; information literacy at The Citadel,

323–324; institutional mission connection to, 2; international perspective of, 201; in IT, 278–280; library role in, 148; planning process for, 299; qualitative/quantitative evidence in, 146; qualitative/quantitative research method in, 146; rubrics in, 8, 9, 146, 190; validity in, 148

Student testing: ACT, 99; as assessment strategy, 107–108; ETS ICT *Literacy Assessment*, 197

Think-aloud protocols: at Carnegie Mellon University, 298, 300; definition of, 298; usability studies in, 299; Web-based resources in, 299

Tools/measures: cost-effectiveness of, 22–23; ethics in, 23; quantitative/qualitative, 23; systematization of, 23

T-test: as inferential statistic, 126

Type I error, 126; ANOVA and, 126

Type II error, 126

United Kingdom: assessment in, 221–222, 236–237; higher education in, 211–214; institutional audit in, 215; quality assurance in, 211–214; standardized learning outcomes in, 221–239; university libraries in, 212–213

University libraries: in Australia, 206–207; in South Africa, 209–211, 216; in United Kingdom, 212–213

University of Nebraska at Lincoln (UNL): assessment matrix use by, 81–82; efficacy of assessment pattern of, 81–82; shared responsibility pattern of, 82

U.S. News & World Report: *America's Best Colleges*, 43, 58

Validity, 118, 339; criterion-related, 128–129; in research design, 128; in student learning outcomes, 148; types of, 128

Variable, dependent/independent, 126

Web courseware systems: for academic library, 281; in IT, 273, 275

About the Editors
and Contributors

JUTTA AUSTIN teaches languages at the Adult Community College Colchester in Essex, England. She also works in the college's quality assurance and staff development department where she is involved in developing, implementing, and maintaining assessment methods and training tutors in these methods. She began her career as a librarian and lecturer at the Royal School of Librarianship in Copenhagen, Denmark. During that period, she was involved in research into multilingual subject indexing and lectured in this field in many countries. After a career break to raise her family, she turned to the linguistic side of her interests and became a language teacher.

SANDRA BLOOMBERG has been Dean of the College of Professional Studies, New Jersey City University, since 1998. She has served in the capacity of faculty member, chairperson, and associate dean at several colleges in the Northeast. Since 1982, she has focused her efforts on issues related to student and program assessment. As early as 1983, she worked with colleagues to identify cross-curricular competencies that were then systematically integrated into core courses of a major urban-based health-care management baccalaureate degree program. Her work at New Jersey City University has largely focused on encouraging an environment in which student learning is at the center of the teaching-learning process; where evidence is consistently used to inform teaching, learning, and programmatic change; and where faculty and students view each other as collaborators in learning.

MARTIN CARROLL is Audit Director and Business Development Manager with the Australian Universities Quality Agency (AUQA). His responsibilities include leading institutional audits of the quality systems in place in Australian universities and state-based higher education accrediting agencies. This role and his broader speaking and consulting activities have taken him to many countries throughout the world, including the United Arab Emirates, Oman, the United States, China, South Africa, Spain, and much of Southeast Asia, commenting on national and intra-national systems and investigating the efficacy of quality assurance in transnational education. Mr. Carroll has led the establishment of Australia's national database of good practices in higher education. He also instigated and chairs the Australian Universities Quality Forum, which has now become the premier annual national event for discussing quality issues in higher education. His research concerns developing a theory of knowledge-sharing as a learning experience. Mr. Carroll is a member of the Advisory Board of the National Institute for Excellence in Institutional Assessment, an Associate of the Education Policy Institute, and provides consulting services for the International Institute for Quality (all based in the United States). Prior to joining AUQA, he was the Quality Manager and Chief Internal Auditor in the Office of the Vice-Chancellor at Victoria University of Wellington, New Zealand. He has been a National Evaluator and Team Leader for the New Zealand Business Excellence Foundation and is a trained ISO auditor.

ELIZABETH CARTER is Associate Professor and Head of Reference and Instruction at Daniel Library, The Citadel. She holds a B.A. degree in art history from Agnes Scott College and a master of librarianship from Emory University, both in Atlanta, Georgia. Her main areas of interest and research are the study of teaching and learning and assessment of the instruction process, and she is the author of numerous published papers and conference presentations on these issues. She is active in The Citadel's Communication Across the Curriculum and Citadel Academy for the Scholarship of Teaching, Learning, and Evaluation (CASTLE; http://www.citadel.edu/carnegie/index.htm) groups, and is a member of the college's Citadel 101 faculty. She is a member of Phi Kappa Phi and is active in state and national library associations, having held a variety of section, committee, and executive board positions in the South Carolina Library Association, including president and chapter liaison to the Association of College and Research Libraries.

ROBERT E. DUGAN is the Director of the Mildred F. Sawyer Library at Suffolk University. In his career in librarianship, which spans more than thirty years, he has been a reference librarian, director of public libraries, head of statewide library development, a state librarian, an associate university librarian, and college library director. He has co-authored eight books and more than fifty articles on topics such as information policy, technology, outcomes assessment, and library management and operations.

KATHLEEN DUNN is Librarian Emerita, University Library, California State Polytechnic University, Pomona. Dr. Dunn, who received her Ph.D. from the University of Southern California in 1984, was Assistant University Librarian for Reference, Instruction, and Collection Services at California State Polytechnic University from 1995 to 2004. Prior to this she was head of Reference and Instruction Services from 1986–1995, and served as Chair of the California State University Information Competence Assessment Taskforce from 1998–2002. She wrote "Assessing Information Literacy Skills in the California State University: A Progress Report," which appeared in *The Journal of Academic Librarianship*.

PATRICIA M. DWYER is Dean of Teaching and Learning at Shepherd University. Before assuming this position in 2002, she was Director of the Honors Program and Director of Assessment at Shepherd University as well. She received her master's degree in English from the Bread Loaf School of English (Middlebury College, Vermont) in 1986 and her Ph.D. in American literature from the George Washington University in Washington, D.C., in 1995. She has presented papers on assessment of student learning at several national and international conferences, and has recently had an article on assessment published in *To Improve the Academy*.

CAROLE A. GEORGE is a Human Factors Researcher with the Carnegie Mellon University Libraries. Her work has focused on usage and usability studies related to Web site design, the development of online exhibits, and user studies related to the libraries' services. She has experience with survey and questionnaire design and conducting focus group interviews. Her research interests and efforts have been directed toward user-centered interface design and information behavior studies. She is currently involved in the Graduate Student Interviews, a study to gain a better understanding of how graduate students seek and obtain information to support their research. Before joining the University Libraries, Ms. George was a Research Associate at the Learning Research and Development Center, University of Pittsburgh. She holds an M.Ed.

in research methodology and evaluation and an Ed.D. in administrative and policy studies.

PETER HERNON is a Professor at Simmons College, Graduate School of Library and Information Science, where he teaches courses on government information policy and resources, evaluation of information services, research methods, and academic librarianship. He received his Ph.D. from Indiana University in 1978 and has taught at Simmons College, the University of Arizona, and Victoria University of Wellington (New Zealand). He is the coeditor of *Library & Information Science Research*, founding editor of *Government Information Quarterly*, and, for nine years, Editor of *The Journal of Academic Librarianship*. He is the author of more than 240 publications, 44 of which are books. Among these are *Outcomes Assessment in Higher Education* (Libraries Unlimited, 2004), *The Next Library Leadership* (Libraries Unlimited, 2002), and *Assessing Service Quality* (1998).

RENÉE N. JEFFERSON is an Associate Professor in the School of Education at The Citadel, where she teaches courses in data collection and analysis, and applied measurement techniques. Her research interests include the repeat testers of college admissions tests, information literacy skills of undergraduate and graduate students, and professional ethics of graduate students. Most recently, she coauthored *Ethical Perspectives of Graduate Library and Information Science Students in the United States* (2005). She was formerly a faculty member at the School of Library and Information Science at the University of South Carolina, where she taught courses in research methods and information sources and services. Her professional library experience includes Head of Reference Services at California State University, San Bernardino, and Social Sciences Librarian at California State University, Long Beach. She received a B.S. degree in statistics and her master's in library and information science from the University of South Carolina, a master's of science in industrial/organizational psychology from California State University, Long Beach, and her doctorate in educational measurement and statistics from the University of Iowa (Iowa Testing Program).

HEIDI JULIEN is an Associate Professor at the School of Library and Information Studies, University of Alberta. Previously, she held academic appointments at Dalhousie University, Halifax, Canada, and at Victoria University of Wellington, New Zealand. She holds a B.Ed. and

M.L.I.S. from the University of Alberta, and a Ph.D. from the University of Western Ontario. Dr. Julien has taught at the graduate level in the areas of management, reference, information literacy, and information policy, and actively publishes in the areas of human information behavior, information literacy, and information policy. She has been invited to present numerous talks on her research, and to conduct workshops in the area of information literacy instruction. Dr. Julien's contributions to the library and information science community include active participation in the Association for Library and Information Science Education (ALISE) and the Canadian Association for Information Science (CAIS). She was one of the original founders of the ALISE Doctoral Students' SIG Poster Session, and chaired the ALISE Organization, Bylaws, and Resolutions Committee from 2000–2002. She was elected to the ALISE Board (Director, External Relations) for 2005–2008, President of CAIS in 2001–2002, and Program Chair of the Association's 2004 conference. Dr. Julien is editor of the "Research News" column of the *Canadian Journal of Information and Library Science*, and sits on the journal's editorial board. She is a member of the Information Literacy Working Group of the Canadian Association of Research Libraries.

MARTHA KYRILLIDOU is the Director of the ARL Statistics and Measurement at the Association of Research Libraries. She was hired to establish the ARL Statistics and Measurement research and analysis unit in 1994 and has been the editor of the longest and most prestigious data series describing library trends, including: *ARL Annual Salary Survey, ARL Statistics, ARL Preservation Statistics, ARL Academic Law Library Statistics, ARL Academic Health Sciences Library Statistics, ARL Supplementary Statistics*. She has interdisciplinary experience in libraries and evaluation and measurement, with specialization in the application of quantitative and qualitative research methodologies in libraries. She is responsible for all aspects of the production and publication of ARL's annual statistical surveys, including the data used to describe trends in scholarly communication as manifested by the rapidly increasing costs of serials and monographs, and data that describe trends in expenditures, resource allocations, demographics, and compensation issues in academic and research libraries. Ms. Kyrillidou has worked in developing new methods for measuring the effectiveness of libraries through the ARL New Measures Initiative. In particular, she is project manager for the LibQUAL+™ suite of services, the most widely used protocol for evaluating library service quality across libraries and over time in North America and expanding internationally. She has also worked in supporting the e-metrics set of activities focusing on developing measures that can describe the role and contributions of libraries in the electronic environment. She is the project manager for the NSF/NSDL grant to modify LibQUAL+™ for the digital library environment; and, she is working to implement MINES (Measuring the Impact of Networked Electronic Services), a transaction-based pop-up survey of electronic resources, across sixteen libraries in the Ontario Council of University Libraries, Canada. She is currently one of the co-principal investigators for a national study to develop workforce projections, a two-year collaborative IMLS grant-funded activity.

BONNIE GRATCH LINDAUER, Coordinator of Library Instructional Services at the Rosenberg Library, City College of San Francisco, has authored several books and many journal articles on issues related to information literacy, outcomes assessment, reference services, and research design. In 1999, she won the Association of College and Research Libraries (ACRL) K. G. Saur Award for her article, "Defining and Measuring the Library's Impact on Campus-wide Outcomes" (*College & Research Libraries*, November 1998) and in the following year she received the ACRL Instruction Section publication award. She was the project leader for a two-year test development project, the Bay Area Information Competency Assessment Project (http://www.topsy.org/ICAP/ICAProject.html). She is currently serving on the Executive Committee of ACRL's Institute for Information Literacy, and is also active in the California Academic and Research Libraries chapter of ACRL.

CECILIA L. LÓPEZ is the Vice President for Academic and Student Affairs at Harold Washington College, one of the City Colleges of Chicago. For twelve years (February 1991 to February 2003), she was the Associate Director of the Higher Learning Commission of the North Central Association of Colleges and Schools (NCA). Dr. López received her B.A. and M.A. degrees in English from Florida State University, with the generous assistance of the Southern Scholarship and Research Foundation and the National Hispanic Scholarship Fund. She earned her Ph.D. in Educational Technology, Instructional Design and Learning from Arizona State University. Dr. López has taught at Chabot College, Florida A&M University, and Arizona State University, West Campus. She serves on the executive Committee of the Council for the National Post-secondary Education Cooperative (NPEC) and served on the Board of Trustees of the Association of American Colleges and Universities (AACU) from 2000–2004. She is a member of the National Advisory Board for the NSSE/AAHE project on promoting student success through using student engagement data, the Advisory Board for the Academy of Excellence in Institutional Assessment at North Carolina State University, and the National Advisory Board for the Policy Center on the First Year of College. Dr. López served for ten years as reviewer for *Educational Technology, Research and Development* (ETR&D) and now serves as a consulting editor for the *Assessment Update: Progress, Trends, and Practices in Higher Education.* In March 2000, the Hispanic Caucus of the American Association for Higher Education (AAHE) selected her as the first female to receive the Alfredo G. de los Santos Jr. Award for Distinguished Leadership in Higher Education. Her research on issues affecting higher education, particularly issues relating to assessment of student learning and general education, has been published in articles appearing in *Liberal Education* (Summer 1988 and Summer 1999) and *The Journal of Academic Librarianship* (November 2002), and in the numerous papers she has presented at international, national, regional, and statewide conferences on the assessment of student learning.

PEGGY L. MAKI, is a higher education consultant. She specializes in assisting institutions, higher education boards, and disciplinary organizations as they integrate assessment of student learning into educational practices, processes, and structures. Her work also focuses on assessment within the context of accreditors' expectations for institutional effectiveness. She has recently been named to the Board of Contributors of *About Campus* and to the Advisory Board of the Wabash Center for Critical Inquiry, and is Department Editor of Assessment for *About Campus* and Assessment Field Editor at Stylus Publishing. She serves as a faculty member in the Institute on General Education of the Association of Colleges and Universities (AAC&U), has served as a faculty member in the Carnegie Foundation's Integrated Learning Project, and teaches graduate-level seminars focused on assessment. Formerly Senior Scholar and Director of Assessment at the American Association for Higher Education (AAHE), she has served as Associate Director of the Commission on Institutions of Higher Education, New England Association of Schools and Colleges (New England's regional accrediting body); was Vice President, Academic Dean, Dean of Faculty, and Professor of English at

Bradford College, Massachusetts; Chair of English, Theatre Arts, and Communication, Associate Professor of English, and Dean of Continuing Education at Arcadia University, Pennsylvania; and is a recipient of the national Lindback Award for Distinguished Teaching. Dr. Maki has conducted over 350 workshops and keynote addresses on assessment both in the United States and abroad, including New Zealand, Hong Kong, Mexico, Greece, Bulgaria, British Columbia, and Malaysia. Additionally, she conducts writing-across-the curriculum workshops that develop and document student learning. Her publications on assessing student learning have appeared in AAHE's *Bulletin*, AAHE's Inquiry and Action series, *About Campus, Assessment Update, Change Magazine, The Journal of Academic Librarianship, Leadership Exchange, NetResults*, and *Proceedings of the International Conference on Teaching and Learning*. She is in the process of editing a book on assessment practices at the doctoral level and another book on assessment practices at community colleges, and recently published a handbook on assessment, *Assessing for Learning: Building a Sustainable Commitment across the Institution* (2004). She is currently working with the three public higher education and K–12 institutions in Rhode Island, under a grant awarded her by the Board of Governors to integrate assessment across K–16.

TERRENCE MECH, D. Ed., has been Library Director at King's College since 1982. He also served as the college's Vice-President for Information and Instructional Technologies (1994–2001). Dr. Mech holds graduate degrees from Pennsylvania State University (higher education), Clarion State College (library science), and Illinois State University (sociology). He was a member of the Middle States Commission on Higher Education Advisory Panel on Information Literacy that prepared *Developing Research & Communication Skills: Guidelines for Information Literacy in the Curriculum* (2003). The Jossey-Bass monograph, *Information Literacy: Developing Students as Independent Learners*, which he edited with Donald Farmer, received the Publication of the Year Award in 1993 from the ACRL's Bibliographic Instruction Section. Most recently, he has been conducting workshops on information literacy and assessment.

OSWALD M. T. RATTERAY has been the Associate Director for constituent services and special programs, Middle States Commission on Higher Education since 1994. He has joint responsibility for the commission's incoming information, collecting and analyzing the data that colleges and universities are required to submit annually as well as occasional surveys on such special topics as the self-study process, peer review, information literacy, and outcomes assessment. He is also responsible for coordinating the commission's outgoing information in the form of training workshops, annual conferences, conferences on special topics, print publications, and World Wide Web publications. A graduate of Howard University, he worked as a wordsmith in Washington, D.C., for twenty-seven years, specializing for much of that time in corporate management and summarizing information. He also served on the task force, sponsored by the Association of College and Research Libraries, to Develop Information Literacy Standards for Higher Education (2000).

GLORIANA ST. CLAIR is the Dean of University Libraries at Carnegie Mellon University. Her current interests center around issues of scholarly communication in the academy, building the digital library of the future through initiatives such as the Million Book Project, and creating a library organization through strategic planning, quality assurance, strong consultation with faculty and students, active support of diversity, dynamic fund-raising, and creative leadership. Prior to her appointment at Carnegie Mellon, she held administrative library posts at Penn State University, Oregon State University, Texas A&M University, the University of Oklahoma, and the University of California at Berkeley. Dr. St. Clair was a founder and the editor (2001–2003) of *portal: Libraries and the Academy*. She is the author of more than hundred articles, editorials, and presentations. From 1996–1999, she edited *The Journal of Academic Librarianship* and from 1990–1996, she edited *College & Research Libraries*, the official journal of the ACRL. She earned a bachelor's degree in English at the University of Oklahoma (1962), a master's degree in library science at the University of California at Berkeley (1963), a doctoral degree in literature at the University of Oklahoma (1970), and a master's degree in business management at the University of Texas at San Antonio (1980).

CANDY SCHWARTZ is a professor at Simmons College, Graduate School of Library and Information Science, where she teaches courses in the organization of information resources, including subject analysis, classification, Web development, information architecture, and digital libraries. Dr. Schwartz received her Ph.D. from Syracuse University in 1986. She is the coeditor of *Library & Information Science Research*, has published articles in journals such as the *The Journal of Academic*

Librarianship and the *Journal of the American Society for Information Science and Technology*, and is the author or co-author of several monographs, including *Sorting Out the Web* (2001). Dr. Schwartz has held numerous offices in the American Society for Information Science & Technology (ASIST), including Director and President, and has received local and national ASIST awards for teaching and service.

LINDA SUSKIE is Executive Associate Director at the Middle States Commission on Higher Education. Her nearly thirty years of experience in college and university administration include work in assessment, institutional research, strategic planning, and quality improvement. She has been Associate Vice President for Assessment and Institutional Research at Towson University and Director of the American Association for Higher Education's Assessment Forum. Ms. Suskie has taught graduate courses in assessment and educational research methods and undergraduate courses in writing, statistics, and developmental mathematics. She holds a bachelor's degree in quantitative studies from Johns Hopkins University and a master's in educational measurement and statistics from the University of Iowa. Ms. Suskie is an internationally recognized speaker, writer, and consultant on a broad variety of higher education assessment topics and has been an active member of numerous professional organizations and groups. Her latest book is *Assessment of Student Learning: A Common Sense Guide*. Among her other publications are *Assessment to Promote Deep Learning* and *Questionnaire Survey Research: What Works*.